GOODBYE RELIGION

SECULAR STUDIES
General Editor: Phil Zuckerman

Losing Our Religion: How Unaffiliated Parents Are Raising Their Children
Christel J. Manning

Race in a Godless World: Atheism, Race, and Civilization, 1850–1914
Nathan G. Alexander

The Varieties of Nonreligious Experience: Atheism in American Culture
Jerome P. Baggett

None of the Above: Nonreligious Identity in the US and Canada
Joel Thiessen and Sarah Wilkins-Laflamme

The Secular Paradox: On the Religiosity of the Not Religious
Joseph Blankholm

Beyond Doubt: The Secularization of Society
Isabella Kasselstrand, Phil Zuckerman, and Ryan T. Cragun

Goodbye Religion: The Causes and Consequences of Secularization
Ryan T. Cragun and Jesse M. Smith

Goodbye Religion

The Causes and Consequences of Secularization

Ryan T. Cragun *and* Jesse M. Smith

NEW YORK UNIVERSITY PRESS
New York

NEW YORK UNIVERSITY PRESS
New York
www.nyupress.org

© 2024 by New York University
All rights reserved

Please contact the Library of Congress for Cataloging-in-Publication data.
ISBN: 9781479825295 (hardback)
ISBN: 9781479825301 (paperback)
ISBN: 9781479825349 (library ebook)
ISBN: 9781479825332 (consumer ebook)

This book is printed on acid-free paper, and its binding materials are chosen for strength and durability. We strive to use environmentally responsible suppliers and materials to the greatest extent possible in publishing our books.

Manufactured in the United States of America

10 9 8 7 6 5 4 3 2 1

Also available as an ebook

For Heather and Wendy

CONTENTS

1. Introduction 1
2. Who Is Leaving? 32
3. Why Are They Leaving? 60
4. Where Do They Go? 122
5. What Happens to Them? 151
6. How Is This Affecting Society? 207
7. Conclusion 250
   Acknowledgments 273
   Appendix: Methods 275
   Notes 287
   Index 329
   About the Authors 343

1

Introduction

I'm not religious, [but] I may say, "Well I was raised Jewish" . . . I stay away from "atheist" because that sounds like a group and I'm not really interested in joining anybody's group. I don't feel like fighting religion. I just feel like it's not necessarily for me. . . . On holidays, I would certainly play along [and go to synagogue], I don't want to upset my parents and my grandmother . . . but kind of like I said earlier, I'm not really looking for anything. I'm not looking for an "answer." I'm not looking for acceptance. I'm not looking for guidance.
—Zeb

Religion does a lot of great things for people . . . I mean they help each other; they help their community. I've seen people that are able to get through a very difficult situation because of their belief in God and I think that's fantastic if that's what it takes for them to get through and to be able to hang on and to be able to rationalize the loss of their family or something like that. I'm all for it, I have no problem with that at all.
—Kevin

My atheism comes up pretty often. Especially when people at school ask me about my major. It comes up pretty often in conversation because people often assume I'm religious. But I'm very public about it. I'm going to be a part of the Freedom from Religion Foundation for the "Coming Out of the Closet" billboard campaign . . . they are doing this [atheist] billboard campaign in Chicago and I applied to be on one of the billboards, and they accepted it, which is going to be awesome!
—Cynthia

Zeb, Kevin, and Cynthia are very different individuals, with highly varied backgrounds and experiences. Zeb is a 33-year-old man who was raised Jewish and lives in the Southeast. He's married now and has a career as a radio producer. He's an independent thinker, but simultaneously doesn't want to rock the boat. Kevin is in his 50s, transgender, born and raised on the West Coast, and used to be a Protestant Christian. He's sympathetic to religion and sees its value in the lives of others, despite no longer believing the central religious tenets he grew up with. Cynthia, 21, is Hispanic and a former Catholic. She's a single college student from the Midwest and very vocal about her views. To her, hiding or even downplaying her secular beliefs is unthinkable and she's keen to share her views with anyone who will listen.

Each of these people is at a different stage of life and they find themselves in unique circumstances. But one thing they have in common is that they have all left religion. They are religious exiters. But even here, they exited religion in different ways, for different reasons, and with different consequences and implications for their personal lives. The stories of Zeb, Kevin, and Cynthia, as with other participants described in this book, represent three different pathways to religious exiting: *religious indifference, religious-secular liminality*, and *secular activism*. These can be viewed as a kind of continuum, with religious indifference at one end, and secular activism at the other. Religious indifference is the simplest to define. It just denotes a lack of interest or concern with religion. Religious-secular liminality suggests a more complicated relationship with religion, where there is a kind of tension regarding values about religion. Here, people sympathize with or find some value in religion, if not for themselves, then for society at large.[1] Secular activism refers to being open and public about one's secular beliefs or nonreligious identity, which can involve actively promoting secular beliefs and criticizing religious ones. We'll refer to these pathways throughout this book.

This book is about people who say goodbye to religion; but to describe this phenomenon well we discovered it necessary to analyze comparison groups, including those who were never religious and those who were raised and continue to be religious. In describing pathways to religious exiting, we want to be clear, pathways to religious exiting are just that, pathways. They do not represent fundamental *types* of Americans who were formerly religious, nor are they universal *categories* to be cleanly applied to every person who's ever left religion. The dynamic, fluid social processes that underlie this phenomenon are more complex than a three-part typology can capture. What we're calling pathways are simplified descriptions of patterns we've identified in our data that are useful for thinking about the mechanics of religious exiting in the American context in the twenty-first century.

As we hope to demonstrate throughout, our pathways typology is useful for several reasons. One of these reasons is that, in addition to describing the different positions and dispositions of religious exiters, it has the advantage of helping to explain their motives and trajectories at different stages in life. These pathways, much like the social forces that shape them, are dynamic. As with religious conversion, switching, and commitment,[2] it's possible for individuals to explore each of the pathways out of religion at different points in time. Our goal here is to give scholars and the public a better sense of not just what religious exiting is and looks like, but, more broadly, what's happening with religion and secularity in America today, and what to expect in the future.

We explore multiple dimensions of religious exiting—who is leaving, why they left, where they end up, and what the implications are for society. We have a somewhat unique perspective on religious exiting. To illustrate our position, we are going to present two alternative and hypothetical perspectives against which we will contrast our own—the view of those who have left and the perspective of those who are still religious. These two perspectives are often so distantly related that they could comfortably marry without worrying about having an incestuous relationship. Yet, we will argue that neither perspective provides a full or accurate picture of what is actually happening.

The writings and talks of religious leaders and apologists as they discuss why people are leaving religions illustrate that many of these speakers are blinded by their own devotion.[3] They often attribute people leaving the religion to lack of faith, being offended by other members, having a poor understanding of doctrine or scripture, or a desire to act in ways that run counter to the moral teachings of the religion (a.k.a. sin). All of these arguments have one characteristic in common—they blame those who leave but fail to suggest that religions have any responsibility for why people might be leaving. From this perspective, if someone lacks faith, that is clearly their fault (perhaps the result of their critical style of thinking)⁴ and not the fault of the religion in question. People who leave religions because they were offended by the behavior or actions of other members lack charity and grace, or perhaps are immature and unwilling to forgive others. Some apologists would have us believe that their interpretation of their religion—just one interpretation of one religion of the thousands that exist—is so clear and compelling that only individuals who are willfully ignorant would reject their arguments.⁵ And it is certainly not the fault of religions if people want to engage in lascivious behaviors like promiscuous sex and recreational drug use. Such individuals are endowed with agency and are free to make bad choices. Clergy bear no responsibility for the immorality that leads people to leave religion. From the perspective of many clergy and apologists (though certainly not all feel this way), religion itself is blameless.

As social scientists, we understand why these individuals take rose-colored perspectives on their religions. Who wants to belong to an institution that is deeply flawed, unethical, or preaches dubious dogma? Most of us do not, as it would challenge our image of ourselves. In order to maintain a positive self-image, religious leaders have to construct a version of their religion that affirms its truthful, charitable, and beneficial nature. To that end, individuals who reject the religion must be the problem, not the religion itself. Such individuals must be ignored or even denigrated in the pursuit of the greater good—maintaining the faith and allegiance of the individuals who remain. From the perspective of those who remain religious, those who leave must do so for reasons other than the religion itself being the problem.⁶

Not surprisingly, examining the reasons given by those who leave religions for why they left is almost like looking in a funhouse mirror in which everything is turned upside down relative to the claims of religious apologists and leaders. Such individuals describe the lack of evidence provided by religions for their teachings, the hypocrisy and immoral behavior of members of religions, horribly flawed and illogical doctrines and scripture, and the archaic moral prescriptions of religions that condemn ordinary twenty-first-century behaviors like premarital sex as the reasons why they left.⁷ Those who leave religion are constructing a narrative that creates a positive self-image—a narrative that corresponds to that of people who remain religious. In their version of reality, they are truth seekers and freethinkers who, through hard work and dedication, have emancipated themselves from deeply flawed, immoral, and dogmatic institutions.[8] All the problems are with the religions, not themselves, and that is why they left.

Readers may be wondering with whom we are going to side at this point: Are religious leaders correct? Or are those who left the religions correct?

In typical academic fashion our answer is: Both are correct and both are wrong, but not in the ways they think they would be right or wrong.

This gets us to our perspective on this issue, which is rooted in our disciplinary approach. As sociologists, we are trained to look for external explanations for human behavior. Our sister discipline, psychology, focuses on internal factors that explain human behavior. If we want to believe that humans are nothing more than biological creatures functioning in cultural vacuums who are completely unaffected by the people with whom they interact on a daily basis, then psychology and biology are all that is needed to explain human behavior. But humans are social animals with culture. And even though we humans construct and maintain our culture, our culture acts on us, influences us, and molds us in ways we rarely recognize and often don't want to admit.

An example may help illustrate this perspective. Imagine you are on vacation in southern Norway in a small city like Kristiansand. Toward the end of a lovely day doing whatever you like doing on vacation, your biology tells you that you need to eat. You begin examining your options. In a smallish city, the restaurant choices are limited. There are several ethnic restaurants, including Indian, Japanese, and Italian. There are also several restaurants serving traditional Norwegian fare and a couple of American fast-food restaurants. Of course, you could also stop by a grocery store and make your own food. However, your food choices are not infinite; they are limited by the context and environment. There are, for example, no Ethiopian or Mexican restaurants in town. At a minimum, then, your behavior has already been determined by the environment in which you find yourself. Short of hopping on your private plane and flying to Ethiopia for dinner, Ethiopian food is not an option. Your psychology then combines with sociology to influence your behavior. Perhaps you are more adventurous and decide to try *sursild* (pickled herring). Just one of the Norwegian restaurants has *sursild* on the menu, which determines your choice of restaurants. Alternatively, you may be overwhelmed by all the cultural differences and decide that a meal that aligns more closely with the food you ate growing up sounds really good and comforting, leading you to choose the American fast-food restaurant (assuming you're from the US). Our point, of course, is that biology dictated that you need to eat, but it played a minimal role in determining which type of food you would eat. To understand the choice of restaurant, a combination of psychology and sociology are necessary.

That is precisely the argument we aim to construct throughout this book. A sociological perspective on why people leave religions will be far too simplistic if we only examine the narratives those who left construct to bolster their positive self-image. Likewise, if we base our entire understanding of why people leave religions on the claims of those who have remained religious, we'll be beholden to the worldview such individuals construct to justify their continued adherence to religions. Both groups are constructing narratives that justify what they have done.[9] As sociologists, we value personal narratives. They tell us something important about why individuals leave religion; thus, we incorporate them throughout this book. But we also want to understand what *underlies* those narratives. We are interested in the forces and environmental factors that influence people's behavior even when they are unaware of those forces. To help set the context, we now turn to a discussion of US culture during the twentieth and twenty-first centuries.

Early European settlers to America brought with them their religion, and religion was a prominent feature in the original colonies.[10] There is a long history of religious discrimination in the US. A widely taught myth about European settlement in America is that many of these individuals were fleeing religious persecution and, coming to the US, immediately adopted a more open attitude toward religion. Historians have now discovered that that notion was largely false.[11] Early European settlers in the US did not allow religious freedom. Some may have fled countries where their religion was the one being persecuted. But that didn't translate into a robust understanding of freedom of or from religion. To the contrary, most of the original thirteen colonies had an established religion that was mandatory and individuals who did not respect that religion were punished or even executed.[12] It was in large part because the early colonies couldn't agree on which religion would be the official one for the United States after the Revolutionary War that a religion was not chosen as the official religion and we got the First Amendment to the constitution, "Congress shall make no law respecting an establishment of religion, or prohibiting the free exercise thereof." Read in this context, the First Amendment makes a lot more sense—Congress cannot "establish" a state or official religion. While there are millions of Americans who wish their religion was the established religion in the US,[13] lack of agreement early on prevented this. However, the first amendment did not immediately translate into widespread acceptance of all religions and definitely not acceptance of nonreligious folks. Thomas Jefferson, the third President of the US and a "Founding Father," had to fend off accusations that he was an atheist.[14] From the beginning of European settlement in the US, nonreligion was frowned upon and atheism was reviled. There have been periods of greater and lesser acceptance, but dislike of atheism continues through the early twenty-first century.[15]

However, after the founding of the United States and the expansion of Europeans west into additional Native American lands, it was often the case that individuals on the frontier were less concerned with having a specific affiliation. Certainly, many were religious, and some of the religiously devout worked in conjunction with government and even railroads to ensure that there were Christian churches in most every town.[16] Even so, in the eighteenth and nineteenth centuries in the US, while most people held supernatural beliefs, having a religious affiliation was not considered a requirement to be American.[17] There was even a brief period at the end of the nineteenth century and the beginning of the twentieth century when one of the most popular and famous orators in America, Robert Ingersoll, was openly agnostic and regularly railed against religion in public lectures to sold-out audiences.[18]

This period of freedom of and from religion ended, however, with the rise of communism in the early twentieth century and opposition to Roosevelt's New Deal among wealthy capitalists and corporations.[19] The theorists who came up with communism as an economic system—Karl Marx and Friedrich Engels—were quite critical of religion.[20] Marx famously described religion as the "opiate of the people."[21] He was far more concerned about economics than he was about religion, but his concern with religion was that it was a distraction from economic exploitation and oppression. If people were primarily focused on getting rewards in heaven, they wouldn't fight for fair wages and economic equality in this life. The politicians who implemented communism embraced the anti-religious elements of Marxist thought as well, resulting in widespread persecution of religions and atheist indoctrination under communist regimes.[22]

Communism and socialism did, of course, make inroads into the US, even though the US overwhelmingly embraced capitalism and was largely run by proponents of liberal capitalist economic policies. Substantial steps toward centralized government took place under the Roosevelt administration in the 1930s, including the implementation of the Social Security Administration, substantial economic and financial reforms for corporations and the banking system, and help for the young, the old, and the poor. While these programs were a far cry from the creation of a socialist or communist government, there was substantial opposition to these policies by wealthy industrialists, among others. That opposition resulted in efforts and campaigns to weaken the changes. Many of the initiatives to weaken the social welfare system of the New Deal were blanketed with religion, which conveniently aligned with broader efforts to distinguish the US from its Cold War enemy, the Soviet Union.[23]

The US government slowly and intentionally undertook a number of efforts to combat the appeal of communism, from encouraging Americans to own their own homes[24] to trying to infiltrate communist groups and harassing their leaders.[25] The fight against communism gained momentum during World War II and in the Cold War afterward, as the US government came to realize that the Soviet Union was attempting to spread communism around the world, including to the very doorstep of the US in Cuba.

To combat the spread of communism, the US government engaged in concerted and intentional propaganda efforts to convince the American people that they were at war with "godless communists." Constructing the Soviet Union as the archenemy of the US required a counter narrative—that Americans were religious and democratic. This, of course, led to McCarthyism and the Red Scare; this period—the 1950s—is also when "In God We Trust" was added to US currency and "under God" was added to the Pledge of Allegiance. It was during the Cold War that it became normative in the US for citizens to be religious.[26] Revealing that you were an atheist or even nonreligious during this time was often immediately followed up with a question about whether you were also a communist.[27] Atheism and communism were linked in the minds of Americans and, as a result, it was expected that every "good" American was also a religious American, even if their religiosity extended only so far as saying they had a religious affiliation.

The first modern cracks in this cultural expectation of religiosity may have begun in the 1960s.[28] The 1960s saw the beginnings of a rejection of Christianity in some countries—particularly in Europe. But, more importantly for the US, the 1960s was when reliable birth control became available and eventually legal in the US.[29] Reliable birth control granted women a degree of autonomy they had rarely had over their fertility. At the same time, resistance to the Vietnam War led to a shift in cultural values. Young people increasingly wanted autonomy to make their own decisions.[30] While it would take another 20 to 30 years for this cultural and values revolution to begin to openly undermine self-reported religious affiliation in the US, the foundation of religious decline in the US may very well have been laid in the 1960s.

The Cold War between the US and the Soviet Union continued and the 1980s saw an escalation as the two competing countries engaged in an arms race, a competition that contributed to the economic collapse of the Soviet Union and the eventual end of Soviet domination.[31] During this same period, a political shift occurred in the US that saw the alignment of conservative Christians with the Republican Party,[32] setting up an eventual collaboration of the nonreligious with more progressive views and the alignment of nonreligious individuals with the Democratic Party.

When the Soviet Union finally collapsed in 1991, the link between "godless" (i.e., atheist) and "communist" pretty quickly began to dissolve in the minds of Americans. America was no longer at "war" with the Soviet Union. The US and its allies had won the Cold War—at least, that was the conclusion at the time. Even though it translates into millions of Americans who identified in surveys as having no religious affiliation during the 1970s and 1980s, the percentages of people identifying this way were only between 5% and 7% of the US population. That changed dramatically starting in the early 1990s.[33]

It's hard to argue what, precisely, led to the very dramatic increase in people identifying as nonreligious during this decade. The collapse

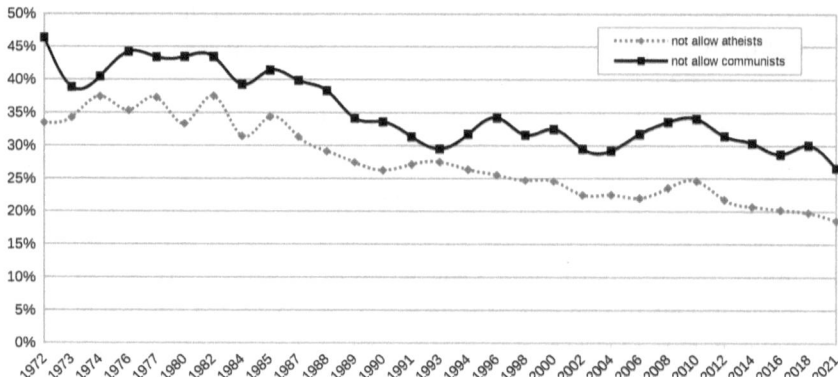

Figure 1.1. Change in Attitudes Toward Allowing Atheists and Communists to Speak Publicly, 1972–2021. (Source: GSS 1972–2021)

of the Soviet Union is likely one factor, but it cannot be the only factor as a number of other countries, like Canada, were also engaged in that Cold War and the rise of nonreligion had already started at that time.[34] It is likely that the disentangling of atheism from communism changed the environment such that individuals who didn't regularly attend religious services—which was around 60% of the US population through the 1980s—were more comfortable admitting that they were not actually religious. As figure 1.1 illustrates, attitudes toward atheists have improved since the 1970s. In 1972, almost 35% of American adults did not think atheists should be allowed to speak publicly, and over 46% of American adults did not think a communist should be allowed to speak publicly. This view stayed fairly consistent for both atheists and communists through most of the 1980s, but then dropped for both. As of 2021, just 18% of American adults didn't think atheists should be allowed to speak publicly, a change of close to 17%; the corresponding number for communists was 27%. While atheists continue to be disliked in theory by many Americans, attitudes have clearly shifted over the last 50 years.

Just as other developed countries around the world were beginning to secularize, so too was the US, but it was not socially acceptable to admit that you were not religious or not a believer. When the Cold War ended, there were already tens of millions of Americans who were functionally and practically secular in beliefs, values, and behaviors but had been using a claim of being religious for cover. This argument is no doubt an oversimplification of all that happened. Even so, the growth of nonreligion over the ensuing decades was accompanied by—and perhaps facilitated by—a number of other changes in American society.

The 1990s saw the birth of the internet, changes in parenting practices, the growth of cohabitation, and the beginning of shifting attitudes on lesbian and gay rights and pre-marital sex. Many of these trends were reflected in traditional media. Top TV shows of the period included *Seinfeld*, *Friends*, and *Beverly Hills 90210*, all of which depicted young people who were regularly engaged in sexual relationships outside of marriage. These shows rarely discussed religion; it was not a central element in the lives of the characters. And all of these shows began to engage with lesbian and gay issues at various points. By the end of the 1990s, *Will & Grace* aired, which featured an openly gay character as one of the two leads in the series.

These cultural shifts continued apace in the early 2000s. Again, mainstream media reflected the cultural zeitgeist when it aired the series *House*, the lead character of which was openly atheist. Religion did figure more prominently in this series because of the main character's atheism, but House's atheism didn't dampen enthusiasm for that Emmy-winning series. An increasing number of movies and TV shows throughout the early 2000s and 2010s featured nonreligious characters. The culmination of this transformation is perhaps an episode of the TV series *Silicon Valley*, called "Tech Evangelist," which aired on April 15, 2018.[35] In that episode, one of the main characters of the series, entrepreneur Richard Hendricks, accidentally outs the CEO of a gay dating app, not as being gay but as being Christian. This twist illustrates just how much has changed in the US over the last 30 years. In the 1980s, the US was still at war with godless communists, and admitting to being an atheist was tantamount to calling oneself a traitor. By 2018, religiosity had so dramatically declined in parts of the US—particularly along the coasts and in specific sectors of the economy—that outing someone as being religious, while meant to be humorous, was comedic precisely because it reflected a growing reality.

We're not trying to suggest here that mainstream media has driven the rise of nonreligion, so much as we are arguing that it reflects the changing environment in which Americans can make decisions about their religiosity. It may be the case that criticism of religion by traditional media has led some people to question their religion, but that is a difficult case to make. Our point is that scrutiny of popular television shows and movies illustrates that there has been a shift away from religiosity and toward secularity, with fewer and fewer shows focusing on religion and religion increasingly being criticized openly, particularly obscure religious groups.[36]

Of course, this is happening in the same country where we still have people who are hunkered down in enclaves trying to avoid all the change that is taking place outside their bubbles (in some cases, these enclaves are literal—like those of the Amish and the Fundamentalist Latter-Day Saints). We also have a country that subsidizes religion to an enormous degree and actually has a minimal wall of separation between church and state.[37] Basically, religions have structured the US government and law to favor religion. Any concession on this front is a hard-fought battle, chipping away at the pillar that is religion in American life. It's in this context that secularization was delayed for quite a while but is now catching up to that in other parts of the world. It may still come as a shock in some parts of the country if someone openly announces their atheism, but such a statement wouldn't get so much as a raised eyebrow in San Francisco, New York, Seattle, or even parts of Salt Lake City. The rapid rise of the nonreligious has occurred in this context. With all the changes that have taken place in the US, some of which came through the countless legal challenges by the secular vanguard, it is perhaps easier now to leave religion than ever before.

Before we begin examining in greater detail the causes and consequences of religious exiting in the US, it is important to detail our terminology and describe our methodology.

Defining Our Terms: Religion, Nonreligion, Religious Exiting, and Variations on 'Secular'

> "Atheists have an active belief system with views concerning [human] origins . . . no life after death; the existence of God; how to behave while alive; and so much more. Honest atheists will admit their worldview is a faith. Atheism is a religion!"[38]
> —Ken Ham

"Atheism is a religion like abstinence is a sex position."[39]
—Bill Maher

Ken Ham is a famous fundamentalist Christian, young-earth creationist, and founder of the organization *Answers in Genesis*, which most notably operates a Creationist Museum in Kentucky. Bill Maher is a famous comedian, commentator and TV personality who is not shy about his atheism. Two very different views from two very different public figures. So who is right? Are atheists religious? By extension, are those who leave religion or come to claim some secular identity actually religious, just in a new or different way? We don't think so. But at least some of this disagreement is understandable, given how different people think about the concept of religion. Indeed, a persistent challenge in the study of both religion and nonreligion lies in the problem of definition. To what, exactly, do these concepts refer? How are they related? What does it mean to say a person is religious, or formerly religious? Does it have to do with an "active belief system," as Ham suggests? Is it a matter of holding certain opinions, an ideology, a disposition, or engaging in specific behaviors? Does "religious exiting" refer to people who have undergone first conversion to, and then conversion from, religion? What is the connection between individuals leaving religion and societal-level secularization?

There's not much new or anything profound about this litany of questions; scholars have grappled with them since empirical studies of these phenomena began.[40] Researchers, including ourselves, have already helped codify the menagerie of concepts contemporary scholars of religion, nonreligion, and secularity are working with, so we refer readers to this literature.[41] But of course, we also can't skirt our obligation to nail down the essential concepts for those less familiar with these terms. To that end, we offer concise definitions and set the conceptual framework necessary for explaining why and how people leave religion and what consequences this has for both individuals and American society.[42]

Religion, Religious

Historically, many definitions of religion have been on the menu. Philosophers, psychologists, sociologists, anthropologists, historians, religious studies and comparative religion scholars each adopt distinct definitions, offer unique perspectives, and focus on different aspects of religion. The nineteenth century cultural anthropologist Edward Tylor famously stated that religion is, simply, "Belief in spiritual things."[43] Enlightenment philosopher Immanuel Kant defined religion as "[the] recognition of all our duties as divine commands."[44] American sociologist Milton Yinger considered religion "[a] system of beliefs and practices by means of which a group of people struggle with the ultimate problem of human life."[45]

So which is it? Is religion at base about belief, moral obligation, or collective practice and struggle? Pragmatist-psychologist William James was on to something when he opined, "The very fact that they are so many and so different from one another is enough to prove that the word 'religion' cannot stand for any single principle or essence, but is rather a collective name."[46] Fair enough. Religion then, must involve a constellation of human beliefs, dispositions, and behaviors; it doesn't mean any one thing. In this sense, all of the above thinkers are correct in some way. But it's just as important to understand that this doesn't make religion anything or everything. If it's to be a phenomenon amenable to empirical study (and we think it is), we need to set some parameters; otherwise, "religion" is really just an empty concept, and it doesn't make much sense to talk about people leaving it.

For their part, sociologists of religion have played an important role in defining religion as an object of scientific inquiry. Empirical analysis of religion becomes possible when we have a clear conception, however broad and inclusive, of what it is. A common convention in sociology is to delineate three types of definition: *substantive, functionalist*, and *symbolic*. The first is captured in Tylor's definition, and deals with what is essential to religion (e.g., belief in spiritual beings); it tends to focus on the substantive beliefs and doctrinal claims of religions. The second examines not what religion *is* substantively, but what it *does* practically. Yinger's emphasis on how people collectively approach "the ultimate problem of human life" fits the functionalist definition. The last attempts to bridge both the substance and function of religion by exploring its symbolic, integrative dimensions (more on that in a moment).

Sociologist Emile Durkheim famously defined religion as "a unified system of beliefs and practices relative to sacred things, that is to say, things set apart and forbidden—beliefs and practices which unite into one single moral community...."⁴⁷ Durkheim's statement crosscuts both substantive and functionalist definitions. He was interested in what religion does for social groups, and what role it plays in orienting people on his famous sacred/profane dichotomy. Although "sacred things" often implies a supernatural component, for Durkheim, it doesn't have to. That is, religion is about fulfillment of human needs and desires by way of certain social interactions and collective arrangements. Providing a moral framework for understanding how to live with fellow human beings is what religion does.

In contrast, the symbolic definition is best expressed by another, more recent scholar, Glifford Geertz. He defined religion this way:

> Religion is (1) a system of symbols which acts to (2) establish powerful, persuasive, and long-lasting moods and motivations in [people] by (3) formulating conceptions of a general order of existence and (4) clothing these conceptions with such an aura of factuality that the moods and motivations seem uniquely realistic.⁴⁸

Geertz's deftly-worded definition is useful because it integrates (1) the symbolic dimension of religion, which includes not just religious symbols per se but everything from sacred texts, to rituals, to origin myths, with (2) an ethos—or moral framework for behavior based on "moods and motivations" and (3) a worldview that explains existence and our relationship to the cosmos. This symbolic definition makes room for both substantive and functional aspects of religion, but also integrates them into a general model of any religion, as depicted in the figure below.

But what about "myth," the "numinous," "mystical," and the like? Isn't this what distinguishes religion from nonreligion? Magical thinking from scientific thinking? There's long been debate about whether supernaturalism is essential to defining religion, the sacred, or the idea of the holy.⁴⁹ Yinger argued that it's not belief in the supernatural that matters, but that humans are given to constructing and *believing* their stories—inclusive or exclusive of the supernatural—about reality and our place in it. Myth, for example, in this context, isn't about empirical or historical validity; it's about a story from which people derive meaning. The focus

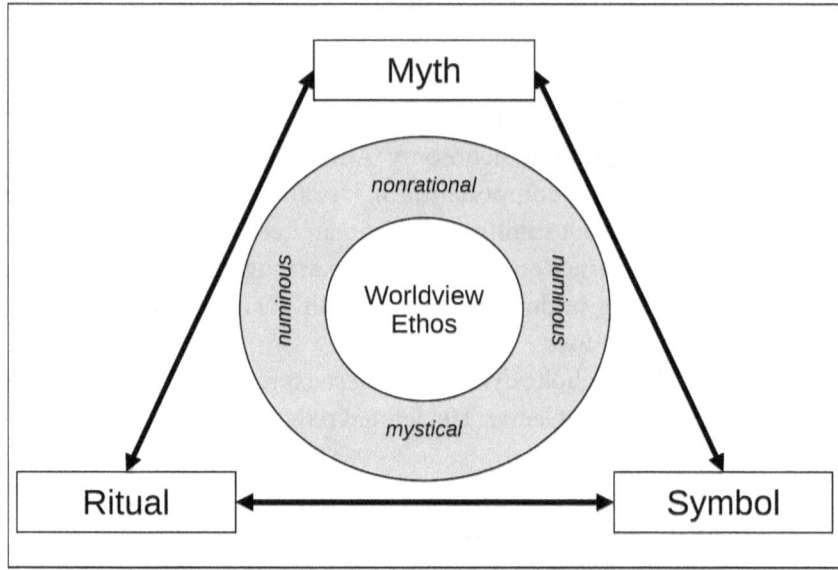

Figure 1.2. Integrating Elements of Religion.[50]

for scholars who take this position tends to be on "lived" or "everyday religion."[51] That is, religion is less about traditional substantive religious claims than everyday practice—practice that's often dissociated from conventional, institutional religion, its doctrines, and the dictates of religious leaders. Individuals engaged in lived religion will identify with and borrow from organized religions, even traditional religions, but they do so in a way that customizes religious beliefs, behaviors, and identities to suit their own needs and preferences. Taking interest in everyday practice, in what people actually do, and in how they create meaningful lives from either (or both) religious and secular norms and values, does of course have merit. One of us (Smith) has even written about a "nonsupernatural sacred" that orients some secular people in communal contexts.[52]

However, talking about secular "versions" of the sacred can quickly devolve into a tangled game of semantics, confounding any coherent definition of religion, so it isn't the line we take in this book.[53] This would take us afield from our purpose, which is to understand how and why people leave religion as it is understood by our participants and most Americans themselves (not imaginative academics). Likewise, we don't downplay the role of the supernatural in religion. In our view, it's not all just about "practice." Beliefs and the claims religions make absolutely matter. And if those beliefs are purely terrestrial in nature, if they have *nothing* to do with the supernatural or otherworldly, we don't call it religion. But as we will see, at least some of the integrated elements outlined above are applicable to some religious exiters. They still have an ethos and a worldview after religion—and rituals, symbols, and myths can play a part in producing them. But given the contents and the meaning these elements take on, it's no longer accurate to call them religious. They are secular. They are nonreligious.

To be clear on the position we take in this book, to be *religious* is to align with, enact, and/or subscribe to the supernaturalism or otherworldliness, doctrines, behaviors, and expectations of a religion, with varying levels of intensity and commitment. If individuals don't do any of this, they are not religious. When we talk about leaving religion, we are talking about individuals disengaging from and/or rejecting these things. Now, admittedly, our book is generally about people leaving conventional religions and their associated traditions. And given the geographic and cultural context of our study, we're talking mostly about people who leave Christianity. But we think there's good reason to expect that the basic causes and dynamics of religious exiting are also applicable not just to other Abrahamic religions like Judaism and Islam, but other non-western, non-monotheistic religions too. We explain why in the conclusion.

Finally, we understand there is gray area here. We can't and don't try to track every belief or behavior that would problematize our definition of religion or what it means to be religious. For example, an atheist who believes in an afterlife, practices witchcraft, supports various secular causes, and loves New Age thinkers, doesn't fit neatly into our framing. However, despite the potential for a definitional rabbit hole, the good news is that between the substantive, functionalist, and symbolic definitions, and a sociological picture of religion in general, we've captured much of what most lay persons and scholars *mean* by religion. That's both a reasonable and useful point of departure for an exposition on how and why some people say goodbye to it.

Nonreligion, Nonreligious

Given the preceding discussion, it might seem equally reasonable to expect that *nonreligion*, since it contains the prefix "non-," just means the absence of, or negation of, religion. But that's not quite right. Following Lois Lee, Johannes Quack and others, there is general consensus among sociologists and other scholars that nonreligion should be defined as that which is, yes, *not* religion, but is nevertheless *related to* it in some way.[54] In other words, nonreligion is not merely a description of what is not religious; it is itself—in at least some minimal way—a product of engagement with the "stuff" of religion. Nonreligion then, is not any one thing, but a concept subsuming a variety of related phenomena; those who study it are examining diverse sets of people, practices, and beliefs that are not themselves religious, but are related to religion in some way, be it discursively, descriptively, or practically. After all, it stands to reason that if religion means many things, this must also be the case with nonreligion.

The key point here is that what makes nonreligion a coherent idea, and, like religion, a phenomenon that can be empirically studied, is the way in which it is tethered to religion and religious phenomena. So even though to be nonreligious is to not have religion, it is also some kind of positive differentiation from religion, not just a "lack" of it. Put differently, whether a person consciously decides to leave religion with great fanfare, or slowly drifts away from it without noticing, the process nevertheless involves changes in beliefs, behaviors, and identities that stand *in relation* to previously held religious beliefs, behaviors, and identities.

In defining it this way, it's important to emphasize that it would be a mistake to make nonreligion strictly beholden to any specific substantive aspect of religion by dint of its relationship to it. Just as we argued above that we can't do with only a substantive definition of religion (e.g. belief in the Christian god) we shouldn't be content to understand nonreligion as simply "not that." We need something broader; something that captures the myriad actions, beliefs, values, and worldviews that express a nonreligious orientation. Lois Lee's concept of *existential culture* is useful to that end. In her book *Recognizing the Nonreligious: Reimagining the Secular* she defines existential cultures as the sets of ". . . ideas about the origins of life and human consciousness and about how both are transformed or expire after death."⁵⁵ Similar to philosopher Paul Tillich's notion that religion is about things of "ultimate concern,"⁵⁶ existential culture points to big questions about human origins and destiny and the ways in which social groups go about responding to these questions. What makes for nonreligious existential cultures instead of religious ones? The answer to that comes from parsing the definitions of religion and nonreligion offered above. To be succinct, it has to do with whether the beliefs people subscribe to and the behaviors they engage in are based on supernatural or otherworldly explanations, rites and rituals, or not.

Lee's point about what people believe about human origins is illustrative. Take Ken Ham and Bill Maher, whose thoughts on atheism we mentioned above. Ham, who believes the earth was formed by the Christian god some 6000 years ago and that that god likewise created human beings to populate the earth, has appealed to a religious, supernaturalist explanation of our origins. Maher, accepting scientific consensus, believes humans evolved over millions of years on a planet billions of years old. Both are explanations that answer existential questions and involve beliefs about the way the world is, but only Ham's is religious. Of course, these two personalities won't represent your average religious or nonreligious American; there is wide variation of belief and practice among and between the religious and nonreligious.

Happily, the concept of nonreligion as defined above neatly maps on to the topic of this book, because to study religious exiting *ipso facto* means we are examining people for whom religion was a part of their lives (however saliently) but who underwent a process of change in leaving it. This is different from studying those who never had religion in their lives and were always indifferent to it. A person born to devoutly Christian parents, who spends their early life as a sincere believer, and pursues a career as a minister before leaving religion is obviously very different from someone born to parents wholly secular who never had even curiosity about religion.

This isn't to say those who leave religion can't become more-or-less indifferent to it, or that they're always thinking about or "relating to" religion as they navigate their lives. Nonreligious Americans, including those sampled in this book, range from passionate atheist activists to the religiously indifferent and—more often than not—are something in between. The common denominator for the subset of the nonreligious population of interest in this book is that these individuals identified with religion and were religious but later abandoned this identity and became nonreligious.

This book therefore occupies an important space, as it is a study of both religion and nonreligion. Inspecting what happens after people leave religion, what they come to believe, what identities they adopt, how their behaviors change (or don't) is an exercise in the study of nonreligion, since our participants are best described as nonreligious, be they atheists, agnostics, humanists, freethinkers, secularists, naturalists, skeptics, or something else. Yet, there's no denying that their experience with religion is an important part of how they became nonreligious. Couple that with our goal of understanding what this all means for both religion and society and it's clear we're dealing with the domains of both religion and nonreligion.

Religious Exiting

Having fleshed out what we mean by religion and nonreligion, religious exiting should be pretty straightforward. There's general consensus in the literature that religious exiting refers to, "the social and psychological process by which an individual exits a religious identity, ideology and/or community."[57] Religious exiting is thus transitional. It marks the move and space between being religious and nonreligious. One might wonder about individuals who leave one religion to join another or about abandoning some religious beliefs or behaviors in favor of new ones. These processes describe the concepts of religious switching, religious preference, or religious conversion.[58] But they aren't examples of religious exiting because the individual hasn't actually left religion. They've moved around within it. As the title of this book makes clear, our focus is on religious exiters,[59] which is what our interviewees are. They were once religious but no longer are.[60] We aim to describe why and how.

Secularity, Secularism, and Secularization

There are other kinds of phenomena that are not religious, but that don't bear on or relate to religion in the way we have just defined nonreligion.

We'll conclude our discussion of terminology with three variations on the word secular. It will become clear early on in this book why these are important for the study of religious exiting.

Like "nonreligious," the adjective "secular" at base refers to that which is not religious. But unlike "nonreligious," it doesn't need to imply any relationship to religion. Running is a secular activity, not a religious one. But it's also unrelated to religion (unless perhaps your run was inspired by the 1973 Shirley Caesar song, "Running for Jesus"). This is the basic difference between nonreligion and *secularity*, the noun form indicating a state of being secular. As we'll see, it's useful to have both terms for studying those who leave religion. This is because religious exiters have a relationship with religion, but some number of them also take up a positive secular identity and worldview, irrespective of how little or much they come to care about religion.

Secularism is related to, but has a different implication from, secularity. Though based on the same root word, it has a more political meaning. We'll use the term here to refer to the constellation of attitudes, values, and social actions that promote the political separation of religion from the state and its various institutions. Coined by English author and secularist George Holyoake (1817–1906), secularism embraces pluralism, including freedom and diversity of religion, but underscores the need for a secular and open society to accomplish this. Most secularists, including many of the religious exiters in this study, would be comfortable with less religion in society, which brings us to our final term.

Secularization. This concept has been hugely important not just to sociologists of religion, but to the history of modern sociology itself.[61] Secularization theory, the claim that religion declines as societies undergo modernization, has been of central concern to sociologists and other scholars of religion, both to those who accept and who reject its basic premise. It's uncanny how scholars and researchers can examine the same evidence and come to opposite conclusions about secularization, but there has indeed been disagreement among scholars about the nature, extent, or even existence of secularization, with some arguing that the opposite is true—that the world is better characterized as undergoing *de*secularization and religious resurgence.[62] This scholarly argument has historically been phrased as the secularization debate.[63]

We'll go on record and state that we think there is strong evidence of secularization, both throughout the world and in the United States, which is often cited as an exception to the clear secularization of other advanced democracies, especially those in western Europe. More to the point of this book, the patterns of religious disaffiliation and the rise of the nones (those who claim no religion) in America and elsewhere that have been making headlines over the last two decades are part and parcel of secularization—the decline of religious authority, participation, belief in religious claims, and other dimensions of religion as a consequence of the forces of modernity. Secularization is complex and uneven, and "modernity" means a lot of different things. We'll spell this out more systematically in the coming chapters, but it's worth noting here that we see religious exiting as an important part of the broader demographic trends regarding the nonreligious in America, and we argue that it is both cause and consequence of secularization.

Belief, Behavior, and Identity

Belief, behavior, identity. These three terms will recur throughout this book and are as important as the definitions just outlined. We'll discuss them explicitly where necessary, but they're also implicit in almost everything there is to say about religious exiting. *Belief* refers to the cognitive acceptance of specific claims about the world. Religious beliefs, as discussed earlier, include supernatural claims that are believed to be true by adherents of the religion. Beliefs involve the world of ideas, which can't be observed directly. When an individual gives assent to a supernatural claim about reality—for instance, that Jesus performed miracles, that there is an endless cycle of rebirths into different animal forms, or that sacred writings on golden plates were delivered to Joseph Smith by an angel—we're in the domain of belief. *Behaviors* are the observable actions of individuals and groups that are informed by beliefs, values, and identities. Importantly, we can empirically measure behaviors in a way we can't with beliefs. Church attendance, praying, fasting, and an array of other rites are subsumed within behavior. Concisely, it's the things people actually do.

Readers familiar with the sociological literature on religion will already have noted that, instead of using the "3 Bs"—belief, behavior, and belonging—we have proposed a modification by replacing "belonging" with "identity." We are convinced that this approach[64] is an important advancement in our understanding of religion and nonreligion. For many individuals, including many scholars who study religion, being religious is often assumed to be the default or base state of being.[65] This is reflected in the language people use generally, but also in the language that we are continuing to use in this book, as we noted above that we are interested in "nonreligion" in contrast to religion. What "nonreligion" as a term does is continue to privilege religion as the default and situate those who are not religious in relation to religion. As one of us (Cragun) with Kevin McCaffree argued in a recent publication, this is extremely problematic and not actually reflective of reality. This is most readily observed when thinking about religious belonging.

Religious belonging has generally referred to someone's religious affiliation, which is whether someone self-identifies as having a connection with an organized religion. From nominal identification, to loose affiliation, to full and active membership, belonging is an indication of an identity-commitment (whatever its strength) to a religious group, organization, or tradition. Is someone Catholic, Muslim, Buddhist, Hindu, a Hutterite? And, if so, how strong is that identity relative to other identities the individual holds? That is certainly a dimension of religiosity and is important to consider. But focusing on whether or not someone belongs to a religion is shortsighted and misses a massive amount of information about people. For instance, in Estonia, roughly 16% of citizens "belong" to Eastern Orthodox religions, another 10% are Lutheran, and another 3% to 4% "belong" to other religions. That accounts for close to 30% of Estonians. But roughly 70% of Estonians either refuse to answer the question (~16%) or report having no religious affiliation (~54%). In other words, the majority of Estonians don't "belong" to a religion. If we focus only on belonging, we effectively have no information about the identities of the majority of Estonians because belonging is only about their identity vis-a-vis religion. Many of those nonreligious Estonians are humanists, but they are also materialists and naturalists and environmentalists and so much more. They have identities—many identities—but they are just not religious identities.

By broadening this area of focus from just religious belonging to identities instead, we can focus on the positive content of who someone is rather than what one lacks. Additionally, and more importantly, doing so situates religious belonging as a subset of identities and de-privileges religion. Identities become the baseline or default. All people have identities; some people have religious identities.

Rather than refer to these three dimensions of humans as the "three Bs," then, we refer to them as belief, behavior, and identity, or "BBI." Accounting for BBI in the analysis of religious exiting is essential for two reasons. First, whether we are talking about religious or nonreligious individuals, or religiosity and secularity at the societal level, they represent key dimensions of private and public life. Traditionally, belief, behavior, and identity are used to reference religious life specifically,[66] but those who leave religion, and nonreligious people generally, are never without beliefs or behaviors, those beliefs and behaviors are just not religious. On identity, as with beliefs and behaviors, our focus is on individuals who were once religious but later became nonreligious. It's certainly relevant, categorically speaking, whether an individual belongs to a religious group or not, but we're especially interested in the *transition* people make out of religion. Studying this liminal space might actually tell us something about the nature and role of religion in public life that we can't learn from studying the religious and/or nonreligious in an either/or sense. As we'll argue, for some religious exiters, it's not just that religious beliefs, behaviors, and identities are abandoned, and that's the end of the story. Rather, religious exiting can be an expression of an intermediary stage before the adoption of explicitly *secular* beliefs, behaviors, and identities.

The second reason BBI are essential to our analyses is that they link up to all the other concepts outlined in the previous section. If we want to have a theoretical explanation of the causes and consequences of religious exiting we can't merely rely on descriptive accounts of individual religious exiters, be it through surveys or interviews. As we have noted, religious exiting, as personal as it may be for the individual, is not a product of individuals, unconnected from broader social forces, simply deciding to leave religion out of purely rational self-interest. We don't live in an atomistic society; individuals leave religion in contexts and by dint of cultural processes unfolding all around them. To uncover the social and psychological processes at play, to find common patterns of experience and the cultural conditions in which those experiences emerge, and to make informed judgments about what causes religious exiting, we need to pay keen attention to changes in BBI at both the individual and societal level.

Throughout the following chapters, while we focus on religious exiters, we compare three groups—those who left religions (i.e., religious exiters) those who were never religious, and those who have stayed religious or joined religions. We classified individuals into these groups solely on the basis of religious identity. The overlap between identity, belief, and behavior is not perfect, but it's actually quite substantial. In other words, if we know that someone identifies as Catholic, that can tell us a fair amount about their beliefs and their behaviors. Likewise, if we know that someone has no religious affiliation (i.e., they are a "none" or "nonreligious" or a secular humanist), that, too, tells us quite a bit about their beliefs and behaviors. Of course, knowing someone's identity by no means perfectly predicts their beliefs or behaviors. Someone may indicate they do not have a religious identity but they still believe in a monotheistic, Judeo-Christian god and pray to that god. Inversely, there are many people who report a religious affiliation but never attend religious services and/or do not believe in a god or higher power. Even so, in our methodological appendix, we show that identity works fairly well at capturing belief and behavior, which is why we have opted to use that as our primary tool for delineating between exiters, the never religious, and those who have stayed or joined religions.

Methodology

No one research method can fully explore or explain something as complex as why and how people leave religion. This is why we've adopted a mixed-methods approach to understanding this topic. Survey data and quantitative analysis of it is essential for understanding the role of demographics, social context and background, and the many variables that correlate with the process of religious exiting. Multi-year field research, interview data, and field note data work in tandem with what we know from surveys (and a few field experiments), and qualitative analysis of data collected from these methods deepens this knowledge and provides fresh insights. We want to understand the social and cultural conditions that shape individuals and their relationship with religion, answering questions about why they leave religion and what this looks like. But we're also interested in the consequences this has for religion and society. Assessing that is a tall order, and it takes a multi-method approach to fill it. We agree with Becker's[67] point that the similarities between quantitative and qualitative approaches to understanding the social world are at least as important as their differences. In a sense, each relies on the other, and there's no necessary epistemological divide between quantitative and qualitative methods. As he said, "I think the same epistemological arguments underlie and provide the warrant for both [methods]." This gives us confidence that our combined methods and styles of analysis point to the same underlying reality of religious exiting.

Throughout this book, we draw on several well-known and publicly available surveys. Our primary quantitative source is the General Social Survey (GSS), a long-running (1972 to the present) survey fielded by the National Opinion Research Center with funding from the National Science Foundation. Scholars consider the GSS to be the gold standard when it comes to high quality survey research for a variety of reasons, including the very high response rates, the careful survey construction, the inclusion of identical survey questions for decades, and the representativeness of the data. The GSS includes data to address many of the questions we'll discuss in this book and, whenever possible, we will draw upon it because it is such a high-quality and reliable source of data. However, there are times when we will turn to other surveys, particularly when those surveys include greater detail related to a question of interest, like the World Values Survey. With all of these data sets and our analyses, we provide relevant documentation and citations so anyone interested in our analyses can replicate them.

Regarding our qualitative data, we draw on 120 in-depth interviews with individuals from a wide range of backgrounds (see the appendix for a full description of our sample). Interviews took place in clusters at different points over ten years, from 2008 to 2018. This range provided an opportunity to see important cultural and political shifts take place in American society that bore on the religious exiting of participants. Our interviews traverse the end of president George W. Bush's administration, the whole of Barack Obama's, and the beginning of Donald Trump's. Legislative actions including the federal legalization of same-sex marriage and other important cultural developments occurred during this time and we found that they were connected to religious exiting. Perhaps most significantly, our interviews occurred alongside the most significant change in religious affiliation patterns in American history, the rise of the nones.

All formal interviews were in-depth; they lasted from 40 minutes to 2.5 hours, allowing religious exiters to develop their thoughts and share many details about their experiences leaving religion. About half the interviews were in-person, while the other half took place over phone/video conference or chat. It also bears mentioning that both authors of this book have had countless informal interviews over many years with individuals who have left religion. Though most of these weren't recorded and transcribed, they have helped flesh out the context of our thinking and analysis.

Our interviewees ranged in age from 18 to 92 years old. The different authors used different methods to recruit participants. For instance, Smith established himself as a researcher and fieldworker at a number of secular organizations, primarily in Colorado and Michigan, where participants were recruited based on their interest in the study. In Colorado, Mountain West Freethinkers[68] was a primary source of interviews. In Michigan, participants were recruited from a chapter of the Sunday Assembly,[69] a network of secular congregations. The second part of recruitment involved a self-referral system where respondents referred others for interviews. This expanded the sample to include individuals from many different US states and regions of the country, broadening the context for a more meaningful sample (though our sample is neither random nor representative in a statistical sense). Importantly, about half of the referrals were self-identified nonreligious individuals who had minimal involvement with secular groups.

For the interviews conducted by Cragun, participants were recruited differently. A short survey was approved by his university's ethics board and links to it were posted on Craigslist. Participants were told that, if they qualified for and participated in an interview, they would be paid $50. Several hundred individuals completed the survey. Cragun then used a diversity sampling approach to select individuals who reported no religious affiliation and no connection to a formal secular organization. Importantly, these individuals add to those who did not have an association with secular groups and who were interviewed by Smith;

such individuals represent the majority of the nonreligious. Combined, we have 120 rich interviews with various types of nonreligious individuals in the US.

Many other kinds of qualitative data beyond interviews were collected and analyzed for related research projects over the years that led to this book. We collected and analyzed hundreds of hours of participant observations; methodological, empirical, and analytical field notes; memo-writing; and many relevant websites, podcasts, emails, pamphlets, working papers and other kinds of grey literature from secular and freethought organizations and ex-religious support groups. In short, though aspirational more than practical (or possible) we took the disposition shared by many researchers with regard to one's research topic, following Barney Glaser's dictum that "all is data."[70] This is a useful position to take when the goal is not just to describe, but *explain* the phenomenon of religious exiting.

Finally, analysis of our qualitative data followed the logic of Grounded Theory (GT), which is to say, the data were systematically organized and coded such that the concepts, categories, and themes described throughout the book were developed over time through an inductive and iterative process.[71] The goal of GT is to ensure that arguments and explanations, however abstract they become, always remain grounded in the data. For instance, we did not impose categories like "moral push factors" (chapter three) from the outset, and we did our best to keep our preconceptions about why people leave religion to a minimum. Rather, the various parts of our theory of religious exiting emerged through a process of coding and recoding data, whereby comparisons across transcripts and other information led to the ideas we use to explain what's going on in the data. However, we also needed to assess how and when the qualitative data confirmed (or didn't) what we know from surveys. We tried to ensure that both our qualitative and quantitative data were in constant conversation, rather than exist as isolated sets of data. We did this by comparing: (1) individual interviewees' stories as told by them, with (2) the sociological interpretation we developed from these stories through the inductive process, and (3) the responses from surveys and a range of demographic variables. As suggested above, the surveys we use aren't narrowly focused on religious exiters. We work with data that allow us to draw comparisons between those who have left religion, those who have stayed with religion, and those who were never religious. When combined with our interviews, this proved very useful for addressing the questions we pose in this book and for making sense of the data that address them.

Where We're Headed

Though ours is not the first study of religious exiting in the United States, we think our use of the literature, and the arguments we make throughout, advance our understanding of the subject in a way that's beneficial to scholars and lay readers alike. Rather than attempt an exhaustive literature review up front, we've integrated all the important empirical studies that bear on our topic throughout the book. What follows is a very brief description of the subsequent chapters.

We have organized the chapters with a series of simple and logically-ordered questions that address the phenomenon of religious exiting. We want to know which Americans are leaving religion (chapter 2), why they are doing so (chapter 3), where they are going (chapter 4) and what happens to them after they leave (chapter 5). These questions address directly the social, demographic, political, and psychological forces at play in the lives of Americans as they exit religion. The first question recognizes that some are more likely than others to leave religion. Are there demographic forces that explain this, that tell us who is most likely to leave? What variables are at play by way of race, class, and gender, and how do these shape the process of religious exiting? Chapter 2 sets the stage for the rest of the book by outlining just who it is we're talking about when we refer to religious exiters.

We then extend the implications of this into chapter 3 by asking the "why" question. Is it just the stereotypical white, young male with no children and lots of education who's saying goodbye to religion? Here we show that this caricature is just that, a caricature. Though this demographic is certainly part of the story, it's by no means the end of it, or even most of it. In fact, the data show that the demographic characteristics of religious exiters are increasingly matching those of the population at large. This leads to the questions we address in chapters 3 through 5. If it's not just a narrow slice of the population who is leaving religion, what other factors are leading people of all backgrounds and social positions to leave? This takes us to in-depth discussions of the social and psychological motives for leaving religion. There are various push and pull factors at play. Changing social networks, increased education, questioning religious claims, the internet and social media, and the intermingling of specific historical and political forces all combine to help explain why more Americans are leaving religion.

Once they have left, where do they go? Chapters 4 and 5 take up these (much less researched) questions. Do people seek out other kinds of social relationships or groups to replace their former religious ones? How do religious exiters spend the time formerly spent on Sundays at church? Studies have shown the significant time investment that religion demands of many Americans.[72] What happens when this time simply opens up for people who leave? In short, how does belonging and behavior change when individuals enter a post-religion space in their lives? We show in these chapters a range of outcomes on this question. Some formerly religious individuals pursue new interests, take on new commitments, or take up old interests or commitments that they now have more time for. Many religious exiters simply give up religion, finding freedom from it without changing their lives in any appreciable way. Others join explicitly secular groups for support and friendship, or join secular and humanist organizations that take up the task of promoting secularism, defending the separation of church and state, or fighting discrimination against the nonreligious.

The final chapter asks a more abstract question about what religious exiting *means* for society (chapter 6). That is, we move beyond individuals and their social contexts, and seek to explain how society might change as a result of this new landscape and the fact that the fastest growing "religious group" is now populated by those who claim no religion at all.[73] What does it mean for American society when so many Americans do not need religion, are indifferent to it, or have a newfound freedom from it? Should we be worried—as apparently so many people, including researchers of the very topic, are[74]—that lack of interest in religion will mean a diminishing of our intuitions for charity, volunteer work, community, social cohesion, the pursuit of social justice, and human progress? Could it mean the collapse of individual and collective morality or even civil society if Americans continue to leave religion at the rate they are now?

Chapters 2 through 6 are empirical chapters; they present a lot of data and analysis, and they ultimately ground our arguments regarding these and all the substantive questions that frame this book. In the conclusion we summarize our findings, but we also take the opportunity to hover just above that ground and speculate a bit on "what all this really means" and what the current data may suggest about the future. It's always a risk making predictions, especially about something as controversial and consequential as the fate of religion in America. But we also think it's worthwhile; it pushes the conversation, spurs new questions, stretches our thinking, and will clarify at a later date where we were right and where we were wrong, which can in turn help guide the efforts of future research.

2

Who Is Leaving?

Technically, I was raised Lutheran. My dad was a Lutheran. My mom was nothing really. She hadn't gone to church since she was about 12. But my dad thought that whole, you know, better safe than sorry type of thing (laughs). So that's how it was for a while. We'd go to church during Easter and Christmas and stuff like that. . . . My parents believed that should we ever choose any religion, [that] it was certainly up to us; they would support us in whatever we wanted because who were they to say we had to believe in a particular religion? . . . Then Pastor Jim—our church's pastor—he was a cool guy, we all liked him a lot. Even he knows I don't believe anymore, and he's cool with that. But then we moved to England and my mom decided that she was going to be a Wiccan (laughs); I was like eight at the time. She said she could feel the spirit through the trees and I didn't know what she was talking about, but I did know I didn't believe in god anymore . . . that's when [I decided] religion just wasn't working for me.
—Ken

I was raised [Christian] and [was] born in China and came here when I was five. But we started going to church when we moved to Memphis and there was a pretty tight-knit Chinese community that was centered around a church. There was a lot of overlap between the first Chinese Baptist church and this Chinese school that ran on Saturdays, and there [was] church on Sunday, and you saw the same people. I was pretty hardcore about it I guess. I was baptized when I was eleven and people were telling me that I should wait until I was older so that I could decide or whatever, but I was like, "I already know" (laughs). And I really like it. I still like Bible trivia; you know, all the sort of interesting details

about biblical history and who did what and yeah. . . . [But] I guess I've given up trying to figure out what is "true" [with respect to religion] and I'm at the moment more curious about how physiologically, mentally, neurologically, we think about things that are true and [our] beliefs, or what's important in meaning and religion.
—Monica

As a Black female, especially in my age group amongst my peers . . . I have three characteristics that really make them uncomfortable. First, I chose not to have children. There are some undercurrents in Black subculture about making those choices. I never even pretend to be a theist, even when I've gone to people's churches. I don't participate in prayers, and a lot of times I don't even bow my head, to show how irritated I am that people are putting pressure on me to conform. I have not hidden my intellect, and that has caused issues. So I tend to get dinged on those three things among my peers. I try to be nice about it, but as I get older, I'm a bit tired of it (laughs) you know, enough already! I'm heading towards 50, I don't think someone's going to be able to change me. I've had two prayer circles for me at Heritage Christian, which cracks me up. You know, they were going to pray and bring me to the fold. And I say, "Well thank you, but save it for someone who's in dire need!" (laughs).
—Torin

As with the vignettes in our opening chapter, the individuals here—Ken, Monica, and Torin—represent widely different backgrounds. The stories they shared again illustrate our three pathways, *indifference*, *liminality*, and *activism*, respectively. Their experience with religion, how they left it, and how they feel about it now, are in some ways as disparate as the backgrounds from which they came. Their biographical stories, in one sense, couldn't be more different. Ken was 18 at the time of our interview. His Scandinavian heritage tracks in an almost stereotypical way regarding his disposition toward religion.[1] He was noncommittal and unimpressed with religion, even as a child. He appreciated that his parents would let him choose his own religious path, he liked his pastor and had no discernible problem with religion; it just wasn't for him, and he figured this out early in life. Monica, an Asian American woman in her 30s, values her religious upbringing a great deal, despite the fact that she left Christianity after high school. For her, so intertwined were religion, ethnicity, and community, that she sees value in religion, sympathizes with the religious, and does her best to withhold judgment—even on religious "truths"—though she herself no longer believes its core claims. Torin was in her late 40s when she was interviewed. An African American woman, she was raised Baptist but left the church, and all religion, in her 20s. As her statement suggests, she has often dealt with friends and family trying to bring her back to the fold, despite her having left many years ago. Torin has lived in various parts of the country (and, in her words, "didn't do well in the South") and was a double major in college, leaving with degrees in journalism and management. She's been divorced, and by her own account is a person who speaks her mind. She unyieldingly resists people who make assumptions about her beliefs because of her race and gender. This has led her to being very open about her atheism and feelings about religion.

So, who is leaving religion in America? Everyone. Well, not *everyone* of course, but with respect to the sociodemographics of religious exiting, it's not just one category of people who are leaving. It's not only young, white males with lots of education.[2] Increasingly, religious exiting cuts across every racial, ethnic, gender, and age category.

How Many Are Leaving?

Before we discuss the characteristics of exiters, we want to make clear why this book is needed, and why we should be examining those who leave religion, by showing the magnitude of this trend. Figure 2.1 shows the percentages of the never religious, religious exiters, and those who have stayed religious or joined by decade using the GSS.[3] In the 1970s, 94% of Americans[4] had either stayed religious from their childhood or joined a religion. Just 0.8% of Americans had been raised without

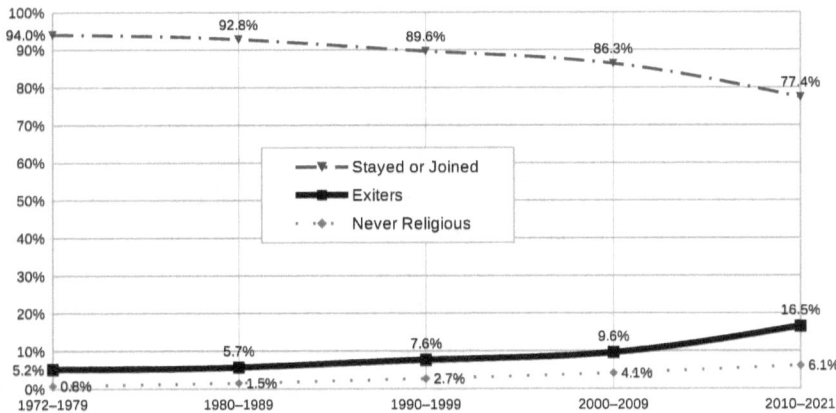

Figure 2.1. Exiters, Never Religious, and Religious, 1972–2021 by Decade. (Source: GSS, 1972–2021)

religion and 5.2% were raised in a religion but left. Looking at adult Americans, that would translate into just under 8 million who had left religions in the 1970s. As of the second decade of the twenty-first century, 16.5% of Americans had left the religion of their childhood, which is about 38 million people. These are estimates drawing on roughly a decade of surveys, which means the number of Americans who were raised religious and now do not identify as such is likely higher as of the writing of this book.

Small groups or categories, like individuals who enjoy professional wrestling[5] or furries,[6] are often studied because they tend to be unique and, as a result, are interesting. In the 1970s, exiters were a relatively small group, though still larger than Mormons and Jews combined. But today, exiters are not a small group. As of 2023, there were more religious exiters in the US than Southern Baptists and almost as many exiters as Catholics. When groups are small, they are fascinating because they tend to have unique characteristics. But as groups grow larger, they tend to become less unique and reasons for studying them shift from, "Oooh, look how strange these people are," to "This group or category could be influential in politics or social life generally and we should probably understand who they are." That is where we are with religious exiters—they are no longer a small, esoteric group of individuals. Who, then, are religious exiters?

Who Is Leaving?

Recent research has suggested[7], and the data we show in this chapter agree, that in some ways, religious exiters were more unique fifty years ago.[8] They tended to be younger and disproportionately male. But as the number of Americans who have left the religions of their childhoods has increased, exiters have come to look increasingly like other adult Americans. Not to give away the primary finding of this chapter at the beginning, but it is now the case that the basic demographic characteristics of individuals are not all that useful in predicting who might leave. In other words, anyone could be an exiter. Religious exiters are anywhere and everywhere.

Age

A lot of studies that examine either exiters or the nonreligious generally have noted that they tend to be younger than religious people.[9] Inversely, there are many studies that find religious individuals, particularly in mainline denominations, are substantially older than those without a religious affiliation.[10]

Figure 2.2 shows the average ages of religious exiters, the never religious, and the religious by decade in the GSS from the 1970s through 2021.[11] In the 1970s, when religious exiters were a much smaller percentage of the population than they are today, their average age was 35.9, compared to 45.2 as the average age for religious individuals in the GSS, a gap of just over 9 years. As the figure illustrates, that gap has shrunk over time. In the most recent GSS data, the average age of exiters had increased to 44.7 while the average age of the religious was 51.3, a gap of 6.6 years. Religious exiters are still younger than the religious, but that difference is diminishing. Why might this be the case?

It isn't often thought of this way, but an argument can be made that leaving a religion is a type of innovation. There is a substantial body of research examining the diffusion of innovations and who is likely to be at the forefront of adopting novel social and technological developments.[12] Young people are more likely to adopt new technology, like electric cars and virtual reality headsets, than are older individuals. There are many reasons why that might be the case, but one big reason is that younger

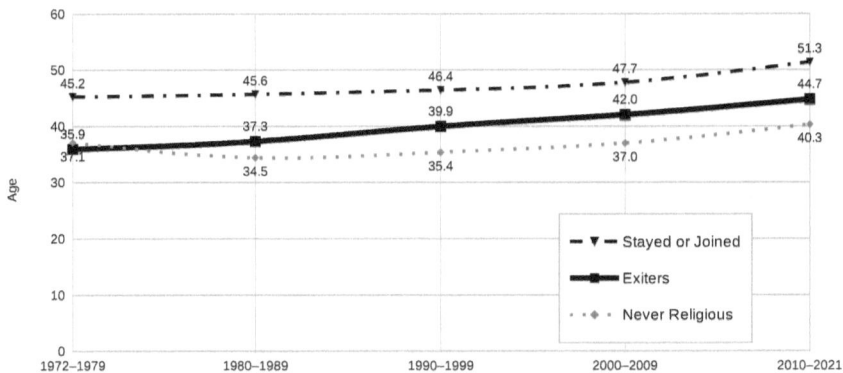

Figure 2.2. Average Age of Exiters, Never Religious, and Religious, 1972–2021 by Decade. (Source: GSS, 1972–2021)

people are less risk-averse than older individuals. Younger individuals are more willing to accept that their behaviors can result in opprobrium, ranging from social disapproval to potentially running afoul of the law.

As we noted in the previous chapter, there was a strong sentiment in the US during the Cold War that atheists were also communists and that "good Americans" were religious Americans.[13] Openly expressing that you were not religious during the Cold War could and did result in discrimination,[14] which is definitely a form of opprobrium. As recent research has illustrated,[15] individuals who are the least likely to experience marginalization and discrimination in most aspects of their lives—like young, affluent, white men—can "afford" the greater risk of experiencing discrimination. We are not suggesting that young individuals leave religions because they want to experience discrimination but rather that they are better situated to cope with, compensate for, or deal with any discrimination they may face because of their younger age. This may explain why, in the 1970s, exiters were much younger than the population generally.

Even so, as figure 2.2 illustrates, exiters remain younger than average. Why might that be if exiting is diffusing throughout the population? First, exiters are still a minority, even if they are closing in on 20% of the US adult population. Statistically, as exiters become a larger percentage of the population, they will increasingly look like the rest of the population. That's basic math.

But there is another reason why exiters will likely remain younger for a while. Exiting always involves a rejection decision, even if that decision is just to lose the inertia involved in maintaining a nominal religious identity. The decision to reject one's religion typically involves rejecting the religion in which they were raised. In other words, it is most often children rejecting the religion of their parents. Sometimes, children deciding to leave can result in the parents deciding to go with them.[16] But usually this means that it is children who are leaving and parents who are staying. Thus, so long as exiting primarily involves the rejection of one's childhood religion, and we do not group exiters in with those who were never religious, exiters will likely continue to be younger than the national average.

That exiters continue to be younger than average raises another question. Don't some people return to religion as they age?[17] Are people afraid of death and using religion to cope with their mortality, as some scholars have argued?[18]

Figure 2.2 alone does not refute that argument. It could be the case in our data that young people leave and older people return to religion, which would result in a lower average age for the religious exiters, as we see in the figure. The GSS only tracks religious affiliation at two points in time—at 16 and at the time they participated in the survey—so we don't have the additional information needed to determine how often people change their affiliation.

However, figure 2.1 at the beginning of this chapter and additional data near the end of this chapter provide some evidence to suggest that, even if some people who had exited religion return to religion later in life, that is not the case for most people. How is that observable in figure 2.1? Stephen Merino[19] showed that nonreligious individuals are more likely to raise their children into adults who are also nonreligious than are religious individuals to raise their children and have them remain religiously affiliated, which aligns with our data. The increase in Americans who are being raised without religion, shown in figure 2.1, from just 0.8% of Americans in the 1970s to 5.3% in the most recent waves of the GSS, illustrates that many of those who exit religion remain nonreligious and raise their children that way. As we show near the end of this chapter, retention isn't great for lots of religions. If exiters were returning and/or those raised without religion were raising their kids with religion, the nonreligious would not be growing. But both are growing, which supports the idea that nonreligion is "stickier" than is religion in the twenty-first century in the US. It also suggests that once people leave, they tend to stay out of religion.[20]

Skeptics might point out that our argument in the previous paragraph is not definitive evidence that religious exiters do not return to religion on their deathbeds. That's true. We do not have data tracking people's religious affiliation from birth to old age and every moment in between; we don't know definitively that people in their golden years don't turn to religion as they contemplate their mortality. But there is a growing body of research looking at elderly nonreligious individuals that indicates many of these individuals are not afraid of death and have no interest in turning to religion for comfort in their final days, a topic we return to later.[21] In fact, some research suggests that nonreligious individuals are better able to cope with death than are religious individuals.[22] In line with that research, our interviewees, while they were not on death's door when they participated in our study, were not looking to return to religion to cope with death.[23] Some had left religion 20, 30, or even 40 years before they were interviewed and had not experienced any desire to return to religion. We're not trying to claim that no one who exits religion ever returns; certainly, people do. But the statistical data suggest returning to religions is not offsetting religious exiting.

Race

At least since the 1970s, scholars have suggested that white individuals are more likely to leave religions than are Black individuals or individuals of other races.[24] The assertion that white individuals were more likely to leave religions doesn't quite capture the full picture. Figure 2.3 shows the percentage of exiters who were white by decade, from 1972 through 2021. Across all five decades of the GSS, exiters were slightly more likely to be white than were the religious—about 3% to 5% more likely. That gap has stayed consistent over time.

Obviously, one way to interpret figure 2.3 is to infer that white individuals are more likely to leave religions than are Black individuals. But we think the small, consistent gap over time is actually more interesting, as it is indicative of two things. First, even in the 1970s, Black individuals

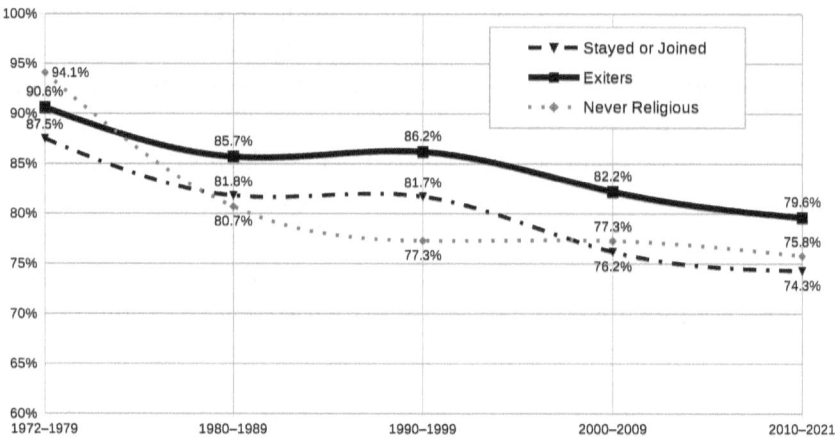

Figure 2.3. Percentage of Exiters Who Are White, 1972–2021 by Decade. (Source: GSS, 1972–2021)

and individuals who identified their race as "other" were still leaving religions and were doing so at just slightly lower rates than white individuals. Second, the small, consistent gap illustrates that religious exiting is not exclusive to white individuals in the US. It is a universal phenomenon affecting people of all races.

At least since the 1970s, Black individuals have been close to proportionately represented among exiters, and clearly are today. While it may seem as though Black individuals in the US are more religious—and, in fact, a slightly higher percentage of Black individuals are religious compared to white individuals—race is not a strong predictor of who is or is not going to leave religion.

As far as we know, there have always been people who are skeptical of religion, at least since the dawn of history.[25] Black Americans—and Black women in particular—are often simply presumed to be religious.[26] There is no reason to believe that Black individuals are inherently less skeptical than white individuals when it comes to religion;[27] suggesting otherwise is a racist trope. Torin's exasperation about this is telling. She recalls openly questioning Jesus's miracles at age three, and she can't really recall a time when she wasn't skeptical of religion or its claims she was taught to believe as a child. She'd get frustrated by people, including some of her Black friends, for assuming that, deep down, really, she must be religious; it's just that she's lost her way and needs to come back to the fold: "People were really trying to recruit me, and get me to church because again, I'm this odd person. They had never met anyone, *especially* a Black female, who wasn't religious. So that became an uncomfortable situation down there [the American South]."

Because the percentage of Black Americans who are exiters is slightly smaller than that of white Americans, Black Americans have been largely erased or simply ignored as a percentage of the population that has left religion. Very little research focuses on Black individuals who have left religions or who are openly nonreligious.[28] Outspoken and uncompromising atheists like Torin may be somewhat unusual, but, historically, it's simply not been clear how many Black Americans shared Torin's skepticism of religion while all along being *assumed* by others to be religious. In fact, one recent study shows that Black atheists experience "racial identity denial" from other Black individuals, whereby the nonbeliever is seen as "less Black" than their religious counterparts.[29]

This relates to an important factor at play when it comes to leaving religion in the US: one's willingness to accept the risk of discrimination.[30] Leaving religion or outing oneself as a nonbeliever carries a risk of discrimination in the US (and in many places around the world). There is a robust scholarly literature on the risks associated with identifying as nonreligious or an atheist.[31] Importantly, some people are better able to manage such risks.

Avoiding prejudice and/or discrimination in the US is kind of like riding a bicycle. When riding a bicycle, there are lots of risks: tipping over, running into something, someone running into you, bike failure, etc. There are a number of ways to mitigate those risks as well: wearing protective elbow, knee, and wrist pads; wearing a helmet; riding in specific locations; and having a well-maintained bicycle. While most people riding bicycles want to minimize risks to avoid injury, there are some individuals who are willing to take risks, competing in events like the X Games. These risk-takers have typically found ways to minimize as much risk as possible—practicing for years; using high-end, specialized equipment; and wearing protective gear. These individuals also tend to be young, healthy, and athletic. But the individuals who take these risks do so knowing that they are exposing themselves to potential harm.

In a similar fashion, individuals who leave religions or individuals who are open about their atheism are exposing themselves to risk.

Having left religion or not believing in a god isn't a stigma that everyone can see. It is easily concealable.[32] In the hierarchy of American society, the individuals at the top of the hierarchy—and generally at the lowest level of risk of discrimination—tend to be well-educated, affluent, white men. They are unlikely to experience discrimination due to their race, sex, education, or income. Such individuals can, therefore, afford to risk discrimination by leaving religion. This helps explain why so much of the scholarly literature on atheists tends to focus on affluent white men—they were in a social position to accept the risk of being openly atheist.[33] A clear illustration of this are the often-cited New Atheist authors—Sam Harris, Richard Dawkins, Christopher Hitchens, and Daniel Dennett. All are well-educated, affluent white men.

Black individuals in the US have an open stigma—their racial classification. It is a stigma they typically cannot hide and it is a stigma that results in discrimination ranging from microaggressions to police brutality and racially motivated murder.[34] Given the risks such individuals face, why would racial minorities increase their risk of facing additional discrimination by leaving religion? Certainly, many Black individuals have done so.[35] Torin is a good example. Recognizing her stigma, she decided to take the risk, in spite of the cost. When asked why she was willing to out herself, she replied:

> Well, it didn't really help me to hide, when I was the only Black person in an all-white situation. I was going to get noticed. My personality really doesn't lend to being toned down because it didn't matter if I tried to tone down; there were going to be things that would happen just because of my characteristics. I'm a weird mix of that, because in a sense I come off as arrogant, but I'm not trying to be arrogant, it's just that I really have a strong sense of self in what I believe and how I feel, and I'm not easily swayed just because it might make you comfortable. And I've had to pay the price for that.

Torin went in the opposite direction, reasoning that, though she could stay quiet about her atheism and having left religion, given her other characteristics (and personality) she might as well be open and add one more "discrediting" aspect to her identity.[36] But, in the context of managing stigma, it makes sense that most Black Americans would be more reticent than white Americans to expose themselves to a higher risk of discrimination, as this compounds their risk. This also helps explain why Black Americans may be less likely to indicate they have left religion or are atheists than are white Americans—it is a risk mitigation strategy, and it makes one wonder how many others share Torin's views, but are disincentivized to openly admit it. There are, in fact, well over a million Black Americans who are nonbelievers but who are not open about this.[37] There are also millions of Black Americans who *are* increasingly open about having left religion, and for some of these individuals, this comes at significant personal expense.[38]

In sum, while white Americans are slightly more likely to leave religion, there is also less risk to them in doing so. For Black Americans, leaving religion adds another basis for discrimination on top of their race, which may very well account for their marginally lower self-reported rates of religious exiting.

Gender

The relationship between gender and exiting religion is similar to both age and race, but for different reasons. Figure 2.4 shows the percentage of exiters, never religious, and religious who were male by decade from 1972 through 2021. As with age, in the 1970s, there was a substantial gap; 62.8% of exiters were male while 44.5% of the religiously affiliated were male, a difference of 18.3%. That gap has declined over time, such that in the latest GSS data, 53.6% of exiters were male while 42% of the religious were, reducing the gap to just 11.6%. Much of the prior research on religious exiting has focused on the fact that men have been more likely to leave religion than women.[39] We think it is important to note that, even in the 1970s, just under 40% of those who had left religion were women, and today, it's close to 50%. In other words, the nonreligious were never all men. Figure 2.4 raises two questions. First, why is the gap shrinking over time? Second, why might men have been more likely to leave religion than women?

As we suggested with age, the shrinking gender gap in religious exiting is likely due to the increasing prevalence of religious exiting. As more individuals leave religions, exiters will look more and more like the population, generally. That has increased the average age of religious

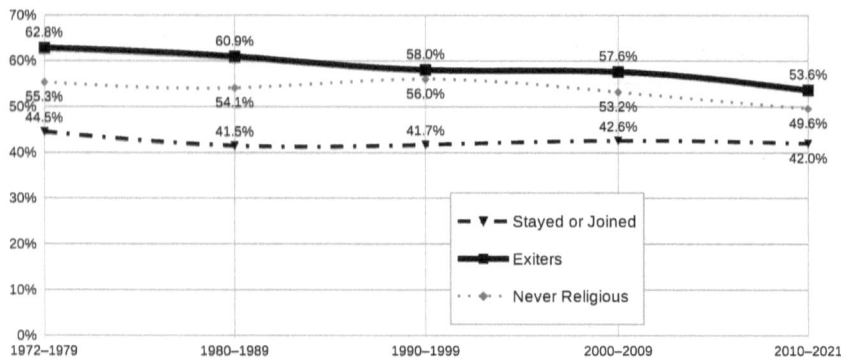

Figure 2.4. Percentage of Exiters, Never Religious, and Religious Who Are Male, 1972–2021 by Decade. (Source: GSS, 1972–2021)

exiters over time and has reduced the gender gap as well. Additionally, as not having a religious affiliation becomes more common, it will also become more widely accepted and less stigmatized, which leads to the second question.

Just as we argued above concerning race—that Black individuals were in a more precarious position when it comes to prejudice and discrimination and were, therefore, less likely to adopt another stigmatized identity—there is evidence to support this argument for women in the US.[40] Women in the US face prejudice and discrimination because of their gender—they are often paid less, overlooked in hiring practices, denied opportunities, harassed, and abused.[41] There is no reason to believe that biological or social differences between men and women would contribute meaningfully to differences in religiosity, despite some research suggesting so.[42] To the contrary, women, of course, are just as capable as men in thinking about, evaluating, and making decisions regarding their continued affiliation with a religion. However, so long as being nonreligious or identifying as an atheist carries with it the risk of added discrimination, it makes sense for women to conceal their nonreligion or atheism to avoid added discrimination. If the US was truly egalitarian when it came to race and gender, we would be surprised if there were any significant differences in religiosity between white and Black individuals (as well as other racial groups) or between men and women.

In some ways, we are actually somewhat surprised that Black individuals and women in the US are as willing to leave religions as they are, given the inequality that exists. At the risk of overstating our case, we think Black individuals and women may actually be more courageous than white men in their willingness to face the discrimination that comes with rejecting religion. For white men, particularly young, well-to-do, heterosexual, highly educated white men, rejecting religion is now almost normative. But for women and Black individuals to reject religion when there is still widespread prejudice against atheists and the nonreligious takes real courage. Scholars studying Black atheists have noted the importance of religion among Black communities and the substantial risks such individuals take when they reject religion.[43] Likewise, gendered expectations concerning religion make it more challenging for all but highly educated, affluent white women to reject religion.[44] For other women, to reject religion has required serious mettle.

Yesenia is one such example. Born to low-income immigrant parents from Mexico, when asked about why she chose not just to leave the Catholic faith she grew up with, but to identify herself to family, friends, and others as an atheist and humanist, she responded this way:

> I'm Mexican American, and so in that way, I was raised Catholic. It's a Catholic country, my parents are immigrants. . . . I was actively going to church between 14 and 16. I completed my first communion and confirmation, mostly because I thought it was something I *ought* to do, and that was kind of it. After that, I was in high school and by the time I started college I would just check off a box that I was Catholic. . . . [Now] I mostly use "atheist" because I feel like that's a term most folks are familiar with and requires less explanation than saying, "I'm a humanist." I *am* a secular humanist. My beliefs are and what I want in my life is more and more [in line] with humanism. So it's not just a lack of god, it's social justice. I want to act, not just think alike; you know and help those people who are struggling. So it's not just the absence of god, I still want to do something positive and have (pause) . . . I want to be a good person. I want to help other people without this kind of threat or promise of heaven or hell in the end. That's what I explained to my mom, who's a Spanish (only) speaking immigrant, and she still doesn't really get it . . . she just doesn't really understand why I don't believe in god.

Yesenia's gender and ethnicity, her disenchantment with religion, and desire for social justice all combined such that, for her, she felt compelled to make her views known and to "do something about it." As we saw earlier, it's more acceptable for most Americans today than it was fifty or even twenty years ago, to claim no religion. Even outing oneself as an atheist doesn't carry with it the stigma it once did.[45] Both Torin and Yesenia found that taking the social risks was acceptable, even necessary. But it's reasonable to think that for many minorities in similar situations, the costs that come with violating these cultural expectations continue to be prohibitive.

Scholars have long believed that race and gender prominently contribute to one's likelihood of being nonreligious or an atheist.[46] While such arguments were bolstered by data indicating that white men were more likely than others to identify as nonreligious, white men were never the only individuals leaving religion in the US; they were always accompanied by Black individuals and women, as well as other racial and gender minorities, though data on those latter groups are more challenging to find. Additionally, from a purely mathematical perspective, white men have to make up a smaller proportion of religious exiters as more and more people reject religion. As a result, the gap in religiosity between men and women and between Black and white individuals in the US is going to continue to shrink as nonreligion becomes more normative. Using race and gender to predict who is going to leave religion may have seemed useful in the past, but neither was ever a reliable predictor.[47] Other factors are far more important.

Class

One demographic characteristic that doesn't factor very prominently in understanding religious exiters is social class.[48] Social class is more than just how much money someone has, though it is often measured in that fashion. Social class is really the culture—beliefs, values, and behaviors—someone holds, particularly in relation to their income and wealth. Measuring someone's culture is challenging, which is why social scientists often turn to more simplistic measures like income to attempt to capture social class.

When we write that social class is often overlooked when examining religion, it's because the relationship between social class and religiosity

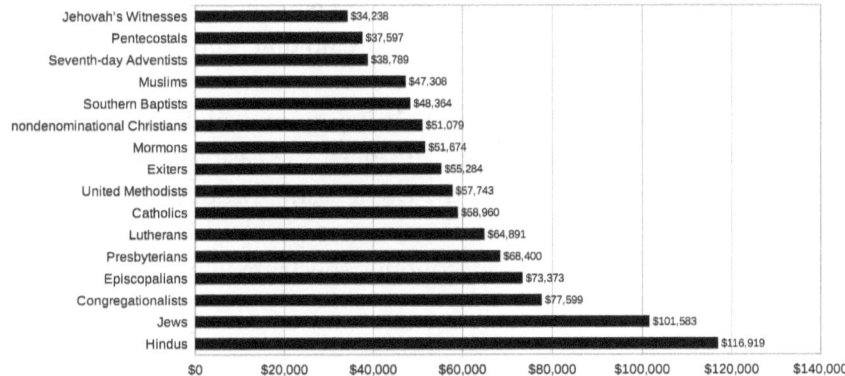

Figure 2.5. Average Income by Religious Affiliations—Inflation-Adjusted, 2010–2021. (Source: GSS, 2010–2021)

is complex and social class does not tend to be predictive of religiosity. Historically, that wasn't the case,[49] but in recent decades, whether someone has more or less money is not a strong predictor of how often they attend religious services, whether they hold religious beliefs, or whether they report a religious affiliation.[50] We examined the average incomes of religious exiters, the never religious, and the religious in the GSS, from 1972 to 2021. The differences between the three groups were small in the 1970s and grew slightly smaller over time, but they were never meaningful differences.

What does this mean as far as being able to single out who is going to leave a religion and who isn't?

Nothing, really.

Well, more accurately, what this means is that religious exiting is not a phenomenon that disproportionately occurs among the wealthy or the poor. People of all social classes are leaving religions, and that has been true for the last 50 years. That, of course, is interesting in itself. As we noted at the beginning of this chapter, pretty much anyone with a religious affiliation could leave. This certainly holds when it comes to social class.

Figure 2.5 provides additional information on incomes by religious affiliations in the US. Hindus and Jews have the highest average incomes in the most recent waves of the GSS while Jehovah's Witnesses and Pentecostals are at the bottom. Exiters are almost precisely in the middle of the groups examined. While we argued above that income or social class is not predictive of people leaving, and we stand by that assertion, that is not the same as saying that there are no differences in income by religious affiliation.

Some scholars have suggested that being nonreligious is an elitist phenomenon.[51] It has, historically, been the case that atheists are wealthier than average.[52] But, in the US, it is simply not true to suggest that religious exiting is an elitist phenomenon tied to social class. There are people from across the socioeconomic spectrum who leave religion.

Education

Unlike social class, there is or at least was a relationship between education and religious exiting, but it is complicated. Some scholars believe that education leads to secularization, and they have found evidence to support that assertion.[53] But it's also quite complicated and the causal direction can be confusing. Some religions—particularly conservative, sectarian religions like Jehovah's Witnesses and some evangelical religions—discourage members from pursuing an advanced education.[54] In those cases, it is not education that reduces religiosity. It's the opposite; religiosity prevents education, particularly higher education like college and graduate school. Religions that discourage advanced education, however, may be more the exception than the rule as many religions—particularly mainline Protestantism, but also Catholicism and Judaism among many others—encourage advanced education.

Some studies have indicated that higher levels of education result in lower levels of religiosity.[55] But there are more recent studies that suggest education does not have a clear, linear effect on religiosity.[56] In fact, the effect of education on religiosity is a good opportunity to illustrate the importance of separating out belief, behavior, and identity. Some studies have found that higher levels of educational attainment are associated with higher religious service attendance.[57] These studies typically attribute that to the fact that people with more education tend to have higher levels of civic engagement, generally.[58] In contrast to attendance, education does appear to reduce orthodoxy of belief.[59] In other words, people with more advanced education tend to hold less literalistic views of scripture or more nuanced understandings of their god or a higher

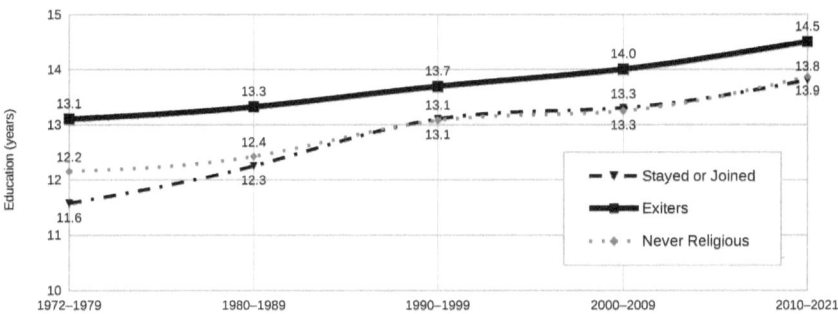

Figure 2.6. Average Years of Education of Exiters, Never Religious, and Religious by Decade, 1972-2021. (Source: GSS, 1972–2021)

power. As a result, the relationship between education and religiosity is too complex to simply say that education increases or decreases religiosity.

When it comes to increasing the odds that someone will leave religion, figure 2.6 suggests that education may have been associated with religious exiting in the 1970s and 1980s, but is decreasingly a useful indicator of whether or not someone will leave religion.

The average level of education of exiters in the GSS in the 1970s was 13.1 years, which is about a year of college, compared to 11.6 years of education for the religious, which is just below a high school diploma (i.e., 12 years). A roughly 1-year gap in educational attainment between exiters and the religious continued through the 1980s, but had declined to about half that by the 1990s. In the most recent waves of the GSS, the gap is about half a year of education.

Education, like gender and age, may be a characteristic that mattered more in the past than it does today. When exiting was less common, it appears as though education was more likely to lead people to leave religion. In more recent years, religious exiting has spread so widely throughout the US population that educational attainment is less predictive of people leaving religions.

As we will see, many of our interviewees noted that education was influential in leading them to leave religion. But there were also many who indicated that they lost their belief as children or adolescents, well before they went off to college or graduate school.

Region

Different regions of the US are known for varying in their religiosity.[60] Many Southern states are grouped together and labeled the "Bible Belt" for high rates of affiliation with particular denominations of Protestantism and, increasingly, non-denominational Christianity. The Intermountain West has a disproportionate percentage of Mormons, due to their early settlement of the region in the nineteenth century.[61] The upper Midwest has historically been known as Lutheran, a result of the settlement in that region of many migrants from Scandinavian countries. Large numbers of Episcopalians and Catholics are located on the East Coast and in New England, as Episcopalians were among the first European settlers in what would become the US, and Catholics migrated to the East Coast from Europe.[62] Methodists tend to be found in the Midwest, as Methodism was often associated with migrants who traveled west during the Great Expansion.[63] The Pacific states have the mixed reputation of being a place for religious innovation but also of lower levels of religiosity.[64]

Americans have been more likely to leave religions in certain regions of the US since the 1970s, as table 2.1[65] below indicates. Three regions of the US have had higher levels of religious exiting: New England, the Mountain States, and the Pacific states. In New England, this is often attributed to the greater population density and higher levels of urban living,[66] an argument we examine in greater detail below. In the Mountain and Pacific regions, lower levels of religiosity have often been explained by a settler mentality that values autonomy and/or an outdoor-oriented lifestyle that appreciates the beauty of nature.[67]

Of primary interest to us are two elements of table 2.1: regional differences and the trend over time. Given that there are regional differences, those may help explain religious exiting. Why are people more likely to leave religions in some regions of the country than in others? The nice thing about this question is that the answer is unlikely to be individualistic but rather contextual, which makes this very much a sociological question. In other words, context matters for religious exiting, particularly when religious exiting is unusual. People will be more likely to leave a religion when it is less likely that they will experience discrimination and stigma, which is the case in the three regions previously mentioned. Why might there be a lower likelihood of discrimination in these regions? The coasts tend to be more progressive politically, and more multicultural.[68] Some of that multiculturalism comes from very large cities that serve as safe places for diverse populations.[69] Leaving a religion in a large, diverse city carries a lower risk of stigma precisely because of the diversity. This is the same reason why LGBTQ individuals tend to congregate in specific cities; cities tend to be more accepting of diversity than rural areas.[70]

The culture of the Mountain states, while somewhat conservative, also has libertarian tendencies that place more emphasis on autonomy.[71] Freedom from religion is one manifestation of that autonomy and, while not everyone may accept it, it is a cultural value that may help explain why rates of exiting are higher in those regions. In fact, this autonomy can be seen in other data from the GSS. The GSS includes a question asking participants whether they think atheists should be allowed to speak publicly. Looking at just data from 2010 to 2021, 84.9% of individuals in New England, 84.2% of individuals in the mountain states, and 82.7% of individuals in the Pacific states think atheists should be allowed to speak in public. In the east south central states, the corresponding percentage is 67.8%.

The second element of table 2.1 that is of interest is the trend over time. If religious exiting was restricted to just one region of the US, or just limited regions, that would suggest that context plays an extremely important role in religious exiting. However, examining table 2.1 closely reveals that, over time, religious exiting has increased in every region.

TABLE 2.1. Percentage Exiters by Region, 1972–2021, by Decade.

	1972–1979	1980–1989	1990–1999	2000–2009	2010–2021
New England	8.2	6.6	9.7	13.0	19.7
Middle Atlantic	5.2	6.0	6.7	9.2	16.5
East North Central	4.1	5.8	7.2	9.6	16.7
West North Central	4.0	4.1	6.3	9.5	20.2
South Atlantic	3.4	4.3	5.3	7.4	13.4
East South Central	3.4	2.7	4.0	4.6	10.5
West South Central	3.0	4.0	6.1	7.5	12.1
Mountain	7.4	6.5	11.7	12.6	22.8
Pacific	10.6	10.5	13.3	14.3	22.4

This aligns with the general findings of this chapter—that religious exiters are everywhere and can be virtually anyone. There isn't a region of the US where religious exiting has not increased since the 1970s. Even in the historically most religious parts of the US, like the Southern states, religious exiters make up at least 10% of the population in the latest waves of the GSS.

Rural/Urban Environments

In addition to looking at the regional variation among religious exiters, we examined whether there are differences in the population density where individuals live. Are individuals who live in larger cities more likely to leave religions than those in more rural areas, as we alluded above?

The GSS includes a variable capturing the population density where participants lived at the time of the survey. The variable is a little problematic because it is heavily skewed by very large populations. In other words, most American adults do not live in cities with seven or eight million people, but cities of that size pull the average city size up, making it seem as though most people do live in very large cities. To address this, we considered both the mean city size and the median, which gave similar results. In the 1970s, there was a gap between exiters and the religious in terms of the size of the city in which they lived, with exiters living in much larger cities than the religious, but that gap has basically disappeared over time such that there is no difference today.

What both the average and median location sizes suggest is that religious exiting may have been more common among city dwellers fifty years ago, but, as we have suggested with other variables, as exiting has diffused through the population, leaving religion is now increasingly common in both rural and urban areas. And, as noted above, it may have made more sense when religious exiting was less common for people in multicultural and diverse cities to leave as cities tend to be more accepting of diversity.[72]

LGB

Recent research has shown that sexual minorities, specifically lesbian, gay, and bisexual individuals, are less likely to be religious.[73] Given many religions' positions on LGB involvement,[74] it's not all that surprising that some LGB individuals choose to exit religion altogether (an issue we return to in Chapter 3).

GSS data support the idea that LGB individuals are more likely to have left religion. The GSS added a question about sexual orientation only in 2008, so the data we have on this item do not track all the way back to the 1970s. Even so, there is pretty clear evidence that LGB individuals are more likely to have left religion than straight individuals. Roughly 16% of straight individuals in the US were exiters in the latest waves of the GSS (i.e., 2010 to 2021). The GSS separates out lesbian and gay (LG) individuals from bisexual (B) individuals, so we can report those percentages separately. While the samples are quite small (they are aggregated across all the GSS waves from 2010 to 2021), 29.9% of lesbian and gay individuals were exiters and 29.6% of bisexual individuals were exiters. LGB individuals are almost twice as likely as straight individuals to have left religion.

How religions think about, treat, and often work against the rights of LGB individuals has likely played a role in driving people out of religion, a topic we return to in the next chapter.[75]

Prior Religious Affiliation

The last variable we consider in this chapter is the religion of someone's childhood. As noted in chapter 1, the GSS includes a measure of someone's religious affiliation at age 16, which we used to determine whether or not someone exited religion. We can also use that variable to explore whether there are different rates of religious exiting by religions. In other words, are people more likely to leave the Catholic Church than, say, the Jehovah's Witnesses?

Roughly 55% of religious exiters were raised as Protestants and close to 40% were raised Catholic, which makes sense given that those are close to the percentages of the population that adhere to those religions among the religious. Smaller contributions come from Judaism (~2%) and other religions (~4%) and there is very little variation in this over time.

Admittedly, "Protestant" is a very big category and includes a lot of different religions, as does the "Other" group. Because the specific denominations within those categories may be significant, we dug a little deeper into the GSS data to see if we could determine which specific groups were losing the highest percentages of members. We looked only at data since 2010 (i.e., 2010 through 2021). How we calculated the percentages that follow is fairly straightforward. We'll use Catholics as an illustration. During the 2010s, there were a total of 5,103 individuals who were raised Catholic who participated in the GSS. Of those, 1,025 reported they no longer had a religious affiliation, which is 20% of individuals who were raised Catholic. The corresponding percentage for Jewish individuals is 14.7% and for Protestants, broadly, is 17%.

Within the Protestant category, roughly 11% of individuals raised Southern Baptist left the religion (for Baptists, collectively, it was 14% who exited). The percentages raised in other Protestant denominations who left are all also in the double digits: Methodists—17%; Lutherans—16%; Presbyterians—20%; Episcopalians—25%; and non-denominational Christians—21%. Do keep in mind that each of these groups had over 100 individuals raised in the religion who participated in the GSS from 2010 through 2021. When the numbers are smaller than that, we need to be more circumspect with the estimates. As a result, we chose to report just a handful of additional religions where there were at least 50 participants in the GSS who were raised in those religions. Around 36% of individuals raised as Jehovah's Witnesses became nonreligious. For Mormons, 30% left. The corresponding percentages for other groups with enough participants to report include: Church of Christ—11%; Congregationalists—19%; Pentecostals—13%; and Seventh-day Adventists—15%. We report these percentages as rough estimates, recognizing that some of them are based on very small samples.

A follow-up question is how religious these individuals were before they left. The GSS provides some information on this. In limited years (1991, 1998, 2008, and 2018), the GSS asked respondents how often they attended religious services when they were young, how often their mother attended, and how often their father attended. On average, exiters reported attending religious services about two to three times a month, just slightly lower than those who remained affiliated or joined, who reported, on average, attending nearly every week. Mothers for both exiters and those who remained religious or joined were reported as attending roughly two to three times a month, and fathers for both groups were reported attending roughly once a month. On all of these measures, for those who ended up leaving religion, their home environment was just slightly less religious than for those who stayed religious or joined, on average.[76]

Pew's Faith in Flux data, though now just over 10 years old, suggests the same. Pew asked respondents how strong their faith was as a kid, ranging from "very strong" to "didn't have religious faith." Exiters, on average, reported their faith at just below "somewhat strong" while those who stayed or joined put their faith as just above "somewhat strong," on average, though both would round to "somewhat strong." Both groups indicated they attended religious services roughly once a week as kids. However, the frequency of attendance for exiters was slightly lower than for those who stayed or joined. The difference in attending religious education classes was pretty small—both reported attending slightly more often than "occasionally." Exiters were somewhat less likely to be part of a religious youth group (41%) versus those who stayed or joined (52%). By their teenage years, differences had started to increase a bit. Attendance for exiters was slightly lower, at roughly once or twice a month, than it was for those who stayed or joined, at roughly once a week. But the strength of their faith had dropped for exiters by their teens. Exiters, on average, reported that their faith was "not too strong," while those who stayed or joined still reported "somewhat strong" faith.

Admittedly, in the previous discussion, we mostly focused on averages. It's likely that kids raised in very secular homes will be more likely to grow up secular.[77] But the more important point here is that knowing how religious someone was in their childhood is not a great predictor of whether they are going to leave religion as an adult. As with so many of the demographic variables we have examined in this chapter, the takeaway is generally that it is not easy to predict who is going to leave religion. People of all ages, races, genders, sexualities, social classes, and levels of educational attainment, in all parts of the country, even those with dedicated religious upbringings, are leaving.

Conclusion

We wish we could conclude this chapter with some sort of definitive statement that it is easy to predict who is going to leave a religion and who isn't, based just on demographic characteristics like age, race, gender, or where people live. But, as the data provided in this chapter illustrate, that just isn't the case. To make this point even more clearly, we put together a mixed effects logistic regression model with religious exiting as the outcome. In simpler terms, we developed a statistical model that draws upon almost all of the variables in this chapter to see how well we can predict whether someone is going to exit religion using just demographic variables.[78]

If we didn't think this was important, we would not include the following rather technical description and table, but, for those who appreciate statistical models, we hope this will reinforce the arguments of the chapter. In order to examine whether there are differences in probabilities of religious exiting by period (i.e., decades), we used a mixed-effects logistic regression model with period (1970s, 1980s, etc.) as a random effect and age (standardized and centered), race (white = 1; other = 0), gender (male = 1; female = 0), income (standardized and centered), education (standardized and centered), region (dummy codes for each region; New England is the reference region), and population density (standardized and centered) as fixed effects. Table 2.2 shows the results of the regression.

There are a number of elements in table 2.2. that are important, but we're going to try to keep this simple. An interpretive guide may help. The coefficients shown in table 2.2 are odds ratios, which can be interpreted as follows: If the value is above 1.00, that variable increases the odds of religious exiting. If the value is below 1.00, that variable decreases the odds of religious exiting. With age, for instance, the coefficient is 0.69 ($p < .001$), which indicates being older reduces the odds of religious exiting relative to younger individuals. Education (1.19, $p < .001$) increases the odds of religious exiting, as does being male (1.69, $p < .001$), and being white (1.49, $p < .001$). Living in any region except the Mountain and Pacific regions reduces the odds of religious exiting relative to living in New England; there is no difference in the odds of religious exiting between New England and the Mountain states, but people in the Pacific states are even more likely to be religious exiters than are those in New England (1.18, $p = .039$). Finally, the intercept reflects the period effects and is statistically significant, but there is more information about the period/random effects at the bottom of the table. For instance, the ICC shown in the table (0.05) indicates that the period

TABLE 2.2. Mixed-Effects Regression of Religious Exiting, 1972–2021.

	Odds Ratios	CI	p-value
Intercept (Period)*	0.06	0.04–0.10	< 0.001
age	0.69	0.65–0.72	< 0.001
education	1.19	1.14–1.24	< 0.001
income	0.96	0.93–1.00	0.045
location size	0.85	0.81–0.88	< 0.001
sex (male = 1)	1.69	1.58–1.82	< 0.001
race (white = 1)	1.49	1.35–1.64	< 0.001
Middle Atlantic†	0.74	0.62–0.87	< 0.001
East North Central	0.72	0.62–0.85	< 0.001
West North Central	0.61	0.50–0.74	< 0.001
South Atlantic	0.57	0.48–0.67	< 0.001
East South Central	0.43	0.34–0.54	< 0.001
West South Central	0.54	0.45–0.65	< 0.001
Mountain	0.98	0.82–1.18	0.858
Pacific	1.18	1.01–1.38	0.039
Random Effects			
σ^2			3.29
τ_{00} PERIOD			0.17
ICC			0.05
N PERIOD			5
Observations			37,487
Marginal R2			0.09
Conditional R2			0.134

* The periods are: 1972–1979, 1980–1989, 1990–1999, 2000–2009, and 2010–2021.
† The reference region is New England.

is not a strong predictor of religious exiting. That is confirmed with the pseudo R²s at the bottom of the table. The marginal R² is the amount of variation in religious exiting that is accounted for or explained by the fixed effects or all the demographic variables we included but not the period variable. In this model, demographic variables explain about 9% of the variation in religious exiting, which is not a lot. The conditional R² is the amount of variation in religious exiting explained by the entire model. In our model, it's just 13.4%, which suggests the period in which someone participated in the GSS explains about 4% of the variation in religious exiting (Americans were more likely to exit religion in later waves of the GSS).

We are not including this model to make the argument that we can predict who is going to leave religions. Some scholars would point to the statistically significant coefficients (i.e., anything with a probability of occurring that is less than .05) and argue that they had found something important. We don't count ourselves among those scholars. To the contrary, we're including this model to make the point that, even with a high-quality sample of tens of thousands of adult Americans across nearly 50 years, our ability to predict who is going to leave religions based on demographic data and period effects is not very good. We can explain about 13% of the variation in who is going to leave, leaving roughly 87% of the variation in who is going to exit religion unexplained. It may technically be accurate to say that younger, white, well-educated men living in urban areas on the coasts are more likely to be religious exiters, but just barely. How we interpret our model is really that we can't predict who is going to leave religion using these variables alone.

We interpret this model as indicating that religious exiting is not happening just among small subsets of the US population. At the beginning of the twenty-first century, pretty much anyone and everyone in the US could become a religious exiter. Many of the impediments that once prevented people from leaving religions have disappeared, and the impediments that do exist are no longer as powerful as they once were.

Over the last three decades, the decreased stigma associated with claiming no religion has led to more people reporting they have no religious affiliation. With the threat of being labeled a traitor or communist for rejecting religious claims disappearing, and generally declining religious authority,[79] it's not surprising that people feel freer to criticize religion. Rather than seeing religion as the most important institution for fostering community, a sense of purpose, and moral solidarity—and associating with it a sign of being a true American[80]—people more readily acknowledge that the good life is obtainable without religion. It's not that such doubt and criticism of religion is new, or that some radical paradigm shift has occurred in the last 30 years. Rather, it's that the *conditions*—the cultural and sociopolitical conditions incentivizing religious belief, behavior, and identity—have changed.

In the following chapter, we offer some additional clues as to who is going to leave religion. But we encourage readers to keep their expectations relatively low concerning how well we or anyone else can do this.

3

Why Are They Leaving?

My parents were both Catholic and I was brought up in the Catholic Church, but they weren't very religious as far as going to church on Sundays. They would go sometimes for the big holidays like Easter and Christmas and they weren't big into the church, neither one of them. There were times where they would just take us to church and so we could go to catechism and then come back and pick us up after Mass. So we didn't really, it wasn't a big part of our family when we were growing up, as far as there were no Bible [studies], we were not reading scripture and all that kind of stuff. And so then once I got to be I'd say like around 15, 16 I began to question the Catholic Church and I just kind of [pause]; even though I went to like a Catholic high school I just became disenchanted with the church and so I didn't really go much.
—Pam

I remember pinning my dad in the corner and calling him out for his hypocrisy, and demanding an apology.
Interviewer: Was any of this [reaction] directed toward religion in general?
Oh yeah. Just that I was able to call him out on his abuse and tell him he was wrong. I made a lot of jokes about religion which really gets under his skin. And at that time—my senior year of high school, I started dating this guy, who, I liked him because he was really dark and he was a musician, and he was really deep. He always said he was a Satanist, and I thought that was stupid too! (laughs). He had the same type of upbringing, he was from a fundamentalist [Christian] background too, and his dad was abusive . . . I think that relationship gave me the courage to be really independent and in-your-face about it [no longer being a

Christian]. I was calling myself a non-believer, but it was really an angry kind of thing. I mean, it was very different from now. Now I say I'm a non-believer, but I don't feel the anger.
—Noelle

From the fall of 1970 to Christmas eve of 2010 . . . I was working at churches on Sunday morning, sometimes full time, sometimes part time. But I worked damn near every Sunday for 40 years. I decided in 2010 after being in the same church for 21 years that it was time for me to basically stop doing that because I wasn't dealing with my own atheism. That was a door in the back of my mind that didn't really get opened, until I was ready. . . . So you know, that [Christianity] was my culture and I retired on Christmas Eve 2010. And within, well the very next Sunday—see you got 41 years of doing the same thing every Sunday—and I'm sitting at home and I got coffee and I'm in my little record studio and just hanging out and I'm going, "Wow, I don't miss church at all!"
—Don

In some ways, this chapter represents the key to understanding religious exiting. We know from the previous chapter that many Americans are in fact leaving religion, and we have discussed who those people are. But much turns on the *why* question. Why are more Americans leaving religion? What forces actually motivate a person who was socialized into religion to want out? As one might guess, the reasons are manifold. Sometimes those reasons are relatively straightforward, while other times they're very complicated, even opaque. Pam, Noelle, and Don each left religion for different reasons at very different stages of the life course. Pam's relationship with Catholicism, despite doing catechism, Mass, and going to Catholic school, was tepid. Her parents raised her Catholic, but weren't themselves all that committed. Her "disenchantment" early in life isn't very surprising. Pam's path out of religion is common. Noelle, on the other hand, was raised by fundamentalists. She had a fraught relationship with her parents, in which religion, and the expectations placed upon her, played a central role. The hypocrisy she perceived cast a long shadow over anything of value she saw in religion, and it took years for her resentment to dissipate. Noelle was more than a decade older than Pam when she left religion, and her (Noelle's) exit was more deliberate and dramatic. In contrast, Don was an ardent churchgoer for decades. A musician, he played church music and held several leadership roles in the congregations he belonged to. His whole life was invested in his church and he never imagined, even into middle age, that he would abandon religion altogether. But that's exactly what he did. In his 60s he finally "dealt with" the atheism lurking behind the backdoor of his mind. After doing so, he joined secular groups, began playing music for them, and became much more outspoken about his newfound secular beliefs than he ever was about his religious ones. He didn't drift away early in life due to lack of interest or commitment. He wasn't outraged by hypocrisy. He wasn't angry. He was just done with religion.

Having such different experiences, are there any common threads as to why Pam, Noelle, and Don left religion? With what appear to be disparate motives and distinct situational factors at play in their respective lives, one might be tempted to think there's not much shared between them. Indeed, their reasons for leaving vary as widely as the timing at which they left. Phil Zuckerman, in summarizing the early sociological work on apostasy,[1] reflected on some of the dynamics germane to our discussion. He distinguished three generic and intersecting axes of apostasy. The first is *early* vs. *late*. The second *shallow* vs. *deep*. The third *mild* vs. *transformative*.[2] We won't spend time here fleshing each of these out, but as suggested by the typology itself, we need to point out that the when, where, why, and how of religious exiting matter a great deal. It will characterize the nature of the exiting process. Don's longtime commitment to religion no doubt shaped both his leaving it and the life he went on to live post-religion. This is different from Pam's indifference to and disconnection from religion as a teen, or Noelle's strong push back against the fundamentalism she grew up with. Our focus in this chapter is on the most salient factors we've identified that motivate religious exiting, many of which are shared by our participants, notwithstanding the clear differences just mentioned.

A useful way to begin is by offering a brief aside on the dissertation work of one of the two authors (Cragun), which focused precisely on the topic of the present chapter: why people leave religion in the US.[3] In his dissertation, he developed a statistical model that attempted to include the many factors that contribute to people leaving religion. While his dissertation research was sufficient to earn him a PhD, it had a major flaw. The statistical technique he used assumed that people left religions for generally the same reasons.[4] It took several years to realize why this assumption was erroneous, but subsequent research has revealed something important: there is no comprehensive model or explanation for why people leave religion. People leave religion for many and varied reasons. As a result, it is extremely challenging to capture why all people leave religion with a single statistical model (i.e., a top-down or deductive approach). Instead, what is necessary is trying to understand why individuals leave religion and then generalizing the specific to broader explanations for why certain groups of individuals leave (i.e., a bottom-up or inductive approach).

Importantly, participants' narratives express the beliefs, behaviors, and identities discussed in our opening chapter. Every interviewee in our study underwent a process of social and psychological change that tracks along these three dimensions. In fact, in one sense, to trace the causes of religious exiting is to simply account for the changes across these dimensions. Although varied in relation to each other, no dimension is left untouched when a person says "goodbye" to religion.

Our study isn't the first to discuss the reasons people give for leaving religion. A growing number of studies have done this as they seek to describe the dynamics of religious exiting.[5] These studies, and ours, consistently show individuals' intensifying problems with a variety of religious doctrines, their observations of hypocrisy among religious peers and leaders, growing disparity between their personal political positions and those held by their religion, widening concerns about identifying with organizations perceived as flawed or corrupt, changes in typical and preferred behaviors, and other personal and social fissures that culminate in leaving religion altogether. This process, and the felt needs of some people to divorce themselves from religion, unfold in response to a set of distinct, though related, push and pull factors. We discuss salient factors suggested in the broader literature, drawing on a variety of data sources. While we have attempted to be fairly comprehensive, this chapter cannot capture every cause for religious exiting. It does, however, provide a foundation for understanding some of the primary reasons. We draw on quantitative and qualitative data to highlight both individuals' motives for leaving religion and underscore the social forces at play as they do so. Our analysis expands on recent work on the nonreligious[6] by moving beyond describing demographic trends and explaining the social and psychological motivators behind leaving religion.

Push and Pull Factors

When studying people who emigrate from one country to another, demographers often think about the forces involved as falling into two categories: push and pull factors. Push factors are the aspects of life in the resident country that are driving the individual to leave that location. Pull factors are the aspects of life in the target country that are drawing the person toward the country. In the case of immigration, push factors might include: war, famine, disease, poverty, or lack of economic opportunities. Pull factors could include: high level of technological development, social safety net (e.g., universal health care, unemployment benefits, etc.), job opportunities, low crime rates, and other appealing characteristics.

A similar logic can be used in thinking about why people leave religion. In the remainder of this chapter, we apply this logic, having developed a list of the most salient causes of religious exiting. However, before we discuss push and pull factors, we think it is important to note that many people just gradually drift away from religion. In fact, that is probably the most common reason why people exit religion in the US. In Pew's 2008 Faith in Flux[7] survey, 71% of those who exited religion reported that gradually drifting away was one of the important factors in them leaving religion. It wasn't *necessarily* doctrines, politics, inequality, abuse, or any of the other major factors we'll discuss below. It was simply a gradual process of moving away from religion without any one specific cause. We don't want to suggest that most Americans who leave religion are doing so in dramatic fashion with a very specific denouement, emotionally charged conversations, tears, and conflict. It's likely that for most people, exiting religion is like someone's hair changing to gray—it starts with just a few hairs, is gradual, is not something they think a lot about, and can take years to eventually make a complete change, often without the person even realizing that it has happened until it is complete.

Why focus on specific push and pull factors if, for most, leaving religion is a gradual process not necessarily based on any one of these factors? Well, that many people gradually drift away from religion doesn't mean those same people are lacking justifications for their secularization—most of them *also* identify the factors below as being important, at least *post hoc*. What's more, that so many people are now just gradually pulling away from religion reinforces one of the primary arguments of our book—the social context has changed, and all the factors we discuss are implicated in that change. In the middle of the twentieth century, there was widespread and powerful pressure to identify as religious and to demonstrate one's religiosity. As we have seen, the US was at war with the "godless communists." But the social context—the environment in which people find themselves making choices about religion has changed. Many forces have come together to change this context, but one important one is economic. Profit-driven enterprises have an incentive to compete with religion, undermining religious authority and dominance along the way. People can choose to tailgate at a National Football League game on Sunday, or attend church.[8] People can choose to go to the gym, the beach, hiking, or a movie on Sunday (or Saturday or Friday, depending on the religion) instead of to a religious service. And those who choose to do something other than religion will no longer be condemned for it. That subtle shift in the acceptability of doing things other than religion has opened the floodgates for people to just gradually drift away. Millions of Americans are doing just that. But of course, for many others, leaving religion is more complicated, as we detail below.

Push Factors

The factors that push people out of religion are moral teachings, doctrines, policies, political statements, and issues with religious leaders and other members of the religious community.

Morality

A primary push factor driving people out of religions is their moral teachings. Rather than being the source of people's morality in the twenty-first century, many Americans look at religions and see organizations that espouse sexual and gender inequality,[9] racial inequality,[10] and morally suspicious and highly restrictive moral teachings surrounding sexual behavior and women's autonomy, among many other issues.[11]

The list of denominations in table 3.1 illustrates this by providing the positions of the 10 largest religious organizations in the US[12] on 3 issues: whether women are allowed to be ordained as clergy (specifically, whether women can hold any position within the religion), the religion's

TABLE 3.1. Denominations—Policy Positions of 10 Largest Religions in the US.

	ordination of women	position on abortion	involvement of LGBTQ individuals
Catholic Church[1]	No	Never	oppose same-sex marriage and LGBTQ individuals in ministry
Southern Baptist Convention[2]	No	Never	oppose same-sex marriage and LGBTQ individuals in ministry; reject TQ
United Methodist Church[3]	Yes	Yes, but . . .	splitting over this issue
Church of Jesus Christ of Latter-day Saints[4]	No	in limited circumstances	oppose same-sex marriage and LGBTQ individuals in ministry; reject TQ
Church of God in Christ[5]	No	in limited circumstances	oppose same-sex marriage and LGBTQ individuals in ministry
National Baptist Convention, USA[6]	congregation specific	congregation specific	oppose same-sex marriage and LGBTQ individuals in ministry
Evangelical Lutheran Church in America[7]	Yes	in limited circumstances	congregation-specific
National Baptist Convention of America[8]	No	Never	oppose same-sex marriage and LGBTQ individuals in ministry; reject TQ
Assemblies of God[9]	Yes	Never	oppose same-sex marriage and LGBTQ individuals in ministry; reject TQ
Presbyterian Church USA[10]	Yes	Yes	congregation specific

1. Regarding the ordination of women in the Catholic Church, see: *Ordinatio Sacerdotalis*. Dated May 22, 1994. Accessed January 23, 2022. https://www.vatican.va. On the Catholic Church's position on abortion, see: the section titled "Respect for Human Life" in the *Catechism of the Catholic Church*. Accessed January 23, 2022. https://www.vatican.va.

2. Regarding the ordination of women in the Southern Baptist Convention, see the "Resolution on Ordination and the Role of Women in Ministry." Dated June 1, 1984. Accessed January 23, 2022. https://www.sbc.net. For the Southern Baptist Convention's position on abortion, see: "On Celebrating The Advancement Of Pro-life Legislation In State Legislatures." Dated June 1, 2019. Accessed January 23, 2022. https://www.sbc.net. Regarding

the Southern Baptist Convention's position on LGB individuals, see "On Sexuality And Personal Identity." Accessed January 23, 2022. https://www.sbc.net.

3. Women have been allowed to preach in the United Methodist Church for a very long time. See: "Timeline of Women in Methodism." Accessed January 23, 2022. https://www.umc.org. On the issue of abortion, the United Methodist Church discourages abortion but allows it. See: "What is the UM position on abortion?" Accessed January 23, 2022. https://www.umc.org. The United Methodist Church allows LGB members to participate but does not allow them to officially hold leadership positions. See: "Human Sexuality." Accessed January 23, 2022. https://www.umc.org. However, this issue has become so contentious that the denomination is now splitting over it. See: Hahn, Heather. 2021. "Conversations Address Going Separate Ways." UM News. Accessed January 23, 2022. https://www.umnews.org.

4. The LDS Church's position on women holding the priesthood is clear in the study manual "What Does It Mean to Be Ordained to the Priesthood?" Accessed January 23, 2022. https://www.churchofjesuschrist.org. The LDS Church's positions on abortion, homosexuality, and transgender individuals are detailed in its General Handbook. Accessed January 23, 2022. https://www.churchofjesuschrist.org.

5. We were unable to find a clear statement on the ordination of women on The Church of God in Christ's (COGIC) website. Instead, we cite the University of Southern California's Center for Religion and Civic Culture report on the denomination, which details that women are not allowed to be ordained. "Report: Church of God in Christ." Accessed January 23, 2022. https://crcc.usc.edu. COGIC opposes abortion. See: "Church of God in Christ Reaffirms Pro-Life Stance." Accessed January 23, 2022. https://www.cogic.org. COGIC rejects all but heterosexual relations. See: "Same-Sex Marriage and Homosexuality," Dated 13/04/2004. Accessed January 23, 2022. https://www.cogic.org.

6. The National Baptist Convention USA allows individual congregations to determine whether women should be allowed to be ordained. See the University of Southern California's Center for Religion and Civic Culture website, "Report: National Baptist Convention." Accessed January 23, 2022. https://crcc.usc.edu. Likewise, the National Baptist Convention USA does not dictate what individual congregation's positions on abortion must be. See: Masci, David. 2016. "Where Major Religious Groups Stand on Abortion." Accessed January 23, 2022. https://www.pewresearch.org. The National Baptist Convention USA's denominational leadership officially opposes homosexuality but does not dictate what individual congregations are allowed to do. See: "A Statement on the Same-sex Marriage Issue, Voting and Christian Responsibility." Dated 06/21/2012. Accessed January 23, 2022. https://www.nationalbaptist.com.

7. The Evangelical Lutheran Church in America (ELCA) allows women to be ordained. See "45th Anniversary of the Ordination of Women: Executive Summary – Clergy Questionnaire Report 2015." Dated June 2016. Accessed January 23, 2022. https://download.elca.org. The ELCA discourages abortion but allows it. See "Evangelical Lutheran Church in America: A Social Statement on Abortion." Dated September 4, 1991. Accessed January 23, 2022. https://download.elca.org. The ELCA recognizes that there is a diversity of views regarding LGB individuals and allows individual congregations to address this issue. See: "A Social Statement on Human Sexuality: Gift and Trust." Dated August 19, 2009. Accessed January 23, 2022. https://download.elca.org.

8. The National Baptist Convention of America opposes the ordination of women. See: Durso, Pamela R. 2015. "She-Preachers, bossy women, and Children of the Devil: A History of Baptist Women Ministers and Ordination." Accessed January 23, 2022. https://bwim.infof. We were unable to find official policy positions for the National Baptist Convention of America on abortion or LGBTQ issues. This article indicates that, as part of the broader Baptist Fellowship, the National Baptist Convention of America continues to oppose LGBTQ rights: Roach, David. 2018. "CBF Nixes 'Absolute' LGBT Hiring Ban, Maintains It For Leaders." Accessed January 23, 2022. https://www.baptistpress.com.

9. The Assemblies of God has long allowed women to serve in leadership roles. See: "Leadership and Governance in the Local Church": https://ag.org. Accessed 01/23/2022. The Assemblies of God opposes abortion in virtually all circumstances with the possible exception of the mother's life being threatened if the pregnancy continues. See: "Sanctity of Human Life: Abortion and Reproductive Issues," (adopted August 11, 2010). https://ag.org. Accessed 01/23/2022. The Assemblies of God opposes LGBTQ participation and identities. See "Homosexuality, Marriage, and Sexual Identity" (adopted August 5, 2014). Accessed January 23, 2022. https://ag.org.

10. The Presbyterian Church USA (PCUSA) allows women to be ordained. See this report: Android, Angie and Coe, Deb. 2016. Gender and Leadership in the PC(USA). PC(USA) Research Services. Louisville: Kentucky. https://www.presbyterianmission.org. Accessed January 23, 2022. PCUSA's official position on abortion allows women to make this decision. See "As abortion debate grows, Stated Clerk reminds church of General Assembly policy." Accessed January 23, 2022. https://www.pcusa.org. PCUSA allows individual ministers and congregations to make decisions regarding LGBTQ individuals. The denomination as a whole is affirming of LGBTQ participation in the religion. See: "Sexuality and Same-Gender Relationships." Accessed January 23, 2022. https://www.presbyterianmission.org.

position on abortion, and the religion's position on same sex marriage and participation of LGBTQ individuals. These three issues reflect views on sexual and gender equality and women's autonomy.

Of the 10 largest religious organizations in the US, five prohibit the ordination of women and one has made this a congregation-specific issue. Seven of the 10 largest religions in the US continue to view homosexuality as sinful, oppose same-sex marriage, and prohibit LG individuals from serving as clergy, and some have released statements explicitly rejecting transgender and queer individuals (bisexual individuals are typically ignored in all of the position statements).[13] Of the remaining three, two have limited support for same-sex marriage and/or allow LGBTQ individuals (really LG individuals) to serve as clergy. This issue has wrought havoc on moderate religions in the US. LGBTQ issues led to the split of the United Methodist Church, beginning in 2019, which divided members, congregations, and resources between the more conservative and the more progressive wings of the religion. Just two of the religions on the list support a woman's right to choose an abortion. Four oppose abortion under all circumstances—including incest, rape, or when a woman's life is in danger. Three religions allow abortion in those limited circumstances.

As this table makes clear, most of the largest religions in the US continue to adhere to social values that were widespread in past centuries. Their policy positions do not align them with the majority of Americans on any of these issues. As of 2021, 62% of Americans do not think homosexual sex is wrong *at all*; 85% of Americans think abortion should be legal when the mother was raped, 78% think it should be legal if there is a genetic problem with the child, and 90% think it should be legal if the woman's life and/or health is in danger; and 80% of Americans disagree or strongly disagree that a woman should stay home and a man should work.[14] The 10 largest religions in the US are almost completely out of touch with the American people when it comes to these moral issues.

Certainly, there are some religions in the US that have modernized, receiving substantial criticism from more conservative religions in the process. But those religions tend to be smaller. Why might more socially and morally progressive religions be smaller than conservative religions? Consider the option facing those who leave conservative religions: Do they leave religion altogether or do they switch to a religion that more closely aligns with their moral views? Freedom of association in the US means religious affiliation is voluntary and people can choose *not* to affiliate. What is the incentive to affiliate with a religion, even if it does align with your morals and values? While religions may offer a sense of community, that comes with a cost—donations to the religion and time commitments, at a minimum. And what if one finds little in common with the other people at one's local church, synagogue, or mosque? Might it make more sense to simply give up religion altogether if there is no longer a social cost to doing so and find a community of like-minded individuals playing in an amateur soccer league, role playing Dungeons & Dragons, or boating?

The inverse is also true: Those who harbor unpopular moral views have a much greater desire and/or need for religion. Individuals who do not favor gender equality or who think all abortion should be illegal or want LGBTQ individuals to be marginalized have an incentive to surround themselves with other like-minded individuals. What individuals holding unpopular opinions on moral issues get by maintaining an affiliation with a religion that shares their perspective is justification and validation. While the majority of society is telling such individuals that they are bigots or cruel or antiquated or evil, within their religious community, they are righteous warriors defending religious truth.[15]

What this reflects is value misalignment. Value misalignment is, we believe, a meaningful push factor when it comes to religious exiting. To illustrate this even more clearly, we created several charts showing the values of those who left religions, were never religious, and those who have remained religious. Because the data we used to create these charts is cross-sectional and not longitudinal, we cannot argue that value misalignment is causal. It may be the case that people leave religion for some other reason and then their values shift. But the figures below make it quite clear that there is a gulf in values between those who have left religion or were raised without religion and those who remain religious in the US.

In figure 3.1, 79% of those who have left religion do not consider homosexual sex to be wrong at all. The corresponding percentage for the religious is 45%—a difference of 34%. Likewise, as figure 3.2 shows, 71% of those who have left religion think abortion should be legal for any reason while just 42% of the religious agree. There is more agreement

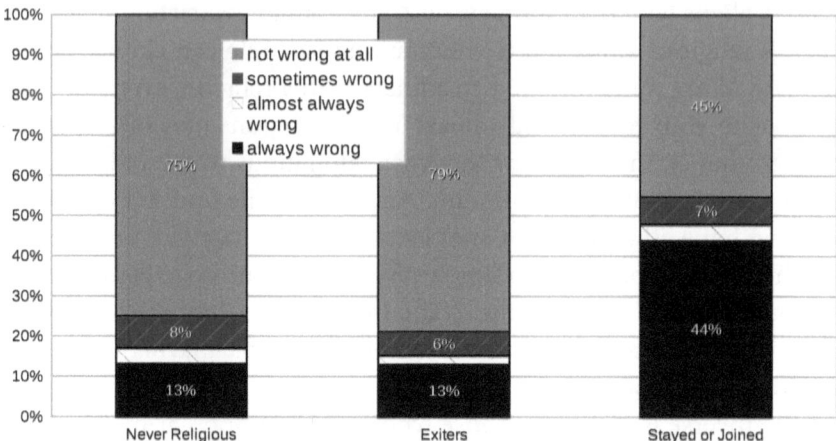

Figure 3.1. Views Toward Homosexual Sex Among Exiters, Never Religious, and Religious. (Source: GSS, 2010–2021)

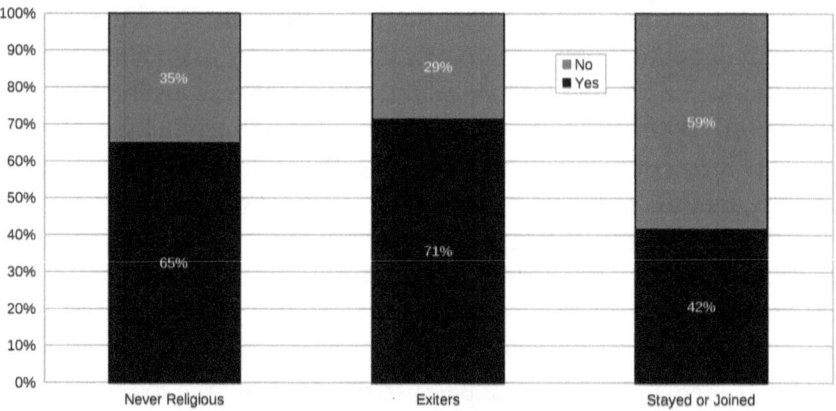

Figure 3.2. Views on Whether Abortion Should be Legal for Any Reason Among Exiters, Never Religious, and Religious. (Source: GSS, 2010–2021)

between those who have exited and those who are religious on the roles of women in society, but a small gap remains here as well. As figure 3.3 illustrates, among those who have left religion, 41% strongly disagree that men should work and women should tend home and 44% disagree; among the religious, 24% strongly disagree and 46% disagree.

While our data cannot establish causality, our interview data strongly suggest that value misalignment is a contributing factor to religious

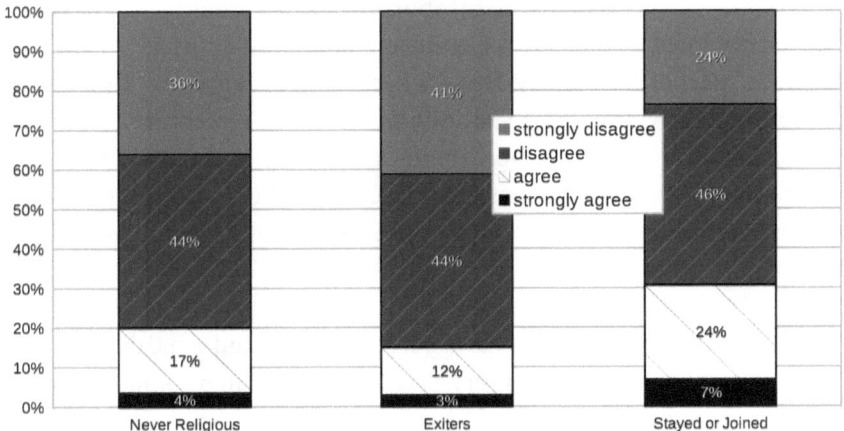

Figure 3.3. Views on Whether It Is Better for Man to Work and Woman to Tend Home Among Exiters, Never Religious, and Religious. (Source: GSS, 2010–2021)

exiting. Nearly all of our participants discussed one or more of these topics during interviews. From abortion to gay marriage, from gender relations to global warming, it's clear that moral issues were motivating forces in their decision to leave religion. For instance, roughly a third of participants talked at some length about their distaste for conservative religion's resistance to gay rights and marriage equality. Noelle, who figured in one of the vignettes at the beginning of this chapter, is a 31-year-old single mother who grew up in a strict Catholic family, who was vexed for years by what she was taught about gay people when she was young:

> The gay rights issue really bothers me. I mean I have some really good gay friends that are awesome people. And when I think about the fact that— like my dad's harped a lot about gay marriage and every time it's like a sword in my side, I just. . . . The hypocrisy! I mean he's so Christian and dysfunctional, and yet so anti-gay marriage. And when I hear that, that's something that really gets my blood boiling, and almost makes me think that he's gay (laughs) . . .

Noelle came to resent the ten years she spent in Catholic school, and her relationship with her father soured when she became an adult. She left Catholicism for good in late adolescence.

For forty-seven-year-old Kim, abortion was a similarly salient issue. Kim is divorced and has three children. She grew up in a "very Irish-Catholic" part of New Jersey. Despite her Jewish background, Kim found herself regularly attending Catholic Mass and felt pressure to believe in the Christian god from her friends and others in the neighborhood where she grew up. Even now, after decades of being nonreligious, it's still apparent how much moral issues like abortion played in her deciding to leave religion for good:

> I mean, I'm certainly passionate about some things, and some things are very—you know, abortion is very, very foundational in my mind. If you can't get pregnant, you should not vote on whether abortion is illegal. That's just how it should be, to me. . . . And like I said, the things that I think a lot of Christians would find immoral, aren't even concerns of mine. But with [abortion], you know, if a young woman gets pregnant and has an abortion, that's a decision she has to make. Having a baby's a really big fucking deal. Trust me. I had three of them. And you know, nobody should—should have to do that, if that's not what they want to do. And so that's not immoral in my mind. But it is in religion's mind. Most religions anyway . . .

Then there's Taren, who was sixty-five at the time of our interview. She grew up in a military family and traveled all over the US. Her family raised her in a fundamentalist Church of Christ congregation where she was taught very conservative positions on a range of moral issues. This continued into early adulthood, where she attended a college in Tennessee run by the Church of Christ. She later came to see the moral teachings she grew up with as thoroughly misguided and all too obsessed with sex:

> I heard that [religion is the basis of morality] on Dr. Laura[16] one time. And she was so adamant about it that I was just flabbergasted. And I hadn't really thought about it in the past. I must have heard this sometime around 1995. And I've thought about it quite a bit. . . . But I have decided that any good in religion comes from the morality that is inherent in people in the first place. And that . . . I long ago concluded that the so-called "morality" that is evidenced in religious circles is all to do with

who is sleeping with whom. Because it's all about pre-marital sex. It's all about fornication. It's about abortion. It's about homosexuality.... That's their morality!

Taren left the Church of Christ after finishing college and moving to California. The last time Taren set foot in a church was when a friend from that college came to visit her and insisted they go to church together, "And so I went. And I was very disgusted by it. I didn't wanna go, and I was very hostile and barely made it through the whole thing. I just, I thought it was just total shit."

Like Taren, many participants simply got fed up with their respective religions' teachings on these and other moral issues. The topic of morality seemed to emerge naturally in almost every interview, but as it became apparent that this played a major role in many of their stories, we began asking participants more directly about how moral issues were connected to their leaving religion. For example, consider an exchange with Kent, a single, retired entrepreneur. Raised Catholic, he went to Catholic schools from elementary school right through his second year of college before he began to question his religious upbringing. At the tail end of president Bush's administration in late 2008, Kent had this to say about why he left not just Catholicism, but rejected religion in general:

> Well, one of the long simmering issues [for me] has been abortion. And the opposition of religious people to abortion. I strongly believe in a woman's right to choose, so that's been simmering in the political system for like 40 years, I guess. Ever since Roe versus Wade.[17] But no, just the ascendancy of the Religious Right. Especially with the election of the first—well, I don't know if "election" is the word—the first ascendancy of the current inhabitant of the White House. It was 7 and ½ years ago that that happened. But it had been going on before that to some extent. And there was ... there was a kind of precursor of that, I guess it was in the 80s, with the Moral Majority. The so-called Moral Majority. And the prominence of TV evangelists, and so forth.

It was the moral issue of abortion (among other things) and the role of conservative religion and the political right that pushed Kent out of religion.

Monica, a Pacific Islander woman in her early thirties from Georgia who spent time as both a Baptist and later Methodist before leaving religion, had an experience similar to many participants who came from Christian backgrounds. In her case, she became skeptical of her religious socialization much earlier than Kent. And it wasn't, as it was for Kent, politically-framed moral issues like abortion that drove her away. Rather, she found the very concept of the Christian god at odds with her intuitions about what it means to be moral:

> It [leaving religion] was kind of like, took a few years. So in middle school I read this book called *Jacob Have I Loved*, and it's one of those Newbery Children's Books and it is basically about Jacob and Esau. . . . It's told from the point of view of the Esau character; and she's ugly; and she's not smart; she's not as popular. And her grandma would quote the Bible to her where God said, "Jacob, I have loved; Esau I have hated thee." And I read that, being a Christian and I was like, what?! God can hate somebody? And I was so like . . . I went in the Bible and looked for it. You know, it's in there twice. So when I was in seventh grade I went to a private Christian school . . . and I got the courage to ask my teacher. I didn't want to seem like sacrilegious or whatever but I asked him, "Look. Here in the Bible it says God hates Esau, what's up with that?" And his response was like, "Some scholars believe what they actually mean here is that God chose Jacob, and Jacob's name changes to Israel, he's the father of all Israel, so God chose these people and not the other people." And I walked away thinking like, how is that better than basically saying God completely rejects an entire group of people, [based on] just one person? So from there I was just like, I don't know about this God.

As Monica's narrative illustrates, there was value misalignment between her understanding of what a god should be like—loving of all people—and how the god of the Bible was described. For her, a child, to observe this, makes it clear the moral teachings of many religions are so misaligned with prevailing mores that even young people steeped in religion see how problematic religious morality can be.

Don, whom we met at the beginning of this chapter, was passionate about his role in providing music for the several Protestant groups he used to belong to. Now an atheist, he struggled for decades with the moral teachings of Christianity, for which he never found resolution while a Christian. He is now a member of The Clergy Project,[18] a support network for religious leaders who no longer believe in the supernatural claims of religion. His summary, in part from a journal entry he read to us, of why he became a nonbeliever highlights the importance of morality in his decision to leave:

> They [religious friends and family] say, "The Bible is our source of morality." And I will say, "Tell me something in the Bible that informs your life and morality." And none of them know. They say, "Well, thou shalt not kill." Oh, really? So you have to go to the Bible to know that? Let me just read you a quick thing I wrote: "My morality comes from my upbringing with mostly secular parents and the experiences of life in what I believe I could become. Morality is based on the ideas that are as old as humankind, when our ancestors figured out basic rules for supporting each other's survival and procreation. I start with the basics: I prefer life over death and assume that others do. I prefer to be treated kindly and assume others do. I understand that killing, enslaving, raping, repressing, stealing from others is not a way to sustain a culture. And personally deeming those behaviors reprehensible, I don't participate in them. I choose to do good and remain neutral in relation to others and avoid causing harm. The Bible and religious dogma do not inform my own sense of morality, but they're contradictory and often immoral teachings. My morality is in no sense based on the teachings of the church or the word of a deity nor is it motivated by the promise of eternal reward or the fear of eternal punishment. I don't believe in either. I'm moral on my own and can happily be without god."

Don made clear in his exit journey his realization that religion was neither required for morality nor a good source of it. For our interviewees, the Bible or any other book of scripture is not necessary to justify prohibition against murder. Religious teachings are not necessary to arrive at the conclusion that being nice is generally a good idea. As Frans de Waal has illustrated, our primate relatives have morals that are superior to those in the Bible.[19] And, while some people have found ways to selectively interpret the Bible to validate gender and sexual equality, it's much easier to advocate for gender and sexual equality without trying to reconcile such a position with a book that considers women chattel and inferior to men and advocates capital punishment for homosexuality.

For many people, the conflict between the morals taught by their religion and the morals they hold serve as push factors driving them away from religion. It's much easier to live day-to-day feeling like your morals are validated by those around you than it is to be constantly challenged to change your moral views.

Intriguingly, this is a catch-22 for religion. If religions advocate antiquated morals, they will tend to alienate young people and people who hold more egalitarian views. But if religions modernize their morals, they lose one aspect of what makes them distinctive in the modern world. The appeal of some religions in the twenty-first century for some people is precisely that they subordinate women and/or denigrate LGBTQ individuals.[20] There is still demand for such institutions, as our figures in this section illustrate. Religions provide a supportive community for individuals who hold such views, allowing them to feel validated and justified.[21] If religions shift their morals, they lose their niche appeal.[22] Yet, religions that continue to advocate antiquated moral positions find themselves in a constant rearguard action: they are glacially modernizing their morals, all the while fighting against their more conservative members who want no change and their more progressive members who want faster change.[23] This catch-22 for religions is one of the reasons why secularization *seems* inevitable: regardless of what religions do, change or not, they are likely to lose their appeal to many in the modern world.[24] By "modern" we are referencing the argument made by Kasselstrand et al.[25] in delineating secularization theory, where they defined modernization as "the transition from a traditional, rural, non-industrial society to a contemporary, urban, industrial (or postindustrial) society." Modernity is obviously going to vary by context and geography, with some societies being more modern than others.

This leads us to our first general proposition regarding religious exiting:

Proposition 1: *Ceteris paribus* (all else being equal), individuals who hold more modern, egalitarian views will be more likely to leave religion than those who hold more traditional views.

Political Push Factors

The connection between politics and leaving religion is complicated. Before we get into it, we'll note one fact that is quite clear—there are very few nonreligious people—either those who have left religions (~8%) or those who were never religious (~12%)—in the Republican Party. The alignment of the Republican Party with conservative Christians in the US has alienated the nonreligious from that party. But precisely how politics relates to religious identification is complex.

Several connections between nonreligion and politics are apparent in qualitative and institutional membership data. Philosopher Sam Harris, who rose to prominence in the early 2000s, made it very clear in his first book and in subsequent work that he was spurred to write about religion in large part because of the September 11, 2001 attack by Muslim fundamentalists on the US. Harris is not alone. Leaders of secular organizations in the US like American Atheists, the Freedom from Religion Foundation, American Humanists, and the Council for Secular Humanism, all noted that there was a large increase in dues-paying members and subscribers to their magazines and other publications following the September 11th attack.[26]

There was another political component that was motivating the nonreligious at that same time—George W. Bush was President. While a Methodist, President Bush was also an evangelical Christian and held many views that would classify him as a "fundamentalist Christian,"

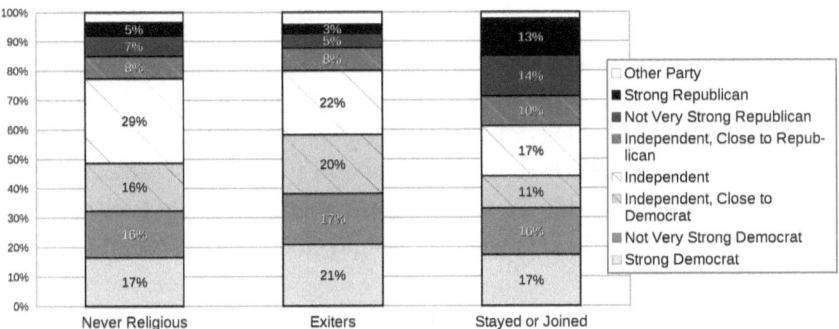

Figure 3.4. Political Affiliations of Never Religious, Exiters, and Religious. (Source: GSS, 2010–2021)

including a literal interpretation of scripture and a belief that the world is starkly divided between good and evil. Bush's close alignment with conservative Christians along with the attack on the US by fundamentalist Muslims strongly intimated to many nonreligious Americans that their secular values were under attack. As a result, they became more vocal, politically engaged, and organized.[27] This is illustrated in our dialogue with many participants, including Noelle, who, though she left religion in her late teens, only found reason to join a secular group during the Bush Administration years later:

> Q: You left religion a long time ago. But you mentioned you adopted the term "atheist" only about two years ago. What brought that about?
> A: Well . . . (long pause) I guess the main thing that made the difference for me, and which I haven't mentioned yet, is the past eight years of hell (Bush administration) we've been in. And I see the huge impact that the fundamentalists have made in this country trying to strong-arm everybody into doing their will; and that invoked a whole lot of bad memories for me.

Billy, a young college student, was similarly suspicious of the link between Bush, his policies, and evangelical Christianity, even drawing a comparison between Bush and Ahmadinejad, then president of Iran. Billy had traveled extensively as a child because of his father's work, spending years in Germany, China, and other countries. This exposure to different cultures informed his thoughts on religion when he got older:

> And then here [the US], being atheist is suspicious. Because then you're not on the same, you know, page as society. Especially when you have a demagogue like George Bush in office. That kinda seems to affect the whole sort of psychology of people. . . . They are—they have so many things in common. Or even like Ahmadinejad and George Bush in some respects you know with the fear mongering and the call to arms. And the call to God. And rallying people around God; they have so much in common.

As these and other interviews throughout this chapter show, our data suggest that the alignment of conservative Christianity with the

Republican Party had the consequence of driving nonreligious people out of the Republican Party and led them to become more politically active. Not all of these individuals became Democrats. As figure 3.4 above illustrates, exiters and those who were never religious are particularly likely to be political independents. There are, of course, still political conservatives among the nonreligious, but many of those individuals identify as Libertarians.[28] It is also the case that many political moderates and politically independent individuals who are nonreligious side with Democrats in the US in many elections because Democrats are more likely to advocate for their values. Our interview data reflect this, and it is, in some sense, a microcosm of broader trends. Most identified as liberal/progressive or politically independent, but few valorized the Democratic party, though they sided with them when it came time to vote. No one identified with the Republican party or political conservatism (see the appendix for more details on the political affiliations of our interview participants).

There is another theory that is popular among some academics that warrants discussion here. Several scholars have gone so far as to suggest that the alignment of the Republican Party with conservative Christians has actually contributed to the rise of the nonreligious.[29] We have always found such arguments lacking. The basic idea is that the linking of the Republican Party with evangelical Christians, the Moral Majority, and other conservative religious groups during the 1970s and 1980s led Americans in the 1990s to stop identifying as religious. Yet, why would the alignment of one major political party in the US with a specific strain of religiosity lead tens of millions of Americans to leave religion entirely? This argument has always seemed like a leap in logic to us, as though those suggesting it missed at least one piece of the puzzle. The more obvious consequence of such an alignment would be that individuals who reject conservative Christianity would leave the Republican Party and become politically independent or join another party (the argument we made above), not that they would reject religion.

It is possible that religious moderates and liberals who left the Republican Party as it was taken over by religious conservatives also switched their religious congregations and affiliations in order to feel more comfortable with a religious home more closely aligned with their values. A large percentage of Americans—close to 40%[30]—switch religious affiliations during their lifetimes. Such a switch could then lead these individuals to eventually leave religion altogether if they found when joining a more moderate or liberal religion that there wasn't much about organized religion worth keeping. This would be the missing piece to the argument. But we are hard-pressed to believe that Americans see the alignment of Republicans and conservative religious folks and immediately decide, "Well, that does it. I'm no longer religious." However, it could lead such individuals to: (1) leave the Republican Party, (2) switch to a more moderate/liberal denomination, and *then* (3) decide that they no longer need religion. Step two has been missing from these arguments for a long time (though see below for other possibilities).

Why might step two lead to step three? That liberal religion in the US functions as a halfway house for people on their way out of religion was suggested as early as the 1960s.[31] As a number of scholars have noted, religion in the US is a marketplace.[32] Religions compete for "consumers." This has led to all sorts of innovations and changes in religiosity. The Catholic Church switched their mass from Latin in the 1960s as a result of this. Many religions modernized their music in the late twentieth century. Megachurches with highly entertaining services have gained prominence as they try to compete with other forms of entertainment vying for people's attention, like the NFL.[33] With all of these innovations to help distinguish themselves in a competitive religious marketplace, there are important characteristics that can help keep religion relevant: they need to provide their "consumers" (a.k.a. adherents or followers) a sense of community and a worldview that helps them deal with both everyday life and existential concerns.[34] If people can find community outside of organized religion, which is most assuredly the case today and was predicted over a century ago,[35] then this essential component of religion is no longer a motivator to remain religious. And if modern society can provide a worldview that helps people address both immediate concerns (e.g., How do I determine what is right and wrong?) and existential concerns (e.g., What happens when I die?) what does religion have to offer that one cannot get elsewhere?

This suggests that conservative religions have an advantage over liberal religions in modernized societies: as we have seen, some individuals retain values and beliefs that do not align with broader social values. If someone doesn't believe men and women should be equal (ignoring or rejecting non-binary individuals altogether) or if someone doesn't think lesbian, gay, and bisexual individuals deserve equal rights, they can find support for those beliefs in conservative religious communities. Both women and men who think it is best for women to stay home with kids while men work have their values affirmed in conservative religious communities.[36] What values do liberal religions support that are not supported by the broader society in the US? While there may be some exceptions (e.g., the pacifism of Quakers), most of the values held by liberal religions are also those advocated by broader, mainstream society and are manifest in movies, TV shows, on the news, in books, and in all sorts of media. Thus, from the perspective of *homo economicus*, what is the "value added" of liberal religion in a modern society?

We do not mean to suggest that there are no benefits from liberal religions. To the contrary, what progressive religions offer is actually an intriguing combination of potentially lower costs than more conservative religions, but with similar benefits. Progressive religions can still provide supportive communities, engaging services, existential security, and a number of other benefits. At the same time, progressive religions can reduce some indirect costs of religious participation. While it may still require expenditures of time, money, and other resources to participate, there is a possibility that affiliating with a progressive religion reduces the stigma of association with conservative religions that is growing in the US today.[37] In other words, in certain locations and circles (e.g., San Francisco, New York City, Seattle), it may be costly socially to identify oneself as an evangelical Christian or a Pentecostal or Jehovah's Witness. But identifying as an Episcopalian, Lutheran, Presbyterian, or Methodist may not carry the same level of opprobrium as do other labels that imply conservatism.

This argument does raise an interesting possibility that, to our knowledge, has not previously been suggested. It could be the case that the alignment of the Republican Party with conservative Christianity has resulted in general stigma among left-leaning individuals that all religion is detrimental to society. Given the low levels of knowledge many people have regarding religion,[38] it's possible that people could hold binary views towards religion: religion is either good or bad, harmful or beneficial. For individuals who consider religion generally to be more harmful than beneficial—a view now widely held in some parts of the world—they may consider all religious people to be questionable.[39] The implication here would be that, when someone identifies as a Jew or a Mormon or Hutterite, the distinction between these religions is completely lost and the person hearing the identification hears only, "That person is religious and religious means conservative Republican."[40]

While by no means a definitive test of this idea, we did find some data that speak to this possibility in the American Trends Panel Wave 30 from Pew[41] that included the question, "Considering everything, what impact do churches and religious organizations have on American society?" Response options included: (1) "They do more harm than good," (2) "They do more good than harm," and (3) "Don't make much difference." Overall, just 21.1% of Americans reported in 2017 that they thought religion did more harm than good while 55.5% reported that they thought religion did more good than harm; 22.5% indicated they didn't think religion made much of a difference. Looking at just those individuals who say they think abortion is morally acceptable (a proxy measure to single out left-leaning individuals), 36.7% reported that religion did more harm than good, 38.7% responded that they thought religion did more good than harm, and 22.9% said they didn't think religion made much of a difference. These data suggest it could be the case a small percentage of Americans hold generally negative views of all religion and would be critical of anyone who said they were religious, but it is not the case (or was not in 2017) that a majority of Americans view religion negatively and not even a majority of left-leaning Americans stigmatize religion such that simply identifying as religious would lead people to wonder if someone was also politically conservative.

This returns us to the original assertion by Hout and Fischer[42] that the alignment of the Republican Party with conservative Christians led to the rise of the nonreligious. We are not convinced this was the direct cause of people leaving religion, but it could have indirectly contributed to this by encouraging people who had previously attended conservative religions to switch to more liberal congregations, only for those individuals to realize that liberal religions didn't offer them much in the way of community or inspiration that they couldn't find in their local bowling league, community garden, or book club. It may also be that, in some social circles, reporting a religious affiliation—any religious affiliation—results in a general sense of disapprobation, leading people to feel social pressure to leave religion. Thus, it could be the alignment of Republicans with conservative Christians indirectly contributed to people leaving religion in the US, but it is doubtful that it was the proximate cause of the rise of the nonreligious.

There is one other possible pathway by which the alignment of the Republican Party with conservative Christians may have increased religious exiting. Several scholars have recently argued that political affiliation has become something of a master status or primary identity.[43] These scholars suggest that one's political identity is so powerful that it can actually result in people changing other identities they hold, including their race, ethnicity, sexual orientation, and, of course, their religious affiliation. These scholars have mustered some evidence for this idea, but their evidence is only suggestive that this might apply to a very small group of people, is preliminary, and has not definitively ruled out other possible explanations. For instance, when Egan[44] showed that individuals who were closely aligned with the Democratic Party were more likely to change their sexual orientation over a four-year period, he noted that bisexual individuals were the most likely to change their identity to either lesbian or gay and did not show that large numbers of heterosexual individuals were changing their sexual orientation. Likewise, the data upon which he drew did not include more deeply probing questions that could capture whether these individuals had been closeted and only changed their self-reported sexual orientation once they were safely ensconced in a community that was more accepting of their sexual identity. The same arguments apply to those individuals whose affiliation with the Democratic Party changed their religious affiliation to none—it's a small number, they may have already been religiously disengaged, and they may also have been closeted about their nonreligion. As recent research shows, there continues to be widespread prejudice and discrimination against the nonreligious, particularly among Republicans.[45] While an intriguing line of research, we are skeptical that the alignment of Republicans with conservative Christians explains the rapid rate of secularization that has occurred in the US since 1990.

If the Republican Party continues to align itself with Evangelicals and religious conservatives, it will continue to alienate most of the nonreligious. It doesn't require much foresight to realize what this is going to mean: Evangelical Christianity is not growing in the US. It's declining.

The nonreligious are growing rapidly. Millions of people are exiting religion in the US every year. The new base for the Republican Party is shrinking and it will likely continue to do so.

More to our point, religions are stuck in an awkward position. As we have seen, if a religion tries to remain socially and politically conservative, it will remain relevant for a shrinking percentage of the population that finds validation in such institutions. If, however, a religion tries to adjust to shifting mores and norms, it becomes less appealing to conservative individuals and more progressive individuals don't need the same validation of their morality and worldview because their worldview is legitimated by broader society. The question for religions, then, is how do they walk the line between modernizing and remaining supportive of their conservative members? The religions that seem to be surviving in the face of rapid secularization are those that do slowly change their morals (and concomitant doctrines), but they do so well after those values have changed in society, generally. These religions tend to have members who are quite conservative. Progressive individuals, on the other hand, are being pushed out of these institutions by the outdated moral and social views of the religions. This is part of the reason for the generational gap observed by researchers who have found that American youth are less religious, more likely to be suspicious of religion, and less likely to adopt theistic views than earlier generations.[46]

This leads to our second general proposition:

Proposition 2: *Ceteris paribus*, individuals who have more progressive social and political values will be more likely to leave religion than will individuals who have more conservative social and political values.

Doctrine and Dogma

A major contributor to why people leave religion is that they stopped believing in the claims and teachings of the religion in which they were raised. This might seem obvious or overly simplistic, but it is definitely a factor that contributes to religious exiting. More than fifty years ago, when the phenomenon of religious exiting was barely on sociologists' radar, it was noticed that coming to reject specific religious doctrines

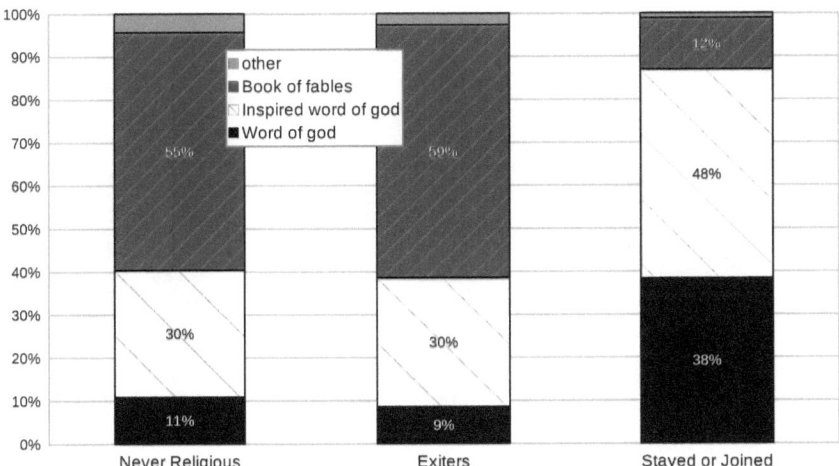

Figure 3.5. Views of the Bible Among Never Religious, Exiters, and Religious. (Source: GSS, 2010–2021)

indeed helped spur the process of leaving religion. For instance, Armand Mauss, based on his study of Mormons and other groups, called the abandonment of religious beliefs the "intellectual dimension" of "religious defection" and discussed its relationship to two other dimensions in his typology, the social and emotional.[47] Claims, and belief in those claims, matter. Many religions make claims that, in the light of modern understandings of nature and the universe, are absurd, such as asserting that a worldwide flood occurred,[48] that the earth is 6,000 years old, or that humans did not evolve and do not share a common ancestor with other primates. There are, of course, millions of Americans who continue to hold such beliefs, but those numbers are declining and it is becoming harder to believe such claims in light of the pervasive evidence and narratives to the contrary.

To illustrate that exiters have rejected some of the core elements of traditional religion, we begin this section with three charts showing how exiters differ from the religious on three beliefs: their view of the Bible—whether it is the literal word of god, the inspired word, a book of fables, or not really relevant to them; whether they believe in an afterlife; and whether they believe in hell.

Figure 3.5 shows that there are massive differences between exiters and stayers when it comes to their view of the Bible. While 38% of the

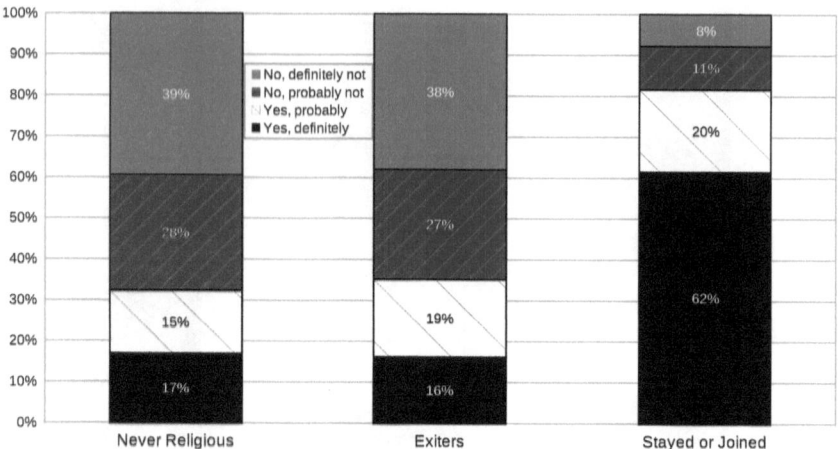

Figure 3.6. Belief in Hell Among Never Religious, Exiters, and Religious. (Source: GSS, 2010–2021)

religious believe the Bible is the literal word of god and just 12% consider the Bible to be a book of fables, among those who have exited religion, just 9% retain a literal interpretation of the Bible while 59% consider the Bible to be a book of fables. The majority of exiters reject the idea that the Bible is an inspired book and put it on par with the *Iliad* and the *Odyssey* as a work of fiction.

A minority of exiters believe in hell (35%), as shown in figure 3.6, in contrast to the 82% of the religious who reported that they definitely or probably believe in hell. In contrast to their view of the Bible, where a majority of exiters do not consider the book to be religiously inspirational, just over half of exiters do believe in an afterlife, but nearly 30% fewer exiters believe in an afterlife compared to the religious (57% vs. 86%, respectively).

At a very basic level, then, those who leave religion are much less likely to hold traditionally religious (primarily Christian, in this case) beliefs. In religions where right belief (orthodoxy) is heavily emphasized (e.g., Protestantism), it is more difficult to "pass" as a nonbeliever than in religions where right behavior (orthopraxy) is more heavily emphasized (e.g., Judaism). For many of our interviewees, once it became clear that they did not share the beliefs of the majority of the people in their religion, they decided to leave.

As we noted earlier, it's not uncommon for those who remain religious to attribute negative motives to those who leave—like a desire to have sex before marriage or use alcohol or drugs. A large percentage of those who leave attribute their decisions to something entirely different—the teachings of their religion. Figure 3.7 draws on the Pew survey discussed earlier in this chapter—the 2008 Faith in Flux survey—that asked a number of questions of people who had left the religion of their childhood. In figure 3.7, we included just those who had left religion and not joined another religion. The reason most commonly given—by 38% of the respondents—for why they left religion was the teachings of religions. It is the case that the rules and rigidity of the religion are a problem for some people; 8% indicated as much. But far more common are problems people have with theology.

For many religious exiters, they stopped believing at a fairly young age but only had the autonomy to exit religion once they left their parents' home. Before that point, their parents insisted that they continue attending religious services and activities.

As we hope we've made clear, the causes of religious exiting are manifold; not many people leave religion for any one reason. Historical, societal, psychological, and other forces (summed up by the concept of

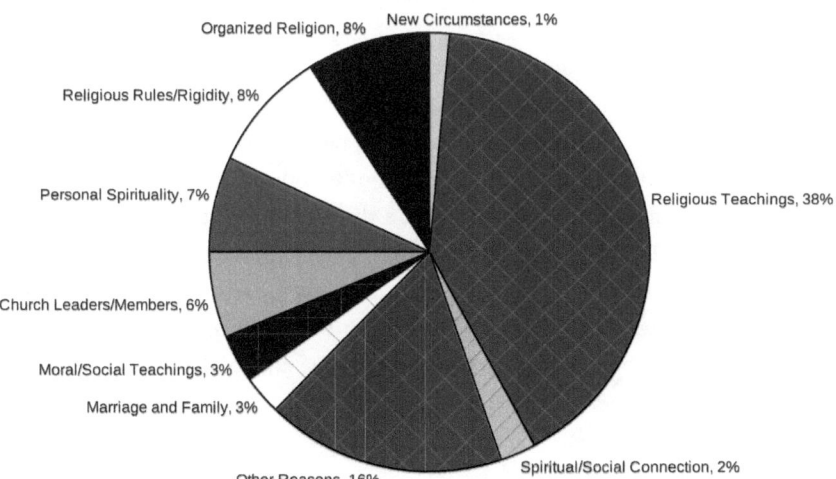

Figure 3.7. Reasons Given for Religious Exiting. (Source: Pew Faith in Flux Study, 2008—weighted)

secularization) all converge to produce the phenomenon we're calling religious exiting. But as the data suggest, it really is the case that intellectual curiosity and honesty, an inclination to question, and disagreement with and disbelief in the metaphysical claims of religion play a decisive role. Some scholars are suspicious of this, perhaps because it's obvious, or seems too simple.[49] However, consistent with survey data, the words and experiences of exiters themselves make it difficult to argue that disbelief in religious doctrines isn't a major contributor to religious exiting.

Our interviewees help illustrate the role beliefs play in religious exiting. Identifying as gender-fluid, Claire was in her twenties, married, a mother of two, and a school teacher at the time of our interview. Born in Kansas, she spent most of her life in California. Raised in the Foursquare Church, an evangelical pentecostal denomination, she was intimately familiar with Bible camp, speaking in tongues, and the importance of doctrinal truth. She didn't have a negative experience in her church. In fact, she was fond of the people, and at one point described it as ". . . a really good church" where she had "a good experience." The problem was the doctrine of hell. After questioning her faith as a teenager, she came across some videos by Rob Bell, founder of Mars Hill Bible Church, a Christian megachurch in Grand Rapids, Michigan. Bell encouraged his listeners to reconsider the conventional notion of hell as a literal place of unending conscious human physical, emotional, and spiritual torture.

> One of the biggest questions I heard was, "What's up with this whole cosmic transaction thing? Couldn't god have just avoided this whole big show? Why did god need blood money to pay for our sins?" Those three questions. And it solved for me the fear of hell through the work of Rob Bell, particularly a video which took a different look at the atonement. So that was definitely one of the final things [that caused her to leave religion], and then the last nail in the coffin was the argument of free will and whether we have it. And when a friend argued convincingly to me that they didn't believe that human beings have enough free will to make it justifiable to send them to hell . . . that was it. I think it was the death of hell that won me over.

Consider Fatima, a multiracial woman in her late 50s who was raised (mostly) Lutheran. When she was asked directly about what finally led her to leave religion for good, she reflected on the problem of hell in the context of her conflicted multi-faith family situation growing up:

> I was going to a church that said, "If you don't believe, well. . . ." (pause). It's interesting. She's [her mother] very Christian. My father is from India, he grew up Hindu. So basically, the message I got was if you don't believe, you're going to hell. So I thought for years my dad was going to hell. I have three siblings and I think we all had to deal with that message, and how were we [to] reconcile that? And I had a couple of friends in high school who were atheists and I had the sort of chance, or message maybe, that if you once believed and turned away, you were kind of doubly damned. So it took a lot for me to say, "I can't believe this." I mean, I can't adhere to this and I've got friends who are really good people, and a father, who's a really good person, and they're going to hell, you say? And so I thought, well, I finally decided that if they're going to hell, it can't be too bad a place (shrugs), and so I gave it up.

For Claire and Fatima, as for many religious exiters, the traditional Christian conception of hell is untenable, immoral, and evil. This developed in both of them a powerful motivation to drop religion that embraces a belief in hell as a core doctrine.

As with disbelief in religious scripture and the doctrine of hell, skepticism abounded regarding traditional religious views on an afterlife, though some were open, more philosophically than doctrinally, to the idea of consciousness in some form surviving death. Claire's view is illustrative of what many had to say on this question:

> I believe we have one life and this is the life we have and this is the one earth that we have and we are somehow mandated by ourselves by this innate drive for our species to survive and for us to survive to make this world the best it can be because nobody can do it for us and we can either help ourselves and raise ourselves out of the dirt or just let ourselves just fall.

What's the basis of Claire's and other participants' belief that "we have one life and this is the life we have"? Unsurprisingly, a commitment to evidence and a scientific outlook, coupled with basic inferences about the nature of biology and life itself led most to a similar conclusion. Here's Matthew, a retired science teacher and freelance writer. His incredulity is clearly based on science and evidence, to which he defers on the question of an afterlife:

> Physicists are pretty confident that there is no means by which certain sort of psychic or paranormal phenomenon could take place. So no existence beyond death, no telepathic communications or telekinesis, not any of that stuff. It just isn't possible from a scientific standpoint.

Notice Matthew's response bundles various purported phenomena. Psychism, telepathy, and the paranormal are, for him, all on par with the idea of an afterlife. Skepticism, the debunking of religious claims, and myth-busting all have an affinity with a secular and scientific worldview, and the nonreligious in the main are more likely to embrace such a worldview.[50] Perhaps rejecting the supernatural is seen by many as a prerequisite for being nonreligious. However, the context here is interesting. Bader, Baker, and Mencken[51] show that belief in supernatural and paranormal phenomena, including encounters with ghosts (taken as evidence of an afterlife), palm reading, alien abduction, and even Bigfoot is much more widespread in the US than one might think. This may seem surprising, especially in light of the secularizing forces we argue are the source of increased skepticism of religion and religious exiting. One might assume that disbelief in the supernaturalist claims of religion would coincide with giving up other dubious claims that lack evidence and scientific validation. However, leaving religion doesn't always mean abandoning all such beliefs. As noted above, the *majority* of both religious exiters and those who were never religious believe in at least one of these unprovable claims, that life continues after death.

None of our interviewees actually stated that they definitely believe in an afterlife. But some were open to the idea, or simply acknowledged that they don't know, or aren't that keen to guess. Judy's framing (and good humor) is illustrative of the "official" position many took on this issue. After a period of what she called "almost psychotic religiosity" in her youth, she left Catholicism to try several other religions including Quakerism. None of them took. In her 70s at the time of the interview, she was a self-described scientific-pantheist. Her "death assessment" left open the possibility of an afterlife, though she thought there was good reason not to expect one.

> You know, my death assessment at the moment of what exists and what doesn't exist; I'm currently thinking that my ashes are going to feed the trees, and that's all I know. But, you know, it's possible; if there happens to be another life, I just hope it'll be a good one. But it's just something that . . . (pause), it's not something that seems *likely*. I think there's better explanations of how the world was created, and how we came to be, and how it might [end].

Whether they thought there might be an afterlife, most tended to argue that what matters is the here-and-now. A few used the humanist refrain, "Let's care about the one life we *know* we have."

Intellectual and moral problems with the Bible, heaven, hell, and a litany of other doctrinal issues are not incidental but rather central to religious exiting. It's of course possible for some (perhaps many) religious individuals to have real doubts about the doctrines of their religion but stay the course because of family, friends, community, and other social connections. Other religious doctrines, such as the idea that doubt itself is a critical part of an earthly test—thus the necessity for faith—can keep one committed to their religion. But religious exiters are different. They are willing to sacrifice the comforts and benefits of religion, and sometimes important relationships, in order to remain honest in their beliefs and committed to what they see as the truth.[52]

Hypocrisy

While family, friends, community, and social connections can keep people in, those same forces can drive people out of religion. How?

Hypocrisy!

Hypocrisy functioned as a push factor among our interviewees. It was often rooted in a combination of morality and doctrine. Much of the responsibility for this push factor lays at the feet of religious leaders. Many religious leaders have asserted that the divine forces they represent are the source of morality. Revealed scripture or divine inspiration then serve as the basis for the religion's moral teachings. An essential part of the message of many religions is that they can delineate for members what is right and wrong. That would not be a problem . . . IF the religious leaders teaching these moral messages and the most devout members adhered to those teachings. Some religious people distinguish between what they perceive to be a good system of moral guidance and the people who are supposed to enact it, recognizing that people are flawed, even if the moral system is divine. But other members assume that those preaching the moral message should also live it. And when they observe leaders and presumably devout members of their faith failing to uphold the moral teachings they espouse, the disconnect is often jarring.

Probably the most glaring illustration of hypocrisy, which has received widespread attention over the last 30 years, is pervasive sexual abuse. Dozens of Catholic dioceses in the US have filed for bankruptcy as a result of sex abuse lawsuits.[53] The Catholic Church is not the only religion that has been sued for covering up sexual abuse; it's just the largest and has received the most press. Nearly every major religious denomination in the US, from Scientology to Orthodox Judaism[54] and from nondenominational Pentecostal congregations to Unitarian Universalists[55] have faced charges and convictions due to sexual abuse by clergy.[56] When the moral messengers are also the most morally bankrupt, it's not surprising that our interviewees noticed the hypocrisy and then continued that line of reasoning: if even the *leaders* of the religion aren't following the moral teachings, maybe the problem is with religion.

Hypocrisy came up in some of the data we analyzed. In figure 3.7 described above, 6% of those who had left religion noted that church leaders and members were the primary reason they left. It's not entirely clear from the survey responses whether this reason for leaving is situated in interpersonal conflicts or hypocrisy, but it's likely a combination of both. Even so, hypocrisy came up in our interviews too. For instance, Liv, who was 62 at the time of our interview and lived in Texas, was raised Catholic. She attended Catholic school, most of the people she knew were Catholic, and she always felt pressure in her youth to "do what she was supposed to." Though her parents required the whole family to be active churchgoers, she didn't actually see her parents as being particularly religious. As she moved into her teenage years, she began to suspect that religion, for them, was more about appearance than substance. When asked about why she left Catholicism, it became clear that hypocrisy played a basic role. She observed it not just in others, but noticed it in herself too:

> I think one of the things was the more that I went to church and got to know about other people that were going to church, especially people . . . acting holier than thou, being on the front pew of the church and acting *so* religious, and going to confession, and going and getting communion, and all this. And then [find out] they were having affairs or they were cheating on this or just doing all these things is quite. . . . (pause) How hypocritical is that to be doing that? And these were sometimes, they were like very important people in the church and I just didn't understand. I can't accept that. And then also just going through confession and saying you go and you say "Forgive me Father for I have sinned and I will sin no more." It was like, as I'm saying the words I say well, I'm being a hypocrite because I know I'm not . . . when I leave here I'm going to be a hypocrite because I'm going to be going out and doing those things that I just said I wasn't going to do. And just so many more things; at that time you didn't really hear about say like [the] priests, the scandals with the priests as far as them molesting kids and stuff like that. I don't know, there was just a lot of, to me, hypocrisy about the church.

Liv felt like the disjuncture between who she actually was and who she was expected to be by her Catholic family and community set her up for hypocrisy. She didn't want to be a hypocrite; and she got tired of seeing the hypocrisy around her.

Rodney is a man in his 50s who was raised in a small nondenominational Christian sect. His father was the minister of their church. His mother was as religiously devout as his father and they were both very strict parents. His observation of hypocrisy was very close to home as he witnessed the contradiction between what his parents—especially his abusive mother—would preach at church and how they would act at home. This, combined with his reading of the Bible, pushed Rodney away first from his parents and then the church:

> My mother was quite violent. So I think the hypocrisy between talking about peace and "turn the other cheek" and all that. [This] was telling me

that it clearly doesn't work for her. So to me it was supposed to be this magical thing you know, it's what they were telling me. It's such a magical thing, he died to save us from our sins . . . [but] everyone still seemed to be acting very sinfully and I couldn't understand what the difference was. They didn't seem any better than anybody else . . . I was really disgusted by what I read [in the Bible] and the lack of wisdom. There's a few gems here and there, no question about it, but overall, not a whole lot.

Across all interviews, how prevalent were all the above push factors—including perceived hypocrisy—in explaining why these individuals left religion? In a word, pervasive! However, this is not to suggest either (a) homogeneity of experience for everyone who leaves religion, or (b) universal application of these particular push factors. It's possible that none of the above is at play for some religious exiters. What we do get, though, is a snapshot of some of the central social, moral, psychological, and intellectual proximate causes for leaving religion as told by exiters themselves. What's more, despite the caveats offered in the introduction, there's good reason to take participants at their word for why they left religion, since this rarely suggests superficial engagement with arguments for and against religion. To the contrary, these respondents, irrespective of their religious upbringing, initial religious commitments, and level of religiosity, thought carefully, often for long periods of time, and with varying levels of anxiety and strain to relationships, about whether to stick with religion. In the end, they chose not to. The seriousness with which they approached the problem and that characterized their decision ultimately to leave should inspire at least some confidence in the words they share.

This leads to our third proposition:

Proposition 3: *Ceteris paribus*, individuals who reject religious doctrines and teachings will be more likely to leave religion than will individuals who accept religious doctrines and teachings.

Pull Factors

When thinking about immigration, there are not just push factors that drive people out of a country. There are also the factors that pull people toward a new location. The same is true of becoming nonreligious.

Although various push factors have been emphasized in the literature, there's very little research that focuses on what "pulls" people out of religion. According to our interviewees and our research, there are many characteristics of the nonreligious life that are appealing, though that is not how religious exiting is depicted by religious leaders. Many religious individuals paint dark fantasies of what life is like for the nonreligious. Those without religion are believed to be alcoholics and drug addicts who have no moral compass, are criminals, are physically, emotionally, psychologically, and economically impoverished because they lack the blessings of the righteous and are constantly buffeted by Satan.[57] It is a fantasy that is painted to convince religious individuals that there is only misery awaiting them outside religion.

These imaginings may even have seemed compelling to our interviewees . . . until they turned on the TV, got on the internet, or went to school. All it takes is meeting one well-adjusted nonreligious person to plant a seed of doubt about these dark fantasies of how horrible secular life is. In reality, leaving religion behind came with many benefits for our interviewees, all of which function as pull factors that facilitate religious exiting.

Better Things to Do

A significant pull factor according to our interviewees is that they no longer have to spend their time attending long religious services, engaging in religious rituals, or reading archaic texts that have little relevance to their lives. Instead, nonreligious people can spend their time how they want. Whether that involves reading a novel instead of studying the Bible, going to the beach instead of synagogue, hiking instead of praying, the point is that there is no longer an obligation to do or think of things that they do not want to do.

In an earlier study, one of the authors (Cragun) asked religious college students to choose between attending religious services or a variety of alternative activities. The study was designed so they were able to choose between religious services and each alternative, allowing us to determine which of the 20 activities they would choose over religious services. Of the 20 activities contrasted with attending religious services, 50% or more of respondents preferred 17 of them, including listening to music, reading a book, spending time with their pet, going to a bar, going to a museum, going shopping, exercising, going to a movie, staying home and relaxing, going out to eat, sleeping, going to a professional sporting event, going to an amusement park, going to the beach, spending time with friends, going to a concert, and spending time with family. Only playing video games, watching TV, and surfing the web lost to attending religious services, but more than 40% still chose those over attending religious services.[58] Keep in mind, these were the students who reported a religious affiliation. Imagine how those who are nonreligious would respond. The point here is fairly clear: divesting religious obligations frees up time to pursue other, often more enjoyable and fulfilling activities. One of the factors pulling people away from religion is all of the alternative ways they can spend their time.

Given our recruitment strategy for our interviews, our sample over-represents those who replace church and other religious activities with explicitly secular ones, like joining secular groups. There are religious exiters who fill at least some of their freed-up time with things like monthly secular congregational services or involvement with humanist or skeptic groups. However, even here, other than those who lead such groups or who are actively involved in secular activism, the time spent in this space compared to what their former religious involvement entailed is quite trivial. What most of our participants were left with, as we've suggested, is more time with their families, and to pursue their interests, whatever they may be. Our interviewees discussed what they did with their time now that weekly church services were no longer on the menu (see the next two chapters for more on this).

Let's examine two cases. Audra, a divorced woman in her 60s, wasn't raised with religion, but for nearly two decades, in her 30s and 40s, she began a spiritual quest where she spent a lot of time trying out different churches and groups of religious friends. She came to realize the only thing she truly enjoyed about religion was the non-church-service socials where they got to spend time outdoors. When asked what she does now that she's no longer connected with any church group, she said she looks forward to spending more time with her grandkids, and also:

> I like to go on road trips. I'll do something at the last minute if it sounds good. . . . I'm a spiritual person, you know? I love nature, and I love going

hiking. I love animals and people and so anyhow, you know. . . . Like there's a homeless [service] thing this weekend. And then I'm going hiking Saturday, and [then] going to this thing with my theater group, I'm going to see a play in Coronado.

Or consider Chelsea. Now in her late 70s, she grew up Catholic and was actively involved in the church until her late 20s. In the context of her now being retired, one of us (Smith) casually suggested that maybe she misses church? Even if for purely social reasons, or for something to do. With an incredulous tone she made clear she has plenty to do thank you very much. For instance, she recently reached out to some friends, because "we are starting a book group. We got people signed up [for that] and also [for] a game night. I get support from other people. I take care of myself. I like to run and think and relax."

The first thing Smith (who himself likes to run) thought was, "Wow, I hope I'm still running in my 70s!" But what became clear was that neither Audra nor Chelsea seemed to have any difficulty finding meaningful things to do, pursuing their interests, spending more time with the people they love, or building new relationships since they left religion. In fact, none of our interviews suggest that religious exiters become isolated, unusually lonely, or have difficulty filling the time that used to be occupied by religious services or activities. To the contrary, as with Audra and Chelsea, our participants were drawn out of religion as they came to focus more on what they wanted to spend their time on.

To be clear, we're not suggesting that no one loses anything when they leave religion, or that it's always a smooth transition. Indeed, the break up with religion can be painful, in no small part because of lost social connections or changes in what one does with their non-working life and leisure time. What we are claiming is that there is no good reason to think that religious exiters are at a unique disadvantage, or that they aren't able to find better things to do with their time.

This pull factor leads to a structural proposition related to secularization:

Proposition 4: As societies modernize, people will increasingly find secular ways to spend their time rather than engage in religious behaviors.

Autonomy

Underlying the factor above is autonomy. Autonomy means choosing what you want to do. But autonomy also means being able to choose what you believe, what you value, what to think, how you decide what is right and wrong, and how you think about the world.

For some of our interviewees, the idea that they could construct their own morality and worldview was terrifying. Life, the universe, and what to make of these is challenging and complex.[59] It may seem like other, more qualified individuals should provide some guidance on how to live, on how to know what is right and what is wrong, and on what people should do. But for other interviewees, autonomy and freedom were extremely enticing. Nonreligious individuals have no obligation to oppose birth control because their religion does. They have no obligation to avoid pork because it is not kosher or halal. They do not have to fear that they will go to hell because of their mistakes or that they will be reincarnated into a lower life form. They are able to construct a worldview without religious constraints.

For many, they came to realize that religious clergy were rarely more qualified to make decisions than they were. Some clergy have no training and simply assume the mantle of leadership because they have been "called."[60] While other clergy do have training, it is commonly in theology, and perhaps some training in counseling. Even with that training, this does not make clergy experts on morality, the origins of the universe, philosophy, comparative religion, or even on the history of their own religions. Why, then, queried our participants, do clergy have any more authority on ethical or metaphysical questions than do lay individuals?

Admittedly, as academics, we have a personal stake here. We do think it is important to recognize that some people are experts and that expertise does matter. We need biologists, physicists, engineers, physicians, lawyers, political scientists, psychologists, therapists, etc. But many nonreligious individuals are reluctant to suggest that theology is akin to these other disciplines or professions. In our research, it wasn't uncommon for nonreligious individuals to offer sentiments aligned with H. L. Mencken's take on theology, "Theology: An effort to explain the unknowable by putting it into terms of the not worth knowing."[61] For many nonbelievers, theology is a game of make believe. From that perspective, what makes someone an expert? Presumably it is that there are some people who are more or less knowledgeable about what other people have made up. That doesn't mean someone with no formal training in theology cannot come up with something just as compelling, as has been done by many of the leaders of new religious movements.[62] If it's made up, why is formal training necessary? This is the realization that many nonreligious individuals come to: they don't need clergy to tell them what to believe. They are perfectly capable of arriving at beliefs on their own.

Glen, a gay man in his mid-50s, was raised a fundamentalist Baptist. His father was a minister, and when Glen came out at age 14 he was rejected by both his father and his church community. Thrown out of his house, and homeless for a time, he had many difficult years ahead of him as a result of his religious upbringing and the prejudice he faced. He tried different, more inclusive versions of Christianity before realizing he didn't need a religious authority (starting with his father) to structure his beliefs. He outlined the logic of religious authority, which he came to see as both false and pernicious:

> Before I could even understand culpability or sin, you know, I made a public profession at age six, because that's what my parents wanted. I look back and all I wanted to do was love my parents and do what they and God wanted me to do. So I had my little altar call experience as a very young child and I don't know, this dad thing was always (pause), you never questioned it, because they never questioned it, and if you understood, it wouldn't be called faith. That was their response to anything that you asked, or if you tried to rationalize or ask too many questions, you're questioning God's minister, which is God's anointed, who gets his authority from scriptures, *sola scriptura*. They take the literal translation of the scriptures and if it's not in God's word, then they have no use for it. And when [you] question an anointed minister, you're questioning his authority, which is scripture, which if you question scripture, you question their authority, which is God. Therefore, you're a heretic.

Glen had a better life at the time of our interview. He was in a good relationship, had a stable job, and enjoyed a kind of cognitive freedom he

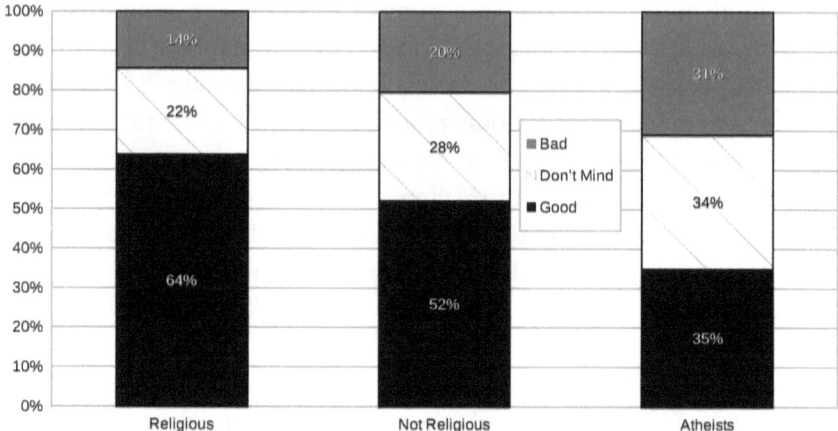

Figure 3.8. View of Whether Greater Respect for Authority in the Future Would Be Good or Bad Among Religious, Not Religious, and Atheists. (Source: WVS Wave 7)

never had while in the church. Granted, his situation was more extreme than most. But his desire for autonomy—intellectual, emotional, sexual—and his reasoning about how he had to break with religion to achieve it, was echoed by many participants.

The desire for autonomy is an observable distinction between those who have left religion and those who stay. Figure 3.8 shows the results of a question from the World Values Survey asking participants whether they would like to see greater respect for authority, which is the inverse of autonomy. The World Values Survey doesn't allow us to parcel out those who have left religions, as we were able to do with the other surveys, but it does contrast religious individuals with both nonreligious individuals and atheists. As the figure illustrates, 64% of religious individuals think it would be good to have greater respect for authority in society. Just 35% of atheists agree that would be good, with the nonreligious falling in between.

We should note, of course, that among the religious there is a percentage that values autonomy. It's just a smaller percentage than among the nonreligious and atheists. We mention this for a couple of reasons. First, we do not mean to suggest that everyone with a religious affiliation is opposed to autonomy. There are many people within religions who value autonomy and who question authority. A clear illustration of this is the percentage of Catholics who reject the idea of papal infallibility.

In the 2021 GSS, 17% of Catholics said it was probably or certainly false that there are times when the Pope speaks infallibly on matters of faith and morals. Another 40% were uncertain that this was true, while 43% of Catholics reported they thought the Pope was probably or certainly infallible at times. Among Catholics in the US, more than half question or reject a key Catholic doctrine, illustrating that there is questioning of authority among the religious.

The second reason this is noteworthy is that there is some evidence that it is those individuals who question their religion and place some value on autonomy who are most likely to leave religion.[63] This question about papal infallibility is particularly interesting in this regard because the percentages holding various perspectives have changed over time. The question was first asked in 2004 and has been asked in every wave of the GSS since then. In 2004, 11% of Catholics said it was probably or certainly false that there are times when the Pope speaks infallibly while 54% were at the other end, asserting that it was probably or certainly true that the pope speaks infallibly at times. Interestingly, millions of individuals left the Catholic Church in the US between 2004 and 2021, presumably many who questioned papal infallibility. Yet, even with those most likely to question papal infallibility leaving, there has been an increase in questioning Catholic doctrine. What this change suggests is that there has been a shift toward more secular views even within religion over time.

In a way, religious exiting is kind of like harvesting strawberries. Not all strawberries ripen at the same rate. As the workers pass over a plant, they look for strawberries that have a specific color, indicating they are ready to be picked. The workers pick the ripe strawberries and leave those that are not sufficiently ripe, giving them time to ripen so they can be harvested at a later date. Of the strawberries that remain after the first harvest, some will ripen in time for the second harvest, and so on. Some strawberries will never ripen and will stay on the vine until the plant dies or is removed to make way for another planting season. Our analogy here isn't perfect, but the general idea is pretty accurate. Those who leave are like the ripe strawberries; they are ready to be "harvested." Others will ripen over time. And among those who remain, there is always a shifting hither and yon, but the general direction over time is away from obedience to authority and toward autonomy.

This autonomy can, of course, lead to behaviors some might question. Nonreligious individuals are more likely to report spending time at bars and are more likely to report having used illicit drugs, though these differences are not large and likely have only minimal effects on health.[64] Autonomy also allows nonreligious individuals to reject the moral dictates of religion, freeing them up to have pre-marital and extra-marital sexual relations without concomitant guilt or feeling like they have sinned, which, again, nonreligious individuals are *slightly* more likely to do than are religious individuals.[65] We want to be careful in how we phrase the above findings. Siding with recent scholarship, we would agree that excessive drinking and the use of some illicit drugs (e.g., heroin) are not healthy.[66] But we don't mean to suggest that premarital relationships are unhealthy, only that many religious people consider such behavior immoral. As we will see in chapter 6, there are important differences in how religious and nonreligious people think about morality; premarital and extramarital sex are less a health issue than a moral one.

Recognizing these differences in behavior, there is an issue surrounding causality. Most of the social scientific data we have is cross-sectional, not longitudinal. As a result, it's not always clear which way the causal relationship works. For instance, does someone who is religious meet someone, develop a relationship, then decide to move in with them only to feel guilt because of their religious worldview then jettison their religious worldview to no longer feel guilt? Or have such individuals already divested themselves of their religious worldview, allowing them to cohabit with their partner without guilt?[67] In reality, it's probably both scenarios. Even so, the autonomy to make such life choices without moral condemnation and guilt make nonreligion more appealing.

In one of our joint publications with another scholar, Bethany Gull, we found that people who had left or were in the process of leaving religions were often inspired by what they perceived to be a search for authenticity.[68] They were finding their true self as they sloughed off all of the elements of religion they had been trained to accept and adopt as children and as part of a religious community. As they slowly disentangled themselves from religion, their authentic self—who they always felt they were and who they truly wanted to be—was revealed. For many, this was the first time in their lives that they got to be themselves.

Both autonomy and the appeal of authenticity can be seen in our interviews. In some cases, they are linked together. For instance, Fatima reflected on what she felt she positively gained having left Christianity:

> There's no requirement (having left religion). There's no dogma I have to suck up to, for you know, "We believe *this*!" And then there's the piece of authenticity. People are, I mean in terms of this, it's sort of outside the group thing, because of religiousness, which is easy, you know you jump into a religion and now you don't have to think. You just take what people say and you can just go, "Okay, the Bible says this, the pastor says that, whatever." These are mostly people who are thinking for themselves about what is good? What is right? I think that the more we connect with our own authenticity (pause), I do believe in the goodness that is inherent in every person; the more that we connect with our authentic selves, the more we are good and moral people.

There is one final point about autonomy among the nonreligious we think is important, and somewhat ironic. Autonomy is valued by the nonreligious. But it is also the case that many nonreligious individuals learn about the importance of autonomy while undergoing socialization into being nonreligious. In other words, nonreligious individuals adopt autonomy as a value in order to *conform* to the norms of being nonreligious; they are autonomous, just like all the other nonreligious people. While that is a bit of an overstatement, we enjoy the irony here.

As with the previously discussed push and pull factors, we have developed a proposition around autonomy:

> Proposition 5: *Ceteris paribus*, individuals who place a greater value on autonomy will be more likely to leave religion than will those who place a lower value on autonomy.

Modern Worldview

We noted above that our participants reflected on the antiquated morality taught by religions, along with doctrines that contradict modern understandings of the world, like young earth creationism. These functioned as push factors driving people out of religion. Likewise, being able to embrace explanations rooted in evidence and logic functions as a pull factor, drawing people out of religion.

Our informants noted that a modern worldview is apparent in something as simple as a basic biology class. The biologist Theodosius Bodzhansky once wrote, "Nothing in biology makes sense except in the light of evolution."[69] In elementary school in the US, students begin to learn about biology. Included in those lessons are discussions about evolution, depending on the teacher and school district.[70] For a young student who has been taught at their church, mosque, or synagogue that a deity created the earth some 6,000 years ago, with their parents reinforcing this idea, learning about evolution and evolutionary time spans—millions and billions of years—will, for many such individuals, lead to serious conflict. We are not of the opinion that such conflicts always have to be resolved. People are able to compartmentalize their beliefs quite well and for long periods of time, so they do not have to resolve these contradictions or the cognitive dissonance it can produce.[71] But our participants indicated there was great appeal and satisfaction in being able to reconcile such cognitive conflicts. As a result, the appeal of a modern worldview can pull people out of religion just as much as an anachronistic worldview can push them out.

Staying with evolution, consider Jacob's experience. Raised in Utah by a Mormon father and Episcopalian mother, he suggested that neither of his parents pushed religion on him, but he does remember as a child assuming they were correct when they told him about the virgin birth of Jesus and other standard Christian doctrines. He was sent off to boarding school at age fourteen. Now a grown man, he responded eagerly to our question about a modern, scientific view of the world, his assumptions about Jesus and miracles now reversed in light of his encounter with science and modernity:

> Q: Are scientific and secular explanations of the world important to you? Are those in any way connected to it [his rejecting his parents' religion]?
> A: Absolutely, and I'm glad you brought it up! I would say definitely. You know, I've read quite a bit about evolution and biology—where man came from. A little bit of Dawkins etc.; I'm not an astrophysicist or anything but I would say it *is* important. But I feel like it's kind of already been proven to that extent. You know, anyone that thinks dinosaurs coincide

with humans (laughs), I mean it's just, like, science handled that issue a long time ago. I think evolution has been proven. Evolution theory is a fact. Magical babies don't come from virgins. There are simply things that do not occur. . . . I think those that choose to think that way—I mean they call it what it is, which is faith. You know and that's the perfect definition. It literally is faith, and I don't know how many more facts you can present to somebody. . . . I mean, a man [can] come back [from the dead]!? I mean not even firsthand account.

Breanna, a woman in her mid-20s, waxed a little more philosophical about the draw and benefits of a modern worldview. She described her household growing up as more spiritual than religious. They weren't consistent churchgoers, but she remembers, at age nine, wondering about the prayers her parents would offer to god before dinner—"Why do we pray before our meals? I don't think anyone is listening. Who is this for?" Like virtually all our participants, rather than feeling threatened by existence absent a god who's established a cosmic plan (let alone listens to dinner prayers), Breanna expressed what she thought a modern worldview has to offer humanity:

> Our purpose and our responsibility in life is to love each other and care for each other and create a better world, *even if* our experience is just totally subjective and cosmically meaningless. And for naturalism, I think evolution is awesome and science is amazing and such a cool tool to figure out how things work, and to be inspired and to be full of awe at the universe because we understand both so much and so little about it!

It's true to say that, however scary or painful it may have been to leave religion or reject the religious worldview they grew up with (not at all for some, a great deal for others) a modern, secular, scientifically-informed worldview was embraced by all our interviewees, and they all thought divesting themselves of religion was a necessary step to this end.

This leads to our sixth proposition:

Proposition 6: *Ceteris paribus*, individuals who hold modern, scholarly understandings of the natural world will be more likely to leave religion than individuals who do not.

All Offense; No Defense

The final pull toward nonreligion is related to the consistency of a modern worldview. However, this one has more to do with how defensible such a worldview is to others rather than the logical consistency it provides to the individual. To illustrate this point, we offer a metaphor.[72]

For any given religious individual debating someone who adheres to a different religious system, they must be figuratively armed with both a sword for offense and a shield or armor for defense. Imagine, for instance, a conversation between a Muslim and a Mormon. The Mormon may argue that Islam is flawed because the Quran has a number of factual mistakes, like claiming that all living things are sexual, "And of all things we created mates" (Quran 51:49).[73] The Muslim would need a shield to defend against this criticism of their scripture. But the Muslim adherent could very easily turn this around and, with their sword, level a similar criticism of Mormonism by noting that the Book of Mormon claims there were horses and chariots in the Ancient Americas, "Now the king had commanded his servants, previous to the time of the watering of their flocks, that they should prepare his horses and chariots, and conduct him forth to the land of Nephi" (Alma 18:9).[74] Both criticisms have merit, as both books of scripture contain scientific and factual inaccuracies. The point is that both the Mormon and the Muslim can attack with swords, but they also have to defend with shields; they are not immune to criticism concerning the flaws in their religions, as is the case with all religions.[75]

Now imagine a similar conversation but between a nonreligious atheist and a Catholic. In such a conversation, the Catholic adherent could attempt criticisms, but there is certainly no founder to criticize and there is also no doctrine to critique. Atheism is a lack of belief, not an affirmative belief. As a result, the atheist doesn't need to carry a shield or even wear armor. There is nothing for others to criticize on this point. Instead, the atheist can wield two swords and attack incessantly while the Catholic individual can do nothing but attempt to parry the onslaught of criticisms.

The point of this metaphor is that nonreligion combined with atheism and/or agnosticism was a defensible position according to our participants because both are absences of positive assertions. There is, quite literally, no positive content to atheism or agnosticism. This is not to say that such individuals cannot adopt a philosophical belief system like humanism (as many of our participants did), which does offer positive assertions about the universe and someone's worldview.[76] But, at base, our participants saw themselves as not having to worry as much about defense as they criticized religion.

The logic and appeal of such a position is observed in our interview with Deion, a Black man in his mid-40s. At the time of our interview, Deion was a chief petty officer in the Navy. Raised by a devoutly Christian mother, he attended worship services every Sunday with her as a child. But ever since he asked his Sunday school teacher, when he was 10 years old, how dinosaurs can be millions of years old if the earth was only six thousand years old, as he'd learned from Bible study, he's been skeptical of all religious claims:

> People are saying dinosaur bones are millions of years old so you know, what's the deal with that? And this Sunday school teacher looked me right in the face and said, "Satan put those bones there" (laughs). I was like "Reeeaally?!" Even at ten years old I knew there was something really wrong with that answer. I've got books and books telling me one thing and I've got you telling me that the devil put bones in the earth . . . ? What?! That was the beginning of my unraveling right there.

After leaving religion, Deion even joined a group called The Military Association of Atheists and Freethinkers, as he was inclined not to hide his views among his mostly religious peers. He had no problem playing offense, and he makes clear what he thinks is going on in the minds of the religious, and why he doesn't feel much need to play defense or rationalize his having left religion. How did he come to such conclusions? When asked about what he's learned from his interactions with the religious, and especially his fellow servicemen, he responded this way:

> I think the biggest problem religion poses is it gives answers that can't be questioned. It gives you this beautiful package that says, "This is the world, and God is the reason why the world is and all you have to do is believe in a certain set of rules and not only will you be saved, you'll live forever. When you die you'll come back to life and you'll live forever and

you'll be at the right hand of God." And they offer no actual proof or evidence for this, but at the same time they are hitting all the good points that people want to hear; nobody wants to die . . . and not know what's going on afterward. They don't want to think that life is finite. . . . Nobody likes that idea—*I* don't like that idea. But once they sell you this proposition that you can escape that, all you have to do is accept a few precepts and not think about it and go to church once a week, and listen to your pastor, and if you do all these things, you will be good to go.

That nonreligious individuals are able to play more offense than defense, doesn't mean they are constantly attacking their religious kith and kin. Religious exiters, of course, were taught and once held many of the same views, so it doesn't make sense that they'd always be looking for a fight. Even for those who do relish a good argument about religion and god, for most, this tends to wane as time goes on.[77] Many just want to move on with their lives and not spend unnecessary mental energy on all that's wrong with religion.

Tesha, a divorced business owner in her 30s, made it plain why she had come to feel her position was more defensible. Born on a military base in Germany, she spent her first 25 years in Alabama, among some very religious people. Raised by a Catholic father and Southern Baptist mother, she recalled her "first strong memory of religion" as a child was being "terrified" at her brother's catechism after she asked, "What happens if you don't take the first communion?" to which her sister replied, "You go to hell."

> It's not that I *believe* that there is no god; it's that I personally don't believe in god. I am agnostic about the question of whether god exists because I have no proof either way. You necessarily have to be agnostic about things for which there is no proof [so] I don't feel an obligation to defend my [nonbelief].

One qualification is needed here before we move on. "All offense, no defense" has to do with intellectual argument, reasoning, and claims-making about religion. Freedom from having to defend religious claims is a pull factor for religious exiters, and one of the benefits of "going nonreligious." But there is one important dimension in which many nonreligious Americans, and perhaps especially religious exiters, *do* feel they have to play defense, and that's regarding the idea that they can't lead moral, healthy, meaningful lives without religion. We address this issue briefly in our penultimate chapter, but for interested readers, we and other scholars have addressed this claim extensively in other works.[78]

This leads to our seventh proposition:

Proposition 7: *Ceteris paribus*, individuals who strongly value logical consistency and reason will be more likely to leave religion than do individuals who are unaware of these ideas or do not highly value them.

Generational Change

Perhaps the biggest reason people leave religion today is not about any specific push or pull factor. It's a move toward secularity for children and young people generally. As figure 3.9 illustrates, every successive generation in the US over the last 50 years has consistently been less religious than the previous generation, as other scholars have noted.[79] We acknowledge the importance of specific push and pull factors at the individual level, as we've done above, but also recognize these are at play against the backdrop of more sweeping social and generational change.

Figure 3.9, which uses GSS data from 1972–2021, shows the percentage of each generation that reports not having a religious affiliation. The figure presents a clear pattern. The earliest generation, often dubbed the Greatest Generation, for which we are considering anyone born before 1927 in the dataset, consistently has the lowest levels of nonreligion throughout the time period. The Silent Generation, those born between 1928 and 1945, fairly consistently have the second lowest levels of nonreligion throughout this time period, followed by the Baby Boomers (1946–1964). Members of Generation X (1965–1980) are more likely to be nonreligious than are all the previous generations, and Millennials (1981–1996) are even more likely to be nonreligious than are members of Generation X.[80] The small number of participants from Generation Z in the most recent waves of the survey make interpreting the initial data somewhat circumspect, but it looks like in the latest wave of the GSS (2021), Generation Z is just as likely to be nonreligious

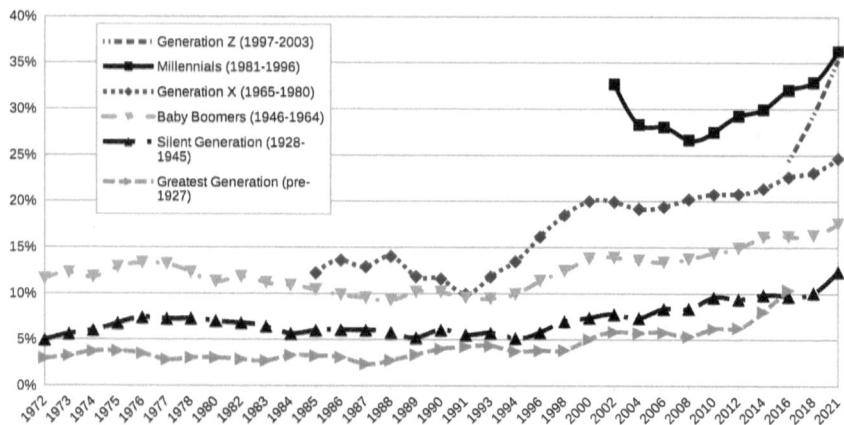

Figure 3.9. Percentage Nonreligious by Cohort Over Time (Source: GSS 1972–2021, 3-year moving average)

as are Millennials.[81] What figure 3.9 illustrates is that, in the modern era, transmitting religion to one's offspring is hard. There are a number of impediments to this that have resulted in increasingly nonreligious generations in the US over time. Also of note is the uptick in nonreligion for all the cohorts starting around 1990 that is shown in figure 3.9, which aligns with the idea we introduced in the introduction about the end of the Cold War and the cultural change that allowed more Americans to identify as nonreligious. In what follows, we discuss why there are such notable differences among generations and how this contributes so substantially to the rise of nonreligion in the US.

Before we delve into why generational change is so important, we first need to wrestle with some language. Many religious social scientists[82] frame what we are calling generational change as, instead, a "failure to transmit" religion on the part of parents.[83] Since we're sociologists who study religion and not religious social scientists, we have attempted to remove the explicit moral valence from this topic. When religious social scientists call this a "failure" they are not hiding their personal views on this subject. To the contrary, they are making it clear that they are blaming parents for their children not being as devoted to religion as these religious social scientists want them to be.

Since we try to be objective, data-driven scientists, we see no reason to continue to use language that privileges religion (it does so in more ways than we take up here). In fact, we are fond of flipping pro-religious jargon on its head. We can very easily see how generational changes in religiosity are not a failure on the part of parents but rather a success. When parents grant their children autonomy in deciding what to believe, whether to participate in religion, or whether to identify as religious, they are actually living and practicing modern, egalitarian values.[84] Parents who compel children, however well-intentioned, to believe certain things or face punishment (in this life or the next) are engaging in a form of coercion, though we fully recognize that not all religious individuals do that.

Granted, as parents, we understand well the importance of teaching and guiding children into certain behaviors. It's important to teach your child not to run into the street without looking. It's important to teach your child not to touch a hot stove or to not eat medicine prescribed for someone else in the family. And there most certainly can be punishments to enforce behavior that will keep children healthy and alive. Such punishments are arguably a form of coercion. But forcing a child to attend religious services on a regular basis, or to pray to certain beings (and not others), or to engage in ritual behaviors like being submerged in water for the remission of their sins. . . . Are these necessary for the health or well-being of children? Will they substantially improve children's mental health? Are these beliefs and actions required to develop well-adjusted, civically-engaged members of society?

Data and years of research on these questions indicate that they will make virtually no difference to the children.

Why, then, compel children to do this? Why consider it a "failure" when parents don't do this? And why not grant children the autonomy to decide whether they will participate or not?

Astute readers will note that we focus primarily on religious *behaviors* in the last few paragraphs. That was intentional. It's really only behaviors that parents can attempt to control. They can strongly encourage beliefs, and they can certainly attempt to indoctrinate children into believing what they, the parents, believe or holding values similar to those of the parents. But any kids connected to the outside world are going to have plenty of opportunities to slough off the beliefs and values of their parents.

Parents can try to inculcate children to believe certain things, to identify in certain ways, or to hold certain values, but there is a very real chance that, assuming they let their kids watch TV or movies, get on the internet, leave their house and play with other kids, or attend schools, their kids are going to reject at least some of the beliefs and values of their parents. What parents can control (to some degree at least) are behaviors. They can insist, as the parents of both authors did when we were growing up, that if we wanted to live in our parents' houses we had to attend religious services, we had to participate in early morning scripture studies, that we could not consume certain substances (i.e., alcohol, tobacco, coffee, etc.), and we could not be sexually intimate until marriage, among other restrictions. Our parents attempted to control our behaviors. Of course, they didn't always succeed (wink, wink). And they definitely failed to transmit their religious beliefs. And that's fine. Because it is not a "failure" when parents are unable to transmit religious doctrines and their personal views when those doctrines and values are misaligned with modern sensibilities. It is, to the contrary, exactly what a modern, rational, evidence-valuing society's view of morality would encourage—letting children think for themselves.[85]

With this clarification out of the way, let's examine what is happening with the transmission of religion from parents to children. The primary way that religion is transmitted around the world is through parental socialization—parents teach, pressure, or even force their children into religion.[86] If parents are religious and their goal is to transmit their religious beliefs, values, and behaviors to their children but they "fail," this interrupts the primary pathway of converting people to religion. Our wording here is specific—no one is born with religion; regardless of the validity of any religious claim, everyone has to be *taught* to believe in Allah, Vishnu, Poseidon, or the healing power of crystals. If attempts to pass religion from parents to children do not result in the perfect transmission of religion—which is highly likely, since we are talking about transmitting all elements of a worldview, identities, and behaviors—children will be different from their parents.

Why is this such a big deal? Why have so many social scientists spent millions of dollars studying this process and written numerous books and articles about the transmission of religion from parents to children?[87] This is a big deal because it is *the primary* way that people become religious. Evangelism and religious proselytizing are increasingly ineffective around the world,[88] particularly in modernized societies. Adults and even adolescents are decreasingly interested in joining religions. If someone's goal is to ensure the maximum number of people are religious, the most effective way to do this is to indoctrinate and coerce children into religion when they are too young to be able to object. But even parental socialization of children into religion is becoming more and more difficult in modern societies like the US.

Why?

As an illustrative example of the problem of religious socialization due to generational change, consider Charlotte. Charlotte was born in 1964. Her paternal grandparents were very strict Catholics. Her maternal grandparents were practicing Lutherans. She succinctly describes how with each generation, religion went from vitally important, to nearly irrelevant:

> My father grew up an only child in Manhattan. Both [his] parents were Irish and had such a strict Irish-Catholic upbringing that they both ended up renouncing the religion; although they did maintain their belief in god, they did not pass on Catholicism to my father. My mother grew up in Germany and Latvia during the war, went to a displaced persons camp, finally came over to this country when she was in college on an athletic scholarship. She was raised Lutheran, believes in god, but did not pass any of that on to her children. I'm the youngest of four children; of the four children, none of us were baptized or ever taken to church by our parents, nothing. My oldest sister is an atheist, my brother is probably agnostic; my sister who's just two years older than me, she has a belief in god and has periodically during stressful times in her life become a churchgoer. Otherwise, she doesn't, so it's somewhat hypocritical. And then I of course am an atheist.

Save one sister's tepid and sporadic involvement, across the generations, religion for Charlotte's family essentially dropped off the map. Belief in a god remained for some of them. The fact that three of the four children Charlotte's parents had are both nonreligious and nonbelievers when their grandparents were devout believers seems remarkable, but is exactly what we would expect given the shifts in society in recent years. And as the data show, they are part of a much broader trend in the US.

Many different factors account for this. Charlotte's grandparents were born in an era when their Catholic religion was important to their parents, their identities, communities, and worldview.[89] Charlotte mentioned how their indoctrination and the strict demands of the religion caused them to question organized religion and then leave the Catholic Church, though they still remained believers (presumably in the Christian god). Charlotte's grandparents had kids, including her mother, who came of age in a period where it became increasingly common to question religious authority.[90] Feeling no real connection to Catholicism or any other religious organization because of this break in tradition and religious socialization, her own mother and father were believers in only an undefined and noncommittal way. Religion itself was not passed on. Charlotte discussed how both her parents always made clear their children could choose which religion they belonged to, if any. She goes on to give more context with respect to her own coming of age:

> In high school once I remember giving—you know how they had classes on birth control, they were discussing homosexuality, gay marriage and all that. This was back in the '80s, but in my town it was pretty good at an educational level; all of my parents' friends were like engineers and things. I remember once they brought in a priest or something, who was representing a religious [group], and he was talking about abstinence and things like that. But I went up to him and asked him, "How do you know? How can you definitively know that there is a god and that these things will happen . . . how can you say there's one way?" and he goes, "Well it's like that chair, you want to go sit in that chair, and you have to have faith that the chair will be there and will hold you." And all I thought to myself was, "What a crock!" The chair's going to be there because one, I see it. I have experience telling me that the chair is there, that when I sit in it, it will hold me and there is no one around who is going to pull it out from me!

Charlotte's skepticism as a youth carried through as she became an adult and went off to college. The Cold War had ended. The symbolic link between communism and atheism had weakened. By the time Charlotte had her own children, they were raised with lesbian and gay (LG) individuals on TV and in movies. Norms had shifted. The idea of gender equality had gained real traction. Educational attainment was increasing. Creationists had lost in the courts. Modernization was spreading throughout the US and much of the world, and then the internet became widespread. A growing number of people were already leaving religions, increasing the odds that Charlotte's social network included nonreligious people (see chapter 5 for more discussion of social networks).[91]

What has Charlotte's lack of religious socialization, and her skepticism of religion meant for her relationship with her own children as they come of age? Here's a clue from a conversation she had with one of her teenage sons during the 2008 presidential election:

> I was watching election stuff on TV with my 15-year-old son, who is an atheist. . . . After watching the election he said, "You know mom, I could be president, I'm smart enough, I like the subject matter, I present well in public . . . ," and I said, "Yeah, you could be the first atheist president," and he goes, "Yeah, because I'd ask, 'How many atheists have started religious wars?'" So there's hope (laughs).

Over generations, religion has simply lost its power in Charlotte's family. Though of course it's possible for her or her atheist son to start believing in a god and/or join a religion (maybe even the Catholic church), it seems unlikely. And it doesn't strike us as any more likely that her own kids will suddenly take up religion and pass it along to *their* children. Such is the pattern of secularization across generations at the level of family socialization.[92]

As Charlotte's example illustrates, it doesn't take much for an entire family to exit religion over the course of a couple of generations. Changes in the environment and in societal values make it increasingly challenging to transmit religion intact from one generation to the next. This leads us to proposition 8 (our final proposition, number 9, we save until chapter 5):

Proposition 8: *Ceteris paribus*, individuals with greater exposure to modernity will be more likely to leave religion than individuals with less exposure to modernity.

Returning to the issue of transmitting religion, were Charlotte's parents "failures"? If you are a religious social scientist and think everyone should be religious, then yes, absolutely. Such scholars might insist that Charlotte's parents should have been more forceful in getting Charlotte and her siblings to fully participate in all of the rituals of the Catholic Church.[93] These scholars don't prioritize autonomy in children; what matters most is that children are adherents of religion. Religion is the priority; humans with modern secular views are the problem. Of course, if you hold modern values, Charlotte's parents were not failures at all. They recognized that certain beliefs, values, and behaviors were important to transmit to children while others were not. As a result, Charlotte's parents chose not to force the beliefs they were taught as kids onto their own kids.

It should be obvious at this point why transmitting religion from parents to children is so important. When parents endow their children with autonomy, children often reject traditional, organized religion. According to our interviewees, organized religion is not only antiquated and typically misaligned with modern values, it is boring. Of course, this is going to vary pretty substantially by the religion. Many religions have changed their style of music, have incorporated videos and presentations into their sermons, and some invest heavily in engaging activities for children and young people to make religion attractive.[94] Even so, the appeal of secular activities is often stronger than that of religious activities. If a child can choose between playing Fortnite or reading Harry Potter versus attending hours of lectures about arcane topics based on a book that is thousands of years old and at odds with modern sensibilities, which are they going to choose?

We have tried to be careful in describing what happens with parental socialization by noting that it is virtually impossible to perfectly transmit religious beliefs, behaviors, values, and identities so long as parents live in the modern world. Of course, there are some parents who try not to live in the modern world, or at least minimize their children's participation in modernity. The growth of homeschooling and religious private and charter schools attest to this. While not all parents who home school or send their kids to religious schools in the US are doing so to avoid modern beliefs and values, many of these parents are doing so precisely because they are afraid that a secular education will change their children.[95] They are right. Secular education will result in their kids being more secular than their parents.[96]

There are also the more extreme religions that attempt to avoid modern life altogether, like members of the Fundamentalist Church of Jesus Christ of Latter-Day Saints.[97] Such groups do all they can to isolate their members and children from the modern world to prevent them from adopting modern values, beliefs, and behaviors. Their logic isn't flawed. If a parent wants to prevent a child from seeing the benefits of equality, autonomy, technology, democracy, and education, the best way to avoid that is to prevent children from observing any of it to begin with. Inversely, kids raised without religion aren't particularly likely to find religion later in life in secular societies.[98] It's not that secular parents do much to "inoculate" their kids from religion or try to critique or attack religion.[99] But being raised secular is a pretty effective inoculation against religion. This was not always the case, but is increasingly so. Children raised nonreligious in the twenty-first century are very likely to stay nonreligious.

We mention the more extreme religious groups only to illustrate that resistance to modernity is a continuum. Some parents fully embrace modern sensibilities; some parents completely reject them. Most parents fall somewhere between these two extremes. If the parents allow even the slightest exposure to modernity, the end result is more than likely going to be higher levels of secularity and lower levels of religiosity, which is precisely what figure 3.9 above illustrates.

What does this ultimately mean for the future of religion in the US? Young people are much less religious than are older generations. While some religious social scientists have hoped for decades that the lower levels of religiosity among young people will disappear as young people age and begin to worry about death,[100] we don't think this is correct. Most people who become secular never return to religion. If more than 40% of young people in the US today are secular and are going to remain secular, raising their kids secular, and a growing number of those who report a religious affiliation are going to leave religion and have kids who leave religion, the future will be one with even lower levels of religiosity. This is a trend that is unlikely to reverse itself.

The assumption sociologists in the "failure to transmit" camp have long held—that young nonreligious individuals will eventually embrace religion—isn't totally baseless. The kernel of truth is that some research has found those who were raised with religion as children (however tepid or severe their parents were about it), but rejected it in their youth, sometimes *do* return to the fold in later life.[101] However, this not only doesn't capture the dramatic rise in youth raised without religion in the first place, but even for kids brought up religious it appears to be increasingly unlikely. And when scholars say that "young people" are less religious than older people, we aren't really saying that it's youth itself that is the cause. Various push and pull factors, generational change, and the forces of secularization offer a better explanation of why young and old alike are increasingly nonreligious.

Since we've made such a big deal about the pro-religious framing surrounding the transmission of religiosity from parents to children, we should also discuss whether it is a "failure" when secular or nonreligious parents have children who convert to religion. Given the arguments we made above about how autonomy is a modern value, we think that children raised in secular homes who end up religious are another indication of successful, modern parenting and are, by no means, a failure. From our perspective, transmitting religiosity or secularity is a failure based not on the outcome, but rather on the process and values that are transmitted as a result. If parents must rely on coercion or force to transmit their values, that is a failure. If parents discourage autonomy in their children, that is a failure. The aim of parents who value instilling autonomy in their children should not be creating religious or nonreligious clones of themselves but rather providing their children with the knowledge and values that help them make good, informed decisions of their own.

Our participants' lives reflect this. Though it's true many began questioning religion in their youth, nearly 40% didn't finally leave until their late 30s, or even early 40s or later. As with Charlotte quoted above, it just doesn't seem likely that these religious exiters or their children will feel the need to take up religion. Extending this issue a bit further, we turn our attention now to something we mentioned earlier, almost in passing. Perhaps the primary reason scholars (and others) assume people will come to need religion or look to a god late in life is because of fear of death.[102] At first blush this seems a plausible theory, and we've no doubt that some people are in fact motivated to become religious for this reason. But this is by no means universal or even common, especially with religious exiters. We've already gotten a sense of how our religious exiters think about death by way of what they've said about the afterlife. But consider those in their 60s, 70s, and beyond. Their life trajectories and their attitudes about death simply undermine the argument (or assumption) that increasing awareness of one's own mortality is likely to frighten individuals into returning to or embracing religion.

Luke makes this clear. At 65 at the time of our interview, he had thought a lot about death, particularly after the deaths of both his parents. His father died relatively young (57), and it was unexpected. Both his parents were raised religious, but neither of them were dogmatic or "took it [religion] very seriously." They took him to church as a kid. He remembered with some fondness going to the Unitarian church—"probably because they could get a 'church-like experience' without being required to [hold] dogmatic beliefs." His mother had confessed her atheism to him later in life and he was inspired by her attitude when she was dying of lung cancer:

> My mother was totally fearless. She was dying of lung cancer and when she went into the hospice, she was funny, she was peaceful, and fearless and I found that to be pretty inspirational, you know. They were making her comfortable. She was going to be out of pain. She really looked forward to that and I can remember them asking her what would you like for dinner Joan? And she would say, "Sherbet and morphine please!" and laugh.

Though Luke admitted he couldn't be certain he'd respond the same way when it's his time, he took his mother's example as something to emulate. When asked directly about his own mortality, he responded:

> I'm very comfortable with it. My religious friends will often ask me, "Well what about when you die? You don't think there's anything after death?"

And for me, I tell them no. I find that completely comforting. Other than the fact that dying could be uncomfortable, I find there's nothing to be afraid of because there's nothing, there is nothing after you no longer live. There is nothing to be afraid of.

Like Luke, most of our participants held a similar attitude and outlook regarding their own mortality. They simply accept it as a natural part of life. They find neither comfort in religion nor do they think it would provide them convincing answers about death. They take a post-religious, naturalist view on the question, and this doesn't appear to add any more distress than is "normal" when one contemplates one's own death. They care about life, find it meaningful, and are happy to live it. Many religious exiters view our existence as a gift, even a kind of "miracle," just not one bestowed by an external authority.

To be clear, we are not arguing that as people age they don't reflect more on the lives they've lived, or the people they've loved, or what they'll leave behind, or what happens after death. It's not that religious exiters like Luke are impervious or indifferent to these personal and existential questions. To the contrary, as human beings they ruminate on such things. Although some remain open and/or agnostic on things like an afterlife, this doesn't move them to embrace religion, the supernatural, or any other idea they found implausible, unreasonable, or immoral for most of their thinking adult lives simply because they know they're nearing the end of their own.

Conclusion

We have argued in this chapter that there is no single reason why people leave religion. A simple way to think about people leaving religion is to use the push and pull approach common with migration—some forces push people out of religion and some forces pull people toward nonreligion. Morality, politics, and problems with religion push people out. The appeal of getting to choose what to do instead of participating in religion, developing one's own worldview, accepting modern values, and embracing reason and logic are all factors that pull people toward a secular worldview. Additionally, so long as parents allow any degree of contact with modernity and autonomy, the odds are quite high that younger people will be less religious than their parents, grandparents, and so forth. Collectively, there are many forces leading people to exit religion.

With massive numbers of people leaving religion in the US, this raises obvious questions that we address in subsequent chapters: Where are religious exiters going? What are they doing? And what does all of this mean?

4

Where Do They Go?

Interviewer: Since leaving religion, what do you do with the time you used to spend at religious services or otherwise practicing religion?
Well. I interact with my family. I deal with friends. I prepare for work. I watch a lot of sports, especially on Sundays. I can say Sunday is one of the busiest sports days of the week. So probably more of that, but anyway . . . I am into electronics and computers . . . [Also] trying to be more of a mechanic, but I am not very good at it (laughs).
—Zeb

I still think that that function [of religion] is very important. It's almost like when my son was born we didn't have a Christening because we're not Christian anymore, but it felt like there was something missing because my other Christian friends had their thing and my parents asked if we were going to and I was like, "No, I'm an atheist remember?" But it felt like there was something missing and, you know, I hear about like baby welcoming ceremonies or naming ceremonies, some sort of ritualistic reason for getting friends and families together to celebrate the arrival of a new baby. And so, that's kind of one of the reasons I wanted to go back to something that vaguely resembles organized religion with some of the functions of organized religion, without the god part.
—Angela

I've been really lucky. At this point, you know, by the time I became an activist atheist, I was retired so I've got more [time] and nothing to lose; it's very easy for me to express my views. . . . I accepted a position on the board [of a secular group] and I've been a co-MC for about six months now, and just you know, planning events, I was the planner for

our solstice party and I've now become [a] coordinator so I'm trying to set up, trying to line up volunteer opportunities in the communities, you know, like we don't feel like we've been working enough.
—Jessica

We know from the previous chapter that Americans exit religion for many reasons, so it shouldn't come as a surprise that they also take different paths after they've left. The stories of Zeb, Angela, and Jessica demonstrate this. Zeb's comments concisely illustrate the situation of many participants when asked directly about what they do now to fill the time and space once occupied by religion. They list ordinary things, such as spending more time with family and friends; they engage their hobbies and interests. They get more work done. In fact, after reviewing participants' answers, we can distill many of their responses down to something like the following sentiment: "What do you mean what do I do now? I go on living my life." They just have more time to do that now. They have more time to do the things they want to and focus on the things they care about. For some, like Zeb, our radio producer, they just have more time to do the things they'd be doing anyway.

For the vast majority of people who leave religion, changes in behavior are not huge. They don't transition from spending hours in religious veneration and penitence every week to spending all of that time protesting religious privilege or debating theists on social media. Many religious exiters spent just a little time engaged with religion each week before they left and that time was quickly filled up with secular activities. It's really that simple.

But for others, as we'll see, it's more complicated, and leaving religion does not amount to merely finding more time during the week. It can involve a path where significant time and energy are spent in the secular community and on secular causes where the exiter clearly continues to think about and have a relationship with religion, though in a fundamentally different way. For this segment of religious exiters, "Where have they been, where do they go?" is perhaps the more suitable chapter title.

Though many had responses similar to Zeb's, there were others, like Angela, who actually did feel like they were "missing" something after they left religion. Angela, who was in her early 40s when she was interviewed, was a software consultant and married with two children. She was raised Catholic but left in her late teens because she found she couldn't accept basic Catholic teachings as true. As Christel Manning showed in her research, some nonreligious parents still want to provide "structure," community, and even religion-like practices for their children.[1] Angela was one such parent. This was why she occasionally took her kids to Sunday Assembly services on Sunday mornings. She even mentioned how, along with the community piece, part of her motivation for doing church-like activities was to show her children they could be "good without a god."

A smaller subset of our interviewees, those who take an activist route, go further, taking the time and energy they used to focus on religion to promote secular values and beliefs. This describes Jessica. Though she wasn't raised in a particularly religious household (they did go to church occasionally), she became a kind of religious seeker in her early teens and into adulthood. In her words, she always "flirted with religion." She joined a Pentecostal church in her late teens before dating a seminarian at age 25. She joined the United Church of Christ as a result, but as she described it, "it just didn't stick." She couldn't accept the claims they made. Then she married a Jew, but decided not to convert; by middle age, she was more independent minded and was "done converting." Jessica was in her mid-60s when we interviewed her. She's deeply committed to her family, and has embraced a secular life as fully as she rejected the religious one she attempted several times to live. Retired, and with more time and "nothing to lose" she was actively involved in the secular community through volunteer work, outreach, and the occasional scuffle with religious folks at the "ask an atheist" booth in public parks.

* * *

Just as there are different causes—historical (chapter 1), social (chapter 2), individual (chapter 3)—that explain why more Americans are leaving religion, exiters end up in different places after leaving. That's what the present chapter is about. We examine where people go after leaving religion, what they do with their time, commitments, and relationships, and how this depends in part on the nature of their religious experience, the degree of their previous religious commitments, their changing social networks, and other factors. One central dimension of the "where do they go?" question involves differences that lead some religious exiters to join secular groups while others do not. This is closely intertwined with our three pathways to religious exiting and the character of the religious socialization exiters experienced. Our interview data are telling on this issue, so we spend time on it here, combining this with detailed time-use survey data to flesh out a more complete answer to this chapter's question.

Religious Socialization and Exiting

Religious socialization is a central concept in the sociology of religion. Very broadly, it refers to the transmission of religious beliefs and practices across generations, with most studies focusing on the proximal relationship of the transmission of religiosity from parents to children.[2] Most of what we've discussed already in this book—and especially in chapter 3, where we discussed generational change—has implicated the concept. Religious socialization involves a constellation of complex and overlapping social processes and includes both primary (the family) and secondary (outside the family) forms of socialization. Though things like church attendance and religious schooling are important kinds of secondary religious socialization,[3] we don't examine them directly here. Rather, we're mostly focused on what role primary religious socialization plays in the exiting process.

We're also interested in what differences may exist regarding the trajectories of those who were raised with religion versus those who had minimal religious socialization. For instance, one might ask whether there was a "secular commitment" among those raised in more secular households that was equivalent to the religious commitments of those raised with religion. The answers are a bit complicated here, because it's not always obvious what counts as religious or secular socialization. Socialization of any kind varies in intensity and consistency. There is also variation in the extent to which socialization is explicit or implicit. Unsurprisingly, and as many scholars have observed, the depth and character of one's religious socialization, especially early in life, will say a lot about one's later religious commitments, mental health, relationships, and other factors.[4] There are far fewer studies that examine this directly in the context of religious exiting. Some studies of religious exiting make the role of religious socialization explicit, but most research simply (and somewhat understandably) takes for granted that one's experience with religion will shape if, when, and how people leave it. One survey study of four Western European societies (France, Germany, Great Britain, and Sweden) found that, compared to "lifelong nones," disaffiliates of religion (i.e., religious exiters) had greater "religious residue" later in life.[5] That is, they were more sympathetic to certain religious beliefs even though they didn't practice any religion themselves. The more religious they were as children, the more religious residue in adult life. This might help explain why some of our religious exiters have sought out religion-like secular groups later in life. But it certainly doesn't explain those, like Glen (stay tuned), who are "done" with religion and have little patience or sympathy for any aspect of organized religion.

Whatever the case may be, our interview data likewise suggest that religious socialization plays an important role in the exiting process. First, let's consider those who weren't raised, at least explicitly, with much religion at all. The experiences of some of our interviewees capture well the ambiguity regarding what kind of religious socialization a person is receiving and what the implications of this might be for how they come to reject religion in general. Take Dennis, a man in his 40s who had served in the Navy for five years, and at the time of our interview in 2014 was living with his girlfriend and enjoying civilian life. An only child, Dennis described his upbringing this way:

> I wasn't raised in a particularly religious household. My father was a hippie in the '60s and so he came to sort of Eastern religions. So if I were to say I was raised with anything, I was raised kind of Taoist/Buddhist. But it wasn't in an organized way. He would read books and share ideas with me. We would have sort of these philosophical conversations. I would see a lot of documentaries on many different faiths. And then my mother was raised more Catholic. But she found her way to a more spiritual way, so she believes in spells, and witchcraft and talking spirits and Ouija boards and all that kind of stuff. But from her I didn't receive any sort

of formal or rigid passing down of beliefs either. It [religion] just never made sense to me. I was a curious child, so I read a lot and watched a lot of documentaries. Whenever there was some documentary on Jesus or that kind of thing, I would be interested, but it never seemed like it was the answer, or "the truth" to me.

It might seem, as Dennis suggested, that he was essentially raised without religion, that it didn't have much of an effect on him, and that his experience would be unlikely to set him on a path of "religious exiting." However, his response to a follow up question took a stark turn:

> INTERVIEWER: So you never really had to reject organized religion. It was more an organic process of [finding it interesting] but just being skeptical, is that right?
> DENNIS: Well, I mean I dealt with religious people. I had other religious family members who would tell me that I was wrong, or would say something like "I love you and I'm sad that you're going to go to hell because you don't believe."

There was clearly more to the story. Dennis's reply suggested that even though he didn't receive any proper religious training from his parents, he was still affected by other religious family members in ways that encouraged him to engage religion critically, setting him on a path to rejecting it and becoming avowedly secular. It's not just a question of whether children are raised with religion; in the American context, many feel compelled to respond to the presence and privilege of religion in the broader culture[6] by "exiting" it, even if they were not formally members of any specific religious organization. This reflects the paradox Joseph Blankholm observed in his ethnographic study of secular individuals and organizations:[7] many nonreligious people, regardless of any overt religious socialization they experienced, have to navigate the religious society of which they are a part and construct their own identities within it.

Though Dennis was not actively religious as a child, it was later, during his time in the Navy, that he felt he had to confront religion and more fully articulate his own beliefs. Though he understood and was fine with the fact many of his peers in the Navy were religious, he was critical of the uneven role the military chaplains played and with the lack of representation of humanistic, and even other religious viewpoints in the military. He provided some context for why he came to identify himself as a secular humanist during his 5-year stint in the Navy:

> There is a sort of ever-present belief in God. Every night at 8 o'clock . . . [there] is essentially a prayer that is read over the loudspeaker anywhere you go. You cannot escape it on the ship because it's over the PA. And in general it was a Judeo-Christian message. It wasn't an "our Father" or generic god thing, it was a specifically Jesus-type message. And I didn't like that. I felt like I couldn't escape it or do anything about it. . . . They [the chaplains] are overwhelmingly evangelical. When I went to boot camp, we were—Sunday was kind of a rest day. And one of the things we were allowed to do on the first half of the day was go to a religious service. And I didn't have any interest in going to the evangelical or Catholic services. There were Buddhist and Wiccan services also, and so I went just for a change of scenery, really. But yeah, I'm aware that they're overwhelmingly religious [the military][8] and I do think that has something to do with being in combat. It certainly helps some people deal with the fact that they're there and that they're doing—while it may not be explicit from our government—that we're on a crusade. I think that some people believe that, that what they're doing is God's work.

Religious socialization doesn't end with childhood. Although Dennis's parents weren't taking him to church, his relationship with other religious family members shaped his perception of religion as a child. Likewise, the religious assumptions and expectations Dennis encountered many years later in the military motivated his dissociation with religion.

Like Dennis, Sue, a woman in her late 40s who lives in Los Angeles, by no means received intense religious training as a child. But unlike Dennis, she was raised with a specific religious tradition and she did attend church semi-regularly with parents. However, her parents' religious commitments were surfacy and somewhat opaque, and they didn't apply much pressure on Sue to be religious. In fact, Sue wasn't sure her father really believed what he claimed to. Her parents divorced when she was young and when her father remarried, his and his new wife's attempts to get Sue to embrace Christianity and to attend their church didn't pan out:

> I was raised Unitarian, so I was not raised with religion [laughs]. My mother was liberal; but the Unitarian church was totally about how everyone is accepted and if you believe in that [a higher power] great, but they don't consider that religion. My dad was religious, says he is Christian, if you believe him, but I don't. His wife would take me to Sunday school when I visited there but once I got old enough I would go, "No I don't really want to do this" and they stopped badgering me about it.

Sue simply drifted away from religion, including the kind of liberal Christianity that doesn't make any demands about holding specific religious beliefs. Her exit from the religion she knew as a kid was, in her words, "totally natural," as was her identity as an agnostic, which she adopted in her late teenage years. Per our argument about religion and politics in the previous chapter, there wasn't a lot of distance, in fact, between the open and liberal religious socialization she experienced as a child and the modern secular views she settled on as an adult. More than a dozen of our participants had an exiting pattern similar to Sue's. They grew up with minimal religious instruction, drifted out of religion, and developed a clear articulation of their own secular beliefs along the way. Of the dimensions of religiosity (i.e., belief, behavior, and identity), it's really just the identity component that underwent any obvious change for Sue and those like her. These exiters never had appreciable religious convictions to start with, nor did they practice religion in any significant way, so their later secular values and commitments don't represent much of a break from their pasts.

At the other end of the spectrum are those who underwent intense religious socialization, often in the context of so-called high-cost religions.[9] Such religions place significant demands on members, are exclusivist regarding their culture and theology, and members' identities and beliefs are so interwoven with the religion that both the benefits of belonging and the consequences for leaving are more pronounced.[10] This kind of religious socialization, usually throughout childhood, characterizes roughly a quarter of our interviewees. At the most extreme, six of our interviewees came from religiously fundamentalist homes, where indoctrination, punitiveness, and a literalist interpretation of religious doctrines were upheld. The exit process for these individuals, as with the nature of the religious socialization they underwent, is in stark contrast to what Sue and others like her experienced.

Glen, from chapter three, provides a clear illustration. He grew up in Missouri and was raised in an independent fundamentalist Baptist church. Everything about his childhood centered on his family's church, and his minister father's strict religious views and leadership in that church. Here's how Glen set the stage when asked about his upbringing:

> Well (sigh), we were pretty isolated from secular activities, such as music, television; we went to church every time the door was open, five, six, seven times a week. Satan was controlling public school systems [laughter] and I don't know, Hollywood. It was a pretty strict upbringing. [We used] the King James version of the Bible because it was the only authorized translation. I don't know, the membership at the church was so isolated and segregated that when the Supreme Court ruled on Bob Jones University versus the US in 1984 about biracial couples and segregation—that church had booted the Deacons [and] would not allow Black worshippers to be full members. They couldn't understand communion, they couldn't be in active ministry, they couldn't complete baptism until 1986 . . . that's how crazy it was.

Like most children, Glen believed everything his parents taught him. Every teaching and every doctrine they—and in particular his father— imparted, he accepted unquestioningly. For Glen, all of these claims to religious truth were wrapped in the notion of authority, starting with the authority of his parents, and it was unthinkable to doubt them. It's worth giving more context for a quote of his we offered in the last chapter to get a sense of the religious socialization—or to use his words, indoctrination—he experienced:

> I accepted everything. I believed, you know, I mean why would you question your parents? They love you, supposedly. I don't know, when I look back at it I was just innocent, the whole indoctrination process you know, it was memorizing scriptures and doctrine and we had wall charts that

were 8 feet long depicting the end of things in our classrooms, and it started at a very young age. Before I could even understand culpability or sin, you know, I made a public profession at like age 6 because that's what my parents wanted. I look back and all I wanted to do was love my parents and do what they [and god] wanted me to. So I had my little altar call experience as a very young child and [pause] I don't know, this dad thing was always, you never questioned it because *they* never questioned it, and if you understood it wouldn't be called faith. That was their response to anything that you asked, or if you tried to rationalize or ask too many questions, you're questioning god's minister, which is god's anointed, which gets his authority from scriptures, *sola scriptura*, very verbal, they take the literal translation of the scriptures and if it's not in god's word, then they have no use for it. And when [you] question [the] anointed, the running minister, you're questioning his authority which is scripture, which if you question scripture, you question their authority, which is god. Therefore, you're a heretic, which, I don't know, it's kind of twisted, but you just have to accept what they teach you, the doctrine. It was so ingrained in you from [an] early age.

Despite the intensity of his religious environment and how terrified he was of his parents' reaction, Glen decided to come out as gay when he was just fourteen years old, as he felt it impossible to keep this part of himself hidden. His fears were not unjustified. His church shunned him. His parents disowned him. And before his father kicked him out of the house he actually quoted to Glen the scripture from Matthew 7:23: "I never knew you, depart from me ye worker of iniquity!" Glen was abandoned and found himself without a stable home environment until he later joined the military. One might think, given the trauma of his early religious socialization, that this was when Glen cast off religion. It wasn't. He was still "religious and spiritual for years and years" after losing his family and home life. He dabbled in Wicca and flirted with the Hare Krishnas for a time, but the Christian roots of his upbringing, despite (or perhaps because of) its severity, left an indelible mark on him, so when he discovered a "gay church" after moving to Florida he felt he'd "come home to Christianity." So kindled was his desire to resume a religious life and regain the approval of his father, he took courses in religion for three years with the intention of joining the professional ministry.

It was only then, as an adult, having deeply investigated Christianity that his religious beliefs began to unravel. At the time of our interview in 2017, Glen was avowedly secular, and, in addition to calling himself a humanist, he enthusiastically used the label "DONE" to describe his relationship with religion.

Glen's story, as suggested, lies at the extreme. It's not representative of most of our interviewees, let alone most religious exiters. And yet, as Altemeyer and Hunsberger showed in an early comparative study examining those who abandoned religion after being raised with it, as well as those who converted to religion after being raised without it, the intensity and duration of early socialization can play a pivotal role in the (non)religious choices individuals make in adult life.[11] They argued, as we did in chapter three, that there is a complex interplay between the emotional and social forces that shape the exit process. Their participants, whether they were—to use their phrasing—"amazing converts" or "amazing apostates," experienced many of the same social psychological push/pull factors we outlined, despite the fact there are obvious differences between these groups in other ways.

Though religious socialization during childhood often does have a powerful effect, ramifying different kinds of exiting later in life, not all who break with religion do so in reference to their experience as children. People can, of course, have no religion at all as children, then join and become intensely committed to it as autonomous thinking adults, only to later reject religion and the socialization that undergirded their commitment to it. This shows the potency of the socialization process that's usually thought of in the context of childhood, and that indeed, most studies of religious socialization take for granted.[12]

This also describes Mya's trajectory. Mya was 40 at the time of our interview. Though both her parents were raised in strict religious households (her mother a Christian Scientist and her father a Methodist) they later rejected their religion—her mother vehemently so. Mya was raised in a secular household, and as a young woman she attended Reed College in Portland where, as she expressed it, the unofficial motto was "communism, atheism, and free love." She prided herself on learning, critical thinking, and autonomy. And yet, just before her 30th birthday, after experiencing some turmoil and uncertainty with what to do with her life, she left for Scotland and joined the Findhorn Foundation, an "intentional, spiritual community" that many people would recognize as a religious cult.[13] She'd found a home, became deeply immersed in new age spirituality, underwent a powerful form of religious socialization, and was involved with the group for years before she began to question the "teacher-student" relationship upon which it was structured, and the authority of its leaders.[14] She eventually got out, and although it wasn't a traditional religion that Mya exited (she wasn't sure even while in the group what she thought about a god), she came to be highly critical of religion in general and to identify as an agnostic. She even made a kind of career as an author based on her experience leaving religion.

So far, our examples of religious socialization and the shape of the resulting religious exiting of participants has focused on the extremes. This is intentional, as there is much to learn about the motives and context for leaving religion and what exiters do after they've left, by examining those who underwent more intense forms of religious instruction. However, just as an oversimplified view of religious socialization (e.g., parents "succeeding" or "failing" to transmit their religion to their children) will fail to account for the complexity of religious change over time,[15] these examples won't necessarily provide a good model for the generic religious exiter. What about those who experienced more middle-of-the-road religious socialization? What about those who neither easily drifted out of religion nor experienced a radical break with it? Let's take two more examples that illustrate the middle ground.

Consider Angela, whom we quoted at the beginning of this chapter. She's a former Catholic and mother of two who became a secular humanist. Her Catholic upbringing played an important role in her becoming nonreligious, but she didn't face the kind of pressure or expectations that Glen did. She was definitely raised Catholic, but her parents allowed her to make her own choices, even early on, with respect to religion. Here she described a bit of her rebellious streak and what happened when she told her parents, at age thirteen, that she didn't want to be confirmed in the Catholic church, even after years of preparation:

> My family was very active in my childhood. We went to church every Sunday. I remember my first communion was at St. Mary's. I remember going to Sunday School from when I was really little until I was thirteen.

> And then thirteen is the year you go to confirmation. So I was going to confirmation classes and I told my parents when I started going that I didn't want to get confirmed... then I started blowing off classes. Me and these two other girls who were also not into going to the classes would sneak off somewhere and smoke cigarettes and climb on the roof of the shed and hang out for an hour and we'd come back down when it was time to get picked up. After a couple of weeks the church contacted my parents and said, "Where's Angela been? She hasn't been in class." And they asked me what I had been doing and I told them I would just go hang out and I said, "I *told* you I didn't want to do it." So I got myself kicked out of confirmation class and finally they asked me, "Why don't you want to be confirmed?" I said, "Because if someday I want to be a Buddhist or Lutheran or some other thing that's not Catholic then that would be a problem!" And instead of trying to force me, they just said "ok" and didn't. Because, you know, my father who was never super great at organized religion anyway, he stood up for me... he basically went to bat for me against my mom's whole side of the family who was like, "What do you mean Angela's not getting confirmed?" And my dad's like, "It's religion. Religion is personal. She's thirteen. If the church is saying that she is old enough to make this decision and she is deciding *not* to, then it's not our right to force her to."

Despite her "very active" religious family, Angela's childhood wasn't characterized by total acceptance of and deference to the religiosity of her parents, as it was for Glen and others from fundamentalist backgrounds. She questioned her Catholic upbringing and sought intellectual and behavioral autonomy even as a child. Her father "went to bat" for her, and her parents, rather than rejecting her or the path she was choosing, gave her space to develop her own beliefs and make her own choices.

Many others shared something akin to what Angela experienced. They were raised with religion. They went to church. They adopted the basic religious beliefs of their parents. But at some point along the way they began to question these things and doubt the religious claims of their parents and church leaders. The pressure from family and friends was not so great they couldn't decide to take their own path, a path that eventually led to leaving religion altogether. Indeed, research has shown that religious parents who are more marginally affiliated and less strict about their own religious commitments are more likely to socialize their children in a way that defers religious choice to them, even if that means choosing no religion at all.[16] Granting children autonomy in their religious choices is often enhanced when parents are split in their religiosity—that is, one parent is religious while the other is not.[17]

This describes Calvin's experience. Calvin, age 30 at our interview, was born in Romania but grew up in the Washington, DC, area. His mother was religious and his father was an atheist. He described this as "very rare" for Romanian families where "everybody is religious; it's just a part of the culture." Calvin described his upbringing this way:

> So I was raised Episcopalian in the DC area. It was kind of a new age Episcopalian if you will—you know, not quite as rigid. But my mom was very religious. We went to church all of the time, not just Sundays. It just seemed like we were there all of the time.
> Q: What was the new age part of it?
> A: Well, not new age really. I just think, you know, I had been to other churches, but our pastor just wore regular clothes, and it was kind of a sharing thing, and it was a little bit more relaxed, not the you know, like the Catholics or something. But my father's an atheist. Before, I guess, when my sister and I were born, they [Calvin's parents] made a deal that he wouldn't get involved at all.
> Q: Your dad would stay out of all that? He wasn't allowed to talk about [his beliefs], but your mom could do all the religious stuff?
> A: Exactly. So yeah, I basically grew up in the church. Sunday school, youth groups, I was a camp counselor at one point; that whole thing.

Like so many of our exiters, Calvin simply did what his mother expected of him, and he recalls that, as a child, he didn't find much cause to question religion. As he phrased it, "I didn't really fully buy into it, but I wasn't questioning it much either." What's interesting here, and somewhat unique with respect to our middle-of-the-road framing, is that Calvin's atheist father, though he wasn't around much during Calvin's childhood, may have counterbalanced the effect of his mom's religiosity on him. Even though his father "wasn't allowed" to explicitly socialize Calvin as nonreligious in the way his mother was, he went on to suggest that his father would "still make his comments [about religion and atheism] when my mom wasn't around." Years later, when Calvin left home and went to college, he described the same "slow progression" toward becoming nonreligious that many atheists who were raised with religion undergo:[18]

> In college I still believed in god I guess, but I had no desire to go to church or anything. And then I guess it was just a slow progression, as every year went by the belief was just getting less and less, and then I started getting into astronomy, and at some point I just stopped buying it. . . . You know, I went to college and things changed. . . . I think when I met Jane [his spouse], I was still kind of borderline having some belief, maybe agnostic type thing, and then you know, it finally progressed to "ok, I think I'm just an atheist."

There wasn't any one thing that made Calvin reject the religiosity of his youth. He harbors no bad feelings toward his mom for raising him Christian, and isn't upset by, nor does he regret, being religious in his youth. To borrow a refrain Calvin used himself, "Religion was a social thing; it was just part of the culture."[19] It was some combination of push/pull factors that moved Calvin out of religion. This is characteristic of many of our interviewees. Though they had a long list of criticisms of religion, those who experienced something between the extremes regarding their socialization didn't tend to resent their parents or the religious instruction they received as kids. Instead, this experience simply provided the context for their leaving religion down the road and no doubt helped shape them into the people they are today.

Secular Joiners and Non-Joiners

Having described the relationship between religious socialization and leaving religion, we turn now to two main categories of religious exiters: joiners vs. non-joiners of secular groups. Afterall, we're asking in this chapter where individuals "go" after they've left religion, and a significant part of the answer here involves whether exiters feel the need to join a secular community. By secular joiners, we mean individuals who have sought out and participated in at least one organization, local or national, that defines itself as secular and is geared toward supporting and/or advocating secular values and beliefs.[20] As Joseph Blankholm[21] showed in his study of people who join secular organizations, there's a kind of paradox at play for secular people, where they navigate tensions and apparent contradictions regarding, among other things, whether the nonreligious should organize themselves around common beliefs and interests. Joiners of such groups tend to have more critical views of religion and are more likely to be secular activists. As with those Blankholm studied, scholars have found that exiters who join secular groups tend to be very knowledgeable about religion and articulate well why they left it. It makes sense that those who were deeply invested in religion or raised in strict religious households tend to have more riding on their leaving it.[22]

All three dimensions of religiosity—belief, behavior, and identity—are affected when one exits religion and then is confronted with choices about taking up secular causes. The nature of one's religious socialization and exit from religion can tell us important things about these choices. Indeed, many of our interviewees who experienced intense religious socialization spent the most time critically examining it, and their exiting tended to be more dramatic than those who simply drifted away from religion never having had much commitment to it in the first place. These individuals are often motivated to join a secular community. Glen, from our discussion above, is an excellent example. Recall that Glen was "done" with religion. And yet, he was not done with the need for identity or the draw of community. This brought him to connect with various secular groups including the Center for Inquiry (CFI), the Freedom from Religion Foundation (FFRF), and the Sunday Assembly (SA), where he became a regular participant. Glen also considered himself a secular activist. He donated to secular organizations and charities, he shared his own story and supported others who had left religion, and unsurprisingly, he has been especially keen to help those who experienced the kind of religious indoctrination he did as a child.

Glen didn't join secular organizations for any one reason, and as he pointed out, for him, different secular groups meet different needs. Part of it is simply social. As he put it, "I'm a social being. I consider myself a social person, I need that connection with other people." But it's about much more than being social. For instance, as he was developing his own secular beliefs, he found CFI a useful group because they focus on skepticism and criticism of religion. The work of CFI helped Glen develop and bolster his own arguments about religion's harms, and it helped validate his newfound secular worldview. His experience is consistent with a number of studies that examine individuals who join secular organizations.[23] But when asked why he joined the Sunday Assembly, it became clear there were many factors that drew Glen into active engagement with the secular community:

> Well their [the SA's] focus isn't on discrediting religion. They're "radically inclusive," and you can decide what to believe or what not to believe. We're just together to have a good time, to start new rituals. I think rituals are important and traditions are important, but sometimes those need to be updated and made more relevant. The Sunday Assembly offers us those rituals that are familiar and common to communities and gatherings. There were assemblies long before there were religions. Just to gather as a community to share a meal, or to share information, or to share concerns, or share joys, or listen to music, sing songs, you know . . . [it's] more about getting together and just reconnecting on a regular basis, not so much to discredit religion, which I think a lot of the other organizations are more about substantiat[ing] their anti-theist position, if that makes sense.

Glen's thoughts tell us quite a lot about the motivating forces that land some religious exiters in secular groups. He began with differentiating these groups. Whereas some promote an "anti-theist" message, the SA meets the need for ritual, community, and tradition. Glen went beyond the notion such secular groups met certain needs and were in essence the functional equivalent of religions,[24] to claim that humans assembled for these reasons "long before there were religions."

There are a number of reasons for exiters to join secular groups, and it will of course be a bit different for everyone. But it's not difficult to see how Glen's involvement and his concomitant secular activism were shaped by and through his religious socialization and former religious self. Yet, despite his distaste for religion—especially the religion of his youth—the "familiarity of ritual" and the various social and psychological benefits to be had by joining secular groups (even ones that look like religion) meant Glen had the felt need to join. Indeed, many secular joiners come from moderately or highly religious backgrounds. This is borne out both in our data and in previous studies.[25] But it isn't true that all religious exiters who were formerly highly religious join or even seek out secular groups, let alone become activists like Glen. Nor is it the case that those raised in comparably nonreligious households—and who lack the same psychological motives of those raised in highly religious homes—have no reason for joining secular groups, or becoming serious advocates of secular causes. Our interviewees represent both categories.

Crissy was a good example of the latter. Crissy was a late-middle-aged woman from the West Coast. She was raised, in her words, as a "secular Christian." "Christian" because she was baptized into the Catholic church as an infant (her mother was nominally Catholic), and through a Mormon grandparent she attended Sunday School at an LDS church for a time. She also had some exposure to Lutheranism from her father. Although they may have held some vague theistic beliefs, none of her immediate family took organized religion very seriously. This was evidenced by the fact that when she was in eighth grade, she "announced to everybody at dinner one night that I was an atheist. I think they chuckled and said, 'Yeah whatever, you'll change your mind.' They didn't care, really." Crissy was an interesting case. After leaving home she went to college and earned an advanced degree. It was during this time she began to be interested in and critical of religion. She abandoned what little remained of her Catholic and religious identity, but then also met and married a Jew, and converted to Judaism. On paper, this made her look like a religious convert, not an exiter, but this would be inaccurate as she quickly (and humorously) made clear during our interview that she converted to Judaism "as an atheist." Against the backdrop of this unusual trajectory, Crissy made a career as a secular activist, holding different leadership positions in several secular organizations for decades. How did she get there? Why did she become a secular joiner and activist? Certainly, in sharp contrast to Glen, she was not motivated to join in reaction to or rejection of an intensely religious upbringing. Rather, she simply couldn't square religious teachings with what she came to know through her own intellectual curiosity and education. This all began at a very young age:

I never got into the god thing. As a very young child I would have conversations in my head about, "Well if god created the universe, who created god? Well the god that created god created the universe. . . ." [Laughs]. And it turned into the infinite regression thing. I remember being very young lying in bed and having those thoughts, and this was obviously well before the "age of reason." And I certainly wasn't exposed to a lot of thinkers [at that time]. I think my family was just getting along from one day to the next; nobody in my family is a great intellectual or philosopher-type. When I went off to college, I sort of settled on psychology and that's where I was introduced to a lot of the great philosophers and psychologists. . . . After [college] I ended up being the only white person working in the multicultural educational outreach program for minorities and disadvantaged kids. I've always gone towards more unique populations; I've always been interested in anthropology, race relationships, and human rights. I've always been directed towards how I can go about and save the world ever since I was a little, teeny kid. I don't know where any of that came from.

Crissy's exit seems a natural corollary of her intellectual development and style of thinking. The more she learned about religion as an adult, well after she had ceased any religious practice or participation, the more her secular identity and worldview became the framework for her actions. Her perennial desire to "save the world" was channeled through secular activism, outreach, and education. Regardless of the intensity of their religious socialization and exiting process, our participants who joined secular groups came to share many of the same secular values. This meant that, even if they weren't outright activists and organizers like Crissy, joiners were motivated by things like state-church separation, the rise of the religious right, the threat of conservative religion to liberal democracy, and a wide range of issues where religion and politics are entangled. This is what many secular joiners spent their time on. But as we've already suggested, joiners also want the social and emotional support, friendships, and networks that most people, religious or not, desire. This is why most of the joiners we interviewed were involved with multiple secular groups.

Sue, who drifted out of religion "naturally" as she grew up, went years without thinking or caring about religion, and was content with her identity as an agnostic. But as she moved into her mid-30s, she realized she wanted more of a community. She started remembering some of the positive experiences she'd had, and that perhaps she had taken for granted, when her mom took her to the Unitarian church as a child. She had been sporadically connected to a couple of secular groups in town because she was concerned about church-state separation issues. But these groups weren't enough for her. She didn't feel fully a part of a community until she joined the Sunday Assembly:

> I have been on and off with various secular groups around San Diego and I've gone to a couple different events, but none of them seem to click with me. It just didn't seem fun. It was all intellectual and I don't know, it didn't click with me. So I was on an airplane and I was reading my humanist magazine from the American Humanist Association and I read the article on SA [Sunday Assembly] and I just [pause] by the end of the thing I was like, "Yay! My people!"

Unlike Crissy, who had a personal and political need to spread secularism through activism, Sue's reasons for joining were more about being with "her people." They shared certain values, but the psychology behind their joining differed. Whatever exiters' reasons for joining, one effect of the proliferation of secular groups in recent years that meet the demands for both community and activism is that the nonreligious are much more connected and mobilized than in previous decades. Secular organizing has resulted in groups like the Congressional Freethought Caucus, which was founded in 2018 to promote science, reason, and defend the secular character of the US government[26] by shaping laws and lobbying for the interests of the nonreligious.

Because of our recruitment strategy (see the appendix), a majority of our interviewees fit our definition of secular joiners. But we still have dozens of participants who left religion and never joined a secular group. For a sense of symmetry, our original thought was to provide some data from our non-joiners that might help reveal why they chose *not* to join secular groups. But as it turns out, there's just not much there, and what little is there has already been noted by other scholars.[27] For instance, we had 26 interviewees who, when asked directly, *Have you ever been involved in any secular organization?* simply answered, "No." It became clear that some of our exiters simply gave no thought to this. They had no interest in joining any secular group, and in some cases weren't even aware such groups existed. It was a non-issue. There were a few others who suggested that a social group for nonbelievers sounded strange or even silly.

So how do the non-joiners find community, support, and identity? They do so through other secular groups and connections, and by "secular" here we mean "having nothing to do with religion." They may be into sports, like Zeb suggested, and build community that way by joining fan clubs or tailgating at sporting events with friends. They may develop a strong support network through work, as Durkheim argued would eventually happen.[28] Their identities did not include religion but also did not include opposition to religion. They may identify as hikers, gamers, or runners, or with their work identities as firefighters, lawyers, or coders. Certainly, cosplayers have identities and communities and support networks, as anyone who has attended a Comic-Con can attest. There are countless identities and communities that require no reference to or reliance upon religion.[29] As Langston et al. illustrated,[30] religion *and* nonreligion are just not salient in the lives of non-joiners. They have built lives outside of religion that are so secular that they are also devoid of references to how they are not religious. In other words, such individuals do not embrace nonreligion, which would involve having a relationship with religion.[31] They are secular. This was the case for many of our interviewees who, while they had thoughts about religion when asked—unlike many Estonians[32] and Danes[33]—they were more akin to the religiously indifferent described by Quack and Schuh;[34] religion was irrelevant to how they lived their lives.

From available data we estimate the vast majority of religious exiters never join a secular group.[35] So it's really only the cases of those who *do* join secular groups that give us a sense for the reasons they have for doing so and what differentiates them from non-joiners. So, why do some religious exiters join secular groups while others don't? As we can see from the foregoing discussion, there's no single answer. But what we do have is a varied set of reasons centered on the validation of values, beliefs, and identities, the need to belong, and secular alternatives to religious practices.

Because our interview data tell us the most about joiners, we get a clear picture of the benefits of secular groups: identity, community, support, and even a place of recovery from religion. However, everything is always in motion, and just because someone decides to join a group doesn't mean this is permanent. As with religious engagement, participation in secular groups can wax and wane. The short life of some nonreligious groups is probably indicative of the transient needs of the segment of people who leave religion. After fulfilling whatever it was they were looking for from their participation in a secular group, religious exiters may simply go on with their lives, needing neither a religious nor secular organization to keep them going. One consequence of this, as we discussed in the last chapter, is that, whether they're joiners or not, exiters are unlikely to pass on the religion they inherited to their own children. Put another way, they're much more likely to raise their children secular. Why aren't adolescents and adults raised secular likely to join a religion? By the time they are thinking adults, it's too late. As we discussed previously, it seems the stickiness of religion comes from inheriting it as a child.[36] From what we can tell, this is an important piece of the context that leads to the religious indifference of many nonreligious Americans.[37]

This isn't to suggest that all exiters, whether they're secular joiners or not, are forever done with religion, let alone a spiritual life.[38] Indeed, some of our interview data suggest that a more autonomous and genuine "spiritual seeking" only just begins for some exiters after they've left organized religion. It's also important to acknowledge the possibility that some religious exiters might in fact return to religion, or even rejoin the specific group from which they left, but there's no reason to think this would be more than a small percentage.[39] Finally, by "joiners" we have made reference only to exiters who join affirmatively secular organizations. But there's another sense in which exiters can be joiners—when they join groups that are not affirmatively secular. As we suggested here and in our discussion of "better things to do" in the last chapter, joining a hiking group, book club, bowling league, spin class, or any other group that affords one a sense of community, belonging, and identity—whether based on leisure, entertainment, education, curiosity, or intellectual stimulation—are all ways that religious exiters might use the time they no longer spend on religion. We look closer at this issue next, in the final section of this chapter.

What Do They Do Instead of Going to Church?

Our qualitative data has helped flesh out the details of the religious socialization of exiters and the connection between leaving religion and joining secular communities. Our interviewees were no longer religious and did not attend religious services (excepting funerals and weddings, which are often infused with religious themes). For secular joiners, we know that some of the time they used to spend in religious activity is now taken up with involvement in the secular community. But we wanted to complement and give wider context for our qualitative data with survey data that gives an accounting of what religious exiters—and not just secular joiners—do with their time. The best quantitative data for understanding how Americans spend their time is conveniently called the American Time Use Survey (ATUS). It is run by the US Census Bureau and is sponsored by the Bureau of Labor Statistics. The researchers running the ATUS draw a sample from a different survey, the Current Population Survey or CPS, which is a survey of thousands of US households completed every month.[40] The advantage of drawing from the CPS is that the researchers already have a lot of information about the survey participants. The households that are selected for the ATUS are then called on a random day (after being notified that they will be called) and asked how they spent the previous day in minute detail. For each activity, participants detail what the activity is and how long it lasted. The end result is a careful description of how individuals spent their time. The responses are then cleaned and recoded into specific categories that range from shopping to playing video games to sleeping.

Unfortunately, the ATUS does not include whether someone was raised with a religion or even what their current religious affiliation is. But we can get at this indirectly because it does include time codes for religious activities. Specifically, participants in the ATUS can indicate whether they attended religious services, whether they participated in any religious practices other than religious services (e.g., praying alone, meditating, singing in a church choir, etc.), any time they spent waiting to engage in religious or spiritual activities, any time spent undergoing security procedures related to religious or spiritual activities, whether they participated in any religious education activities (e.g., teaching

Sunday School, leading a religious youth group, attending a Bible study course, etc.), and a catch-all code for any other religious or spiritual activities that were not included in the other categories. Thinking about our different aspects of religiosity, the ATUS does a stellar job of capturing religious behaviors, but has no information about religious beliefs or identity.

Of course, our readers are aware that there are plenty of other surveys that capture Americans' religious identities and beliefs—we have drawn on some of those surveys throughout this book. The ATUS is an opportunity to dig deeper into Americans' religious behaviors. We think what people actually do tells us quite a lot about them, regardless of how they identify or what they believe. Before we turn to the ATUS data on religious behavior, it's important to reiterate that close to 70% of Americans report having a religious affiliation. Whether Americans who report a religious affiliation actually participate in any religious activities related to that identity reveals how salient that identity is to them.

Here's how we approached this question using the ATUS. We downloaded the 2021 ATUS summary file, which contained data from 9,087 individuals on 401 variables. We then created a dummy or binary code to distinguish between Americans who engaged in *any* religious activities and those who did not for all 9,087 individuals. Basically, anyone who spent more than 0 minutes engaged in any of the religious activities captured by the ATUS noted above was coded as a 0 and anyone who did not spend any time at all in any religious activities was coded as a 1. While this does not capture identity or belief, it allowed us to see how people who do not do anything religious spent their time.

This approach is a bit problematic as the majority of the individuals in the 2021 dataset were not interviewed about how they spent their time on Sundays, the day when most Americans would be engaged in religious services.[41] Even so, this initial classification was, frankly, astonishing. When we looked to see how many Americans spent time engaged in any form of religious activity on any day of the week, just 10.4% of Americans reported engaging in any religious activities; 89.6% of Americans reported not spending a single minute during the previous day on anything religious at all.[42] No praying. No reading scripture. No meditating (with a spiritual or religious aim). Nothing!

Keep in mind that in the 2020–2021 wave of the General Social Survey, 30.7% of American adults reported that they attended religious services between 2–3 times a month or more and that 44.5% of Americans reported praying between once and several times a day. This discrepancy is fascinating. Other researchers have discussed it before, though not for almost 20 years.[43] There are a couple of possible explanations here that we will mention, since the discrepancy is not the primary focus of our analysis: either there is substantial response bias among Americans in surveys and they over-report their religious activity, or people don't remember all of the religious activities they engage in when they are asked about the previous day. Both are possibilities, though we, like most scholars, believe it is likely the first explanation.[44] Either way, the ATUS data call into question the oft-repeated assertion that Americans are very religious compared to the rest of the developed world.

Recognizing that Americans are less likely to engage in religious activities on days other than Sundays, we then selected in the ATUS just those individuals who were asked about how they spent their time on Sundays. That left us with a sample of 2,393 individuals. When we examined those individuals to see whether they engaged in any religious activity, the percentage increased to 18.3%. That still means 81.7% of Americans, on a typical Sunday, engage in *no* religious activities.

With this binary code, we could then compare the two groups on what they do on Sundays. Table 4.1 provides a comparison of how those who do not engage in religious activities and those who do spend their Sundays. For those who engage in religious activities, on average they spend 87 minutes in religious services and 20.9 minutes in other religious activities, or just under 2 hours combined. What do those who do not spend time engaged in religious activities do to make up the difference? How do they spend their extra two hours on Sundays?

For both groups, the largest amount of time—close to 9 hours—is spent sleeping. Those who do not engage in religious activities average 21.6 more minutes sleeping than those who do engage in religious activities. The next largest chunk of time, again for both groups, is watching TV. Americans who spend time engaging in religious activities spend just over 3 hours watching TV or movies on Sundays, while those who don't engage in religious activities average about 4 hours watching TV or movies on Sundays, a difference of about 44 minutes.

TABLE 4.1. Comparison of Time Use Between Religious and Nonreligious Americans. (Source: ATUS, 2021)

	Religious	Nonreligious	difference
sleeping	554.39	575.99	21.6
watching TV	196.1	240.01	43.91
eating and drinking	70.35	68.13	−2.22
working	18.54	56.29	37.75
socializing	46.96	42.28	−4.68
cooking	36.71	35.75	−0.96
doing housework	20.68	28.55	7.87
reading	28.08	23.34	−4.74
relaxing and thinking	20.35	20.98	0.63
playing games (including video games)	9.14	20.92	11.78
gardening	8.56	16.62	8.06
doing laundry	10.1	14.75	4.65
caring for children	11.05	11.36	0.31
playing with kids (not sports)	7.22	10.72	3.5
other shopping	10.05	10.57	0.52
on computer (including social media)	8.81	10.56	1.75
cleaning up after meals	9.46	9.49	0.03
household planning	5.66	7.86	2.2
grocery shopping	4.95	7.78	2.83
self-care	1.04	5.88	4.84
walking	5.3	5.46	0.16
self-grooming	6.49	4.88	−1.61
pet care	3.07	4.82	1.75
walking pet	2.49	4.58	2.09
on phone with family	7.8	4.12	−3.68
participating in social event	5.76	3.36	−2.4
exterior of home cleanup	1.92	3.05	1.13
on phone with friends	4.28	2.51	−1.77
listening to music	2.54	2.39	−0.15
exterior of home improvement	1.49	2.27	0.78
doing arts and crafts (hobby)	1.06	2.24	1.18
watching religious TV	5.13	2.09	−3.04
going to restaurants	1.76	1.78	0.02
emailing	1.47	1.69	0.22
hiking	0.96	1.25	0.29
listening to radio	1.69	1.14	−0.55

TABLE 4.1. (cont.)

	Religious	Nonreligious	difference
running	0.16	1	0.84
having sex	0.03	0.91	0.88
attending religious services	87.09	0	−87.09
participating in religious activities	20.93	0	−20.93
Total	1239.62	1267.37	
Unaccounted-for Time*	200.38	172.63	

* The American Time Use Survey includes more activities which account for the entire 24-hour period. We only included the most common activities.

With most activities there are negligible differences. Both groups spend about 70 minutes eating, around 35 minutes cooking, and about 20 minutes just relaxing and thinking. There are negligible differences in shopping, eating at restaurants, going for walks, cleaning up after meals, and taking care of children. However, there are some areas where there are notable differences. Those who engage in religious activities spend, on average, 18.5 minutes working their primary job while those who do not engage in religious activities average 56 minutes of work on Sundays, a difference of 37.8 minutes. Those who do not engage in religious activities spend about 21 minutes playing games (including video games) while those who do engage in religious activities average around 9 minutes of game playing. Smaller differences between those who engage in religious activities and those who do not include time spent doing laundry (10.1 minutes vs. 14.75 minutes), playing with kids (7.2 minutes vs. 10.7 minutes), walking a pet (2.5 minutes vs. 4.6 minutes), running (.16 minutes vs 1 minute), and chatting with family on the phone (7.8 minutes vs 4.1 minutes). Finally, just because it made us laugh when we saw it, we have to note that those who do not engage in any religious activities do spend, on average, more time having sex (.9 minutes) than those who do engage in religious activities (.03 minutes). Keep in mind those are averages across all the participants; let's hope those who do have sex on Sundays spend more than 53 seconds getting it on!

What, then, does the ATUS tell us about how people who are not engaged in religious activities spend their time, since they are not attending religious services or reading scripture or praying? It would have made for more engaging reading if we could assert that they spend all their time getting high[45] or engaging in some lascivious or hedonistic behaviors. But, of course, that's not at all what we found. Those who do not spend any time engaged in religious or spiritual activities on Sundays, which is 81.7% of American adults, fill their time with mundane activities: they do a little work, sleep in a bit more, watch some TV, do more housework and home maintenance, spend a little more time with their kids, exercise a bit, do some shopping, and maybe get lucky. In other words, they live quiet, rather ordinary lives.

Finally, another part of the wider context for the changes we see in the way Americans are spending their time on Sundays (and every other day of the week) and why fewer of them are attending church and engaging in other kinds of traditional religious practice has to do with changes in the cultural and political landscape. We already explored this topic in some depth in the introduction and chapter 3, so we won't recycle those points here. But an additional point bears mentioning. American culture has become more accepting of the nonreligious. No, we're not done with the culture wars, tribalism, and other problems where religion is a source of conflict and fragmentation in society. However, examining the data over decades, the nonreligious (and even atheists—though less so) in general face less suspicion, less stigma, less vitriol, and generally more acceptance than they did in previous generations.[46] This is in part just practical, a function of defining deviancy down[47]—there are so many unaffiliated and nonreligious Americans now, it's just not practical to define them all as outsiders. Although this will vary by region of the country, it's not that shocking to be nonreligious now. Since the early 1990s, a cultural space has been steadily opening for the nonreligious; there is broader acceptance of those who forgo religion or leave it behind at some point in their lives. It's this context in which each of the interviewees we quoted at the beginning of this chapter—Zeb, Angela, and Jessica—left religion. They were at different stages in the life course, had different motives for exiting, ended up in different situations post-religion, and joined or didn't join secular organizations. But there's little doubt that if they had left religion 40, 30, or even 20 years ago, their exiting process would have looked quite different.⁴⁸ Context is everything. And the context of American culture has changed in ways that have made religious exiting more common, and the phrase "nonreligious American" more normative. What this means for religious exiters themselves—their beliefs, identities, the communities they build, and their role in American society—is the subject of the next chapter.

5

What Happens to Them?

Interviewer: What is your general outlook on life now? Any particular philosophy or idea you live by?
I just haven't sat down and put [this] all together. . . . I try to be a good person. You know, I want to do good in this world and be a good person; be kind, treat people fairly, and try to contribute in a positive way. I'm not an outspoken person. I'm more comfortable in the background. But you know, when I talk to my mom about [my beliefs], for example . . . it's just like, I just want to be a good person, I want to do good things and help others, and that's the extent of it. I haven't sat down to do my own little elevator pitch to [myself] about it.
—Yesenia

This is it, this is the community that we want! And it aligns very well with our beliefs—our "nonbeliefs" (laughs). . . . I get to interact with people who want to participate in activities that bind us together as human beings and the characteristics that human beings share. . . . [It's] a manifestation of things like helping other people, developing ourselves, learning about the world. And these are things that all humans have in common so it's invigorating to me to find people who are interested in that same kind of perspective on the world.
—Ronald

We don't really need to look for the supernatural [for things] to be awesome, to have a sense of wonder. There's so many things in the world around us that are so deeply, well even overwhelming, you don't need to look far. . . . [The] cosmos and stars, galaxies and you know, things around us are absolutely wonderful. And the thing that can explain that from

the purely rational point of view, that's something that's absolutely marvelous, because it's not something that [rests] on an omnipotent being that says, "Hey, let it be like this."
—Leon

In the last chapter, we explained how religious socialization connects to the process of religious exiting. We also described the various factors that make an exiter more or less likely to join secular groups. We've attempted to answer, however briefly, the question of where Americans "go" after leaving religion. Although many of the attitudes and predispositions of religious exiters have been described already, and much might be inferred from both the interviews and survey data we've presented so far, the objective of this chapter is to do a deeper dive on what life is like for exiters post-religion. By "what happens to them?"—the penultimate orienting question of this book—we're referring to the actual contents of exiters' intellectual, spiritual, and social lives:[1] what they come to believe, what identities they embrace, what communities they seek out or build, and how they negotiate relationships in the context of no longer being religious. As a result, our pathways read a bit differently in this chapter. The three-part typology—*religious indifference, religious-secular liminality,* and *secular activism*—doesn't map on so neatly here as it has in the previous chapters. For instance, religious exiters can become indifferent to religion—we've covered that—but not many people are "indifferent" to their own lives, and it's difficult to imagine how one can be indifferent to one's own beliefs about the world, whatever they are. So, it doesn't make sense to characterize an exiter's overall experience or view of the world as "religiously indifferent." That doesn't capture how they actually orient themselves in relation to that world. And, at the other end of the spectrum, although the participants in our study who are secular activists indeed share many things regarding their beliefs, identities, and relationships, giving primacy to the label "secular activist" doesn't adequately convey where they find themselves post-religion; nor does it do justice to the varied worldviews and lifestances they develop or the ways they go about living their daily lives.

Most—nearly all, in fact—of our exiters arrived at what might broadly be described as secular and humanistic worldviews or lifestances.[2] Worldviews are the ways humans reflect on big questions like what exists, what is good, what should we do, and how do we know what is true.[3] Lifestances is a newly re-introduced term that refers to the behaviors, relationships, and beliefs related to one's orientation to life and existence.[4] We don't want to paint too homogeneous a picture, or imply that all or even most religious exiters become affirmatively secular. They don't. Religious exiters in general can and do of course hold many different beliefs and take many different lifestances.[5] But if our interviewees basically converge on a secular belief system, what differences did we find, given the diversity of their backgrounds and experiences? Mostly, the differences lie in how developed and explicit their secular lifestances are. Our opening vignettes provide some clues. Yesenia's words, for instance, reflected her basic desire to be a good person and live a good life. Her response to our question was pretty generic and didn't depart much from the normative values most Americans hold, religious or not. As she herself admitted, she had not fully thought through what her post-religious beliefs were or how they connected to an overarching worldview, and she wasn't all that keen to figure it out or explain it to anyone, including herself. Yesenia, you'll recall from chapter two, was a young, Hispanic, lower-middle-class woman from California. She grew up Catholic and remembered well her catechism classes, confirmation, and first communion. Being Mexican-American and the daughter of immigrants, she did those things because "that's what you do" and "it felt right at the time." But once she moved out, went to college, and began thinking critically about religion, she dropped her Catholic identity and declared herself a humanist and atheist. She knew what she was not—Catholic or religious—but in terms of articulating her beliefs at the time of the interview, she just "hasn't put it all together." Despite her interest in social justice and her activism (e.g., she participated in both the Women's March and March for Science shortly before our interview), she described herself as somewhat of an introvert, and someone who "likes to stay in the background."

Ronald is a middle-aged man from the South. His father is one of fifteen children from a strict Catholic family. But Ronald described his upbringing as "basically unchurched." As he put it, "I think my dad just kind of assumed like through osmosis that I would somehow inherit his religious tradition, which I did not, happily for me, unhappily for him." Any sense he had of being Catholic or a religious believer of any kind evaporated by the time he got to high school. That is when he came to realize that the claims of religion were "all just a story." But he and his formerly Baptist wife wanted a community, one that aligned with both their values and beliefs. Despite his criticism of organized religion, he saw the value of a church community for the individual, and he felt the need to organize his life in part by incorporating and expressing his worldview in a collective context.[6] More than Yesenia, he needed to connect the dots between his beliefs, values, and practices—the integrating elements of worldview we discussed in the first chapter (see figure 1.2)—in a concrete, coherent, and personally satisfying way.

Leon, a man in his 30s and a native of Poland, is a scientist with a doctorate from a prestigious university overseas. He spoke enthusiastically and had a sense of energy—even urgency—during our interview. He approaches life in a very systematic way. Always analytically-minded, he prizes logic and empirical evidence, but he also connects emotionally with the "human experiment," and likes to think about the biggest cosmic questions. His sense of his own beliefs was one of the more fully developed, relative to our other interviewees. In contrast to Yesenia and those who were comfortable not having the clearest picture regarding their post-religious worldview, Leon was keen to articulate to himself and others the details of his. He does this in both his work and relationships. His secular worldview seems every bit as natural and important to who he is now as was his former Catholic belief system, which he was, to use his words, "pretty intense about."

Of course, personalities play a part in how much time and energy religious exiters will put into constructing and expressing a nonreligious identity and worldview. Yesenia's default introvertedness, and the natural gregariousness of Don (whom we met in chapter 3), no doubt had some effect in terms of their differences on these points. But we didn't administer personality tests and won't speculate on how individual psychological traits shaped our interviewees' lives after religion. Rather, at the end of this chapter, after having outlined participants' own descriptions of their beliefs, behaviors, and identities post-religion, we'll make a more sociological argument, connecting factors like the life-course, social networks, and other aspects of our exiters' experiences.

* * *

As we've noted, the nonreligious—and in particular those who identify with labels like "atheist"—face prejudice and sometimes discrimination as a result of the general distrust many religious people feel towards them.[7] Leaving religion can be accompanied by a range of outcomes, negative and positive, with respect to one's relationships, values, and sense of self. Beliefs, behaviors, and identities are implicated to varying degrees. As we've shown, depending on a variety of factors, when one leaves religion, one may indeed lose, if only temporarily, an important part of one's identity, or even one's family, or an entire community. But some scholars seem to suggest that those who abandon religion are left with god- or religion-shaped holes in their lives. A sense of meaning or purpose has been diminished or lost. They're now missing something essential. Life holds less value. Personal wellbeing is undermined.[8] By virtue of this loss, perhaps, in time, a sense of spiritual yearning will accrue and will need to be cashed out in some way, maybe by returning to religion.

What is the evidence for this? How do exiters address these issues? We'll rely mostly on our interviews to scrutinize these questions, but it's worth making an obvious point first: people raised without religion in the first place haven't "lost" these things, and there's no evidence that the least religious societies on earth are in worse shape than the most religious on these questions.[9] Even in the US, where so many commentators express deep concern over religion's decline and where some scholars anticipate that the product of this decline will be no less than a widespread crisis of meaning, recent studies have shown essentially *no difference* on various measures of meaning between the religious and nonreligious.[10]

Of course, some individuals who leave religion will return to it again later in life. Some who leave early or had weak religious socialization as children may even actively seek out religious groups as teenagers.[11] However, most survey data show (as does figure 3.9 in Chapter 3) that from millennials on, young people in America are simply less interested in religion than previous generations. Young Americans don't show any conventional signs of wanting religion, like joining a religious organization.[12] This appears to be the case even for millennials and Gen Zers who *were* raised with religion, so it's doubtful, as we noted in chapter 3, people in these cohorts who weren't socialized into religion would be inclined to take it up later. Are these people bereft of meaningful relationships or a sense of identity? Does, as some scholars suggest, their self-esteem suffer, and they're just less positive about life in general because they're not religious?[13] We don't think so. But our question here is about religious exiters in particular. Maybe those who leave religion do experience a sense of loss.

Let's see.

What do the actual thoughts of religious exiters themselves suggest, over a time horizon of years, about what, if anything, has gone missing in their lives since leaving religion? We'll start by examining an important dimension of what changes when one leaves religion: identity and community. We'll then discuss the role of values, beliefs, and worldviews before concluding this chapter with a discussion of how exiters negotiate their relationships and what the broader implications might be. This will provide a few seeds that will germinate in the next chapter on how all this is affecting American society at large.

Identity and Community

Conceptually, identity and community are discrete phenomena with their own definitions. Most people share common intuitions about what these things are. Across the social sciences there is some convergence on the meaning of each. Briefly, identity at the individual level is the more-or-less stable sense of who one is based on internalized roles, personal characteristics and preferences, social positions, and other constructed categories. We all have many identities, and they can be configured into a kind of hierarchy with those at the top being of greatest importance to the self.[14] They can change or be rearranged throughout one's life based on life course events or transitions and other personal and external changing conditions. Community, on the other hand, simply refers to a collective of individuals who find themselves linked together based on some shared personal or social characteristic. A church group or book club are simple examples, though communities come in many different forms. People don't need to physically congregate on a regular basis to feel or be a part of a community. Indeed, some communities are simply imagined; they function as socially constructed reference categories for individuals to identify with.[15] Both concepts are so often interwoven that it can sometimes make sense to treat them as two sides of the same coin. Here, we'll discuss each in turn, drawing connections between them.

Religious exiters occupy a revealing space when it comes to identity and community. Let's revisit our definition of religious exiting from the introductory chapter. It's the "social and psychological process by which an individual exits a religious identity, ideology and/or community." Leaving religion, by definition, entails changes on these axes. It's not then surprising that our interviewees had a lot to say about both subjects. Much of the time, the conversation naturally steered toward identity, and our interviews suggest this is a salient topic for these exiters.[16] If respondents didn't bring this up on their own, we'd ask directly, with some version of "How do you primarily identify yourself? Is there a term that best defines you with respect to your no longer being religious?" For some, it was complicated (stay tuned), but in many cases, participants answered confidently and concisely.[17]

Don is a great example of the latter. As he declared: "I'm an atheist. I do not believe in any gods. I'm an atheist in the purest sense of the word, I don't believe in things without evidence. I don't believe in any of it [religious claims], anymore." Like Don, some exiters held identities that stood in reference to religion. Glen, for instance, first identified himself as "done." By this he meant done with religion, which he thought was "all about power and control." Religion, for Glen, was a kind of spell needing to be broken in order for humanity to make progress in the world. But Glen was an outlier. For most, there's a kind of balancing act going on where they'll feel the need to articulate what they *do* believe in addition to declaring what they don't. It's not all about opposing religion. Even those who were not shy about calling themselves atheists were keen to adopt more "positive" terms, terms that don't carry the negative connotations of rejection-based identities. Sociologist Jacqui Frost's phrasing for this is "rejecting rejection identities."[18]

Examples from our interviews of the multiplicity and multifaceted use of identities abound. We'll focus on just a handful. First, let's take a few examples from those who identify primarily as an atheist. Here again is Crissy, our middle-aged woman who was baptized Catholic, but went to the LDS church for a time, before marrying a Jew and becoming a secular activist:

> I'm an atheist. Around people that understand—[hesitates]—around people that I think I might be offending, I will use the term "non-believer." And I might use that to describe other people, in case those other people don't want the term "atheist" associated with themselves. But I have no problem with that. But when people want to talk about what I [do] believe in, I would point to the humanist manifesto with its list of values and priorities. I identify completely with that [humanism].

Even as an outspoken secular activist, Crissy is attuned to how others might respond to the fact she's an atheist, and adjusts accordingly. But as she implies, "atheist" is more a technically correct description of what she *doesn't* believe; it's a reference to theism. It doesn't capture her "values and priorities." For that, she points to humanism as the appropriate referent.

Sue's internal view of herself tracks closely with Crissy's, except, as Sue considers who she's talking to, it's less about causing "offense" than about simplicity and making herself clear. As she comments: "It depends on who is asking. If it's somebody who I perceive to be more in the liberal spectrum I might even go as far as to say secular humanist because they'll know what that means. But a lot of people don't know what secular humanist means. So, I usually round up to atheist." And it's worth re-quoting part of what Yesenia said back in chapter 2, as she, like Sue, tends to "round up" when identifying herself to others:

> I mostly use "atheist" because I feel like that's a term most folks are familiar with and requires less explanation than saying, "I'm a humanist." I *am* a secular humanist. My beliefs are and what I want in my life is more and more [in line] with humanism. So it's not just a lack of god, it's social justice. I want to act, not just think alike; you know and help those people who are struggling. So it's not just the absence of god, I still want to do something positive.

Crissy, Sue, and Yesenia are far from closeted about their identities as atheists. But there's more to the story. They want others to understand their position, and their identification with atheism accurately expresses that, but only in one dimension—on the specific question of a god. They account for the meaning these labels have, not just for them, but for others. And more importantly, they need additional concepts to capture who they've become post-religion.

Many who identify with the term "atheist" expressed something similar with respect to the distinction between their internal self-representation and the labels they'd use to represent themselves to others. Dennis, the former Navy officer, held a similar stance, except he actually enjoyed the "confrontational" component of identifying as atheist: "I think if I were speaking to myself I would use 'secular humanist.' If I'm speaking really to anyone else, it's 'atheist.' I think that's the clearest way of putting it. The idea of the confrontation that has been associated with that term [atheist] appeals to me."

It's interesting to observe the disjuncture between the identities—the stable, internalized sense of who one is—that religious exiters hold in mind versus the labels they'll deploy to meet the perceived demands of the situation. Most of our exiters don't prefer Dennis's confrontational style or share Yesenia's preference for identifying first and foremost as an atheist. Rather, they'll use terms like humanist, agnostic, skeptic, naturalist, and freethinker to describe themselves. Of the approximately 80 interviewees who indicated they were atheists, the majority of them use other terms when interacting with (a) strangers or someone they don't know well, or (b) family members and other intimates who may or may not know they are an atheist, but they simply decline to use that word. They're engaging in a version of passing (or covering, depending on the situation) if we take a Goffmanian perspective on information control.[19] That is, "naturalist," for example, will pass as socially acceptable in a way "atheist" just won't. In essence, revealing the "true" identity—the one that the person most thinks of themselves as inhabiting—is negotiable when interacting with others.

However—and this is important—our interviews show that adopting and communicating to others a nonreligious identity is about much more than being tactful or trying to avoid prejudice through the strategic use of words.[20] Most of our religious exiters were happy to identify themselves accurately and defend their views if they felt it was safe to do so. After all, many have made a conscious choice to leave religion, and they aren't inclined to hide this fact about themselves. To the contrary, we find the primary reason for the varied terminology participants use is that religious exiters actually *need* a set of identity labels to convey the diversity of their thoughts, dispositions, viewpoints, and values. Having different concepts in hand, all of which "work" in different ways and in different contexts, is part of the identity toolkit for religious exiters. Many, in fact, find equal value and relevance in adopting a multiplicity of identities; not to be evasive, and not only or always strategically, but as an honest expression of the different dimensions of their intellectual and spiritual lives.

Deion, who you'll remember began to question, at age 10, the Christian faith he was raised with, walked us through his reasoning. This was dispositive of many of our exiters, nicely illustrating the way many of them internalize their various nonreligious identities:

> First and foremost I identify myself as a skeptic. I feel that skepticism encompasses atheism because atheism is simply an opinion. Saying that I don't think it is likely that there is a god or goddess based on the evidence, that's all that atheism is, it only tells you [what] I'm not. And then you're just like okay, well, who *are* you if you don't believe in God? Because "atheist" doesn't say anything about who I am. Skepticism encompasses everything. So, if somebody comes to the claim, it's like, okay well, what is your evidence? If somebody says you believe in ghosts, it's like well why do you do that? Why do you believe in ghosts? What's your evidence for that? . . . I apply it to every aspect of my life. So, the skepticism isn't cynicism but an honest questioning of the facts to establish what I view to be reality, I think is integrally important to me. Now, as far as my lifestance, you know, my morality, and how I present my ethics—that would be humanism. I'm a humanist. I follow the humanist code to live my life.

Baxter, a man in his early 40s, was equally clear about the multiple identities he holds. He grew up a devout Catholic. He was orthodox in his beliefs. He eventually attended a Jesuit school, taking courses in physics and philosophy. However, he noticed that everything he learned there tended to validate his Christian beliefs, and so he decided to go deeper, independently and intentionally challenging his religious convictions. "Ironically," to use his word, it was Jesuit school and a "five-year journey" that changed his mind about religion. He left the Catholic church and has been "a secular person" for nearly 20 years. Like Deion, he arranged his identities into a kind of hierarchy, prioritizing them based on his own particular calculus:

> The number one label I use to refer to myself is secular humanist. I think that describes me the best. The term "atheist" to me (pause); I *am* an atheist by definition, but I wouldn't, I don't think it has much content to it. It just means you don't have an active belief in a deity and that's all that means. . . . So [I'm a] secular humanist. I also like the term "skeptic" because it translates into kind of a, I think it, I try to look at the world rationally in all things, not just when it comes to religion.

Amberlee, who grew up Methodist and mostly has fond memories of her church community, had a more complicated, even conflicted view of her own identity. She has thought about identity labels quite a bit and has gone through stages in her life where she tries on different labels in a kind of identity ebb and flow. "My family was religious. I mean my big involvement was the church, I grew up there. I did everything they did. That was my community and that was where my trust was, and that was my family and my identity, and it was great." Despite having "virtually no complaints about [her religious] experience," she just outgrew the dogmas and left religion as a young adult. As we talked, she struggled to nail down how to identify herself:

> That's a tough call. I—it still is a negative connotation for atheists, so it's not something I morally embrace. But I kind of feel like I fit the definition. . . . Also I tell you what [pause], it's a challenging question. I do not believe god exists; however, if there were evidence to the contrary, I would be able to change my position on that. I like "secular humanist," although the context of humanism is kind of weird to me. I don't like the idea of somehow elevating the importance of humans. So I don't know, there are a number of terms that I kind of fit under, but there are none of them where I'm just like, "Hey, that's perfect!"

Of course, religious exiters aren't endlessly ruminating on their identities. They also have lives to live. As researchers, we're prodding their thoughts on this. They might not think too much about their identity until some situation draws it out or they feel compelled to consider it. Jessica, who you'll remember was a kind of seeker, trying out a variety of religions well into adulthood before leaving it entirely, had this to say:

> I really didn't think about religion much at all after [leaving it], except for those bouts of trying to get involved in the faith communities, so, since the attempts to convert to Judaism, which would have been in 1990, I really wasn't thinking much about it either way. But then when I joined this Facebook group, probably two or three years ago, I didn't even know what humanist meant and so that was part of my initial involvement with that group, like, what is it? What's humanist? What's atheist? What's agnostic? I had kind of known about agnostic and atheist and I wobbled back and forth describing myself as one or the other, but being involved with this Facebook group made me have a lot more discussions and considerations and readings on what the labels mean. . . . So I started leaning off saying I'm agnostic when I'm really an atheist, so that's why I settled on this term. And as far as "humanist," I really like to be understood. I like the term because not only do you not believe in god but you believe that humans basically can be good and mostly are, and that we can work to improve human life and life in the rest of the world. So for me, humanism is the positive . . . it's important to me to emphasize who I am.

Not until she joined a Facebook group connecting her with like-minded secular people did Jessica really begin to consider her post-religious identity. Though she had a vague understanding of and "wobbled" between agnosticism and atheism, it was connecting with others and engaging conversation that prompted her to add secular humanist to her repertoire of identities. As we'll argue next, communities are often implicated in the process of an individual adopting any given identity. Though a person can read about or passively encounter a wide range of identity labels—deciding what "fits" them—constructing a nonreligious identity, like so many other identities, is a fluid process of working out who one is, based, in part, on social exchange.

Much of what our interviewees reported suggested that finding—or indeed helping to build—secular communities is part of the process of selecting new identities that are in alignment with their changing beliefs (and vice versa). To that end, let's look closer at community. Community can be thought of as a kind of social mechanism bridging identities, beliefs, and values. We discussed at length joiners and non-joiners of secular groups in the last chapter, so we already know some of the relevant factors at play here. But let's examine more closely the contents of those communities—what they're actually doing, and how they shape the identities and lives of religious exiters. Nearly all of our secular joiners, unsurprisingly, place a premium on community. Amberlee, in explaining why she began attending the Sunday Assembly, summed up well the connection between leaving religion and finding a new community consistent with her beliefs:

> I am looking for inspiration, community, and like-minded people. I was a churchgoer growing up and I liked—I missed what I felt was regular motivational, inspirational, you know, things that inspire you to be bigger and better than you could be by yourself. So it's kind of a higher calling in some sense, even though I don't believe in a higher power like [god]. But the fact that you can belong to a group bigger than yourself and be able to affect positive change because of your group association, ways that you challenge yourself to think about the world, to make yourself a better person. That for me had been lacking since I left religion.

Amberlee's sentiments illustrate what sociologists, going back to Durkheim, have long observed about the nature of collectives. Her language of a "higher calling" and belonging to something "bigger than yourself" expresses Durkheim's fundamental insight about the nature and social functions of groups. The motivation, inspiration, and personal betterment Amberlee was looking for, as she puts it, simply can't be had by oneself. It requires a community. Communities, especially those premised on questions of "ultimate concern" and that embody core values, instantiate shared moral beliefs and a sense of solidarity. It's these contexts that produce the collective effervescence Durkheim observed in his study of religion, and as one of us (Smith) has argued elsewhere, this can be no less the case for some secular people and the groups they create.[21]

Many exiters echoed Amberlee's sentiments about the value of communities. Others, like Amberlee, connected this directly with their former religious selves. Ronald, for instance, put this very plainly: "Ya know, one of the things I miss about church is community. You know it's like I have long moved on from the *belief*, but it was really nice to be able to have friends and support each other." Or consider Baxter, a software engineer in his mid-40s whom we met above. Despite no longer believing any religious dogma, he occasionally found himself in church to support his then wife (they divorced, in part, because of their different beliefs):

> I've been a secular person for pretty close to 20 years now . . . and for a long time I saw a lot of churches. I was going to church with my ex-wife for a few years when we lived in New York and um, I always used to remind people, you know I don't believe any of the dogma, I don't feel at home in a church because I don't believe in their message. I don't think their dogma is true. However, I really admire their sense of community, and all the other benefits of having a church, having like a church hall and a church community. It was like a springboard for fellowship for me. We made friends there, it was a really nice close-knit community . . . but to me, I just couldn't feel at home in an actual church because I just didn't believe in the actual religion. So fast forward to a few years later I heard about the Sunday Assembly from a friend of mine and I said "yes!"— there is one close to me, sign me up, because that is exactly what I've always wanted. I want something that's like a church, with a sense of community, a springboard for fellowship and charity and all that but without the requirement of belief in any kind of deity or anything supernatural like that so it was pretty much exactly what I was looking for.

Should we interpret Amberlee's, Ronald's, and Baxter's experience as evidence that there is, if not a god-shaped hole, at least a religion-shaped hole in the lives of those who leave religion? This doesn't seem totally unreasonable at first glance. But it's not accurate. For our exiters, even those who join communities that validate their secular beliefs and identities, it's not actually about recouping what only religion can provide. In fact, we can flip the roles here and take the view that religion simply claims for itself the positive dimensions of community and the benefits that flow from it as if it is the *source* of these things. But mightn't these exiters' remarks about feeling a part of something bigger, finding social support, fellowship, inspiration, and becoming a better person reflect the intrinsic properties and functions of communities themselves? If these are simply basic elements of human interaction and communal life, then it could be that religious exiters who miss the community religion once provided them, and who seek out or build new communities, are just taking these things back from religion; or more accurately, reclaiming these as human experiences, not religious ones.

Some of our interviewees even stated this explicitly. For instance, in talking about the importance of community and how leaving religion did not mean foreclosure on her spiritual life or her ability to experience profundity, Crissy stated, "[My] view of the nature of reality is that all of these spiritual experiences are simply *human* experiences. They are rare, they might be unique, they might feel transcendent or special given the nature of our everyday, mundane lives, but they are simply human experiences." Deion expressed similar skepticism that religion is responsible for the benefits of community:

> You know, the idea of people congregating together is not a religious concept. It has been around as long as man has been around. People have sought the socialization of it, it's very tribal. We get together, we have common interests, we talk and it just kind of enforces that bond. . . . It allows us to get together to reinforce our bonds and be reminded, you know I'm not isolated I'm not surrounded completely by theists. There are people that think like [me], that want the same things that I want, that think the same things are important. Obviously we have [differences] . . . but at the end of the day we're all working toward the same interest; the betterment of our species. . . . It gives us a place to recharge.

A core aspect of many communities, and what generates the emotional bonds some exiters are looking for, is the collective, patterned, meaningful, and routinized behaviors we call ritual. Though many secular groups are about casually hanging out, talking, or listening to a speaker, others, like the Sunday Assembly and Secular Oasis, are centered on music, dancing, poetry readings, group meditation, and other more formalized activities.

Rodney, who we met in chapter 3, provides a good illustration. Having been, in his words, "pretty heavily indoctrinated," he was nevertheless skeptical of what he was being taught as a child. He recalled actually feeling "kind of embarrassed" about some of the dogmas he was expected to accept. When he was 18, he left home and the church, and went on to "create a new life" for himself. Still, he placed a premium on connecting with others through ritual:

> I find a lot of secular folks . . . seem to be afraid of strong emotion or [are] very skeptical of it, and I understand why, because you grew up with that religious indoctrination. But for me life is both the intellectual rigor *and* the emotional connection with people. The ecstasy of learning something new or watching an eclipse, or you know, I'm not afraid of all those emotions. I want to bring both and have them see each other. . . . I find the singing together fun, enjoyable, and the talks much more interesting and fascinating and so . . . it seemed very clear that it was a powerful community builder in a variety of ways, getting up, moving. Our Sunday Assembly people dance a fair bit, and all those things tend to bring joy, and connection to people. And of course the speakers, intellectual stimulation and all of that helps us to learn how to live better, but literally live better in the moment and build a connection.

For Rodney, there was no bright line between the "intellectual rigor" required of being a rational skeptic, *and* seeking positive emotional states with others through ritual. Both are needed, in his view, to build a community and live a better life. It's not news to researchers that communities and social movements, whatever they happen to be about, require more than just interests and goals. As studies have shown, it's not just rational objectives that guide social organizing; emotional bonds and a sense of solidarity—both corollaries of ritual practice—are required for sustaining a community over time.[22] The secular communities these exiters belong to have goals similar to those of religious groups and engage in similar activities—they hold services, do volunteer work, outreach, education—but what's holding them together are emotional connections and fulfilling relationships.

Recall our discussion of the connections between ritual, symbol, and myth—the integrating elements of religion—from the first chapter (figure 1.2). We explained why this is relevant to this book. Still, readers might wonder whether ritual, symbol, and myth fade away once one is no longer religious. Frankly, the answer, for some, is yes. Good data on this are hard to find. We found some data that indirectly speak to the desire—or lack thereof—for ritual among the nonreligious (not specifically exiters) in the 2008 ARIS survey. The 2008 ARIS survey included a subsample of 1,106 individuals who reported no religious affiliation. These individuals were asked if they wanted to have a religious funeral. The vast majority, 71%, reported they did not; 16% reported they did (the rest were unsure). Admittedly, the question here does not perfectly capture what we want. Individuals with no religious affiliation were asked if they wanted a religious funeral and many said no. They were not asked if they wanted any funeral at all, which is a different question. Even so, the 2008 ARIS data illustrate that people who have moved past religion rarely want *religious* ritual in their lives. These data suggest that overt expressions of ritual, symbol, and myth aren't necessary or relevant for everyone who leaves religion.[23] Indeed, many exiters don't need a community of fellow nonreligious individuals and they don't care much about cultivating a secular identity. Further, not every religious exiter misses the community that religion provided. But for others, including a number of our exiters, these things remain important.

Rituals are a means of connecting with others, but they're also useful for solemnizing important life transitions. For some religious exiters, these elements remain or become once again important. It's not surprising, then, that as the ranks of the nonreligious have grown, so too has increased interest in explicitly secular weddings, memorials, funerals, baby namings and welcoming ceremonies, among other rites of passage or celebrations to mark important milestones.[24] There are increasing numbers of humanist chaplains in the US, and nonreligious people can enroll in formal training to become *secular celebrants* in order to officiate these kinds of events.[25]

Some of our exiters take part in secular ceremonies, and a couple even became certified officiants. Stacy is one example. A former Christian, her father was in the Air Force and she spent time in Saudi Arabia as a child. She remembers wondering how "we [her and other Christians] were the chosen people" while the Muslims she met were not. She quit church as an early adolescent, and now, in her 50s, she's been secular for decades. But she's always loved ceremonies and the emotional experience that accompanies them. So, when she heard about secular celebrants she decided to become one:

> In a year and a half I've probably done three or four memorials and four or five weddings. . . . And it's been, it's just a really powerful thing. I love doing it and I love public speaking and I love being part of emotional events and gosh, weddings and memorial services, right? So yeah, it's just really super powerful. I've gotten such good feedback from people about how I even [pause] okay the coolest thing; so I did a local funeral in this suburb of Nashville and the guys who worked there that carried the woman afterwards said, "This was the most amazing service we've ever seen because it wasn't religious." It was all about the woman who died, right, and then people see how a secular memorial service is and how it is a celebration of that person, not just a bunch of empty prayers; it's just so powerful. So that's been really cool. It's such a tribute, it's so much more, it's a tribute to the *person*.

Essentially, Stacy views secular memorial services as in some ways more authentic than their religious counterparts because of their focus on the person, not as opportunities to evangelize or to express otherworldly beliefs or religious doctrines. Instead of "empty prayers" and rote or conventional religious rituals, the ceremony is focused on the life of the person, sharing in grief at the loss, and celebrating their life. Of those who tended to embrace the ceremonial and ritualistic aspects of secular communities, most shared the sentiment that the point of these things is to make connections with other humans. Though most by no means deride religion for the ways in which it approaches ritual and community, the subtext was that secular approaches were more honest and equally valuable.

As we alluded in the last chapter, one reason religious exiters find themselves joining secular communities is to reflect on and share their transition out of religion. In some real sense, such communities function as spaces to "recover" from religion. This can be an important part of the exiting process itself. Russel, a doctoral student in biochemistry at the time of our interview, grew up in rural Illinois. He had religious family members, but he states that he wasn't raised with any particular religion himself. However, he lived in a very conservatively Baptist area—so much so that he felt the need to start a secular community. He discovered the Secular Student Alliance and did the work of creating his own chapter on a college campus. He was surprised and "impressed with the response." He received emails from dozens of students expressing their interest, and had quite a few join. Those who didn't, as Russel commented, said things like "'I love [that] you're doing this. I wish I could be a part of it, but I'm not ready to come out of the closet.'" His group became the second largest "religious group" on campus, next to Cru, a Christian organization for students.[26] He sums up the role the chapter played for many of its members:

> If you're coming out of—well, we had some people . . . tell their story. They leave their religious community, and they kind of lose their friends, and lose what they do on Sundays. They stopped hanging out at church and with their friends, or their friends stopped hanging out with them. And they just need to go someplace where they know they will be accepted. It's been a safe space for those people. There are other people here that know what they are going through and have the same things in common.

Many of our interviewees who became involved with secular groups shared a similar idea. Stewart, now in his early 30s, was a devout evangelical Christian before leaving religion. He said much the same as Russel with respect to the role that secular communities have, of being an ex-religious support system, but he added that the formerly religious can also share in the "common convictions" of those who aren't formerly religious:

> I think that's one thing that's really nice. When I was really, when I was fresh out of the religious background and admitting that I was agnostic, it was a nice sort of landing place where I can have conversations, [there's a] similar language, and people kind of understand you. And because they've had similar circumstances, whether they came from a religious background or not, they tend to have the same sort of common convictions around why they don't believe in a supernatural being. So that was nice just to have a place where you can go and talk about that.

These kinds of communities shape identity in other ways. For some, an "ex" identity (e.g., ex-Mormon, ex-Catholic, ex-Muslim) remains salient as a kind of reference point; an important plot point in the story of the self. Interviewees would often share stories about their religious upbringing, or the "crazy" things they used to believe, and they would bond emotionally over shared experiences and criticism of religion. There may also be an ethnic element of their religion of origin that remains a part of their identity, influencing many aspects of their lives, including the way they navigate their own mental health and wellbeing; they will always be an "ex," whatever else they've become.[27] Others slough off the "ex" identity entirely and don't often find themselves in situations that would remind them of their former religious selves. In either case, our interviews suggest that new identities emerge in the space that opens when religious identities are cast off.

Before we turn attention to beliefs and worldview, we want to make one more point about identity and community. Many scholars have written about the identities and communities of the nonreligious in recent years. It's therefore reasonable to ask what we are contributing by focusing on religious exiters. Our argument, partially in response to the questions we raised earlier in this chapter about what our exiters have "lost" by virtue of leaving religion, is that, for most (not all) our participants, there is a kind of identity vacuum after leaving religion. Not a vacuum in the sense that they've lost meaning in life, or a sense of their personal value or worth, or what they are to do with their lives now that they're no longer religious. Rather, it's a vacuum in the sense that there is a need to figure out how to represent themselves to themselves (and others). For some, letting go of religion had real implications for their identity. Stewart, whose identity as an evangelical Christian eroded over a seven-year period before he became agnostic, expresses this succinctly:

> The hardest part of that [leaving Christianity] was really kind of the final six months before admitting I was an agnostic, and the first six months after that was a time where I was starting to have a struggle with my identity. I think a lot of the difficulty is wrapped up in that. You have a certain self-concept like this is who I am. I lived my whole life defining myself by my relationship to this god, and how much I care about that, and then you just kind of let that go. It's like a huge piece of yourself that you're leaving behind.

After "admitting he was agnostic" and struggling with his identity for a time after leaving religion, Stewart came across the idea of, and then fully embraced, humanism, and he now identifies as a humanist (though, like so many others, he also retains his agnosticism). This started Stewart on a new path. He became very motivated by his new view of the world, so much so that, like Russel, he even started his own group based on his humanist values.

Some studies have shown that simply finding and applying the "right" identity label—a concept that aligns best with a person's disposition or beliefs—can mark a critical turning point in people's lives.[28] This was certainly the case for Stewart. Even for exiters, like Jessica, who report going some time without thinking much about their post-religion identity, at some point in their lives, it becomes salient. Our exiters have clearly thought about their identities. Some adopt new identities almost immediately after dropping religion. They do so enthusiastically, with clarity and confidence, while others have more mixed feelings, with some even questioning the value of labels at all. We can't know this for certain based on interviews alone, but we suspect that, compared to nonreligious Americans raised without religion, most religious exiters at some point in the life course will grapple with their identity and how it stands in relation to their beliefs about the world and their place in it.

The struggle many exiters face to develop a new identity is not evidence that there is a "religion-shaped" hole in their lives. At the risk of repeating ourselves, the hole was never religion-shaped. There may be an identity-shaped hole that is part of being human. Religion can fill that hole, and it does for many people. But for an increasing number of Americans, religion is not necessary for this. This is not "longing" for religion or "yearning" to return to religion or evidence of humans being innately religious, as some scholars have suggested.[29] To the contrary, it is suggestive that humans may need or perhaps really like having an identity; no religion required.

Beliefs and Worldview

Identity and community are closely associated with beliefs and worldviews. These are mutually reinforcing phenomena. So much is this the case, it can be difficult disentangling any one from the other, since they tend to imply and refer to each other. In chapter 3, we argued that one of the pull factors explaining why individuals leave religion is the appeal of a "modern worldview." Actually, "appeal" isn't quite the right word. Most of our interviewees felt *compelled*, based on their own intuitions and reasoning, to reject religious claims, favoring instead modern scientific ones. Our exiters simply couldn't square their religious beliefs with what is known today about the nature of the world and our place in it. They developed fundamentally new and different worldviews after leaving religion.

Though religious beliefs and worldviews have long been a core interest to scholars, for much of the twentieth century, they essentially ignored those with no religion. Sociologists wrote extensively about secularization and other outcomes of modernization, but in terms of examining the beliefs, values, and lives of the nonreligious, they (with a few notable exceptions) simply overlooked them.[30] Fortunately, today we know much more about this, thanks to a variety of studies in recent years, many of which we've referenced throughout this book. Some of these studies have closely examined the contents of nonreligious belief systems and the ways in which secular worldviews are constructed.[31] Some have argued that, rather than comparing the often-taken-for-granted concepts of religion and nonreligion, the study of worldviews per se will yield the most insight into understanding both religious and secular people.[32] Ann Taves argues that one advantage to focusing on worldview itself is that it helps scholars move past the negative connotations associated with secular belief systems and problematizes what counts as religion, rendering instead different beliefs in and claims about the world themselves as the object of study.[33] Here, we differentiate religious from secular worldviews, but we also acknowledge the value of thinking in terms of worldview itself and try to resist oversimplifying things and assuming it's always an either/or situation (i.e., everyone's worldview is either religious or secular).

Much of this overlaps with the lifestances our participants construct, and we discuss this below. We'll observe here that there are likely important differences between, on the one hand, the "unchurched" and other nonreligious people, and on the other, those who were at one time religious but no longer are. Everyone has beliefs, and constructs some picture of the world they inhabit, but religious exiters, in addition to creating new identities (and, for some, new communities), construct worldviews that are in contact with their former religious ones. Thus, there can be differences between religious exiters and those who were never religious. As we suggested in the last section, although transitioning from a religious to nonreligious belief system can cause uncertainty and ambiguity (and sometimes crisis), it definitely doesn't mean all is lost. Exiters experiment with new ideas and identities, reinterpret old beliefs and, as we'll show next, construct no less than fundamentally different worldviews from those they held previously.

The concept of *worldview* entails a complex set of interrelated ideas. But at base, it simply refers to the way one thinks about oneself *in relation* to the world. It's one's overall picture of reality.[34] Worldview may be thought of as our species' ability to ask about and reflect on the nature of existence itself.[35] Every individual has a somewhat unique worldview, but worldviews and the web of interconnected beliefs and values that undergird them are never created in a vacuum. Private worldviews draw on and are constructed within particular social and historical conditions and broader "worldview traditions."[36] Secular worldviews are distinguished from religious worldviews in that the former are anchored to naturalistic assumptions about the nature of reality (origins, causes, the totality of what *is*) whereas most (not all) religious worldviews are premised on theistic beliefs and/or supernatural explanations of reality.

A hallmark of nonreligious worldviews is humanism. Though most nonreligious people don't explicitly identify with humanism, its basic premise encapsulates much of the architecture of a nonreligious worldview, even if only implicitly. And it unambiguously describes most of our religious exiters. It's worth quoting the American Humanist Association's definition of humanism, as it summarizes the basic position of our religious exiters:[37]

> Humanism is a rational philosophy informed by science, inspired by art, and motivated by compassion. Affirming the dignity of each human being, it supports the maximization of individual liberty and opportunity consonant with social and planetary responsibility. It advocates the extension of participatory democracy and the expansion of the open society, standing for human rights and social justice. Free of supernaturalism, it recognizes human beings as a part of nature and holds that values—be they religious,

ethical, social, or political—have their source in human experience and culture. Humanism thus derives the goals of life from human need and interest rather than from theological or ideological abstractions, and asserts that humanity must take responsibility for its own destiny.

Now let's reference this against the words of our interviewees. Breanna is the young woman (from chapter 3) who at age 9 took her parents to task on the efficacy of prayer. We expand here on a few of the sentences we quoted in chapter 3 when discussing modern worldviews. What she has to say when asked about her overall picture of life and reality nicely articulates the position of many of our participants:

> I really love the aspect of humanism that says, whether or not there is a deity, our purpose and our responsibility in life is to love each other and care for each other and create a better world, even if our experience is just totally subjective and cosmically meaningless. [It's] naturalism. I think evolution is awesome and science is amazing and such a cool tool to figure out how things work and to be inspired and to be full of awe at the universe because we understand both so much and so little about it. I think all of these things are the total picture of what it means to me to not believe in god and to put the human experience and the natural world as the priority . . . being in awe [of] the natural world helps me not to worry about little things. To know that in 10 billion years the whole species will be extinct and maybe the universe won't exist anymore, so you know, who cares if you get a B in class (laughs). . . . Our galaxy is literally bigger than I can comprehend. Like I can say it's 100,000 light-years across but I can't really understand that scale, and that's one of what, a hundred billion galaxies!? That's incredible! . . . I love nature and I love art and I do music and writing and the world around me inspires me so much. And it's something that I want to be able to capture and convey and it gives me immense peace and joy to be in this beautiful world and feel appreciative of all the things I get to experience in my little sentient body. . . . So I think it's kind of grounding . . . to go out in nature and just see how beautiful the ocean is, and feel like, wow what an amazing planet I'm on!

Breanna touches on all the cornerstones of a humanistic worldview. Naturalism, science, art, beauty, evolution, a sense of wonder and awe, that humans need to take responsibility for the planet and their own destiny; this reflects the views of those we studied. In other words, we found that the worldviews of these religious exiters converge remarkably well with modern, secular worldviews from across the globe. As van Mulukom et al. found in their comparative survey of ten countries around the world, nonreligious, nontheistic people hold three overlapping "belief sets" that coalesce around scientific, humanistic, and caring-for-nature-focused worldviews.[38]

In discussing their "big picture" beliefs, many exiters, like Breanna, had much to say, and were quite articulate as they did so. But even those who were terse tended to wax a little poetic as they contemplated our questions. For instance, Kevin, whom we introduced in the first chapter, reflected, "I'm on a little blue dot in an infinite universe, and as you get closer to the dot you can see the water, and you can see the land, and as you get closer to the land you can see the patches; and as you get closer to that you see where I am. And I realize that in the face of eternal time—of infinity, this is all passing [around] me, and I have a perspective on it." When asked what motivates him given our smallness in the vastness of the universe he responded, "I believe in people. I believe in humanity. I believe in the little things people do for each other. . . . That's my guiding principle."

Crissy shared this cosmic perspective, but also developed a sense of the practical; citing the role that the circumstances of birth play and interjecting her existentialism as a means of explaining her lifestance:

> I believe that we create our own lives. We are placed into the world with certain parents, certain communities, certain limitations in our environment and inside, internally we have certain strengths and limitations, you know, we have some unique things about us—but when all is said and done, there is no [intrinsic] meaning in life. I'm an existentialist, there is no inherent meaning. Every person and every generation has to try and find the best way to make it through this existence in this life and I think that over the generations people have learned ways to make life meaningful and valuable and I think our parents hand us those things to make it easier for us. Like, "This is what *we* value, this is what *we* think is important," and that at some point every growing adolescent-adult has to reexamine those things and decide for themselves.

For Crissy and most others, our existence and the problem of meaning are things human beings must grapple with and take responsibility for; "we create our own lives" and must "decide for ourselves" how to live and what is true. The worldviews of individuals don't spontaneously pop into existence. Much about our worldviews is implicit, running in the background of conscious awareness.[39] And of course, not everyone has an equally coherent picture of the world or spends the same amount of mental energy consciously reflecting on the shape and contents of their worldview. In fact, some people, if asked to articulate their "overarching view of reality and their place in it," would perhaps be lost for words. But this wasn't the case for most of our interviewees. Each was prepared to offer a clear and more-or-less well-developed statement of their worldview. This is in part a function, we think, of all the cognitive work they have done transitioning from a religious to a nonreligious belief system. These exiters have undergone a fundamental shift from a theistic to nontheistic worldview. Deion describes this shift as he contemplated what he should do after leaving his Christian faith:

> Like, what do I do now? And a few years later I discovered, completely by accident, I was just doing some research and I found the Humanist Manifesto and it completely clicked. I thought, this is who I am; this is how I've been; this is what I've thought. It wasn't like I found something and then used it; it was more affirmation than it was instruction. So from that point on, everything clicked into place and I was able to shift a lot more of my thinking . . . from when I was a theist, I was able to move on and build a new lifestance and build a new attitude and a new morality for myself.

It's not that Deion had some overnight radical change to his beliefs. Worldview transitions usually *accrue*, slowly, organically, implicitly, and on a day-to-day basis; changes in beliefs over time can be almost imperceptible. It's often in hindsight, through long internal dialogue and reflection or in a process of self-discovery, that one becomes aware their worldview has changed. This isn't to say there aren't important events or sudden flashes of realization along the way to a new worldview. It's just that Deion found himself to be already in possession of the basics of a secular worldview by the time his discovery of the Humanist Manifesto confirmed it. This wasn't uncommon among our exiters.

The above quotes broadly reflect the worldviews of almost all our interviewees. But as we mentioned earlier, we're not suggesting that all, or even most, Americans who leave religion become humanists or that they explicitly circumscribe their values within that framing. Even among our interviewees, many of whom were at least peripherally connected to secular groups, there were a few who didn't consciously subscribe to humanism or any specific affirmatively secular belief system. Consider Ronald, who you'll recall was quite enthusiastic about finding a secular group that "aligned well with [his] beliefs." Yet, when asked directly about his worldview, he had this to say:

> Gosh, you know, I hate to even try and distill it down to like a philosophy. I guess maybe a starting point is . . . (pause), I don't believe I adhere to a specific philosophy that [I'm] aware of. I mean I'm not a humanist, I'm not a secularist, at least the way I understand those. I don't think I'm an atheist; I'm probably an agnostic. But I guess that's even more belief than philosophy. Buddhism kind of comes close until we start to get into the supernatural stuff, which just rubs me the wrong way. I think Buddhism has a lot of value to offer until it starts getting into the supernatural stuff and it's probably because to me, it accurately describes the way that humans operate and the way that we have trouble operating.

So what's going on here? It seems like Ronald is very much intellectually aligned with the core principles of humanism and a secular worldview yet he states he's neither a humanist nor a secularist. The apparent contradiction here between Ronald's stated nonreligious beliefs and participation in a secular community, while simultaneously rebuffing identification with humanism, can be explained by his reticence to take the complexity of his beliefs and "distill [them]" down to any one idea. It's evident he doesn't like the idea of holding convictions based on specific beliefs ("I guess that's even more belief than philosophy"). Even his affinity for Buddhism and the flexibility it offers as a worldview gets qualified. Though Ronald is an outlier in our study, it's no doubt the case that many religious exiters hold similarly ambiguous and uncertain positions when it comes to articulating their worldviews to themselves and others.[40]

Consistent with research on the nonreligious in general, beyond humanism (explicit or otherwise) there are two other basic dimensions from which our interviewees construct and anchor their worldviews. One involves morality; the other science. It's not difficult to notice from our participant's stories how bound up their worldviews are with normative values, specific moral concerns, and a scientific approach to understanding reality. Both moral presuppositions and more fully worked-out moral beliefs are part and parcel of worldview construction. Indeed, worldviews themselves can be seen as a mechanism linking moral judgments with moral behaviors.[41] These religious exiters are keen to have an overarching and coherent *moral* picture of the universe; one that constitutively aligns with their secular beliefs and forms the basis for the moral judgments they make. Those secular beliefs, in turn, are often based on, and informed by, science. In chapter 3 we identified morality as a significant push factor driving people out of religion, so we have some sense already of the moral frameworks exiters use in explaining *why* they left. But let's look closer at the connections between their specific moral concerns and the role science plays in their beliefs *after* they've left. Helene, in her characteristically direct and succinct way, said this:

> So my worldview is driven by science and evidence and I think that's the best way and our hope and our future is to pursue science and closely adhere to our ethical and moral standards that are brought forth in humanism. Those would definitely be the driving force behind what I believe and what I am here to do, which is to serve others and to help others in any way I can. To rectify any suffering that I see or any injustice because nobody else is going to do it. It's like if not you, who? And if not now, when?

And here's Russel. His comments, prompted only by a generic question about his worldview, interweave the topics of science, religion, and morality in an illustrative way:

> I want to believe as many true things, and as few false things, as possible . . . I think that's a great guiding principle. Obviously I have very scientific beliefs. I believe that science is the best method we have to believe as many true things and as few false things as possible. Morally, I'm a consequentialist, a utilitarian. I think any moral philosophy that is of value is a combination of those two. I'm in the Sam Harris camp about

the moral landscape and science, that it can inform our moral decisions. Though, a simple consequentialism in a way that often gets misconstrued, it is not appropriate (pause), the questions are so complex that consequentialism isn't always the most pragmatic way of looking at [things]. When we look at the [relationship] of science and religion I'm not in agreement with Gould's [non-overlapping] magisterium. I believe that religion and science overlap virtually completely, and they are all claims about the natural world and any claim that isn't about the natural world isn't useful to us because we live in the natural world. I mean I'm a scientist, I'm hoping to be a faculty member fairly soon. The question about can you be religious and be a good scientist is a very common one that I wrestle with, and I would agree with what most scientists would say which is of course you can be religious and you can be a scientist as long as you check religion at the door. If you're religious you can be a great technician, you can do experiments, you can publish great work, you can really advance scientific understanding but when you come back to the question if you embody scientific values, if you can think of science with a capital S, religion is counter to that philosophy.

Russel went on to talk about other philosophical issues like epistemology and ontology. As he did, it became clear that "wrestling"—to use his word—with difficult questions was an essential part of the process of fleshing out his own worldview. As a biochemist, he was fully committed to the scientific process, not just as he "does science" in his lab, but as he thinks about the very nature of reality itself, including its moral dimension. Science, for Russel, isn't just a set of procedures or techniques of investigation. It's an intellectual activity and a self-correcting process for understanding the world through reason and evidence. For this reason, science shouldn't be silent on questions of morality or other philosophical domains. He states clearly that he thinks religious individuals can be good scientists, and he implicitly acknowledges the possibility of what sociologist Elaine Howard Ecklund has found in her research on the relationship scientists have with religion—that many scientists have more nuanced belief systems than one might expect, and that even atheist scientists aren't entirely hostile to religion.[42] And yet, Russel has reasoned that, in the end, religion and science make different claims about reality, which of course includes the natural world, and that some of these claims simply aren't compatible, however open we want to be about accommodating multiple perspectives, or however tempted we might be to feign harmony between them.

The vast majority of our interviewees held similar views regarding science. They adhere to scientific explanations of the world, and take science to be a useful—even essential—framework for interpreting many of the big questions in life, including moral questions. Even when not talking about science explicitly, many of our exiters' discussions of morality and the good life implicitly rely on assumptions from a scientific understanding of ourselves. Breanna, for instance, believes humans are "hard-wired" through evolution and other natural forces for compassion, empathy, and other moral behaviors, and that we wouldn't have been able to build civilization if they weren't. Taking a pragmatic approach, she weaves together her thoughts about the role religion plays in morality, using religion as a kind of foil, and in a way that reveals the basis of her own secular moral universe:

> I saw this little comic once where one character says, "I don't steal from people because god says not to and if I want to go to heaven then I need to do what god says and I need to follow god's word." And the next person says, "I don't steal because it's kind of a dick thing to do." And I think, you know doing something because someone has instructed you to do it, or you're afraid of a reprimand, or you're seeking a prize, that's not fundamentally moral behavior. That's conditioning to seek a response. True morality and being charitable is the means, not the end. You do things out of love and compassion and out of empathy and I think if you have empathy, which we are hardwired for as social animals, you know what it is like to be hurt and therefore you don't wish that on other people and you seek a connection to others and one way to do that is to help them. If you look at any holy book there are both really beautiful compassionate things that are said, you know love thy neighbor, faith, hope, love, and out of these the greatest is love and that's beautiful. Let's keep it. But then there is completely appalling Leviticus shit. So, you are applying your own sense of morality to biblical literature in determining which is the stuff to follow and which is not. If you're saying that morality comes from god then you would have no way of discerning that "love thy neighbor" is a better rule to follow than "enslave thy daughter." So, I think the case

for morality being a universal human experience can be made from a lot of angles. I'm not religious and I just spent six years of my life getting an education so I can help people with their health and I love feeling that I can make a positive contribution to the world . . . what we can do now is bring love to ourselves and others. It doesn't make sense to be a bad person. You don't win that way.

Breanna's argument is strikingly similar to the one Phil Zuckerman makes in his appositely titled book, *What It Means to Be Moral: Why Religion Is Not Necessary for Living an Ethical Life*.[43] The main idea is that human morality and our desire to do good isn't a divine gift, not something bestowed upon otherwise amoral beings, but a hard-won treasure, rooted in our biology and evolutionary past, and transmitted through culture. Ethics are codified and institutionalized through effort, reflection, and learning many hard lessons. Science and philosophy are critical mechanisms for understanding all this. For Breanna, empathy is immanent in human beings and doing good an end in itself; these are the conditions of a "true morality." Others, like Crissy, acknowledge that viewing humanity itself—rather than religious or divine edicts—as the source and arbiter of morality may be disquieting for many, but that's the challenge we face in life. After elaborating on the importance of science and then questioning the conventional and religious view of free will, she went on to suggest that, "Where we do seem to have a lot of choice is in making decisions about what we think is important; what we think is valuable; what we think is right or wrong. And I find that this is the great mystery in life; it's the great struggle in life."

One might wonder whether religious exiters simply replace religion with science. Do they just swap out a religious worldview for a scientific one?[44] Did they steal the altar from religion and place it before science? With respect to our exiters, the answer is, no, not really. Certainly, appeals to science are amplified and normative among secular people and communities. In fact, as Baker and Smith argue regarding the "constructive dimensions of [their] worldviews," science, for secular people, is the "primary institution in which they place epistemic authority."[45] Jerome Baggett finds that some American atheists espouse a scientific atheism, which fully buys into the "myth of the conflict between science and religion," while others embrace atheism's "agnostic root," admit their "unknowing" and remain open as to what science can or can't reveal. Either way, science is important to America's nonbelievers. And our interviewees, as we've shown, tend to develop deep commitments to a scientific view of nature and humanity. But lots of people, including most religious people, claim science is on their side. Fascinatingly, even new religious groups with highly non-normative belief systems do this. These are precisely the groups one might expect to be the most anti-modern and anti-science, yet they weave scientific (and plenty of pseudoscientific) findings into their theologies. For example, scholar Benjamin Zeller shows the ways in which the Unification Church, Hare Krishnas, Heaven's Gate, and other new religious movements respond to modern science, not by rejecting it, but by carefully integrating many of its claims and incorporating select scientific insights and findings. This lends greater substance and weight to their unique doctrines, eschatologies, and other aspects of their religious worldviews.[46] We don't have data to measure how committed our participants were to science before versus after they left religion. However, we can state that they unequivocally see science as being the *most* compatible with a secular rather than religious worldview because it (the secular) doesn't also make otherworldly claims that are inaccessible to scientific inquiry. So yes, these exiters put a premium on science, and it plays a fundamental role in their worldviews, but we can't say that they simply "replaced" religion with it.

As our exiters discussed science and morality, this would often lead to other topics that are likewise constituent of their worldviews. We can't possibly be exhaustive here, nor do we need to be, as both of us and others have written on these subjects elsewhere.[47] But let's examine two recurring and related topics from our interviews: meaning and mortality. Once again, there is a convergence between our religious exiters and what researchers have found in studying affirmatively secular people.[48] On the question of the attitudes of the nonreligious toward death, unfortunately, there's not a wealth of good data. For example, compared to the religious, nonreligious people have been underrepresented in the literature guiding end-of-life care, and much of what has been written has been from a religious perspective.[49] Cicirelli compared the "death acceptance or rejection" between the spiritual orientations (essentially, finding meaning in life) of the religious and nonreligious, finding that the latter are more keen to extend life as long as possible, and make it as good as possible, since they have no expectation of an afterlife. The religious, on the other hand, could defer some of this to an afterlife. Interestingly, both groups had similar ethical stances and standards; they were just rooted in different sources. The religious felt the need to care for others because we are all a god's children, whereas the nonreligious cared for others because "we all belong to the same evolving species and depend on each other for survival and continued growth in an ever-changing world."[50]

In their study "Doing Death without a Deity," MacMurray and Fazzino suggest, unsurprisingly, that the pervasiveness of religious language and symbols surrounding death are unhelpful to the nonreligious. That "nonbelievers manage dying and death in a highly privatized religious culture" can mean marginalization and a sense of alienation surrounding death and dying. The nonreligious don't have the same access to the rites and rituals consistent with their beliefs that the religious do (though, as we noted earlier in the chapter, this is changing). On the other hand, contrary to the findings of Cicirelli's study showing that the nonreligious were more keen to extend life as long as possible, a study by one of us (Cragun) revealed that the nonreligious had both less anxiety about death than the religious, and were less likely to use aggressive interventions to prolong life.[51] There are many variables at play, and more research is needed to determine to what extent there exists a stable pattern of differences between how the religious and nonreligious think about and deal with death. The point here is that, as we'll show next, the way in which our interviewees relate to mortality in no way suggests an inability to cope with death, as many religious people imagine.

Our interviews suggest that although exiters are definitely aware of the potential alienation they may face holding a nonreligious view of death in a culture that prizes—and even assumes by default—a religious framing and interpretation of it, they nevertheless develop a picture of mortality that is made meaningful and is nested satisfactorily within their nonreligious worldviews. To put it succinctly, they're okay with death. We touched on this topic very briefly while discussing the afterlife in chapter 3, but let's explore this in more detail by seeing what our participants had to say.

Annette, a woman who at the time of our interview was 74, provides a clear example. Her father was an evangelical Christian, and Annette was baptized in an evangelical church when she was young but later affiliated with Methodism and Presbyterianism before leaving religion altogether. She comments on her own mortality, and shares that she's also had to care and plan for the deaths of others:

> As I get closer to it [death] (laughter)—cause I'll be 75 in August, it comes up more frequently in my mind and all among my friends too. I have friends in their 80s. And so it comes up because of our [age]. I was thinking about this the other day, that I wish we had a date when we were going to die. You know, just give me a date. Mark it on the calendar and then, you know, I can plan better. My inability to plan my finances because I have no idea when it's going to happen, I could live for 10 years or I could live for 20 years and so that part of it is bothersome to me. I don't really care about the afterlife because I don't believe in one. I think that's almost a relief that I don't have to worry about it. I'm going to be dead, so. . . . I just actually planned the cremation of my brother; he's not dead, but he's quite disabled, mentally and physically disabled and I'm his only living relative. That's another way that has always gotten me into helping others because I have this brother who's always been a part of my life. So the home that he lives in right now was something like, what happens when he dies? So I had to arrange cremation and that got me thinking about what I want. But I'm not afraid of death. Before I was born, I wasn't here, and I won't be here after I die. And that's okay.

Annette has spent time reflecting on death, and she's quite matter-of-fact about it. Though some might interpret her words as being cavalier about death, that's not at all the impression she gave. For instance, she went on to talk about how happy and fortunate she feels to have lived as long as she has, and this gratitude tends to motivate her to appreciate life and help others along the way.

Luke, who you'll recall in chapter 3 shared some of his thoughts about the deaths of both his parents, had some interesting thoughts. Luke's parents were both rather liberal and fairly skeptical about conventional religion. He remembers the whole family sitting around the dinner table having philosophical discussions about existence and the idea of an afterlife. Though his family wasn't very religious in the traditional sense, he remembers going to Sunday school as a kid, and later, he attended the Unitarian Church with his dad. After that, though, Luke drifted away from religion entirely. He didn't make a "hard exit" as some others did, but as he's aged, his secular worldview has increasingly informed his view of death. Here is the full quote from which we offered a fragment in chapter 3. This is in the context of describing the discussions his family would have when he was younger:

> And so I continue that [reading and thinking about mortality]. And that's also something that I would say is why I am so happy is because I really kind of developed my own worldview. I'm very comfortable with [death]. My religious friends will often ask me, "Well what about when you die? You don't think there's anything after death?" And for me, I tell them no, I find that completely comforting, other than the fact that dying could be uncomfortable, I find there's nothing to be afraid of because there's nothing, there is nothing after. . . . There is nothing to be afraid of. And anyways, thinking about those big picture ideas helps with my happiness. It's an ongoing thing cause I know there are things that we can never understand. And because I love that intellectual process; good, more questions on the board (smiles).

That Luke finds the finality of death "completely comforting" suggests he's integrated the reality of mortality with his secular worldview. Judy, a former Catholic, felt she had to be similarly frank with others about her view of death. She recounts when her 94-year-old mother was recovering in hospital after surgery for a broken hip—the result of a fall—and she had to negotiate with her Catholic family members about what was the best course of action:

> I went to visit her, and after the surgery she had said that she wanted to die. And, you know, it was very fraught and I [was] trying to figure out what to do. I . . . I wanted to get it across to her that if she really wanted to die she could stop eating, and this led to some conversations with my cousins and I think you know, it's difficult because they have these very different views but I was pretty straightforward, but very mild by saying that I think this should be a personal choice and that whether they might

believe in a god and I didn't that we had a lot of values in common, so there's been instances like that where, you know, I have to be forthright to people despite the possibility of having some extreme disapproval.

Annette, Luke, and Judy are older individuals, and, as with most of our exiters who were beyond age 65 or so, they tended to have well-formed views about death. Perhaps they simply had more experience with death and thought about it more than younger exiters. But reflections on mortality, and this pattern of a high level of acceptance of death, wasn't purely a function of age. Yesenia, for example, found herself thinking about it more since the passing of a close relative:

> I think [about] death more so now. In the last year my one aunt who I was particularly close with and grew up with passed away last year, last summer. And that was the first time I really had to deal with death. Before that, people I had known had died, but no one that I was close to. It was like, you remember such and such, they're related to your cousin, or to whoever, you know so I just didn't have personal connection. . . . And so in the last year since that happened, I thought about that quite a bit but yeah, that part a little more now that my parents are getting particularly older and aging, and not always in great health. But yeah, I just kind of go with the flow and I don't hold on to that piece of it too much.

She went on to suggest that death is just something we have to accept. Yesenia was officially agnostic about an afterlife. But her position is to embrace the life we know we have, and as she says, "go with the flow." Ronald's view of death was even more succinct. He suggested that not only is this life enough, but that the inevitably of death was his motivation to make sure he lives this life to the fullest, "I mean, I know that this life is all I've got, and so if I want something I have to do it now, or try and make it happen *now*." That life is to be lived now and not for a hypothetical future state, one study found, was a common attitude among secular humanists and a basic premise for their finding happiness and contentment in life.[52] This appears to be the case for these exiters as well.

The pragmatic, sometimes blunt stance on death was a motif running through our interviews. Cathy was in her mid-40s at the time of our interview. She came from, in her words, a "strong Polish Nationalist

Catholic" background. As a young child, she spent many hours on multiple days of the week at church with her mother. Those weren't fond memories for Cathy. She began questioning Catholic teachings at age 9, and when she was a teenager, she told her mom she was done with Catholicism. She went to college, discovered other nonreligious folks, and has since described herself as a freethinker. As a physical therapist working in the ICU, she's worked with many individuals *in extremis*. This serves for her as a constant reminder of death, from which she draws a sense of gratitude for life. She's even already planned her own funeral, though she's still many years away from old age:

> I think that freethinkers are deep thinkers. I'm often with people who talk about those things [existence, mortality]. Also, working in the ICU I see death all the time and I see extreme changes in life all the time. Like somebody who was a young kid driving around and all happy and about to get married, and they get into a rotten car accident and now he has a head injury. So I do appreciate life and I think about that and I know that it could be right around the corner and I even planned my funeral and talked about what songs I want played and that kind of thing. I don't think it's morbid, I think it's just planning, just like you plan your day, you plan your dinner, you gotta go grocery shopping first, that kind of thing.

Of course, people have many different and sometimes conflicting feelings about death. And we can't always take what people say about it at face value. One's personal view of death can change over time and context. We're not suggesting that everyone who casts off religion suddenly finds themselves at instant peace with death, or that they become walking embodiments of *carpe diem*. There are no doubt religious folks who are equally content with their own mortality, as death simply represents the next step toward some future state they're sure they'll inhabit. As some research shows, greater confidence in one's beliefs, be they religious or secular, can have a significant effect on reducing anxiety about death. Wilkinson and Coleman argue that convinced atheists are able to cope with aging and find consolation in death in much the same way (or rather, to the same degree) as religious believers.[53] It's not so much the contents of one's worldview as the strength of it that is protective against death anxiety.

Larry, for instance, was less sure than Cathy, Judy, and Sydney, regarding his feelings about death. His comments suggest more ambivalence and uncertainty as to how he should be using his time in life. Larry is a Black man in his mid-40s from the Northeast. His parents were liberal with respect to their religious beliefs and he didn't describe himself having been particularly religious. When he did go to church, it was mostly because he enjoyed singing in the choir. But a few years before our interview, he had "an awakening relative to religion" and decided it did more harm than good, so he left the church. Larry is a musician but also has a degree in electrical engineering, which is his primary occupation. He considers himself lucky; he enjoys stability in his life and has a healthy marriage. Yet, when he considers death, it causes him to worry about how he's lived his life, and it's not clear that having a secular worldview has been a source of solace:

> I guess I'm not sure [about death]. It's hard to put into words. But maybe recently it might be partly my work, and my work wears a bit on my mortality which is starting to bug me now that I'm thinking about death more, fairly secretly. And then thinking about what I've done in my life and certainly I get this feeling that there is certain goals or certain experiences of life that I feel aren't as good as I wish it were . . . going forward I feel that I have a kind of mixed feeling about wanting my life to change in certain ways . . . I'm not sure, to be strong enough for me to actually do it—I get distracted by what's going on now, and then next thing I know it's a new year and [I] didn't do any of that stuff, and it kind of goes on like that.

To be sure, it's common for almost everyone to wonder at times whether they are spending their lives in a way they'll be happy with later. Leaving religion didn't necessarily improve the attitudes of all our exiters on the issue of mortality. What it did do is cause them to reframe their view of death in secular terms. For most, their motivations *for* life shifted. Notwithstanding—and indeed sometimes in part because of—their having left religion, they came to appreciate life and seek meaning in it; they find gratitude in all they have, they embrace the good, and they accept they will die.

How do the nuts and bolts of humanistic values, commitment to science, and view of death shape the sense of purpose these exiters create?

We've been sensitized to this already from the preceding discussion, but let's scrutinize some additional interview data more narrowly focused on this question. We asked participants the following: "How do you respond to the idea that a person needs god and/or religion to find meaning and purpose in life?" It was somewhat surprising to learn that not only had our exiters thought about this in some depth, but many expressed that they had actually had this question in some form put to them directly by a family member, friend, or even acquaintance.

A good example is Leon. He and his family moved to Tennessee when he was young. He remembers his Catholic upbringing well, describing the religious classes he took in school as "borderline compulsory," and commenting that "everyone was indoctrinated four hours a week as far as Catholic[ism] was concerned." Some of that religious instruction "stuck" from when he was a kid, though he has always struggled with accepting Catholic beliefs. He vacillated on religion and the question of god during his youth, but became very religious and committed to faith in college (stating wryly that he "knew everything" then), before finally abandoning religion. He now puts his scientific knowledge (as a microbiologist) to practical use by working with a team on fighting communicable disease. Now an atheist and rationalist, he's thought about it carefully and decided that life's brevity *is* what gives him meaning and purpose.

> I do encounter people who have said some very [pause], I encounter people often who [say], "If there's no god, what keeps you alive and [gives you] purpose; it's very sad we're born and live for 60, 80 years and then we die, and then there's nothing?" And I say, well, *that's* what gives my life purpose. I get to be here for say 80 years. It's a wonderful world. I want to experience it. I want to learn more about it. I want to help contribute to it [for] all the people that come after me. That's what's just, what's right.

Breanna shares Leon's view that purpose is a product of existence itself, and the fact we can't know how long it will last. In her typically frank and pragmatic style, she claims:

> I think that if you're talking about meaning and purpose and what it's all for, my philosophy basically is that we are here, we exist. So, whether or

not it amounts to anything cosmically, whether or not there is any permanence to our impact on the world—right now we exist so we basically have three options: we can kill ourselves and cease to exist, we can exist and be unhappy, or we can exist and be happy. So it seems, if we're going to be here we may as well make the most of it. We may as well have rich, fulfilling experiences, we may as well create love as best we can, and we should spread this to other people so that they can have the same positive experiences. Our lives are made meaningful by the joy that we get out of them.[54]

For Breanna, the point isn't whether the conscious experience of the individual goes on forever. We can't know that; people can only believe it. What we do know is that we exist now, and the rational thing to do is make the most of it. For her, abstaining from the supposition of immortality concentrates the poignancy and "meaning" of life; it doesn't undermine it.

Glen describes how, from his perspective, meaning is to be found in the "little things." After his long and difficult road exiting the fundamentalist Christianity he inherited as a child, Glen has decided that his life can have meaning by doing good, right now, however limited in the grand scale of things that might be:

> My focus has to be that any good that I can do is what I'm supposed to do. You know, it's just how it is. If I wait for an opportunity it's not going to happen, I have to make opportunities, I have to make time, I have to make the effort and it's the whole experience. . . . I can have my quiet little existence and be content with what little good I do, knowing that somehow or other I made somebody's day better. . . . So I guess it's about the little things, it's not the big things, I don't have to change the world. I don't have to find a cure for cancer. It's about just making a human connection and doing something good.

Consider Ahmet's response to the question of meaning. Ahmet was born in Turkey. His grandparents were Muslim, but he described his mother as a deist rather than a theist, and his household as essentially nonreligious, in terms of practice. Still, as a young man after emigrating to the US, he felt the need to join a freethinking group and distance himself from religion. He now identifies himself as a secular humanist. He puts plainly what scholars who study the life course have long observed[55]—the fact that "life is a process" and that one's circumstances, social roles, age, and other factors play a constituent part in what, to use Ahmet's word, "drives" a person and gives them a sense of purpose. But he also isn't as sure as Sydney and Breanna about whether his secularity is the basis for having "all the answers":

> It's [life is] always a process to find meaning in places. I certainly wouldn't consider life meaningless or that I haven't found meaning in anything but things that drive me or don't drive me change over time.... What drives me most is that I'm recently engaged and that leads to me thinking about having children down the road and so being a good dad would be what life is about... 10 or 20 years down the line will things I'm doing equip me to be a good father or raise good children? Perhaps 5 years ago... I was driven by the notion that you only get one life. I do derive some happiness from it and I tried to explore where that comes from and that was the answer I got to 10 years ago. So I don't know, I don't claim to have answers, and I think some people have better answers than others, but nobody can claim theirs is the right one, and I'm not going to claim mine or anyone else's is the right one either.

What Ahmet is sure of is his frustration regarding the conventional idea that one needs to be religious to experience a sense of profundity and wonder in life:

> I certainly consider myself a person with a sense of wonder and I think that's probably the main reason I'm doing science right now. I'm filled with a sense of wonder whenever I look at the natural world or when someone chips away at it and discovers one more puzzle and I get to learn and read about these things and perhaps one day discover a piece of the puzzle of my own. That's certainly driven by my sense of wonder.... It's certainly not the money I can tell you that much [laughs].

Many shared this view and talked about how meaning is derived from having a sense of wonder and mystery about the universe and our place in it. Yes, as other researchers have found, secular people find meaning and purpose in "ordinary" things like parenthood, work, and making a contribution to their communities.[56] But over and above this, these exiters, contrary to popular assumptions, were in no sense closed to the idea of something "bigger than themselves." They spoke of having a sense of profundity and awe at the cosmos and our improbable existence in it. Some even spoke of the idea of transcendence, not in a supernaturalist sense, but in a way that accords with their secular worldviews. Annette, for instance, has come to appreciate her existence all the more as she has aged:

> I'm sometimes just overwhelmed by the awesomeness of just the fact that it's raining or just that I can see clouds moving or, I think that that's transcendent in a way, and that nature itself is pretty incredible. The fact that we are here [and] can really think about your existence; and the fact is that you're one of the billions. . . . I think your life is so much brighter and better if you understand the awesomeness around you.

The "awesomeness" of existence isn't lost on Breanna either. Nor does she hesitate to use the adjective "magical" to describe things. She loves to feel "really connected to the beauty of things, and to things that seem magical in their simplicity or their vastness, and really appreciate the scope of existence." Rodney stated that he's cultivated his connection to nature and the cosmos all the more since leaving his Christian faith. He spoke emphatically, nearly stumbling over his words as he tried to pack in various strands of thought when asked about his appreciation for existence:

> I love it! . . . That's how I've been living my life, for decades . . . (pause) I've done a lot of backpacking, hiking, going out and looking at the stars, you know, so I'm very much experiencing these things and in the communities I've been a part of a lot of connection and excitement about people as well, so nature, and science, and people, and I feel a lot, you know, I practice meditation as well, secular meditation, so I find that I actually spend a fair amount of my time in a very high state, um, not exactly right, I don't mean like *high* [laughter], but a feeling of euphoria. . . . I feel a deep, you know, really almost bliss when I read about new planets being discovered and there's a transcendent awe for me. . . .

So, do people who give up religion give up a sense of wonder or mystery or reverence for existence and their ability to reflect on it? No. Nor anything close to it. This became so clear as interviews went on that we occasionally asked participants directly about whether these things have in any way diminished for them since they left religion. Judy's terse (almost brusque) response is instructive: "I don't know how anybody can stand any more mystery with what we've already got. It's so clearly right in front of our eyes! Why someone would take the time to speculate about non-material beings wandering around somewhere; I just can't. I'm too *full*. I just don't have time for that."

We've been careful throughout this chapter not to imply that all Americans who leave religion adopt the same identities, take up secular causes, or embrace the beliefs of our interviewees. We stress that again here. However, as research in this area grows and as light is shined on the nonreligious in general, the evidence is accumulating that a significant segment of them do. We examine the implications of this more fully in the next chapter. Before that though, let's turn briefly to the implications that leaving religion has for relationships.

Relationships

Much of what we've discussed already is suggestive of the ways religious exiters navigate their interpersonal relationships. Many have faced challenges, big and small, with family, friends, and others as they left religion. And sometimes they'd find support and encouragement from the same. Whatever the specific circumstances, saying goodbye to religion for these exiters was a consequential act that affected not just them, but those they care about. Here we'll focus on how these relationships changed and were managed. The implications of leaving religion ripple well beyond and well after the person has left. We again rely on our qualitative data, because, although there is some quantitative data on the topic—for instance, on religious affiliation and marriage patterns[57]—we simply don't have survey data from which we can draw clear conclusions or infer causal relationships. For instance, are religious exiters seeking out partners and friends who are nonreligious, or are they likely to have exited religion because of the influence of their nonreligious partners and friends? Of course, it can be both. And it's not that our interview data can give us a causal account

TABLE 5.1. Spouse's Religious Affiliation for Never Religious, Exiters, and Those Who Stayed or Joined. (Source: GSS 2010–2021)

	Protestant	Catholic	Jewish	None	Other
Never Religious	11.9	11.3	1.5	69.8	5.5
Exiter	18.3	15.1	1.6	59.6	5.4
Stayed Religious or Joined	53.1	27.6	1.9	9.2	8.2

either. But what it can do is give us a sense of process, revealing the consequences of leaving religion on relationships, and the ways in which religious exiters themselves understand and navigate those consequences.

That said, we do want to start this section with some quantitative data and a brief foray into causality. Table 5.1 presents data from the General Social Survey (GSS) from 2010 through 2021 on the broad religious affiliations of the spouses for the three groups of interest we have examined throughout the book—those who were never religious, exiters, and those who stayed or joined religions. As with many of our other findings, the never religious and exiters look pretty similar, with 69.8% of the never religious having spouses who also have no religious affiliation and 59.6% of exiters having nonreligious spouses, while just 9.2% of the religious have nonreligious spouses. That there is such alignment in religiosity in the US today illustrates the importance of homophily (i.e., the tendency to associate with others like oneself) or homogeneity, particularly in people's worldviews. People will find it more difficult to have a long-lasting intimate relationship with someone when they do not share core beliefs and values, and that is reflected in table 5.1.

The reason we include this table here and not in chapter 2 or 3 is that we cannot compellingly argue a causal relationship. The GSS does not include the necessary questions that would allow us to determine whether someone's social network contributed to their decision to exit religion. What would be needed to make such a determination is someone's religious affiliation as a youth, which the GSS does include, then at least several additional variables would be required to model the influence of social networks on religious exiting: when the respondent met their spouse, what their spouse's religious affiliation was when they met, and when the respondent left religion. With that information, we could construct a model that would allow us to determine whether meeting and marrying someone who was not religious increased the odds of the respondent exiting religion. Without that information, we cannot determine whether the respondent was already nonreligious when they met their spouse or whether their spouse was influential in them leaving religion. As far as we are aware, there are no longitudinal datasets that provide all of these pieces of information. Until we have that information, we are reluctant to include spousal religiosity as a predictor of either religious exiting or not being religious. Some prior research has included spousal religiosity in predictive models and found that it is a strong correlate of religious exiting or being nonreligious,[58] but it's not possible to claim this is causal. Given the limitations of existing quantitative data, we turn, instead, to our qualitative data.

What we find from our interviews, however, is complicated. Most of our interviewees left religion or were in the process of leaving religion before they met their partners or spouses, suggesting that spousal religiosity is not a causal contributor. Of course, some people did enter into an intimate relationship with someone who was not religious before they left religion, which means it may contribute to religious exiting for some. In other words, spousal religiosity can be a causal contributor, but it wasn't for the majority of our interviewees.

At a more nuanced level, we think there is a lot of social network influence that is either mentioned only in passing or ignored by individuals as they discuss their exit from religion. Some did mention such influences when they referenced an uncle, a friend, or other personal contact who was not religious who helped them realize that they were not alone.

A number of studies have examined the topic of nonreligion and relationships, with most of them focused on the social stigma of atheism in particular,[59] the ways in which they manage that stigma,[60] and whether and to what extent atheists[61] and the nonreligious in general experience discrimination.[62] This work informs our discussion, but our focus is not on stigma or discrimination per se; it's on what exiters' relationships look like after they've left religion. In line with the title of this chapter, we want to know what happens to them, and changed relationships is an important part of what happens.

It's been established that religious participation affords various benefits regarding social relationships and networks by way of group membership.⁶³ As we suggested earlier, it's not unreasonable to speculate that leaving religion might undermine both the quality and quantity of interpersonal relationships. But recent studies show this is not always the case; in fact, there are often as many "gains" as "losses" regarding relationships overall, even when the religion being exited constitutes a near totality of the person's social network. This is what one study of exiters of Christian fundamentalist groups found.⁶⁴ The researcher, Andreea Nica, found that, yes, important relationships can be undermined and various stressors and strains to those relationships can last a long time, but new supportive relationships with both former associates and new people are constructed and "reconstructed" (to use Nica's term), and these relationships produce positive impacts on wellbeing. This is certainly the case for our secular group joiners (chapter 4), but even exiters who don't seek out validating social groups still tend to work on existing relationships with spouses, children, and so forth. And, although there is evidence that less affirmatively secular people—and those who don't join groups—don't have as many positive outcomes regarding mental health and other factors linked to relationships,⁶⁵ there is of course no reason they can't, as some of our exiters have done, forge new, good quality relationships without being active in secular groups.

Let's take a somewhat dramatic example first to set the parameters of what our exiters are dealing with. Here's Glen on his relationship with his family. Recall from the last chapter that his minister father kicked him out of the house when he was a teenager. He described a long road back to having even a "functional" relationship with his religious family members:

> It's guarded, but it's functional, yeah. My dad and I, we didn't speak for almost 12 years . . . anyway I finally reached out and said I can't let it continue like that. Because I have resentment stuff out the wazoo and it's actually in my recovery kind of thing; and I reached out to my dad and whatnot, and we agreed that we disagree. I am the topic of every prayer meeting that he goes to, you know, they're still praying for my conversion and they wanted reparation; they wanted reparative therapy, you know, they wanted to change me. We tried counseling and all that. So anyways, it's still, it's guarded, but it's functional, as most dysfunctional families are [laughs].

Glen tries hard to surround the trauma of his religious exit and the knock-on effects it's had on his relationships with a sense of humor and perspective, but it's been very difficult for him all these years later to have a relationship with his family—and especially his father. Note that Glen was the one to attempt some kind of reconciliation with his dad. Knowing that his family and former church community still see him as a lost soul, and continue to pray for his conversion—even wanting "reparations" from him for the damage *he's* done—does bother Glen, but it hasn't stopped him from caring about his family and wanting some kind of relationship with them. A 2015 study tracked the consequences to relationships of eighty individuals who told their religious family members they didn't believe in god. Though some were supportive, and a few even experienced a deepening of their connection, most, at least initially, encountered some combination of disbelief, anger, rejection, hostility, and a loss of ability to communicate effectively.[66] Unfortunately, for Glen, these effects have lasted for decades. Fortunately, for most of our participants, the effects on their relationships haven't been nearly so intense.

Like Glen, Brent grew up an evangelical Christian. Now in their 30s, as a child Brent was trained to be a "soldier for Christ" and used the word "indoctrination" when reflecting on their childhood, though Brent also described themself as "happy" in that role and as a "true believer" in their teenage years. Brent remembers the exhilaration of proselytizing with their fellow soldiers and being among the chosen to spread the gospel. Now a secular humanist and freethinker, Brent comments on both "old" relationships and reasons for creating new ones:

> Having come from an explicitly religious background—and I was homeschooled from kindergarten to high school. So I've never had any formal education as a child. I've only participated in community college so I was very much on the religious side of things. For most of my old connections and relationships I have to own the label of being a secular person because they will just assume that I am the Christian I once was.... I would say it's [joining Sunday Assembly is] for my own development of new friendships. I've been able to develop new relationships that I feel happy about. It's helped me progress in my life and as a person ... although I would be lying if I didn't say I felt the need to make up to some extent for the anti-scientific beliefs and general view that I used to have.

It's interesting that part of Brent's motivation for seeking new relationships is about "making up" for past religious certainties and their proselytization of others to convince them to adopt their religious worldview. In doing so, Brent has had to walk a tightrope with their still religious family and friends. Identifying as gender queer, Brent had to actively seek out relationships with people they knew would be more accepting of *both* their gender/sexuality and secularity. When asked if one has been more challenging than the other as they negotiate important relationships, Brent said this:

> I would say in the context of where I am now, it's harder for me actually to be an atheist than it is to identify as sexually attracted to men. I present very heterosexual, but if I were given the choice, I would perhaps identify more as a female and I'm certain if I were to cross that particular boundary I would very much be labeled more for non-conforming in that sense. But in the context of where I am right now, it's harder for me to be out as an atheist than to be out as a gay person.

We actually weren't surprised to learn that it's been more difficult for Brent to be open about their atheism than their gender/sexuality; studies have shown that identifying with atheism can be more stigmatizing than most other stigmatized categories, given its symbolic power and the fundamental *otherness* many Americans perceive in it.[67] And yet, Brent has made it work; negotiating old relationships in light of their new identities and seeking more supportive relationships with other affirmatively secular people. Clearly, expanding one's social network to include social groups and individuals who will serve as a support with respect to one's identity and worldview plays a critical role in many of our exiters' relationships. Indeed, Brent attributed much of the "progress in life" they've been able to make precisely to these new relationships.

Cynthia, the Hispanic, former Catholic woman in her 20s whom we introduced in the first chapter, likewise attributed some of her best relationships to connecting with people (both religious and nonreligious) through secular social groups: "I've become a lot closer with people who are in that secular alliance group. I don't think they would have been fostered otherwise. As well as in context—I'm on an interfaith council and

I have some really close friends there . . . I would say there are definitely relationships I would not have otherwise."

Sydney described how things changed for her after she left the Free Methodist Church. She was very committed to her church; almost all her family and friends were members. Already questioning her religious beliefs, after finding little support in the church while going through a divorce, she left and eventually became a secular humanist.

> Well after about 15 years, I've managed two kids, you know, very, very active in the church and my entire social life, all my friends, you know, my entire support group was this church. Then my husband had an affair and it created just this catastrophic event in our life and it was actually one of the young ladies that I was working with—shepherding to Christ (laughs), and that was one of the biggest things that happened that started to change the way I was thinking. I felt unsupported by the church, I felt judged and after about five years of trying to repair this marriage, we did divorce. After that divorce, I was pretty much ostracized and I lost the church, my husband—ex-husband—stayed you know. Awful. . . . And so I had to pretty much rebuild my social group from the beginning.

Sydney now has four grown children, and she's worked hard to maintain good relationships with them. She remarried, to a nonreligious husband (former Catholic), and made new friends through a network of different secular groups. It's been by no means easy for her, but she's managed to rebuild relationships and reconfigure her social network in a way that's brought some harmony between her beliefs, her identity, and her community.

Amberlee, who, compared to Glen, Brent, Cynthia, and Sydney, had a very smooth transition out of the liberal religion she grew up with, states clearly the impact of meeting new people and having expanded her social network through social media to include like-minded secular people:

> I'll tell you, Meetup groups! Meetup groups is where we found this [secular community]. This whole community exists, in my opinion, because of Meetup groups. You go in there and there are *so* many groups in our area and you're like, "Holy crap!" And somehow they're all interconnected to

each other and then all of the sudden you have this—not underground community because it's out there—but I feel like you kind of need that... whereby you just have to start somewhere with a group of people who have found each other to build an assembly and have that community.

Amberlee's assessment of the growth of the secular community by virtue of expanding social networks is consistent with research aimed at predicting the growth of secularity in pluralist societies. For instance, one study on religious exiting and social networks finds that, unsurprisingly, families and neighborhood contexts are predictors of religious disaffiliation.[68] What is most interesting, however, is that the authors argue religious exiting might actually have two related phases. The first is that many exiters are "early adopters"—they leave religion irrespective of family and neighborhood contexts and social support. This jibes with our findings from chapter 3, where we explain why people leave religion based on push and pull factors. It also helps explain why one would be willing to reject a former religious identity in favor of a nonreligious one notwithstanding the disinclination of family and others to validate such an identity. The second phase underlines the importance of exiters expanding their social networks post-religion. As the authors put it, "[Religious exiting] spreads as support for it within local social networks widens and it appears more acceptable." Granted, these findings are based on computer simulations of "artificial societies." More research with real-world contexts is needed to have confidence in them. Still, as we argued in the first chapter, and will argue in the next, it makes sense that as people continue to leave religion and raise their own children without it, and as secular networks grow, American society, on balance, should become increasingly accepting of secular people and worldviews.

One important feature of secular community-building in the abstract is the desire to improve the public image of the nonreligious.[69] But we find this is also at play with our exiters at a more concrete and interpersonal level. Megan offers a good example. Megan is a middle-aged woman from the South. Raised Baptist, her family, friends, and neighbors were all religious; most were a part of the same church. As she puts it, "My dad was a deacon, my mother taught Sunday school, and so it was just a big part of our life; that was our community. Pretty much everyone I knew other than family, outside of school, was church friends."

However, she grew skeptical of religion in high school and stopped going to church shortly after. Now a humanist and nontheist, Megan was candid about why she finds it important to be openly secular with her religious family and friends:

> I'm not going to argue them out of it [religion] because it's not the kind of thing I think you can argue people out of. But you can "example them" out of it, and you can be around them until they just recognize that things don't add up for themselves. I mean I like, kind of actually if I'm being honest, enjoying now that my family knows I'm an atheist. I enjoy wondering about how they reconcile that belief because they know I'm a good person, they know about everything I am.

Megan has at least two motives for being open about being nonreligious, and this has shaped the nature of her interactions with family and friends. In addition to wanting to feel authentic, Megan self-consciously, and in some sense strategically, relates to important people in her life in hopes of "exampling them" out of any negative perceptions they may hold about her.

Dennis shared a similar sentiment. After his girlfriend's Christian parents went to see the latest installment of the movie series *God's Not Dead* (based on a popular evangelical Christian author's book by the same name), Dennis explained a surprising conversation he had with her father shortly after:

> Her father was talking about it . . . that all of the atheist characters were cardboard cut-out villains that were very easily explained. And he mentioned that he was in a conversation with people about it, and he brought up [the] point, and he said, "You know, my daughter's boyfriend is an atheist, and he's a good guy, and it's not like that." And so he saw that because I was a good and decent guy in general he saw that I was a good representative of the atheist community.

At the time, Dennis and his girlfriend were thinking about marriage and talking about having children. He appreciated the fact that his potentially soon-to-be father-in-law was willing to defend him and not be taken in by what Dennis characterized as Christian propaganda.

Megan would be pleased with Dennis being a "good representative" and might include this as a small instance of "exampling" others out of their negative views of nonbelievers.

Though it took many of our exiters time to renegotiate their relationships with family and friends, most ended up doing so with at least some success. We underscore this because, despite evidence of, overall, *less* prejudice against the nonreligious today, even the most recent research shows the nonreligious continue to face a "social identity threat" wherein they experience high levels of stigma consciousness, which results in the felt need to conceal their identities and secular beliefs.[70] Granted, there are aspects of our sample that have perhaps selected for individuals who are less likely to engage in this concealment, but as we have both joiners and nonjoiners, activists and nonactivists, representing every region of the country, it's worth highlighting that many religious exiters, with time, become open about their views.

Who our interviewees are open with varies depending on context and the nature of the relationship. Family members are different from co-workers or acquaintances. And the fact that these exiters had to make adjustments to existing relationships, as well as find new ones, doesn't mean all their relationships had to change. Ian's response is suggestive. Ian wasn't raised with any religion, but he embarked on a kind of independent spiritual journey as a young adult, joining what he describes now as a new age spiritual group. He studied Taoism, Buddhism, and other eastern philosophical traditions before joining a local UU Church, which he was active in for more than 10 years at the time of our interview. Now he's a secular humanist, which he sees as the product of his long spiritual exploration. When asked about how these transitions have affected his relationships, he answered succinctly: "I would say that there is kind of a big segregation between my work life, in professional places, and my personal life. So these types of conversation don't come up so much in my work conversations. I mean I don't want to avoid them, but it's not the sort of thing we start off with over coffee in the morning." Which of our three pathways participants are on—and how long it's been since they left religion—will in part determine whether they see their nonreligious status as being relevant at all to their relationships. Exiters of the religiously indifferent type may see no reason to engage others on matters of religion because they just don't care, making it less likely their nonreligious status will bear in any important way on their relationships. Conversely, for some of our activists, their secularity may in part shape almost every relationship they have.

There is another dimension to exiters' relationships that we alluded to at the outset of this chapter. We stated that we wouldn't speculate much on how individual personalities shaped our interviewees' relationships and post-religious lives. But of course, we acknowledge that individual propensities do play a part in relationships. An introvert who has left religion will likely have had a different experience than her extrovert counterpart, and this can matter when it comes to future relationships. As social network analysts observe, one's social network will be influenced by one's personality, preferences, and idiosyncrasies, in addition to the broader structural situations in which people find themselves.[71] Moreover, specific events and circumstances (e.g., getting married, going to college) can elicit or suppress different aspects of one's personality. Among our interviewees, there's evidence these things connect to the nature of their relationships after exiting religion. Judy, for example, shares the way her introversion and being "poor at relationships" in general changed over time, linking this with having left her Catholic faith:

> I think I'm a little poor at relationships. I'm close to my brother and sister and always really have been. The rest of my family? Hmm. I never really was very close to any of them. I was really quite an isolationist as a young person. I think I really changed a lot in my 40s; a lot of things happened between some more intensive therapy and moving to a new place. I didn't like to be in a lot of situations where it felt like I had to follow a particular role, and that goes back to [my] Catholicism and somehow feeling like you had to accept things that you didn't really believe in to get along with people. But I'm much more social [now] and especially just my first marriage in my 40s; Ronan, he's really a little more of an outgoing person than I am, although we're both pretty reserved. But, so he gets me out to meet other people more than I would probably do otherwise.

Though she's still "pretty reserved," Judy's exit from religion, new relationship, and moving opened a space for her socially. She contrasts her past experience as a Catholic with a sense of freedom and being accepted by people, including her husband, who shares her views and values.

Like Judy, Fatima is a fairly reserved person and has had "troubles" with relationships for much of her life. Recall from chapter 3, Fatima is a multiracial woman from a mixed-faith family (her father a Hindu, her mother a Christian). For her, relationships are all about trust. And given the conflicting, sometimes confusing religious messages she grew up with, she had to figure things out for herself. This is why she went on her own spiritual journey, and, as she recounted earlier, continues to think of herself as a "spiritual explorer," and a person who is seeking authenticity in herself and her relationships, which she feels she's been able to make some progress on, in part, because she's tried to develop her social network to include more secular and inclusive people:

> People. Friends. [sigh] I have trouble. I unfortunately don't have a sense of being able to rely on my family emotionally which has been.... I still think I keep trying to go there, which may be related to worthiness and feeling not worthy. You know, the only people who care for me are my family, and then I try to cling to them and they're not there. And I do have very good friends but I haven't created a community, or even just belonging to this community [Sunday Assembly] is really new because I haven't trusted community most of my life, because my first community, my family, wasn't safe emotionally. So it's taken a long time for me to even get to the place of even being able to feel okay in a community.

It's unlikely Fatima's difficulty with trust and feelings of unworthiness have any single cause. Relationships, as everyone reading this book knows, can be complicated. But her religious background and her exit from it has played an important role. In that last sentence, Fatima is referring to the fact that, to this day, she's cautious about the relationships she develops and the social groups she joins. This is in part a function of her past experience with religion and the conflict, both internal and interpersonal, it had inspired. Her relationship with her Hindu father, and her failed attempt to reconcile his faith with what would become of him given her Christian beliefs as a youth (remember, for years she thought her dad was going to hell), continue to influence her relationships today.

Though virtually every interviewee had examples of how their having left religion was a source of conflict with family and friends, the vast majority also conveyed that they had found some equilibrium with those relationships and were generally at peace with them. This appears to be the case whether they had exited religion recently or had been out for 40 years.

Crissy sums up the situation for many as she comments on the early stages of her religious exiting and her relationship with a close relative:

> The most religious family I have is an aunt, and she is very close to me and she's an Evangelical Christian. It was, in fact, her young earth creationism that got me really reading about the controversy. I had no idea that there were really these people that thought the earth was six thousand years old or less. So that has opened up some interesting conversations with her and her husband. But we focus on that we're family, and we love each other, and when they say, "Well, we love you anyway" [even though she's an atheist], I say, "I love you anyway, too" [laughs].

Whether they became secular activists (like Crissy), were largely indifferent to religion, or were something in between, these exiters did what they felt they could in negotiating important relationships. The fact that they left religion wasn't going to stop them from caring about or working on those relationships. As we've suggested, and as related research on religion and the life course shows,[72] *where* exiters are in the life course matters, not just with respect to their feelings about or distance from religion, but in connection to their social networks and relationships. As we explained in the first chapter, though we've presented three distinct pathways to religious exiting throughout, it's probably more accurate to think of these as transitional and fluid, where one can move between them. Could, for instance, the secular groups that many of our exiters joined function as a stopover to religious indifference? Perhaps once the need for social and emotional support is met, religious exiters move on. Though we don't have, strictly speaking, examples of any one exiter who clearly traversed all three pathways, our interviews overall suggest fluidity rather than a straightforward "option" of any one linear pathway.

It's clear that past experiences, specific events, and turning points in the lives of these exiters played a basic role in not just how and why they left religion, but in the quality of their relationships and the directions they took after they left. Relationships with family members changed.

Friendships were lost, added, or altered. Social networks contracted and expanded during and after the transition from religious to nonreligious. Many joined new communities that align with new identities and worldviews. Others had little interest in joining groups, though they still had relationships, old and new, that changed because they left religion. But on balance, these exiters found equilibrium in their relationships.

This examination of relationships leads us to our 9th and final proposition regarding the factors that predispose people to exit religions:

Proposition 9: The larger the proportion of someone's social network that is nonreligious, the higher the odds they will leave religion.

The argument we're making here is tied to the discussion above, which showed the shifting nature of social networks over the life course. As social networks shift—for varied reasons—it seems logical to assert that a network made up of a higher proportion of nonreligious others will be more likely to pull someone in that direction, whereas a social network that is heavily religious will have the opposite effect. In essence, what this means is that joining a network that is made up of more nonreligious folks will have a pull effect toward religious exiting.

We're now in a position to address directly the questions from the outset of this chapter. Does leaving religion fundamentally doom one's relationships in general? No. Are people who leave religion choosing loneliness and isolation? No. Do their lives become deprived of meaning and purpose? No. Though of course leaving religion can affect all these dimensions, if we take the long view and think the experience of these exiters are in any way suggestive of other Americans who leave religion, we can see that they adapt, move on, and create meaningful lives. The foregoing discussion foreshadows what's to come in the next chapter, where we take a wider view and examine the effects religious exiting is having on American society at large.

6

How Is This Affecting Society?

I think [society] is becoming less religious because when we look at the younger segment, people claiming no faith, what that says to me is that probably as they are getting younger and the new generation is getting less and less into faith, I don't know if it will continue and if it does I don't know if it will be full speed ahead like it has been in the last decade, but that seems to be the trend. Looking at some developed European countries, I believe the nontheistic numbers are higher and higher there so maybe we are tending towards that kind of society. And as far as the reasons go, I don't know, it's probably a very complex issue. . . . Maybe, I don't know if this is going to sound extremely arrogant, but maybe that is going to be the natural order, and we will shed the clingings of religion.
—Ahmet

I think that the data shows that people are becoming less religious, but I think people who are religious are more vociferous and more organized than the nonreligious. I think that when it comes to using religion in political ways or ways that shape public policy it is more organized. . . . I don't know if it's [more] people who are less religious or if there are people who feel more comfortable identifying as nonreligious. So I don't know if there is just a decrease in social pressure to be religious?
—Angela

The internet is killing religion. It's really that simple. People have information at their fingertips now and they're starting to form conclusions. . . . And they can see that religious people are acting just like they are. They're not special, they're not better than they are, they're not more "holy" or

more moral. They're just like them and they're doing the same things and then turning around and saying, "Well, you're a sinner." So I think people are seeing hypocrisy now and I think because of that they are turning away from the church. Which you know, hey, I'm good with that. People are starting to wake up. And I think even the folks that are really hardcore are starting to die off and the newer generation is slowly starting to emerge and I think it's just a matter of a couple more generations when you see those numbers start to steepen.
—Deion

Careful readers will note something a bit different, thematically, in our opening quotes for this chapter. As we've seen, there are clear differences between the pathways to religious exiting—indifference, liminality, and activism—and the narratives of our interviewees have demonstrated this throughout. However, irrespective of the specific pathway the above statements represent, our exiters here are in agreement about one thing: religion in the US is in decline. It's as if our participants read this book before we got the chance to write it. To be sure, Ahmet isn't nearly as confident as Deion is on this question, and there is variation among our interviewees on what religious exiting ultimately means for society, but it's fair to say that, basically, they all thought that a growing number of Americans would be leaving religion, and that—again, in essence—this would probably be a good thing for society, or at least not a bad thing. We use this chapter to explore this idea in some detail.

As we've argued so far, a significant number of people have left, are leaving, and possibly will leave religion in the US. While disaffiliation is on the rise, Americans' involvement with religion, at least by one important measure, has been low for quite some time with just 20% to 25% of Americans attending religious services weekly since at least the early 1990s.[1] There is some debate as to whether the rise of those who identify as nonreligious or nones include the (formerly) extremely devout, including those who used to regularly attend religious services.[2] If the extremely devout remain religiously engaged, there really is no reason to think much will change in society. It may be that we are primarily seeing those who were nominally involved with religion distancing themselves more clearly.[3] But there is also evidence that religious behavior and belief are declining even among the most devout.[4] If that is the case, what are the consequences of this for society?

The two ends of the religion/nonreligion spectrum seem to have very different perspectives on what the decline of religiosity in the US might mean for society at large. Many religious individuals, including some religious scholars, are worried that declining religiosity could spell disaster for society, reducing prosocial behaviors like charitable giving and civic engagement and reducing health and happiness.[5]

At one end of the spectrum, there are religious fundamentalists and evangelical Christians like the Pat Robertsons of the world, and other members of what Jacques Berlinerblau calls CRAS (conservative religious anti-secular) movements.[6] These individuals ardently decry and bemoan secularists and other undesirables as eroding the very fabric of American society:

> There will never be peace until God's house and God's people are given their rightful place of leadership at the top of the world. How can there be peace when drunkards, drug dealers, communists, atheists, New Age worshipers of Satan, secular humanists, oppressive dictators, greedy money changers, revolutionary assassins, adulterers, and homosexuals are on top. . . . There is absolutely no way that government can operate successfully unless led by godly men and women operating under the laws of the God of Jacob.[7]

Unequivocally, Pat Robertson believes a decline in religiosity (really, Christianity) spells nothing but disaster for America. A peaceful and prosperous society, in his view, can only be had under a Christian theocracy.

On the other hand, we have secular activists like David Silverman, former president of American Atheists. Though his words are less theatrical, it's clear he expects an improved society as America becomes less religious, drawing comparisons with Canada and Western Europe. At the Reason Rally in 2012, also known as the "Woodstock for Atheists," after touting the rise of the nonreligious and praising those Americans who have had the courage to out themselves as nonbelievers, he opined: "Just look at Canada and parts of Europe . . . religion there is going extinct. I believe America is not far behind. I believe in two decades, we will be in a position where secularism is the norm."[8]

Importantly, both Robertson and Silverman agree that more Americans are leaving religion and that secularization in the US is likely to continue; they just come to opposite conclusions about what this means for society.

Most of our exiters, unsurprisingly, have views that align with Silverman's. They see the decline of religiosity in America as leading to a better world. For many, that world looks a lot like Northern Europe—more progressive values like gender and sex equality, legalizing assisted suicide, and removing restrictions from abortion as well as higher taxes to redistribute wealth through government social programs, among other changes that would terrify Mr. Robertson. We'll take just one example as illustrative from our interviews: recall Sue, the woman who grew up in a liberal Christian family, but now is active in the secular community. She offered this prediction about the future of religion in America:

> I think that it is the beginning of the last gasp of religion. It [the religious right] could be just a big final temper tantrum by a toddler who is not— who finally discovers that not everybody agrees with him . . . I think that the biggest benefit is this is like the next step in making the world a little better, more secular, and now we're starting to get more nonprofits and more organizations that are secular that are driven by secular motivations that are doing great good. . . . I know because I'm intimately tied to international organization[s] and the conversations we've been having are where we stand on social justice and once other organizations come to that conclusion we will be able to have more impact on the world and [be] a platform for social change.

We hate to be the people who rain on everyone's parade, but there is actually very little reason to believe that *either* of these scenarios is likely. We think Pat, David, Sue, and everyone else who espouses similar views are very likely wrong. In our estimation, declining religiosity will not lead to an apocalyptic collapse in prosocial behaviors or declining societal health; nor will it usher in a golden age of progressive values and initiatives or lead to massive reductions in crime or other social problems. As we'll show in this chapter, religion matters a lot less for most of these concerns than people think.

To address this question, we have structured this chapter around ten common concerns people have raised about the consequences of declining religiosity. Where possible, we draw on prior research and existing data to answer these questions and make our case for why both the "disaster" and "utopia" scenarios are unfounded.

1) Will People Donate Less Money to Charities?

While it might surprise people, the short answer to this question is: No.

Indeed, many scholars will doubt or be surprised by our answer, but this is because many scholars have conflated religions *with* charities. Religions are not charities. This is why the IRS classifies them separately.[9] Religions are classified as religions, and that is the basis for their tax exemption, not because they are charities. Certainly, many religions engage in charitable activities and work, but not all do. And, if the criteria for rating charities were applied to religions—the most common criteria being how much of the organization's revenue is spent on the charitable aim of the institution—most religions would get failing grades as at least 70% of their revenue is spent on salaries and overhead and less than 30% goes toward actual charity (for most religious organizations, it is much less than 30%).[10]

The point is that many prior scholars have conflated donations to religions with donations to charities. If you assume religions are charities and then combine donations to religions and charities, you'll reach the obvious conclusion about donations to "charities" when religiosity declines—people will give less money to "charities," but only because people will give less money to religions. That comes awfully close to a tautology.

It is far more accurate to think of most religions as particular kinds of social organizations, such as associations, fellowships, or even social clubs,[11] but not charities.[12] When framed this way, donations to charities aren't declining—religious dues and memberships are declining. The same thing is happening with Freemasonry and with the Boy Scouts of

America—interest in both of these organizations is declining and so, too, are membership dues. Both Freemasons and the Boy Scouts engage in charitable activities, but virtually no one is crying out about how the collapse of Freemasonry and/or the collapse of Boy Scouts will result in the collapse of charitable giving in the US. We would go so far as to suggest that the Freemasons (particularly their charitable arm, the Shriners), the Boy Scouts, and many religions try to make positive contributions to society, though exactly how much of a positive contribution is extremely difficult to calculate.[13] But, it is important to point out that the Boy Scouts of America, Freemasonry, and religions are not charities. In so doing, we avoid the tautological argument that declining donations to these organizations means donations to charities have declined. They may be tax exempt, but they are not charities.

What is required here is to separate out giving to religious institutions from giving to *secular* charities.[14] The real question is whether nonreligious people give as much to secular charities as do religious people. If nonreligious people give as much, then declining religiosity means membership dues to religions are declining, which is a separate issue from the funding of actual charities.

In a separate study,[15] we used the 2018–2019 wave of the Panel Study of Income Dynamics (PSID) conducted by scholars at the University of Michigan to examine this question. The PSID is particularly well-suited to address this question, as it includes comprehensive measures of income and wealth as well as very detailed questions about where people donate money. In addition to asking about donations to religions, the PSID asked participants about donations to numerous secular charities, ranging from educational institutions to community organizations to environmental groups and international peace and humanitarian organizations like the Red Cross.

Given that it is only a minority of people who actually donate money, we used a special form of analysis that takes into consideration data with lots of zeros. After controlling for income, wealth, age, sex, race, family size, and living in an urban environment, we found that the nonreligious and atheists/agnostics did, not surprisingly, give less money to religions. That finding is in line with expectations as they are not members of any religion, and no longer pay their "membership dues." However, the nonreligious and atheists/agnostics were *not* less likely to give to organizations for the needy, health organizations, education organizations, youth organizations, cultural organizations, community organizations, environmental organizations, and international peace organizations. In fact, relative to Catholics, the nonreligious donated significantly more money to environmental organizations, cultural organizations, and peace organizations. Likewise, atheists and agnostics (who were grouped together in the PSID) donated significantly more than did Catholics to environmental organizations, organizations for the needy, cultural organizations, and international peace organizations.

What we found in the PSID is interesting because a number of prior studies have suggested that the nonreligious are less charitable, including toward secular charities. We did not find that. For the most part, the nonreligious were just as charitable as religious individuals (though Jews and Mormons were occasionally more charitable). And, as noted, when it comes to some secular charities, the nonreligious are more charitable than are the religious. It may very well be the case that some religious individuals do not give as much to secular charities because they are giving so much to their religions. In other words, it is probably the case that there really aren't meaningful differences in giving between the religious and nonreligious but rather that the religious give more to religions and the nonreligious give more to secular charities. The implication, of course, aligns with our argument quite compellingly. If more people leave religions, they will give less money to religions, and will give more money to secular charities.

If more and more people leave religions in the US, will donations to religions decline? Yes. Of course. People will stop giving money to religions, just as they would if they ended their gym or yoga studio membership. And that will likely mean decreased revenues for religions and some religions will close.

But does this mean that Americans will stop giving to secular charities? No. Nonreligious Americans still donate money to causes they value. Those causes just aren't religious ones. They donate to help the needy. They donate to their alma maters. And they donate to help the environment, among other social issues.

There is another question here that a few scholars have raised: Don't religions benefit those outside of religions? Perhaps, but this is even more complicated to measure than donations to religions and charities.

Certainly, the primary benefits of religions accrue to those who are members of the religions. That much is obvious. But some scholars suggest that religions contribute to society, generally, through their charitable work and their local economic impact.[16] We acknowledge that some religions do make charitable contributions and some congregations may have an economic impact. But calculating whether religions are a *net* positive contributor to their local community, or actually require subsidies to remain in existence, is very challenging. Consider that religions in the US pay no property taxes, no sales taxes, no taxes on related business income, no income taxes, and no investment taxes. Additionally, clergy can deduct parsonage exemptions from taxable income and they can opt out of social security taxes. By not paying just property taxes, religious organizations in the US receive all of the services local governments provide—police, fire protection, ambulances, hospital subsidies for the poor, education, etc.—but contribute nothing to funding those services. Likewise, religions pay no income taxes but benefit from federal and state programs, like roads, libraries, the postal service, the courts and prison system, the Environmental Protection Agency, the Federal Transportation Administration, the Centers for Disease Control, and so on. Any attempt to calculate whether religions are a net contributor to those outside of the religion in addition to the benefits they provide to their members must also take into consideration all the subsidies that people who are not members of those congregations provide to the religions. When such subsidies are taken into consideration, we are skeptical that religions provide more benefits to those outside the religion than vice versa.

Should we be worried that charitable donations and benefits to those outside of religions will decline if more people leave religions? No.

2) Will People Be Less Moral?

An extensive body of research has now established that the primary motivation for holding more negative views of atheists and other nonreligious people in the US and in many other countries is distrust.[17] The basic idea is that those who believe in gods—particularly the Judeo-Christian god—believe that their god is watching over them, in effect policing their behavior. As a result, such individuals, out of fear that they could be punished, behave more morally than they would otherwise. They also believe that, since atheists don't believe a god is watching their behavior, noting all they do wrong and planning to punish them for it, atheists are therefore less likely to behave morally. Recent research has extended this understanding to the nonreligious, generally, as well.[18]

Is there any reason to believe that people who leave religion will engage in more immoral behavior?

The short answer again is "No," but we will grant that this is a bit more complicated and requires more than a simple yes or no answer.

Here's why it's complicated: Though religious and nonreligious people alike agree on most values and morals regarding things like murder, assault, lying, and cheating, they disagree on the moral status of many other behaviors. For instance, for many religious people, using marijuana is immoral, as is getting an abortion, having sex before marriage, viewing pornography, and masturbating. Of course, there are also more esoteric religious perspectives on morality. Some individuals, based on their religion's teachings, believe the following are immoral: drinking coffee (Mormons), eating pork (Jews and Muslims), wearing the color red (fundamentalist Mormons), using modern technology (Amish), wearing makeup (some Pentecostals), cutting your hair (Sikhs), and stepping on ants (Jain priests). These more esoteric views on morality illustrate that morality and sin are socially constructed and vary by culture and historical moment.[19] Even so, they illustrate an important point: what some religious people consider perfectly acceptable others consider sinful.

This is obviously the case for religious and nonreligious people too. If we use the morality of religious people to judge the nonreligious, there is no question that nonreligious people are more likely to engage in "immoral" behavior since they are more likely to, for instance, cohabit before marriage (and have sex before marriage) and use illicit drugs. Likewise, if we were to judge the morality of religious people by the values of the nonreligious, the religious would be considered "immoral" for marginalizing women and LGBTQ+ individuals and rejecting evidence that contradicts their religious worldview. This disconnect in morality is easily visible in figure 6.1, which draws on data from the World Values Survey. Participants were asked to indicate whether a number of behaviors were "never justifiable" (1) or "always justifiable" (10). The

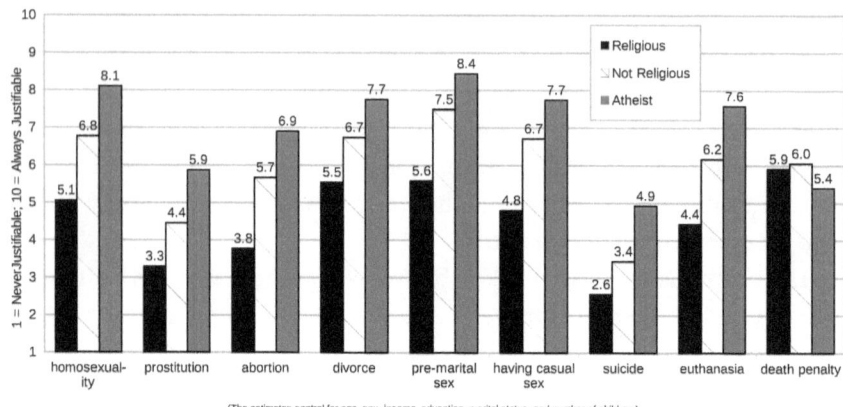

Figure 6.1. Views Toward Various Behaviors Among Religious, Not Religious, and Atheists (Average Marginal Effects). (Source: World Values Survey, Wave 7)

differences between the religious, the nonreligious, and atheists shown in figure 6.1 are after controlling for age, number of children, education, income, gender, and marital status.

As should be clear from figure 6.1, religious individuals in the US are more likely to find all of the following immoral than are atheists and the nonreligious: homosexuality, prostitution, abortion, divorce, pre-marital sex, casual sex, suicide, and euthanasia.

Judging one group by the values of another—ethnocentrism—raises all sorts of problems. What we need, then, are agreed-upon standards for both groups—values that both groups can agree are moral. While there may still be some quibbling on these values for a variety of reasons,[20] figure 6.2, which uses the same approach as the previous figure but with morality issues that are more universal, provides some insight as to where the two groups generally agree.

As figure 6.2 illustrates, the differences between the religious, the nonreligious, and atheists are much smaller when it comes to stealing government benefits, avoiding fares on public transport, stealing property, cheating on taxes, accepting bribes, beating one's wife or kids, or engaging in violence against other people. In other words, when asked to consider moral behavior that is not tied to specific religious injunctions, there are not notable differences between the religious and nonreligious.

Of course, there is a problem with the data from the World Values Survey. It provides us with the attitudes of the religious and nonreligious on a variety of behaviors, but it does not tell us which group is more likely to violate these moral precepts. What we really need are data that speak to the likelihood of engaging in immoral behaviors. Conveniently, many of the behaviors examined in figure 6.2 are criminal. That means a simple metric for determining whether nonreligious people are more likely to engage in immoral behaviors is to examine prison populations to determine if the nonreligious are disproportionately represented among those who have committed crimes and are incarcerated as a result. Alas, data on this question are difficult to find, but what little data we do have suggests that atheists are substantially under-represented among federal prison inmates in the US.[21]

We could try to parse out precisely how big these differences are and what they mean. But that, again, is not our aim. Our goal here is simply to illustrate that this concern is unfounded. Remember, the nonreligious in the US now make up around 28% to 30% of the adult population and atheists, depending on the study, are anywhere from 3% to 12% of the US population. As table 6.1 illustrates, those without a religious affiliation are close to being proportionally represented among federal prison inmates, while atheists are under-represented. If prisons in the US were filled with atheists and nonreligious individuals who were openly stating that the

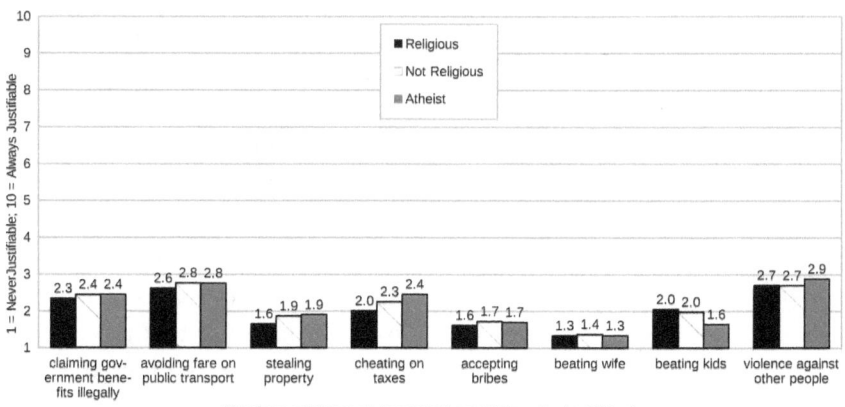

Figure 6.2. Views Toward Various Behaviors Among Religious, Not Religious, and Atheists (Average Marginal Effects). (Source: World Values Survey, Wave 7)

TABLE 6.1. Religious Affiliations of Federal Prison Inmates, 2022.398

Religion	Frequency	Percentage
Adventist	317	0.20%
American Indian	5,121	3.26%
Atheist	134	0.09%
Buddhist	1,315	0.84%
Catholic	23,885	15.21%
Hindu	267	0.17%
Jehovah's Witness	822	0.52%
Jewish	3,868	2.46%
Messianic Jew	3,028	1.93%
Moorish	1,700	1.08%
Mormon	487	0.31%
Muslim	13,078	8.33%
Nation of Islam	1,854	1.18%
Pagan	4,066	2.59%
Protestant	34,030	21.67%
Rastafarian	2,946	1.88%
Santeria	3,123	1.99%
No Preference	46,458	29.58%
Other	5,653	3.59%
Unknown	4,912	3.13%

reason they committed their crimes was because they didn't think a god was watching them, there might be a basis to this concern. But that is not the case. We are also not going to make an argument for atheists being *more* moral than theists. Having interviewed hundreds of nonreligious people—including atheists—for this book and other projects, we know that there are more and less moral atheists. Our point is simple: being religious does not make someone more moral than not being religious.

Do nonreligious people have a different morality than do the religious? In some sense, yes, they do. And this illustrates that morality is socially constructed, since there are also disagreements among the religious as to what is acceptable and unacceptable moral behavior. Judging the nonreligious on the values of the religious is like judging the quality of an apple based on the ideal characteristics of an artichoke.

To answer this question, then, we have to ask a slightly different version: Are nonreligious people more likely than religious people to violate moral codes that are universally accepted? The answer is "No."

3) Will There Be a Decline in Family Values?

This is another concern that requires some unpacking before we can provide an answer based on data. The term "family values" in popular discourse is generally a reference to an archetypal family that consists of a heterosexual couple—a male and a female—with kids, in which the husband works and the wife stays home to take care of the kids. Often included in this notion of family values is opposition to abortion, masturbation, pornography, homosexuality, bisexuality, and gender equality, as well as support for homeschooling and encouraging strict obedience in children. There are a number of organizations in the US that advocate for the above, like the American Family Association, Focus on the Family, and the Family Research Council, among others.

If we assume that "family values" can only refer to the definition above, then it is safe to conclude that secularization and religious exiting in the US will result in a decline in these "family values." As we have detailed in other chapters, nonreligious individuals and those who have left religions are more accepting of abortion, LGBTQ+ individuals, and gender equality.

But this conservative understanding of "family values" also represents an attempt on the part of this specific movement to co-opt the idea that they are the only ones who value the family. And, in a very real sense, this is an illustration of Orwellian "doublespeak," in which their claim that they support family values can often mean just the opposite—they support *specific* values that can result in the destruction of families.

For instance, there are tens of thousands of young people who have come out as gay, lesbian, or bisexual to their conservative Christian parents, parents who adhere to the understanding of family values detailed above. Some of those youth are kicked out of their homes and disowned by their parents who claim to hold "family values," leading to particularly high rates of homelessness, poverty, and suicide among such youths.[23] Another illustration is the dissolution of heterosexual marriages because one of the marriage partners uses pornography and/or masturbates.[24]

And, of course, children who no longer share the religious beliefs of their parents and come out about their nonbelief have had relationships strained or even ruined (as discussed in the previous chapter). We could give quite a few examples of this from our interview data, but here we'll highlight just two.

The first is Tesha, a former Catholic who you'll recall from chapter 3. She's the divorced small business owner whose first memory of religion as a child was being "terrified" at her brother's catechism after she was told that those who don't take first communion go to hell. She reflected on when she told her parents, in her late 20s, that she no longer believed in the religious doctrines she was raised with. The best her parents could do was deny she was telling the truth:

> When I told my parents, that was certainly a negative experience. I told my mom about 5 years ago and I told my dad as well, and I think the both of them were doing the whole cognitive dissonance thing, because they still don't really believe that I'm an atheist. So I think that they are both in some pretty serious denial about it.
> Q: They don't take you seriously?
> A: Initially, I think they saw it as a phase. Now that it's gone on so long, I think they've both just kind of resigned themselves to the denial thing.
> Q: What's your [relationship] like with them [now]?
> A: There have been some rough periods, especially concerning this last election. My dad has been pretty cruel and has sent us some pretty cruel emails about liberals and atheists. . . .

The second example is Madison. She grew up in a fundamentalist Christian family, was a member of a charismatic Pentecostal church, and described her upbringing as "very strict." She faced the "double problem" of coming out as both gay and a nonbeliever within a relatively short time period. Having questioned the Christian faith she grew up with in her teenage years she, in her words, "finally figured out" that she was also gay, and decided to tell her mom, who eventually learned a short while later that she no longer believed in the religion she inherited from them.

> They [her parents] hated gay people. They thought we were horrible people. The only explanation possible for gay people was that they are aliens.

That's how I explain it. But they thought that gays should be killed. And then I realized I was gay, and I thought, "This is fucked up." So I had guilt and shame, and I was suicidal and I thought that I was going to hell even though I didn't really believe in that . . . [but] the guilt is just overwhelming. So I told my mom, and she basically disowned me the day I told her. And then *she* became suicidal too, because it shook her faith. So that was all going on, but I was living with them at the time. They didn't kick me out but—well my dad didn't know at this time, he finally figured it out that I was gay.

Q: You never confronted him about it?

A: No, that would have been really bad. I don't think he would have killed me literally, but I was afraid, because it was a bad thing. My dad was a judge, and he was the number one head honcho at the church and everything. But it was just scary. So I slowly just got away from the Christian thing. . . . I was agnostic for quite a while, I [tried] not to think about it.

In the situations described above, what is actually happening is that "values" are being prioritized above "family," illustrating that the conservative understanding of "family values" is really not always about the family and its importance, but rather the importance of a specific set of conservative values. If a member of the family violates these specific conservative values, their status as a member of the family will be jeopardized. In short, "family values" are rarely about valuing family itself, other than in the very narrow sense described above.

If, instead of the Orwellian "family values" interpretation, we focus on actually valuing the family, there are not substantial differences in how important people consider families to be in their lives. The World Values Survey included a series of questions asking how important six things were in the lives of the survey participants. The results are depicted in figure 6.3:

What we see in this figure is that there are only marginal differences in how important religious and nonreligious individuals consider family, friends, leisure time, politics, and work. The only item on which these three groups significantly disagree is how important religion is.

What about actual family structure? Are the nonreligious and those who leave religion more likely to be divorced than are the religious? Not according to the General Social Survey. Using data from 2010 to 2021

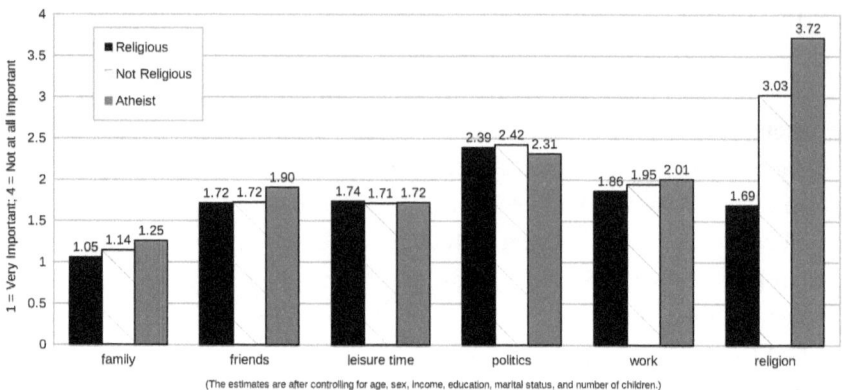

Figure 6.3. Importance of Aspects of Life Among Religious, Not Religious, and Atheists (Average Marginal Effects). (Source: World Values Survey, Wave 7)

on our three groups of interest, the probability of being divorced after controlling for age, education, income, sex, and race is .07 for those who were never religious, .08 for those who left religions, and .07 for those who stayed or joined religions.[25] In other words, after controlling for other demographic factors, whether or not someone left a religion, was never religious, or stayed/joined a religion doesn't change the fact that they have about a 7% to 8% chance of having divorced. The implication here is pretty straightforward—even if the vast majority of people in the US were to be nonreligious, there is no reason to think that this will result in the collapse of families with everyone divorcing. It is likely that fewer people will choose to marry in the first place and more people will cohabit instead, but secularization in the US will not result in the destruction of families.

Are the marriages of religious people in the US happier than those of the nonreligious? The GSS indicates that is not the case either. We compared marital happiness between religious exiters (1.43 on a 3-point scale where 1 = very happy and 3 = not too happy) to that of the never religious (1.37) and those who have stayed religious or joined (1.42). We controlled for age, race, sex, income, and education. For all three of our groups, they report their marriages to be somewhere between very happy and pretty happy with negligible differences between the three groups.

Finally, a healthy sex life has been shown to contribute to relationship quality. The GSS indicates that all three groups are having sex somewhere between once a month and 2 to 3 times a month. There aren't notable differences there, either.

All of the above leads us to conclude that, if one's understanding of family values is the conservative one—anti-abortion, anti-LGBTQ+, anti-pornography, etc.—then, yes, there will be changes in the US as a result of people leaving religion. But if one's real concern about the family is whether people will value families, want to have families, work to maintain their families, and find meaning and fulfillment in their families, there is no cause for concern here.

4) Will Civic Engagement Decline?

Civic engagement is any type of individual or group activity that works toward addressing public concerns, like voting, environmental activism, or charitable work. Generally included in civic engagement is any type of involvement in formal organizations that are designed to benefit the members of those organizations. Attending meetings of a teacher's union or the annual conference of a professional association for accountants would count as civic engagement as opposed to a group of friends who get together to play Dungeons & Dragons or watch a soccer match on TV together. Also considered civic engagement would be volunteering at a soup kitchen or donating blood. There is some research suggesting civic engagement has declined in the US over the last 60 years or so.[26]

An important distinction to note here is that there are at least two types of civic engagement. There is civic engagement designed to primarily benefit the members of an organization. Members of sports supporters' groups, like the Pittsburgh Steelers' Steel City Mafia or The American Outlaws of the US Men's National Soccer Team, participate in these organizations primarily to benefit other members of the organization. Such civic engagement is internally-focused. Secondarily, their participation in these organizations might benefit other fans and potentially raise awareness of the teams they support and of the sport in general. There is also civic engagement that is designed to primarily benefit others. Regularly volunteering at a local animal shelter does not have as its primary aim benefitting the person who is volunteering but rather the animals that have been helped and potentially those in the community who are served by that animal shelter. This is externally-focused civic engagement.

We draw this distinction because much of the civic engagement that takes place as part of religious involvement is internally-focused, though there is some externally-focused civic engagement as well.[27] Many members of religious congregations consider any position they hold in their congregation "service" so long as they are not paid for it. If they are paid, that, of course, is work. Standing in the foyer welcoming people or sweeping up after a social is primarily going to benefit the members of the congregation. Some religions also encourage externally-focused civic engagement among their members. The LDS Church, for instance, regularly highlights on its website[28] their Helping Hands program, in which members of the religion get together to help non-members, particularly after natural disasters.[29] Other congregations run or donate to soup kitchens or other services that benefit the poor or needy.

Drawing a distinction between these two types of civic engagement is not intended as a critique of either type. It is just a helpful distinction to make when considering what the ramifications of declining religiosity might be for the US. If the bulk of the civic engagement that results from religious participation is internally-focused, then, if religiosity declines in the US, what will be lost is civic engagement that primarily benefits those institutions. If, however, most of the civic engagement that is derived from religious participation was externally-focused, that would have more substantial consequences for American society in general.[30] We believe the vast majority of civic engagement that derives from religious participation in the US is internally-focused, similar to what recent research on volunteering in Canada found.[31] As a result, as more and more people leave religions, the primary consequence as relates to civic engagement is that there will be fewer people to volunteer within religions themselves.

Of course, we have some data that can help shed light on this issue. The World Values Survey asked participants about their involvement with a variety of organizations, from religions to labor unions. Participants could indicate whether they were "not a member," an "inactive member," or an "active member." In figures 6.4 and 6.5, we examine just the predicted probabilities[32] of active membership in these organizations by religiosity.

Not surprisingly, a higher percentage of religious individuals are active members of religious organizations compared to nonreligious

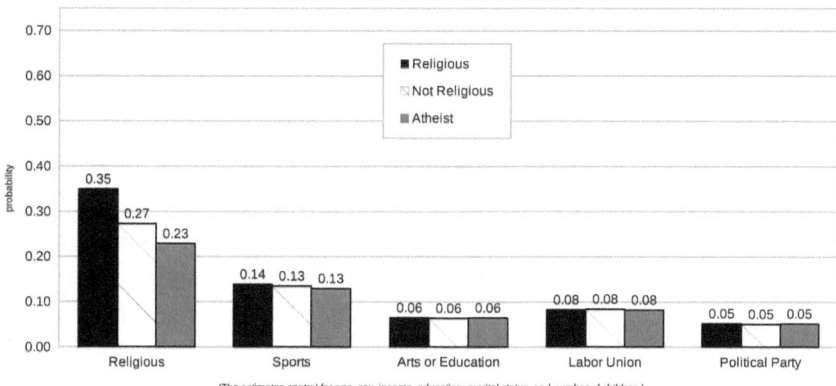

Figure 6.4. Predicted Probability of Active Involvement in Organizations Among Religious, Not Religious, and Atheists (Average Marginal Effects). (Source: World Values Survey, Wave 7)

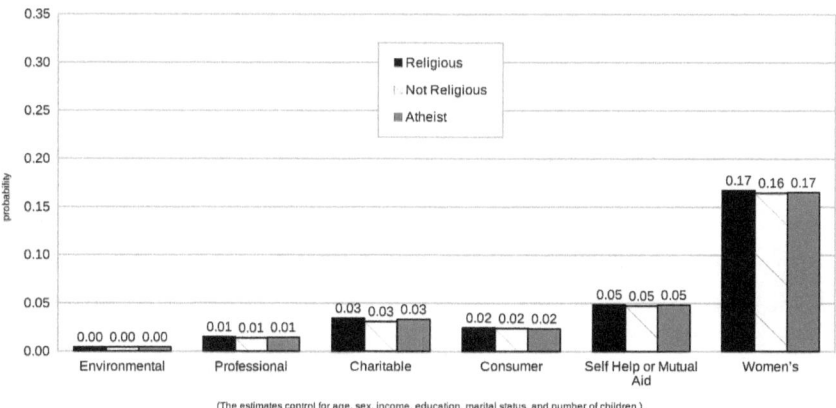

Figure 6.5. Predicted Probability of Active Involvement in Organizations Among Religious, Not Religious, and Atheists (Average Marginal Effects). (Source: World Values Survey, Wave 7)

individuals and atheists. What we want to emphasize, however, is that, for all the other types of organizations, the differences in active membership are basically negligible (apparently American atheists aren't that into sports). Religious and nonreligious individuals are generally as likely to be active members of arts and educational organizations, labor unions, political parties, environmental organizations, professional organizations, charitable organizations, self-help organizations, and women's organizations. The only organization where there is a very large difference is active involvement with religious organizations, which is exactly what we would expect.

What does this mean? With more Americans leaving religion, that last form of civic engagement will decline. It would be shocking if it didn't. However, most of that civic engagement is internally-focused and designed to support the members of religions. Even so, that is a form of civic engagement and it will decline. Despite the decline in religious civic engagement, there is little reason to be concerned about civic engagement generally. Nonreligious individuals are civically engaged, just not with the aim of benefitting religious organizations. Their focus is on a variety of other organizations.

We certainly don't want to ignore all of the good, externally-focused work that members of religions and religious organizations do. In the city where one of us (Cragun) lives, there is a religiously affiliated organization that is fairly well-known for its charitable work, Metropolitan Ministries. Metropolitan Ministries serves about 75,000 meals a month, among its other charitable activities.[33] That translates to about 900,000 meals a year. That is extremely commendable. Also located in the same city—Tampa, Florida—is a branch of Feeding America called Feeding Tampa Bay. In 2020, Feeding Tampa Bay served 66 million meals.[34] In Kalamazoo, Michigan, where the other author (Smith) lives, there is Kalamazoo Gospel Ministries, and a West Michigan chapter of Feeding America that does similar charitable work. Indeed, there are examples all around the country of both religious and secular civic and charitable work. We are not trying to suggest that this is a competition.[35] It's not. Both of these organizations are helping people in need. Our point is simply that there are secular alternatives to religious charities and some of those alternative organizations are already more effective than the religious options. If religiosity continues to decline in Tampa, just like it is in the rest of the US, the hungry will still be fed.

Will civic engagement decline as a result of declining religiosity? Yes. But the vast majority of that civic engagement is internally-focused and designed to maintain the religions themselves. It is not this particular kind of civic engagement that is needed to maintain a cohesive, functioning society. From our perspective, this is not a cause for concern.

5) Will People Have Fewer Kids?

As with many of these concerns, this is a little bit complicated, but, *ceteris paribus*, yes, people who leave religions will probably have fewer kids than those who remain religious.

Why people have kids is complicated. There are a lot of factors involved—age at which they have their first child, health, income, education, race/ethnicity, etc.[36] The factor that interests us here, of course, is religiosity. Why might religious individuals have more children on average? Some religions reject artificial forms of birth control or any form of birth control, including abortion.[37] Other religions teach that it is the responsibility of members of the religion to have children and to raise those children as devout members of the faith.[38] Religions that prohibit premarital sex also tend to encourage their members to marry at younger ages (in part to compensate for the fact that they aren't supposed to have sex until they are married); marrying at younger ages increases the odds of having more kids.[39] There are a number of clear reasons why religious adherents are likely to have more kids than are the nonreligious.[40]

At the same time, there is a nearly universal pressure driving the number of kids people have down: economics. For many people today, kids are a net expense, not a source of financial profit. For those living on a farm, it's possible that kids—working for free or at a substantially reduced wage—can actually help their parents make money. But for most parents today, children cost money—lots of money.[41] As a result of that economic pressure—among a number of other factors—people are having fewer kids. Declining birth rates can be observed among pretty much all religions over time.[42]

We compared the average number of children for our three groups we have been examining throughout the book—those who were raised nonreligious, people who left religion, and those who were raised and stay religious—using GSS data (controlling for basic demographics). Religious individuals average about 1.8 kids, while exiters average 1.4 and the never religious average 1.5.

The difference between those who were never religious and exiters is not statistically significant, but the differences between those two groups and the religious are statistically significant. In other words, nonreligious people do have fewer kids on average than do religious people, as other scholars have found.[43]

One common reason given for why lower fertility rates is a concern is economic. There are politicians and pundits who argue that a declining population will slow or hamper the economy.[44] The argument is simplistic—if there are fewer people to buy things, build houses, travel, etc., demand for goods and services will be reduced. Likewise, there will be more elderly people and fewer kids to pay for them, resulting in a greater percentage of GDP going to elder care.[45] Other macro level concerns that often accompany declining GDP are concerns about countries appearing to be healthy and powerful, declining military might, and declining international influence.

In reality, demographers, economists, and sociologists who actually study fertility are not nearly as concerned about lower fertility rates as are politicians and pundits.[46] Fertility rates decrease *and* increase over time, often without clear explanations. Lower fertility rates in developing countries are often correlated with higher economic growth. There are also potentially other benefits from declining populations, like reducing climate change, damage to the environment, overpopulation, famine, disease, competition over resources, conflict, and war. And even in countries where we have started to see declining populations, like Japan, their GDP hasn't actually decreased, as is so often predicted by the doomsayers.[47]

Keep in mind that GDP is a crude economic indicator that governments use to suggest that they are managing a country well. GDP is also a macro level indicator of just one aspect of the social world—whether a country's productivity is increasing. Once a country is economically developed, GDP says almost nothing about quality of life for individuals. The only real concern then, for which there is currently no evidence, is whether declining fertility reduces individual quality of life. At present, the opposite is more likely to be true, particularly for women, as quality of life tends to improve with fewer kids, not decline.

Fertility rates have declined and the populations of many countries and the world are currently projected to decline by the end of the twenty-first century. Careful planning and considered adjustment may very well result in better quality of life as a result.

Thus, is it a problem if people—particularly nonreligious individuals—have fewer kids?

No.

6) Will People Be Less Informed about Religion?

The answer to this question is complicated for several reasons. First, in a 2010 survey that received quite a bit of attention, Pew found that those most knowledgeable about religion in the US were actually atheists and agnostics.[48] Those who identified their religious affiliation as "nothing in particular" were just below the national average of 16 questions about religion correct out of 32, as shown in figure 6.6.

What Pew's study showed is that, contrary to what one might expect, those who most strongly reject aspects of religion—atheists and agnostics—were actually the most knowledgeable about it. The nonreligious, many of whom are indifferent about religion, did not score substantially below most other people in the US. If we were to go just off of this study from Pew, we would likely conclude that people who leave religion are probably just as knowledgeable about religion as those who stay, if not more so.

But we also want to complicate this question somewhat by asking another one: Why should those who are not religious have any knowledge about religion at all? We are of two minds on this second question. We could argue that there is absolutely no reason to be knowledgeable about religion if you're not religious just like there is no reason to be highly knowledgeable about model horses if you're not into model horses or comic books if you're not into comic books.[49] For many people in highly developed and generally secular countries, religion is only marginally a part of their lives. As a result, there is really no reason for them to spend substantial amounts of time accumulating knowledge about religion when that knowledge will only rarely be utilized. They may periodically encounter references to religion in books, movies, or in the media, but, if it interests them, they could quickly search the internet for a better understanding.

The counter-argument is that religion continues to influence the world in 2023, when we were writing this chapter. For instance, the US

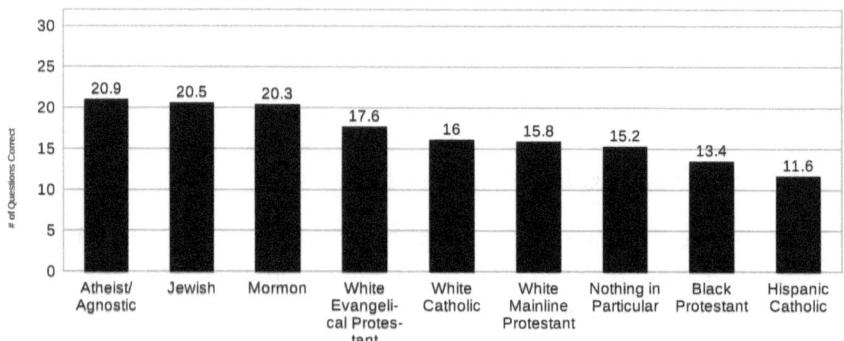

Figure 6.6. Average Questions Correct out of 32 Religious Knowledge Questions by Religious Affiliation. (Source: Pew, 2010)

and its allies recently left Afghanistan, which was taken over by the Taliban, a fundamentalist Muslim group. It would be helpful for people around the world to have some knowledge of religion in order to better understand why the Taliban took over Afghanistan and what they are likely to do with the country under their rule. In 2022 the Supreme Court overturned Roe v. Wade. It is not a coincidence that the six judges who voted to overturn Roe are all conservative Christians. Given that opposition to abortion is largely rooted in religion, it may make sense for people to have some knowledge of religion.

This leads to our last point. In many developed countries around the world, students are required as part of their primary and/or secondary education to take courses in religion; this is often referred to as "Religious Education" or RE. RE in many of these countries is very much like a comparative religions course one might get in college, which examines the beliefs, values, and behaviors of a variety of religions and, increasingly, of the nonreligious. What makes these courses particularly interesting is that they put all religions on an equal playing field; at least, that is what the curriculum requires. In other words, the instructors in those courses are not supposed to proselytize or apologize for specific religions but rather are supposed to simply educate students about a wide swath of religions.[50]

We could be persuaded to support the idea of teaching RE classes that are objective and neutral. We might go a step further, however. One of our sons (Cragun's) recently took a course on Greek and Roman mythology. As a result of that course, he started making connections in literature when characters or stories from those now defunct religions were mentioned. Why largely defunct religions are taught as myth while extant religions are not is an interesting question, particularly when it comes to offering RE courses in countries where anywhere from one-third to more than three-fourths of the students in those courses are nonreligious and nonbelievers. That strikes us as a compelling illustration of religious privilege—showing favoritism toward religion. It would make far more sense to combine RE concerning still extant religions with any discussion of ancient religions. The end result will be populations that are more knowledgeable about religion in general.[51]

7) Will People Find Less Meaning in Life?

There are a number of studies that examine the relationship between having meaning or purpose in life and mental health.[52] What most of these studies find is either no relationship or a very, very small relationship between meaning and mental health. Generously interpreting those studies suggests that there might be some benefit to mental health from having meaning in life or purpose, but such a benefit is, at best, small.

What do we mean by a small benefit to mental health? Imagine we are trying to grow a bunch of tomato plants and we want to find which fertilizers result in the healthiest, best and most productive plants. We find a standard, readily available fertilizer that has a really substantial effect on the plants, increasing their size and yield on average by 50% over using no fertilizer. We should definitely use that fertilizer. Then our kooky friend Alexandra comes by and tells us that she has gotten great results by adding kale that she has chewed for 5 hours to the soil surrounding her tomato plants. While Alexandra is odd and her suggestion is even stranger, we have had some of her tomatoes, and they were pretty good, so we decide to give it a try. But, as data-driven gardeners, we are very careful in our measurements. We measure and weigh every tomato plant at their peak so we can determine how well they do. And, we conduct an experiment. We have 10 plants with no fertilizer or chewed kale (Group A). We have 10 plants with just our really good fertilizer (Group B). We have another 10 plants with just chewed kale (Group C). And, finally, 10 more plants with both kale and the good fertilizer (Group D).

After growing the plants, we find that Group B was, again, 50% bigger than Group A; our fertilizer works. We find that some of the plants in Group C were 1% bigger than Group A, but some of the plants were not different at all, making us wonder about chewed kale as a fertilizer. And we find that all but one of the plants in Group D were the same as the plants in Group B and that one plant was 1% bigger than the others. In other words, we occasionally find that chewing up kale and adding it to the soil might increase our yield by 1%, but only rarely. And spending 5 hours chewing kale is a lot of time for, at best, only marginal improvements in our yield. Would you continue fretting about chewing up all that kale for maybe 1% improvement in yield some of the time?

We apologize for the digression (it won't be our last in this section). We aren't trying to be glib with our metaphor; but this is basically what meaning in life research looks like when it comes to benefits to health. At best, meaning in life accounts for 1% or 2% of the variation in some mental health outcome (e.g., depression, stress, anxiety, etc.) but that effect is inconsistent. That is technical language to say someone with a very clear sense of purpose or meaning in life might experience a 1% improvement in mental health, some of the time, maybe.

Adroit readers might be wondering at this point why we are even discussing meaning in life if it really does *not* matter for mental health. That is a great question. Remember, we indicated these were concerns *people* had.[53] These are not, for the most part, our concerns. Since the claim has been made that people who have meaning or purpose are healthier, we figured we'd take a look and see whether this is true. Some may value having meaning or purpose just because they value having meaning or purpose.[54] However, having meaning or purpose in life really doesn't matter for health.

But let's move beyond any connection to health and talk about meaning more generally. We pulled some data from the General Social Survey that asked about meaning in life. There are two questions, one that is specifically geared toward theists and one that is not. Figure 6.7 shows the results of asking the first question, "Life is meaningful only because God exists" for the three groups of interest—those who were never religious, those who have left religion, and those who have stayed or joined.

Not surprisingly, there are big differences here. Religious individuals are far more likely to agree or strongly agree with this statement, though

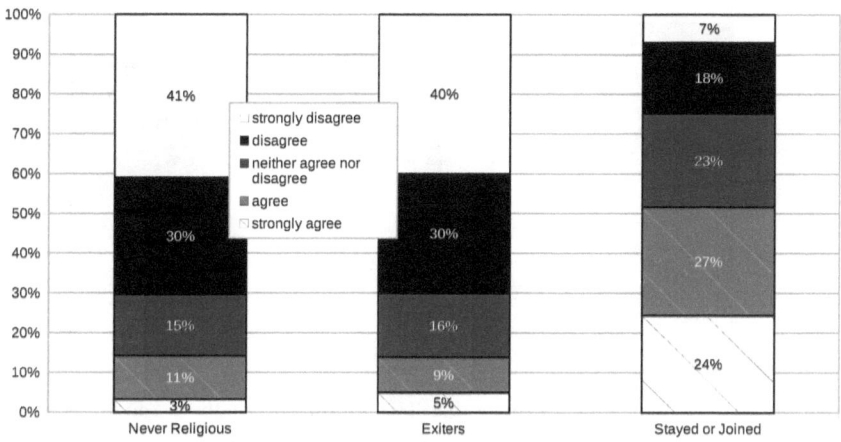

Figure 6.7. Agreement with Statement that "Life is Meaningful Only Because God Exists" Among Never Religious, Exiters, and Religious. (Source: GSS, 1991–2018)

25% of the religious still disagree with this statement and another 23% are neutral.

The second statement participants were given is quite different, "Life is only meaningful if you provide the meaning yourself." As figure 6.8 indicates, the majority of never religious people and exiters agree or strongly agree with this statement.

Neither of these questions directly captures whether there are differences in how much meaning someone reports in their life, but they do illustrate that nonreligious people are aware that they can provide meaning in their life.

The real concern here, of course, is nihilism (specifically, existential nihilism). Nihilism is the idea or perspective that life has no intrinsic meaning or purpose. Nihilism seems to genuinely terrify some people.[55] The idea that we are an insignificant group of sentient primates frantically trying to make a difference on a singular orb that is eventually going to be destroyed by our sun in one branch of one galaxy in a massive universe and most likely none of us will have any lasting impact on the universe can be somewhat disheartening. That doesn't mean it isn't true. For some, it is a bit depressing to realize that nothing we do will really matter a billion years from now or, for most of us, a million or even a hundred years from now. Our lives are, from that perspective,

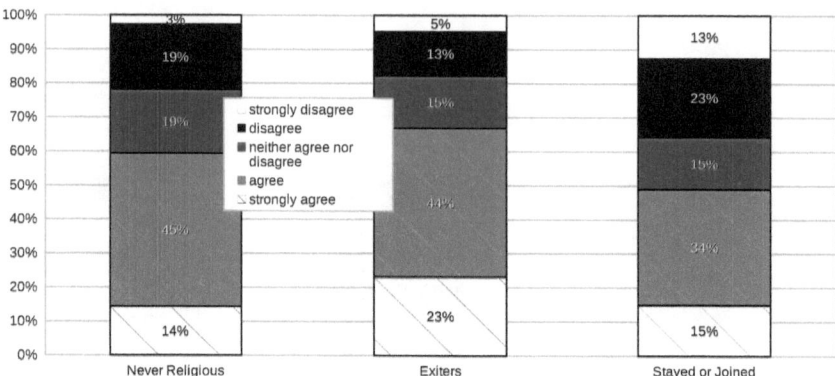

Figure 6.8. Agreement with Statement that "Life is Only Meaningful if You Provide the Meaning Yourself" Among Never Religious, Exiters, and Religious. (Source: GSS, 1991–2018)

completely meaningless. If there is a god, some people believe, then their lives are not meaningless because their lives matter to a god or because they will continue to exist after their physical body has died.

Thinking about meaning from such a long-term perspective can be overwhelming. But that is just *one* perspective when it comes to meaning. If we take a more immediate—or here-and-now—perspective, it's obvious that humans are capable of giving meaning to, or creating their own meaning for, their lives. We are sentient beings—products of the cosmos—capable of reflecting on our lives, and indeed, on our lives *in relation to* that cosmos. In this sense, our lives *do* have cosmic meaning. This may not negate the problem of the meaning of our lives a billion years into the future, but . . . We can matter to our family and friends and they can matter to us. We can try to make a difference in other people's lives. We can make our lives meaningful. Love, kindness, compassion, and every other human quality we care about remains exactly as important as it is—these things aren't diminished in the least should we not find ourselves immortal or part of a divine plan not of our making. And, as the data above indicate, many nonreligious individuals are aware that meaning is something you overlay onto your life, not something that is inherent in life itself.

As some philosophers have argued, it may be that existence is meaningful precisely *because* it ends. The brevity of our existence concentrates its meaningfulness. If it literally never ended (i.e., if, as most religions claim, there's a conscious soul in a perpetual state of existence), could that undermine the meaningfulness of existence? Here's a line from philosopher Ludwig Wittgenstein about life and death that is occasionally referenced by secular people: *"Death is not an event in life; we do not live to experience death. If we take eternity to mean not infinite temporal duration but timelessness, then eternal life belongs to those who live in the present. Our life has no end in the way in which our visual field has no limits."* The essential idea here is that it's the present that matters. It's always the case that it's the present that matters. From this view, which is consistent with the naturalistic worldview expressed by our participants in the previous chapter, nothingness is not something. Nothing, by definition, can't be *experienced*. As the naturalist philosopher Thomas Clark argues (and as Wittgenstein might agree), we *are* eternal from the perspective of subjective conscious experience itself.[56]

We, of course, do not claim to know what, if anything, happens after death. Maybe conscious experience in some way survives the death of the body. Maybe it doesn't. Either way, all living people, including nonreligious people, will carry on creating meaning in life. We can't help it. The "what's it all mean, what's it all for?" question might not even be a valid one. Humans don't much ask this question of non-human sentient beings (e.g., What's the aardvark's purpose in life? Is it extracting meaning from its experience?)[57] and it even feels a bit awkward applying it to the short lives of early humans. In our estimation, questions of existence and the problem of meaning itself are something that arose out of and along with culture and the evolution of our species, not something a priori to our existence as such.

Why the digression on philosophical questions of existence in a sociological book on religious exiting? Well, our research demonstrates that nonreligious people are no less interested in, or capable of, contemplating such questions while creating and finding meaning and purpose in existence. The data, the evidence, and the growing empirical literature on the topic show this.[58] Moreover, the accounts of our interviewees throughout, and the survey findings above in no way suggest religious exiters abandon meaningful lives when they abandon religion. Many of our participants were keen to highlight this. Many, in fact, have thought long and hard about their existence, and, to make an obvious point, they don't see their having lost religion as something that's plunged them into meaninglessness.

Crissy, whom we quoted several times in chapters 4 and 5, offers a compelling illustration. Crissy trained as a psychotherapist and considers herself an existentialist. She spent a lot of time thinking about these things, and she nicely summarized the perspective of many of our participants:

> We have some unique things about us, but when all is said and done there is no *inherent* meaning in life. I'm an existentialist. . . . Every generation has to try and find the best way to make it through this existence in this life and I think that over the generations people have learned ways to make life meaningful and valuable. I think our parents hand us those things to make it easier for us. Like, "This is what *we* value, this is what *we* think is important," and that at some point every growing adolescent and adult has to re-examine those things and decide for themselves. Obviously that will always be a reflection of where [we are] born, who [we are] born to, who [we] grew up with, and the social milieu in which [we] developed. . . . I was a cognitive behaviorist because I realize that our brains are really, really powerful. That certainly we are physical beings and that neurologically we don't have what I would consider free will all the time. There are a lot of things about us that are somewhat determined, that don't necessarily *feel* determined. But where we do seem to have a lot of choice is making decisions about what we think is important, what we think is valuable, what we think is right or wrong and I find that this is the great mystery in life. It's the great struggle in life. I find it endlessly entertaining to observe human behavior and it's very informative for me to study other civilizations, other tribes that still exist on the planet where you think, "Wow!" A lot of different people believe in a lot of different things and are functioning quite well and psychologically they're healthy [though] they believe a lot of different things. I love science. I've always been attracted to scientific endeavors—learning more, exploring more about the universe. I'm very comfortable with not [always] knowing, but exploring. I don't need to have an answer to feel safe but I do always think I should be questioning and seeking and learning more.

Most of our interviewees were not as elaborate on these points as Crissy was, and there's a lot to unpack here. But we can be concise because virtually all our religious exiters shared a few things in common with Crissy regarding meaning and existence. (1) They believe meaning and purpose aren't just "out there" waiting for us to tap into them. We must create it ourselves. Religion is one source of meaning, but not the essential or only one. (2) They have core values. They care about families and relationships and the well-being of humanity. (3) They are focused on the life we know we have. This life. That's what matters. (4) They are okay with ambiguity and uncertainty in life. We should always be questioning and learning, since we don't know everything, and probably never will. Some may still be nihilists, but only in the distal and philosophical sense. In the proximal and pragmatic sense, they are overflowing with purpose.

As most scholars and religious people themselves will be quick to point out, religion provides meaning, purpose, and can motivate behavior. Of course that's true. Our argument here is based on what became clear in our interviews and what is implied in the survey data: that religion is not *necessary* for this. In fact, skepticism about gods, an afterlife, a preordained plan, and other religious claims can itself be a powerful motivator to try to improve the world *now*.

Are, then, those who leave religion, and secular people in general, more likely to reject the idea that there is a preordained, *inherent* meaning or purpose in life?

Yes.

Does this *matter* for living a life that affirms values consistent with being and doing good in the world?

No.

As more Americans leave religion, are they likely to find less meaning in life?

(wait for it . . .) No.

8) Will People Be Less Healthy?

There is a cottage industry dedicated to trying to make the claim that religion—variously defined, measured, and understood—positively contributes to peoples' health. Countless news articles have trumpeted the claim that religious people are healthier than nonreligious people.[59] There is a journal called *Religion and Health* that publishes only research examining this question. And there are scholars who have dedicated their careers to the idea that religion makes people healthier.[60]

These efforts are almost entirely wishful thinking. Before we show data, we want readers to think through these claims with us theoretically, as this is a useful exercise. Again, recall the three aspects of religiosity we've discussed throughout the book—belief, behavior, and identity. Pause and consider for a moment: Knowing what you know about what contributes to someone's physical, mental, or social health, how might religious belief, behavior, or identity lead to better health?

Let's consider identity first. How might claiming a religious identity—Jewish, Catholic, Southern Baptist, Mormon, Evangelical Lutheran Church of America, etc.—lead to someone having better health? Are there group identities in the US that somehow translate into better or worse health? The answer is a very trepidatious "Yes," but really only indirectly. For instance, racial identities have been shown to be related to differential health outcomes.[61] After controlling for all the relevant differences in income, education, and health insurance access, there is often still a residual effect on health from someone's race.[62] The causes for these disparities are probably the result of additional factors we have not captured, including cultural differences and discrimination, recognizing that it is virtually impossible to explain all the differences in outcomes when studying humans. In other words, being classified as white in the US doesn't result in improved health, but being classified as Black results in worse health, likely due to healthcare and other forms of discrimination (net of all the other factors). But race is quite different from religion for one simple reason: most of the time, someone's religion can be hidden from a doctor or healthcare worker. That is much more challenging to do with race. Certainly it is possible for a healthcare worker to find out that someone is a Jehovah's Witness and then choose to discriminate against them when providing care, though more likely targets of discrimination are Jews, Muslims, and atheists.[63] Even so, the only real path by which group identities might contribute to someone's health is through discrimination. Members of marginalized groups or categories might experience sufficient discrimination in healthcare provision or in society generally such that their overall health may be lower than that of members of non-marginalized groups.[64] But this would only matter if: (a) their marginal group identification is known, and (b) if those providing healthcare find that group identification objectionable.

What about religious beliefs? How might, say, believing in a god or higher power contribute to better health over not believing in a god or higher power? Or believing in: heaven, hell, demons, angels, Jesus, Mohammad, Zeus, the Torah, reincarnation, or that a god is married? Can you think of a mechanism by which believing in angels would benefit someone's physical, mental, or social health more than, say, believing in fairies? Honestly, we cannot. There is no reason to think that holding specific beliefs that have traditionally been associated with religions would prove beneficial or detrimental to someone's health. There is no clear mechanism by which this might function. A parallel may help here. Whether or not someone believes aliens have visited earth will make absolutely no difference to their health. People believe weird things. It's only when beliefs translate into behaviors that we might see an effect on health, which leads us to . . .

The final of the three dimensions, behaviors. This is the one area where it may make sense that religiosity could meaningfully contribute to better health. And there are two mechanisms by which this might occur, both of which we will detail here. The first and most obvious way that religious behavior could contribute to health is through getting together with other people who provide a supportive social network. Social support has been shown to improve peoples' social health, and better social health can contribute to better physical and mental health.[65] Keep in mind what we are suggesting here—social support is good for people. Whether that social support comes in the form of membership in a Bible study group at a megachurch, or from friends developed through weekly games of *Magic: The Gathering*, does not matter. What matters is social support. So, if someone regularly attends religious services and, as a result, develops a supportive social network, we can see how that might result in slightly better health. The actual mechanism for improving health is social support, but social support can be derived from religious participation, so religious participation can indirectly improve someone's health.

The second mechanism by which religious behavior might improve someone's health is if a religion prohibits unhealthy behaviors like drinking alcohol, smoking cigarettes, or using illicit drugs. The detrimental effects of all those behaviors on physical health are well-known.[66] As a result, like social support, it is possible that following the behavioral dictates of a religion that prohibits unhealthy behaviors may indirectly result in better health. The mechanism is not the religious behaviors; it is avoiding the unhealthy behaviors. How can we assert this? If an agnostic who has no religious affiliation, has no traditionally religious beliefs, and never participates in any religious services or other activities chooses not to drink alcohol, smoke cigarettes, or use any illicit drugs, will that agnostic receive all the same health benefits as would a Mormon who also avoids these substances because their religion prohibits them? Obviously, the answer is "Yes." And if that is the case, it is not religion that is directly improving health; it is religion encouraging healthy behaviors that then benefit someone's health. The actual mechanism is the healthy behaviors, not religiosity. But we can certainly give religion some credit here if it does in fact increase the odds that someone engages in healthy behaviors.

From a theoretical perspective, religiosity may indirectly improve social health by providing a supportive social network and may indirectly improve physical health if the religion prohibits unhealthy behaviors. Is there any reason to think that religiosity directly benefits health? As the wife of one of us (Cragun), who has a PhD in Public Health, regularly argues, if religions replaced the pews with exercise bikes, the answer might be very different. But, from a theoretical perspective, there is no reason to think that religiosity will directly improve physical, mental, or social health.

Okay. But what do the data indicate? To be doubly certain, we examined variables from both the World Values Survey (just people in the US) on self-reported health (1 = Very good health; 5 = Very poor health), and from the GSS on self-reported health (1 = Excellent; 4 = Poor). After controlling for basic demographic variables in both surveys, there are NO meaningful differences in health. In the World Values Survey, the religious average 2.0, the not religious average 2.0, and atheists average 2.1. In the GSS, the never religious average 2.1, exiters average 2.0, and those who have remained religious average 2.0. Self-reported health isn't a perfect measure of health, but it has been repeatedly shown to be a reasonably accurate measure of someone's overall health. What we find is that religiosity does not matter.

And just to confirm that there are no meaningful differences, we also looked at one other variable in the GSS. Participants were asked how many days out of the last 30 was their physical health poor, which can include illness or injury but also chronic diseases. The never religious averaged 2.7 days out of 30; exiters averaged 2.2; and the religious averaged 2.7 (after controlling for age, race, sex, income, and education). Again, there are no meaningful differences in health based on whether or not someone has exited religion.

To reiterate, we are not claiming that religion makes people more or less healthy. Our argument, which is supported by the data, is that religion may, at best, contribute indirectly to health through reducing discrimination (or, in some cases, increasing it) or by encouraging healthy behaviors. But even those indirect paths toward better health do not appear to matter when you look at data.

Of course, there are other types of health. What about differences in mental health (discussed earlier) or in subjective well-being (a.k.a. happiness)? It turns out that there are no meaningful differences between exiters, those who were never religious, and the religious on these measures either. The GSS also includes a question asking how many days out of the last thirty have participants' mental health not been good. The never religious averaged 3.4, exiters average 3.0, and the religious averaged 3.2. There are not meaningful differences in mental health either.

We also checked to see if religious people were happier than exiters and the never religious. The GSS includes an item asking about participants self-reported happiness that ranges from (1) very happy to (3) not too happy. Net of controls for age, race, sex, income, and education, there is no meaningful difference here, either. The never religious average 2.0, exiters average 2.0, and the religious average 1.9. Religiosity doesn't make people healthier or happier.

If there were large, meaningful differences in physical or mental health or in happiness, we would be concerned. We certainly would not be in favor of people moving toward behaviors or adopting identities that would reduce their health or happiness. We are advocates for healthy behaviors and life choices. And we both draw upon the latest research to guide our own life choices when it comes to factors that will influence our health. However, we see no reason to believe that people leaving religions will be any less healthy or happy than are religious individuals.

9) Will We Move toward a More Consumer-Oriented or Materialistic Society?

Another concern that we have seen, somewhat related to the nihilism question above, is that nonreligious individuals will become more materialistic. The idea here is that, lacking regular reminders about a greater purpose, lacking belief in a divine plan, and/or lacking a connection to the supernatural, nonreligious individuals will instead turn toward consumption and materialism. Unchecked and unexamined consumption is a shallow worldview that focuses only on immediate gratification and fails to take into consideration the impacts of consumerism on the environment and future generations. It prioritizes the consumer's immediate satisfaction and desire over all else, including other living things, the health of the planet, impoverished individuals around the world, and the future.

We worry about this as well. We see people's fixations on consumer products, like those produced by Apple, Nike, and Tesla, and people's slavish devotion to celebrities, like Kim Kardashian, Kanye West, or Neymar, and wonder whether this idolism—of goods and people—is healthy for individuals, societies, and the planet. We have no idea whether the most rabid idolaters are religious or not. But it does seem at times as though these individuals have replaced worshiping deities with deifying companies, products, and sometimes morally questionable people.

In this section, our plan is to determine whether this should be a real concern or not. However, we want to provide an important clarification early on, as there is an unfortunate overlap here that needs to be addressed—the meaning of "materialism." Materialism can mean two things. The first definition is the one we described in the previous paragraph—considering material possessions, like consumer goods, more important than people or ethics or the environment. The second definition of materialism is quite different; it is the belief that everything that exists must be composed of matter. Someone can be materialistic in both ways. For instance, someone who rejects the existence of the supernatural and has built up a collection of rare, unworn Nike shoes while never donating or helping those less fortunate than themselves might fit the bill. But it is also the case that one can be a materialist in the second sense without being a materialist in the first sense, and vice versa.

An individual could reject the existence of the supernatural but find a great deal of satisfaction in helping others, working to reduce pollution or climate change, or trying to change the working conditions of the very people who produce our consumer goods. Or an individual could be deeply spiritual and also be caught up in having the perfect house, clothes, makeup, and aesthetic that helps reflect that spirituality. It is rather unfortunate that "materialism" has two very distinct definitions, one of which is largely considered to be negative (the first one) while the other is neutral (the second one). When those who are concerned about people leaving religion level accusations that religious exiters are materialistic, such individuals may be correct even when they mean something entirely different.

Importantly, then, we are less concerned in this section about the second understanding of materialism—that nothing exists except matter—as that is not a problematic way of thinking about the world. There are many nonreligious individuals who would identify as materialists in that sense. The real concern is whether nonreligious individuals are more likely to be materialistic in the first sense—valuing material possessions over more selfless or altruistic concerns. Is this something that we should worry about as millions of Americans leave religion?

This is a challenging question to answer, as many surveys and studies do not address this directly. One very recent study that addressed this question in part found that atheists were actually more ethical consumers than were theists.[67] The authors compared atheists to theists on four dimensions of consumer behavior and values: actively benefiting from problems (e.g., "Giving misleading price information to a clerk for an unpriced item."), passively benefiting from consumer problems (e.g., "Not saying anything when the waitress miscalculates the bill in your favor."), engaging in questionable ethical behavior (e.g., "Not telling the truth when negotiating the price of a new automobile."), and behavior that does not appear to cause direct harm to providers of goods and services even though it possibly does (e.g., "Watching pirated movies."). While the differences on all of these behaviors and values were relatively small, atheists were more ethical than theists on every dimension.

We found some questions in the General Social Survey that address this question to some degree as well. These questions asked how frequently participants engaged in selfless behaviors over the last 12 months,

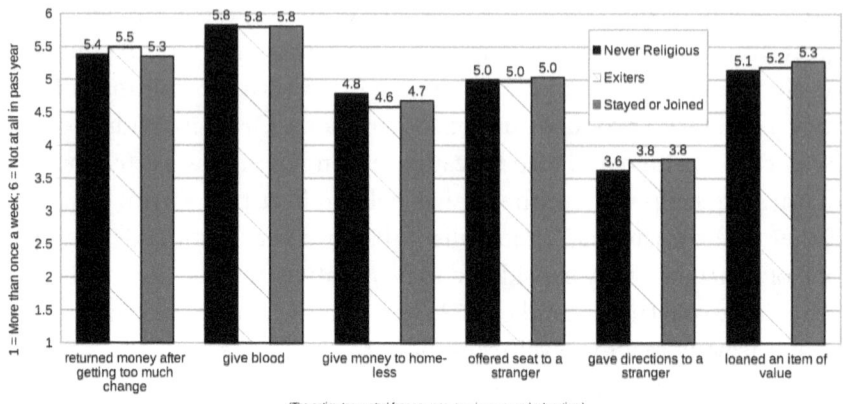

Figure 6.9. Engagement in Selfless Acts Among Never Religious, Exiters, and Religious (Average Marginal Effects). (Source: GSS, 2010–2021)

behaviors that could be considered the opposite of self-interested consumerism. Figure 6.9 below shows the results.

With pretty much all of these behaviors, there are no substantive differences. Nonreligious individuals are just as likely as religious individuals to return money after getting too much change, to give blood, to give money to the homeless, to offer their seat to a stranger, to give directions to a stranger, and to loan an item of value to someone else. If the concern is that people who leave religion will focus on their own self-interest to the detriment of others and society, the data in figure 6.9 above suggest that they are just as self-interested (or, inversely, just as selfless) as are the religious. Once again, though data on the somewhat abstract question of materialism is limited, our conclusion in this chapter is that nothing is likely to change.

We found an additional set of questions in the GSS that seemed to speak to this concern. These questions asked participants about their willingness to make certain sacrifices in order to help the environment (1 = very willing; 5 = not at all willing): would they be willing to pay higher prices, pay higher taxes, and accept a cut in living standards to help the environment. Across the board, there were no meaningful differences on these items between the never religious, exiters, and the religious. The scores for all of them were in the middle of the scale, indicating they were, on average, neither willing nor unwilling to do these things. All three of these questions represent a way in which people are willing to put the environment ahead of what may potentially be their own self-interest. In other words, if those who leave religions are unabashed consumers and materialists, so, too, are the religious.

As the data in this section indicate, a turn toward self-interested consumption and materialism does not appear to be a valid concern as America secularizes. Even so, we think it is worth pointing out what some nonreligious individuals in Norway have done to curtail this possibility. The Human-Etisk Forbund (Norwegian Humanist Association) has developed a civil confirmation ceremony with a corresponding course that focuses on identity, critical thinking, ethics, philosophy, respect, tolerance, humanism, and taking responsibility.[68] This course and the accompanying ceremony are for teenagers, helping young people to reflect on who they are and what they value at an important time in their development. Given that many governments rely upon consumption to boost GDP, it's not entirely surprising that curtailing consumption and trying to help citizens develop greater altruism has been pulled from school curricula. Maybe it's time for that to be added back into what we teach our children.

10) Will People Be as Kind to Strangers?

The Golden Rule is a well-known guideline for how someone should treat others. Many religions have some variation of the rule in a sacred text or in their body of writings. In Hinduism it is worded as "This is the sum of duty: do not do to others what would cause pain if done to you."[69] In Taoism, "Regard your neighbor's gain as your own gain and your neighbor's loss as your own loss."[70] In Christianity, "So in everything, do to others what you would have them do to you."[71] Or the clearest version for the purposes of this section from Sikhism, "No one is my enemy, and no one is a stranger. I get along with everyone."[72]

Many religions have some variation of the idea that you should treat others how you want to be treated included in their teachings. Since it is enshrined in the teachings of religions, one might assume that it is also manifest in the attitudes, beliefs, values, and behaviors of the members of those religions. And that would lead to the concern: If people exit religion, are they going to continue to follow the Golden Rule?

Alas, this concern is rooted in a flawed assumption, namely, the assumption laid out in the previous paragraph. Just because a teaching or belief or value exists within a religion doesn't mean the members of that religion follow it. That turns out to be the case for this teaching in particular. Years of research have shown that religious individuals tend to be more prejudiced than are nonreligious individuals.[73] The exception, of course, is for their ingroup; members of religions tend to favor other members of their religion over outsiders.[74] This isn't particularly surprising, nor should it be, given the large body of research that supports the idea that we favor our ingroups over our outgroups.[75]

For instance, in Pew's 2014 analysis of how Americans view various religions, they provided data on how members of religions rate their own religious group versus how they rate other groups.[76] Pew used thermometer scores that ranged from 0, which means they really don't like or feel really cold towards members of the target group, to 100, which means they really like or feel really warm towards members of that group. Catholics rate Catholics at an 80 on this scale, which is pretty high. But Catholics don't feel as warmly toward other groups: Jews = 61, Evangelical Christians = 57, Muslims = 40, and Atheists = 38. Jewish individuals show the same pattern, rating other Jews at 89, which is the highest ingroup average. But the outgroups for Jews are much lower than that: Catholics = 58, Evangelical Christians = 34, Muslims = 35, and Atheists = 55. The same general pattern holds for all the religious groups examined in the study—ingroup ratings are higher than outgroup ratings.

If, as prior research suggests, religious people tend to be somewhat more prejudiced towards people in their outgroup than are nonreligious individuals, what does this look like for strangers? One example of strangers is immigrants. The World Values Survey includes the question, "How about people from other countries coming here to work. Which one of the following do you think the government should do?" There are four response options ranging from "let anyone come who wants to" to "prohibit people coming here from other countries." The results are shown in figure 6.10.

Religious individuals have the most restrictive views on immigration, followed by the nonreligious; atheists have the most accepting views toward immigration. These differences are somewhat bigger than a lot of those we have examined in this chapter, but they still are not enormous (granted, 48% of religious people say that strict limits should be placed

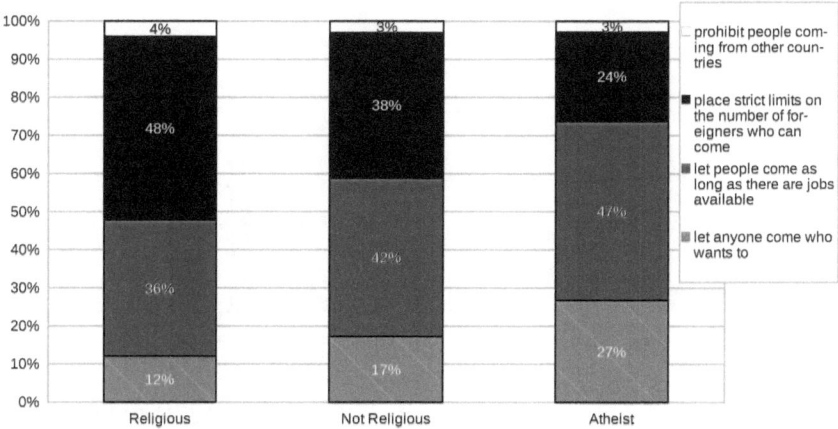

Figure 6.10. Attitudes Toward Immigrants Among Religious, Not Religious, and Atheists. (Source: World Values Survey—US Only, Wave 7)

on foreigners, which is exactly double the 24% of atheists who say the same thing).[77]

What about other strangers? The World Values Survey has another question that is more proximate for individuals. Participants were asked, "On this list are various groups of people. Could you please mention any that you would not like to have as neighbors." Since the Golden Rule often includes neighbors, this question seems to perfectly address the concern at hand. This is also a subtle way of getting at underlying prejudice toward various groups. Figure 6.11 shows the results.

It's pretty clear that no one wants drug addicts, and very few people want heavy drinkers, as neighbors, even though the Golden Rule does not carve out exceptions for those individuals. Among the other target groups, there are very few differences, and most people are fine with all of the following as neighbors: people of a different race, people who have AIDS, immigrants, homosexual individuals, people of a different religion, cohabiting couples, and people who speak a different language. What figure 6.11 indicates, just like so much of the other data in this chapter, is that there are not major differences between the religious and nonreligious on most of these issues.

What can we conclude, then, regarding this concern? Will people who leave religions be as kind to strangers as are the religious?

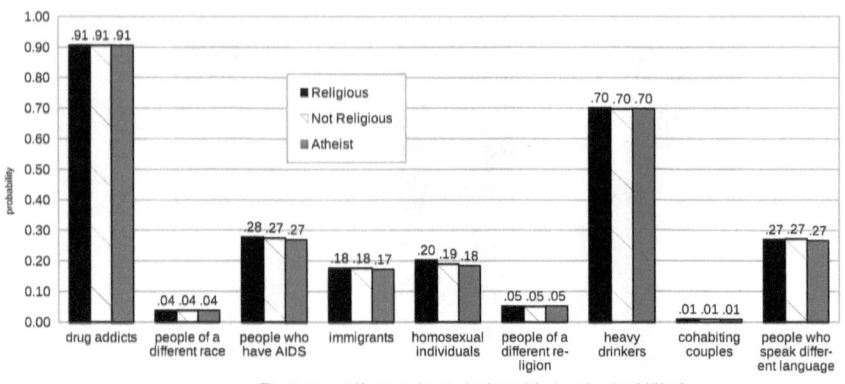

Figure 6.11. Probability of Mentioning Don't Want Various Groups as Neighbors Among Religious, Not Religious, and Atheists (Average Marginal Effects). (Source: World Values Survey—US Only, Wave 7)

If attitudes are a reasonable predictor of behavior, the answer is: at least as kind, if not more so.

Conclusion

We hate to think that this chapter is a disappointment, but we can imagine that it probably was for both the religious and the nonreligious as they read it. We can fully understand the desire to see your "side" come out on top; to somehow be better than the other side. Tribalism is deeply ingrained in us as humans. But data are data, and what some might consider a disappointing chapter we believe is actually a new perspective on people leaving religions. The simplest takeaway from this chapter is that everyone who is worrying about declining religiosity in the US should relax. This might help us (re)focus more attention on the many social problems we *should* be worried about.

We understand that some people will continue to claim that secularization will undermine the pillars of civil society (or at least traditional values), in an effort to scare people and prevent them from leaving religion. We are not so naive as to think that those who stand to lose their livelihood if there is a mass exodus out of the churches, mosques, synagogues, and temples won't just ignore the facts and proclaim impending calamity and doom to keep their revenue flowing. And of course, there are many ordinary religious people whose livelihood does not depend on religions staying in business, and yet they have many of the concerns we've outlined above. Our hope is that this chapter will be shared widely among both the religious and nonreligious, so they can see that they have more in common than they might realize. Yes, there are some differences here and there, but if the pillars of American society include morality, charity, civic engagement, families, education, purpose, health, and kindness, we shouldn't fear more people leaving religion. Life will go on.

7

Conclusion

We have covered a lot of ground in this book. Our central finding is that, since the early 1990s, millions of Americans have exited religion. This represents a monumental change in the US religious landscape. We have examined the causes and consequences of this change, arguing that its implications are important for society and individuals. We'll very briefly summarize where we've been before exploring a few additional implications for research in this area, offering a metaphor, and making a cautious prediction about what the near future holds.

After introducing the topic and setting the context in the first chapter, we provided a detailed look at the demographics of those who are leaving religions in the US (chapter 2). Much of the prior research on religious exiters has suggested that this is a phenomenon led by young, white, well-educated, and well-to-do men.[1] The data we provided illustrate that that is certainly no longer the case—and arguably never really was the case. Religious exiting is happening across all demographics. Since demographic characteristics are no longer particularly helpful when it comes to delineating who is going to leave religion, in chapter 3 we laid out a framework for understanding what factors appear to be contributing to religious exiting. Echoing the way that many demographers think about immigration, we framed the factors as falling into one of two categories—those factors that push people out of religion and those that pull them toward nonreligion and secularity. We illustrated that our interviewees were pushed out of religion for a variety of reasons that crosscut morality, politics, and shifting social attitudes. Our interviewees and survey data suggest that religiopolitical alignment is pushing some people out of religion. Some religions have aligned themselves with one particular political party in the US—the Republicans. While we're skeptical that religiopolitical concordance is a direct cause of religious exiting, it does make sense that aligning a religious institution with a particular political party will work as a push factor for those who hold different political views. Those individuals may not immediately leave religion and instead may switch their religious affiliation to one that more closely matches their political sensibilities. But religiopolitical alignment is definitely functioning as a factor leading people to exit religion in the US.

At the heart of theories of secularization is the idea that modern sensibilities cause problems for religion.[2] Religions that retain literalistic interpretations of scripture, that claim exclusive insight into a god's will or intentionality, or continue to make claims that do not align with a modern understanding of the world are putting their members in a position where they are forced to defend hard-to-defend beliefs. Our interviewees were quick to cite the empirical evidence against many of these truth claims. Some religions seem to be turning to political leaders to help them fend off the "threats" that modern sensibilities pose to the children of the members, by trying to allow for the teaching of creationism or intelligent design in public schools or, since that has largely failed, to use taxpayer money to allow kids to attend private religious schools where they are taught that humans and dinosaurs were contemporaries, that there was a worldwide flood, and that human evolution is a Satanic conspiracy designed to weaken people's faith.[3] Similarly, religious conservatives have stacked the US Supreme Court, which is now reversing longstanding precedent on the separation of church and state, and granting religious individuals greater privileges while also forcing states to fund religious activities.[4] Based on the data we have examined, so long as young people are allowed access to the internet, social media, or mass media, efforts to steer young people into religion will be decreasingly effective.

Hypocrisy was a fascinating push factor for our exiters. We're reminded of the biblical passage from 2 Kings when Hezekiah was ill and near death. Isaiah came to him and said, "Set your house in order, for you shall die and not live." As our interviewees noted, some religious organizations are rife with graft, sexual and emotional abuse, and pervasive attempts to cover up the often unethical behavior of religious leaders and supposedly devout members. When our interviewees observed hypocritical attitudes and behaviors they could no longer abide, they were driven out of their religions. For these exiters, religious hypocrisy undermined any claimed religious moral high ground.

While many religious adherents are being actively, though not intentionally, pushed out of religions, they are also being attracted to life without religion. The religiously unaffiliated now make up nearly one third of the US population. If someone doesn't have a nonreligious friend at this point, they likely will soon. While it is a violation of one of the 10 Commandments, envying the activities of their secular friends or family was a pull factor for many of our participants. Rather than attending religious services, they could have been sleeping in, playing board games with their family, tailgating at an NFL game, boating, skiing, hiking, playing video games, or even just reading a good book. There are an increasing number of alternatives to religious services on offer when those services have to compete in the leisure marketplace, against: farmers' markets, movies, plays, book clubs, exercise groups, and so on. With the decline of blue laws and the opening of Sundays to activities and events that compete with religion, there are plenty of other, "better" things to do than attend religious services, according to survey data and our participants. As we illustrated in Chapter 4, 81.7% of Americans are already not doing anything religious on Sundays. Combine this comparatively superficial reason for leaving religion with the more substantive appeal of a modern, evidence-based worldview that doesn't entail having to defend religious claims about reality, as well as the desire for greater autonomy in one's intellectual, social, and even spiritual life, and it's clear why people are leaving. Religion controls many aspects of people's lives. The desire to be freed from this control, and from the dogmas and dictates of religion, is pulling people out of it.

Granted, this characterization is largely aimed at conservative and evangelizing religion. Don't some religions grant their members greater autonomy and even encourage critical thinking about its doctrines and moral teachings? Yes, of course (more on this below). But our religious exiters, even those who came from liberal religions and who weren't in any meaningful sense "forced" to practice the religion of their parents, tended to speak of an unspoken expectation to accept their religion's claims and adhere to its strictures, whatever they happened to be.[5]

We also argued in chapter 3 that transmitting religion from parents to children is increasingly difficult to do. The transmission of religion is a space where both push and pull factors combine. As parents move toward granting their kids more autonomy, that weakens their ability to transfer their religion to their offspring. Kids that have access to the secular world also struggle to understand why they should hold religious beliefs and morals that marginalize LGBTQ+ individuals, women, racial minorities, immigrants, and so on. In an autocatalytic (i.e., self-reinforcing) fashion, as the number of kids who are being raised without religion increases, religious kids see their friends not attending religious services and instead doing things they are interested in and enjoy. It is increasingly difficult, without isolation and some form of coercion, to transmit religiosity from one generation to the next. As a result, there is a clear pattern of lower levels of religiosity from generation to generation.

What happens when people leave? As we detailed in chapters 4 and 5, some join secular, freethought, humanist, or atheist groups to help them work through the transition. These groups help people deconstruct their old religious identity and build a new, secular identity. They also help them work through any emotional or psychological damage caused by their former religions. But the vast majority of people who leave religions don't turn to these groups. They find identity and community elsewhere—making friends at work, in their neighborhoods, through shared interests, through their kids, and so on. They build new identities as wine lovers, gardeners, hunters, or soccer fans. They build new lives and move on. And, as the time use data from chapter 4 showed, for most Americans, including many who still claim a religious affiliation, this requires virtually no shift in behaviors as they are already not doing anything religious on a regular basis.

Building a new worldview or lifestance, as we described in chapter 5, can range from relatively easy to really difficult. For those for whom this is a challenge, it is also often very scary, transitioning from a religious community where the entire lens through which they viewed the universe was built for them to having to build their own lens on the universe. Others don't think much about it and simply move on with living their lives. And some adopt the tenets of humanism or some other positive affirmations for secular individuals and get to the business of living a life without religion.

Finally, in chapter 6, we tackled some of the concerns people have raised about a society transitioning away from religion. Secular people don't give less money to charities, they aren't less moral, they still have and love their families, they still vote and do service, they have fewer kids but still have kids, they are just as informed about religion (and often more so than are the religious, at least initially), they create meaning, they are healthy, they are unlikely to be more consumption- and materialism-oriented, and they are actually just as nice or nicer to strangers than are the religious. In short, when people say goodbye to religion, there is no cataclysmic collapse of society.

Cliff Diving: A Metaphor for Religious Exiting

Why, then, are people leaving religion? It varies from individual to individual. For any group of individuals, the reason(s) could be wildly different. A gay individual may leave because their religion rejects a core part of their self-identity, their sexuality. A woman may leave because she is fed up with the pervasive misogyny, patriarchy, and inequality of her religion. Someone else might leave because they're just bored and want to do other things. And yet another may run into internal conflict over their understanding of the universe and what their religion teaches. It's very, very difficult to predict why any one individual will leave.

As we thought about this fact, we happened upon a metaphor or parable that we think may be helpful to those who are trying to understand the phenomenon of religious exiting. Imagine a giant pool surrounded by cliffs of varying sizes. Standing on the cliffs above the pool are people of all stripes. The pool represents secularity—a life without religion. The cliffs represent religiosity.

The lowest cliffs are the lowest-cost religions. Some cliffs are just a foot or two above the level of the pool (e.g., Episcopalians), and others have slides directly into the pool (e.g., Unitarian Universalists). For the individuals on these cliffs, getting into the pool is so easy that it's almost like nothing has changed. Many of their friends are already in the pool having a great time. Continuing to hang out on the cliff as more of their compatriots leave makes less and less sense. In fact, as more people enter the pool, the level of the water rises and eventually swamps some of the cliffs for the lowest cost religions, making it so some people who are refusing to jump in are eventually standing in the pool as it overruns their cliff.

The highest cliffs are the highest-cost religions (e.g., Amish, Pentecostalism, Scientology, etc.). Jumping from some of those cliffs takes a great deal of courage as the pool is very, very far below them and very few people are jumping. In fact, some cliffs are so tall that those on the cliff can't actually see the pool, as they are above the clouds. Should individuals on those cliffs choose to jump, they would literally be jumping into the unknown. Yet, people are doing so knowing that they could very well be jumping to their deaths. Jumping from such a height means it likely takes them longer to surface and it's a bit of a struggle, but most eventually do surface, make friends, and join the others enjoying the pool. Of course, there are lots of other cliffs in the mid-range (e.g., Catholics, Southern Baptists, etc.). These cliffs are tall enough that individuals have to jump in the pool, but not so tall that they can't see the pool. And, as more people jump, the pool level rises, reducing the risk of jumping.

Which individuals will jump is very difficult to predict. There are a few factors that increase the odds, but there are no perfect predictors. Some people are naturally risk-averse and want nothing to do with the cliff face, let alone the pool below it. Others don't even hesitate, regardless of the height of the cliff. They would rather go or be anywhere than on the cliff. Some hold hands and jump together. Others take the plunge alone and worry about how those on the cliff will view what they have done. Some are more reticent to jump until a friend who has jumped yells up and tells them how wonderful the pool is. There is so much natural human diversity that it is extremely difficult to predict who will jump and why.

Even so, the pool has always been there and, during certain periods of human history, it was only those most willing to take the risk who were willing to jump. But the pool has gotten cleaner, warmer, and deeper over time. Of course, that is not how religious leaders describe it. They call it a cesspool, and warn people that jumping into the pool will lead to pain, anguish, suffering, and possibly even death. Yet, as the level of the pool rises, the description provided by religious leaders is harder to maintain as more and more of the people on the cliffs can see the pool and all the people in it.

As more people jump in, it is becoming more welcoming and there are more and more people to help the newcomers adjust to life in the pool. It's easier to jump into the pool today than it ever has been and is going to continue to become easier, even though some parents have tried to force their kids to climb to ever higher cliffs to make it harder to jump. The water is rising. The pool is welcoming. Eventually, the pool will get so full that even those on the highest cliffs won't have that far to jump.

We want to be clear that life in the pool isn't perfect. Some people need some swim lessons after they jump, and sometimes there are people in the pool who are exhibiting bad behaviors. The pool is not a utopia. People still have their struggles, some people still cheat, lie, and commit violent crimes. People get sick, people fight, and people die. The secular pool is not the answer to all of life's problems or questions. It's just a different place that is not on top of a cliff and it is just fine.

That's our metaphor for understanding why people exit religion. We cannot perfectly predict which individuals will leave or why, but we know there are some factors that predispose people to leave—the push and pull factors we have discussed—plus a changing cultural environment that makes it easier to leave.

Lived Religion and Functionalist Understandings of Religion

Our cliff diving metaphor (and the basic premise of this book) assumes that there is a real distinction to be made between things religious and not. It takes for granted that there is a thing called religion that people can exit. Let's briefly return to a couple of points raised in the opening chapter, regarding how we define religion and how this connects to contemporary academic understandings of it, before we talk about what the future might hold for religious exiting.

All good social science clearly specifies its object of inquiry and draws appropriate conceptual boundaries around it. Fair enough. But admittedly, this can be more than a little challenging. In chapter 1, we attempted to define our terms and outline the variety of related concepts (religion, nonreligion, secularization, secularism, secularity) that bear on the topic of religious exiting. That's what this book has been about—how and why people leave religion, and what this means for society at large. One problem, however, especially in religious studies and, perhaps only to a slightly lesser extent, in sociology (our discipline) is that religion has occupied a kind of conceptually privileged status for most researchers, even for some who primarily focus on religion's other.[6] This is both a conceptual and empirical problem. Although religion is but one lens through which we humans can view and understand the world, it's been treated by many scholars who study it as though it is the central organizing framework—the focal point to which all other approaches and models for understanding the social world are referenced. Secularization references the decline of religion. The secular references that which stands apart from religion. Nonreligion references social phenomena *in relation to* religion. Religious exiting references the process of people leaving religion. In other words, it's all about religion. Given the social significance and seeming ubiquity of religion throughout human history, this isn't surprising. It even makes some sense.

However, more scholars are realizing that religion is not the inevitable or integral part of the social world that it's often assumed to be, and some argue that traditional models for understanding religion (and nonreligion) no longer work.[7] There are different ways to interpret reality and the world around us, and continuing to presuppose and privilege the category *religion* as a kind of imperative—even just a conceptual one—is a mistake, in part because of what it implies about what we should be studying empirically. To be clear, we're not saying the concept of religion itself is useless, or that scholars shouldn't study religion and employ all the other concepts that relate to it, and that, indeed, have shaped our analysis here. That would be self-defeating; it would undermine our own argument, and wouldn't make any sense. Religion is a real thing. But so are the things that are not religion. What we are saying—and we're definitely not the first writers to say it—is that we have to be clear about what we mean by religion if we want to study it, and its other, effectively. But in light of recent trends in scholarship, we feel we need to stress that religion can't just mean anything we want it to mean, or whatever we find convenient to our argument at the moment. This is why we tried to be careful at the beginning of this book to set up what we mean by religion, before we could talk about what it means to exit it.

This leads us back to functionalism. Readers will recall that we described functionalist approaches to religion in the introduction, when discussing the three common definitional frameworks applied to religion (substantive and symbolic were the other two). To recap in a single statement, a functionalist view of religion focuses on what religion *does*.

There is a long history in sociology of taking, even if only implicitly, a functionalist approach to religion. Indeed, a functional analysis can be, to borrow a phrase from anthropologist Claude Levi-Strauss, "good to think with," since it helps researchers analyze what individuals, groups, and even whole societies actually "get out of" the range of phenomena we call religious beliefs and behaviors. But there is also a significant drawback. Functionalist understandings of religion tend toward being inclusive of a continually expanding range of phenomena, much of which, in our view, cannot reasonably be construed as religious. Take one very simple functionalist definition: "Religion is any attempt to answer existential questions."[8] If this is true, any philosophy or outlook on life that attempts to answer such a question is *ipso facto* religion. As we discussed in chapter 5, virtually all our exiters sought answers to existential questions. Indeed, for many, this was *part of the process* of exiting. They relied on scientific inquiry, and consciously rejected religious claims, to answer questions about, for instance, human origins, or the nature of the cosmos. Forget whether science and religion are compatible; by this definition, science *is* religion. And couldn't we just as easily define philosophy as "any attempt to answer existential questions?"

Needless to say, we don't think this is a very productive way to think about or study religion.

Closely related to the issue of defining the parameters of religion is the concept of *lived religion*, which we, again, introduced briefly at the beginning of this book. Taking elements from both functionalist and substantive approaches, scholars have written about what we might today call lived religion for many decades,[9] but the recent works of Nancy Ammerman, perhaps the most notable proponent of the lived religion approach in sociology, represent its most thorough treatment.[10] Lived religion, despite the wide-ranging phenomena it is meant to capture, is actually, at base, a very simple idea: people make religion their own. Individuals select, borrow, and reconfigure, from the wider sets of collective religious beliefs, symbols, behaviors, and identities available to them via religious traditions, organizations, and the culture at large, in bespoke ways that fit religion to suit their particular needs and interests. Lived religion is about how ordinary people experience, personalize, and express religion in everyday situations. It's not just about religious services or institutionalized spaces—churches, synagogues, mosques, gurdwaras, etc.—where people are "supposed" to have religious experiences. Work, home, play, the grocery store, can all be spaces where religion is lived. Individuals can still be more or less connected to institutionalized and organized religion, but lived religion describes the ways they actually experience it day-to-day, usually in non-institutionalized ways—ways that depart from traditional and orthodox religious beliefs and practices.

Of course we agree that in the twenty-first century, people, in many ways, make religion their own. That's pretty clear. Today a Christian, by virtue of the sheer diversity within Christianity, may adopt, reject, ignore, and negotiate a variety of Christian beliefs, behaviors, and identities. This happens all the time with virtually all religious traditions. And there are many ways in which a more narrowly defined concept of lived religion can be useful—including for the study of "lived nonreligion."[11] But the problem has to do, again, with how expansive we want our concepts to be. What justifies the scope of our object of inquiry, and how should religion (and spirituality) be defined and treated empirically? As with functionalism, one might get the impression, reading about lived religion, that basically anything can be religious. By the most inclusive definitions of lived religion, a 50-year-old agnostic woman, who has never had any religious affiliation, who holds no beliefs in a deity, angels, or anything supernatural, has no expectation of an afterlife, but who loves walking meditations while in nature, and sometimes refers to her awe and reverence for the natural world as "spiritual," will be said to be engaging in lived religion. In our view, this is using the term religion much too flexibly and edges toward the idea that everything is religion. If finding or creating meaning of any kind in life and developing a set of beliefs about the world, if holding values and developing relationships connects and contributes to this meaning-making—if this is, by definition, religion (of the lived variety)—then in our estimation, it's an empty concept. Every one of our religious exiters, in one sense or another, "attempted to answer existential questions." Does this make them religious? If we took this functionalist definition and linked it up with the recent work on lived religion (for which it is well paired), we'd be forced to say, no matter how much they protested, that our participants continued to be religious, even after they abandoned their religious beliefs, organizations, identities, and the rest. But set aside religious exiters. Maybe they're unique in some way. How about the millions of people who grow up without religion at all, who never step foot in a place of worship, never hold a religious identity, never subscribe to a religious creed or doctrine, never feel beholden to the dictates or advice of religious leaders or friends. When they ask themselves and attempt to answer, as most people inevitably will—be it superficially or with great depth—questions about the nature and meaning of their existence, have they suddenly become religious? We don't think so. As sociologist and theologian Anna Sofia Salonen observes, "People—whether religious or not—are today as interested as ever in the surrounding world and give meanings to everyday incidents and perceptions of the wider whole. . . ."[12] People make meaning and they ask questions about life. This doesn't mean this is religion, even lived religion. This way of thinking about religion just doesn't work well and makes it almost impossible to study it coherently. It certainly wouldn't make sense to write a book about religious exiting, because ultimately no one exits religion. Religious exiting can't exist if nothing is not religion.[13]

What Next?

What does the future hold for religious exiting and the growth of the nonreligious? We are social scientists, not prophets. We are not and should not be in the business of telling others what the future will bring. But . . . social science does allow for reasonable predictions with lots of caveats and conditions. Also, we're not the only ones to project the growth of the nonreligious into the future. In a 2022 study,[14] Pew developed their own projections for the religious makeup of the US, which we'll describe in more detail below.

We're going to be extremely cautious here with our projections. Previous scholars who have suggested that religion was going to decline dramatically[15] or completely disappear[16] have been shown to be wrong and are now legitimately criticized. As a result, we're not going to make such a suggestion. Also, we're going to be rather conservative and only project to 2040.

Keeping in mind that all such projections are heavily qualified and contingent, we are going to offer some possible futures for the US religious landscape.

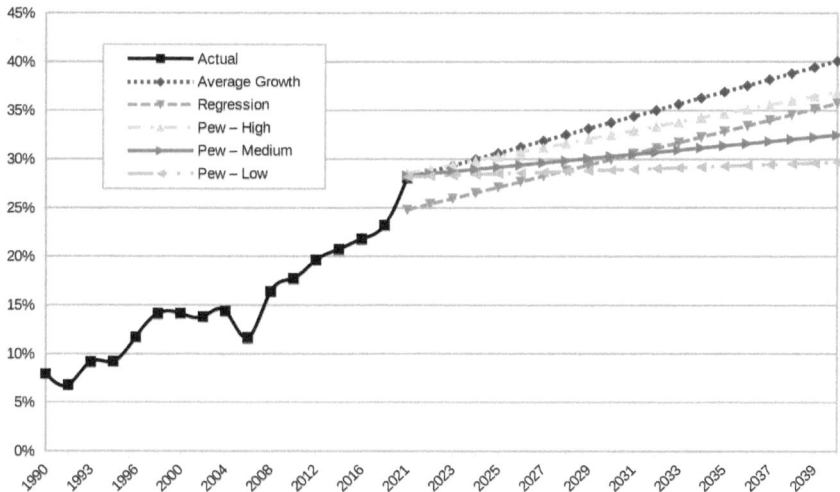

Figure 7.1. Estimates of Nonreligious Growth, 2021–2040.

Figure 7.1 shows the percentage of the US population that reported no religious affiliation from 1990 through 2021, based on the General Social Survey, using a solid black line. Those are not projections but the actual survey results. In 1990, 9% of US adults reported no religious affiliation; in 2021 it was 28%. The 2021 wave of the GSS was the latest wave available when we were writing this book. Everything after that point is a projection of the growth of the nonreligious into the future. We provide 5 estimates—2 of our own and 3 from the previously mentioned Pew study.

First, Pew's estimates include a number of important elements. They included demographic variables in their models, recognizing, as we have mentioned, that the religious tend to have more kids than the nonreligious. As a result, the religious have the potential for more growth because they are having more kids, though the religious are less likely to retain their children than are those with no religious affiliation, so the net flow is away from religion at present. The various estimates by Pew also make certain assumptions. The low model assumes that no person in the US will change their religion after 2020, which is, of course, not particularly plausible. But that assumption does provide a baseline of what could happen should demographic inertia continue into the future. Assuming that there is no more religious exiting in the US, just the continued inertia of nonreligious people raising their kids without religion, that will still result in a very slight uptick in the percentage of the population that has no affiliation through 2040, from 28% to 29%. The mid-level projection by Pew assumes that the switching (really, exiting) that is currently taking place will continue into the future. Under that assumption, Pew projects the nonreligious to grow to about 32% of the US population through 2040, which really isn't that much growth in light of recent past growth. Finally, Pew's high-growth model assumes that the rates of switching (i.e., exiting) will increase, which would result in the nonreligious making up about 36% of the US population by 2040.

We added two models to the three by Pew, both of which use radically simplified assumptions. First, we took the average growth of the nonreligious per year from 1990 to 2021, around .6%, and projected that into the future. That results in the highest estimate in our figure, around 40% of the US population being nonreligious by 2040. Our second model simply regressed the percentage nonreligious on the year (so, on time), and generated the requisite regression coefficients that way.[17] The projected percentage of the population that would be nonreligious in 2040 using this hyper-simplified model is right around 36%, the same as Pew's high-switching model.

While the two projections we have added are very simple, they reflect some basic assumptions. To make those assumptions explicit, our projections can be thought of as reflecting the same social forces that contributed to the increase in religious exiting from 1990 to 2021. In other words, whatever social forces drove people out of religion from that time period resulted in (a) an average rate of religious exiting and/or (b) a trend in religious exiting. If we assume that the social forces driving religious exiting from 1990 to 2021 continue to be in effect through 2040, then it's plausible that the rate of religious exiting will continue apace. Of course, those forces could change. As we noted, our models are contingency models, not prophesies. We are not saying what will happen, only what could happen should certain assumptions hold true.

This leads to one final point here. While we think Pew's baseline model, in which religious exiting basically plateaus, is unlikely (as do they) and the various other projections are more likely, it is also worth mentioning that both our slightly higher projections and Pew's high-switching projection could underestimate religious exiting in the coming years. It is possible—note our switch from "plausible" to "possible" here—that religious exiting and having no religious affiliation are effectively social innovations, like the adoption of CDs over cassettes, or DVDs over VHS tapes, or smart phones or even electric cars.[18] When technological advances take place, there is often a slow build-up at the beginning, when early adopters are really the only ones who are willing to take the risk of adopting the new technology. Once acceptance of the technology hits a certain level in the population, then it becomes more widely accepted and adoption accelerates rapidly, only to plateau once it reaches nearly complete saturation. Effectively, innovations follow an S-shaped curve—slow growth at the beginning, rapid growth in the middle, and slow growth at the end. This can be seen with cell phones. At the beginning, cell phones were expensive and buggy, and were only adopted by a select few. But the spread continued until it hit an inflection point (usually somewhere in the 20% to 30% range). Once enough innovators had purchased cell phones and they were reliable enough, the rate of adoption accelerated until almost everyone had one. There are, of course, still some people who have not switched to a cell phone, but they are increasingly rare.

We realize it might sound strange to compare cell phone adoption with people leaving religion. But in terms of making projections, it's possible that religious exiting could actually follow a similar path, with relatively slow growth for a while, followed by an inflection point when this nonreligious innovation begins to spread rapidly, only to plateau at some point in the future with a minority of individuals remaining religious indefinitely. We are not arguing that an S-shaped curve is more likely than the projections we laid out, only that we and Pew could be wrong and could underestimate the rate of growth of the nonreligious in the US. There is another factor that is important to note as well—older people are substantially more likely to report a religious affiliation than younger people. Thus, in addition to people leaving religions and people being raised without a religious affiliation, those most likely to report a religious affiliation are literally being removed from the population at higher rates through death. As a result, the transition from a predominantly religiously affiliated society in the US to a predominantly secular society may increase through all three social forces—exiting, retention of young people, and the death of the elderly.

As a result, the percentage of the US population reporting no religious affiliation is likely to continue increasing at a relatively quick pace for the foreseeable future.

Finally, astute readers will have noted that we are primarily discussing the nonreligious, collectively, in this section—both those who have exited religions and those who were raised with no religion. We did that primarily so we could draw on Pew's projections, since they did not separate out these two groups. But it is not all that complicated to think about how those two groups will shift over time. At present, the majority of Americans report a religious affiliation, which means there are more people who can and will exit religion than there are people who will be raised without a religious affiliation. Eventually, that will probably change such that there are more people who are raised without a religious affiliation among the nonreligious than there are people who left religion, but that is decades into the future.

We can certainly quibble over the details or try to make very precise projections for the future of religious exiting in the US. But we think it actually makes more sense to simply note that, should current conditions continue through 2040, we would genuinely be astonished if the percentage of the US population that reports no religious affiliation did not continue to increase. We do *not* think that religion, as we defined it in the first chapter of this book, is going to go away entirely, at least not any time soon. There will, in all likelihood, still be many Americans with a religious affiliation in 2040 and beyond. But the future of religion in America in general doesn't look great, as more and more Americans say goodbye to it.

Generalizability

As with any argument, it's always a good idea to tie up loose ends. In the first chapter, we mentioned briefly that we thought our arguments in this book were generalizable to non-Christians and probably to other populations beyond the US. We want to address the generalizability of our arguments at greater length.

In chapter 3, we used a push and pull framework to lay out a number of propositions that we believe increase the odds that someone will leave religion. Here are all nine propositions in a single list:

- Proposition 1: *Ceteris paribus*, individuals who hold more modern, egalitarian views will be more likely to leave religion than those who hold more traditional views.
- Proposition 2: *Ceteris paribus*, individuals who have more progressive social and political values will be more likely to leave religion than will individuals who have more conservative social and political values.
- Proposition 3: *Ceteris paribus*, individuals who reject religious doctrines and teachings will be more likely to leave religion than will individuals who accept religious doctrines and teachings.
- Proposition 4: As societies modernize, people will increasingly find secular ways to spend their time rather than engage in religious behaviors.
- Proposition 5: *Ceteris paribus*, individuals who place a greater value on autonomy will be more likely to leave religion than will those who place a lower value on autonomy.
- Proposition 6: *Ceteris paribus*, individuals who hold modern, scholarly understandings of the natural world will be more likely to leave religion than individuals who do not.
- Proposition 7: *Ceteris paribus*, individuals who strongly value logical consistency and reason will be more likely to leave religion than do individuals who are unaware of these ideas or do not highly value them.
- Proposition 8: *Ceteris paribus*, individuals with greater exposure to modernity will be more likely to leave religion than individuals with less exposure to modernity.
- Proposition 9: The larger the proportion of someone's social network that is nonreligious, the higher the odds they will leave religion.

There are a number of points of clarification that are in order regarding some of these propositions. First, readers will note that almost all of the propositions begin with the caveat *ceteris paribus*, which is Latin for "all else being equal." We didn't include this phrase to pretentiously use Latin. We used it as a qualifier for our propositions. In essence, what we mean is that if we have two individuals who are effectively identical in every respect except the way that is delineated in that proposition, we would argue that the person who differs in the way we suggested would be more likely to exit religion. Of course, "all else" is rarely equal. To illustrate what we mean and the generalizability of our arguments to other populations, we are going to describe several hypothetical situations.

Imagine identical twins, Scott and Steve, raised in a rural town in the Midwestern United States. As identical twins, we can rule out biological differences (for the most part), helping to create our "all else being equal" condition. Their parents are devoted members of a Lutheran congregation and expect their children to attend with them. While they are genetically identical, Scott and Steve have varied interests, which leads one of them—Steve—to develop a different friend group from Scott. Steve's interests lean toward theater and dance. Scott is more interested in business and finance. As a result of their different interests, Steve's friends end up being somewhat more progressive than Scott's and, when they graduate from high school, Steve ends up pursuing a career in theater while Scott attends college to earn a degree in business. Steve's friends and career interests result in a more progressive social environment and Steve ends up adopting those same values (i.e., proposition 2). Scott, meanwhile, has surrounded himself with more conservative friends and does not end up adopting values that are much more socially progressive than those of his parents. In this hypothetical scenario, theoretically, almost everything else is equal because they are genetically identical and they were raised in a nearly identical fashion, but Steve is more likely than Scott to exit religion. Of course, this is just a hypothetical scenario. In the real world, finding such a perfect case to illustrate our theoretical arguments is more difficult. But the intent here is only to illustrate why we included the caveat at the beginning of most of our propositions—rarely is all else equal.

That leads us to our second point—the generalizability of our propositions and findings. We developed our propositions and theoretical arguments based on data from the United States. From its origins as a group of European colonies, the US has been a majority-Christian country. The vast majority of our interviewees exited Christian religions, as did the vast majority of the exiters we were able to examine in the GSS. Given that the bulk of our data derive from formerly Christian individuals in a still predominantly Christian country, it is a perfectly fair question to ask: Do these results generalize beyond such environments and to members of other religions? We believe they do and will use, again, hypothetical scenarios to illustrate why.

Imagine, again, two identical twins, Sana and Sneha, whose parents are first-generation immigrants to the US from India, who live in Charlotte, North Carolina. Their parents came to the US to pursue higher education. One is now a hospital administrator and the other is an MD. They raise Sana and Sneha as Hindus and encourage them to retain their religious beliefs and behaviors. Yet, at the same time, Sana and Sneha are being raised in a highly developed country where elements of modernity are pervasive (proposition 8). When Sana and Sneha complete high school and are considering college, Sneha decides to pursue a degree in computer science while Sana decides she wants to study anthropology. Sneha's career path will, of course, expose her to modern technology and, in all likelihood, will include training in logic and reason (proposition 7). Sana's studies may include training in logic and reason as well (proposition 7), but will most assuredly include training in the history, evolution, and nature of religion, leading Sana toward a clearer understanding of the socially constructed nature of all religion (proposition 3). Both Sana and Sneha are, per our theoretical argument, more likely to exit religion than would be individuals who are not pursuing their career paths. That Sana and Sneha were raised Hindu is unlikely to substantially alter the consequences of their education and training. However, here is where *ceteris paribus* becomes relevant. If, for Sana and Sneha, their Hindu background is more than just a religious identity and is really a cultural or ethnic identity, it is possible that they may both continue to identify as Hindu, despite no longer holding any of the supernatural beliefs or believing in the efficacy of the typical rituals associated with their religious heritage. They may continue to value their ethnic identity and participate in some aspects of their religion because it is part of their identity, but not because they believe it will in any way influence their future through supernatural, divine, or cosmological forces. The point of this hypothetical exercise is to illustrate that the propositions we outlined that increase the odds of people exiting religion are not exclusive to a Christian context but should generalize beyond Christianity to any religious environment.

We offer one final hypothetical example to illustrate the possibility of our theory applying to very different contexts. It does not strain the imagination to think that our theoretical model would be applicable in very similar contexts (e.g., Canada and the UK) or even in somewhat different contexts (e.g., Mexico, Lithuania, or even Israel) that have

Judeo-Christian histories. But what about very different contexts? Do our same propositions hold in, say, Lesotho, Laos, or Libya?

Imagine, again, identical twins, Sengphet and Kham, born to a contentious couple in Laos. Shortly after the kids are born, the parents divorce. The mother moves to Vientiane and marries a highly successful business person, while the father, a local convenience store owner in the small town where the parents were originally raised, marries one of his employees. Both parents, however, are devout Buddhists and raise their children as Buddhists. In the divorce—remember, this is a hypothetical scenario—they decide to split up the twins. Sengphet goes with the mother and Kham goes with the father. Thanks to the affluence of his step-father, Sengphet attends the best schools in Vientiane and is then sent to Europe for college, while Kham is able to attend the local public schools then begins working with his father in the convenience store. Sengphet is more likely, as a result of his education, to be exposed to modernity (proposition 8), and to receive training that emphasizes logic and reason (proposition 7). We believe our theoretical model would apply equally well in a Laotian context as it does in the US. The factors that lead people to exit religion are, we contend, universal. So long as the criteria laid out by one of us (Cragun) in a recently published book on secularization are met—that there is freedom of/from religion and the country is modernizing[19]—then the same general forces that lead to religious exiting in the US should apply in other contexts and environments as well. In essence, Cragun's other book laid out the macro- and meso-level forces that lead to religious decline, while the arguments in this book are designed to explain the micro-level forces that lead to religious exiting.

We included *ceteris paribus* as a qualifier with our propositions. Statistically, it is possible to hold variables constant, which allows us to test the propositions with the *ceteris paribus* qualifier in place. Yet, finding appropriate variables and gathering data that allow for direct tests of these propositions is a work in progress. Many of our propositions were developed initially based on qualitative results; good measures that would capture the variables denoted in our propositions need to be developed and/or more widely utilized in surveys. We invite scholars around the world to develop improved measures and scales to capture the concepts we have described, and to test our propositions at greater length than we have. As should be the case with any scientific theory, we invite testing and replication and will modify and adjust our propositions accordingly.

Finally, one more point when it comes to our theory of religious exiting is in order. We argued explicitly in chapters 2 and 3, as well as above in our metaphor, and implicitly elsewhere, that it is very difficult to know what factors will lead someone to leave religion. The reason this is so difficult is that it is basically impossible to know for any single individual which factor is going to push them over the threshold and out of religion. A clergy abuse scandal may be the deciding factor for one person but not for another. Higher education could completely undermine one religious acolyte's beliefs, while it might strengthen the beliefs of another. Realizing that they are bisexual could be the final straw for some individuals, but have no bearing on the value that others place on religion.

Religiosity is actually preference-based and rooted in subjective values. In this sense, people are religious not because it is logical or reasonable to be so. This runs counter to the claims of some scholars from the 1990s that religion can be understood from a rational choice framework.[20] A close examination of rational choice explanations of religiosity reveals that such models quickly devolve into *post hoc ergo propter hoc* fallacies.[21] Basically, how these models work is that they look to see what someone does and then, based on the outcome, they assume that those are the individual's preferences. When the typical person hears "rational" they assume it means something like weighing costs and benefits—that people will choose the course of action that minimizes costs and maximizes benefits. But how most sociologists of religion actually implement a rational choice framework is to rationalize someone's actions after the fact, asserting that they chose what they did because it was rational to them, making "rational" really mean "subjective." It is the exact opposite of a predictive, theoretical model.

An illustration may help. Imagine a teenager, Samantha, is raised in a very conservative Christian faith that rejects LGBTQ+ individuals entirely. Samantha realizes as a teenager that she is lesbian. If we were to assume that Samantha makes decisions after weighing the costs and benefits and attempts to maximize benefits while minimizing costs, logically, Samantha should leave her conservative Christian faith that rejects a core part of who she is. The costs of staying—regularly experiencing prejudice and discrimination, having members insist that she is evil and influenced by Satan or even possessed by a demon, having the members and potentially her own family reject her, and her developing self-hatred and loathing (among other costs)—are unlikely to be outweighed by the benefits—she retains a community and perhaps her family, albeit a community and family that considers her less than, other, and sinful. Objectively, the costs outweigh the benefits and Samantha should leave. But, if Samantha chooses to stay, advocates of the rational choice model of religiosity would argue that Samantha's decision is rational *post hoc* (i.e., after the fact) because, to her, she found reasons for staying, even if they are objectively irrational.

Our intent here isn't to wade into a debate about the utility of rational choice models of religiosity at length but rather to illustrate why it is so difficult to predict who is going to stay religious and who is going to leave. If people were fundamentally rational in an objective, predictive sense, it would be easier to predict who is going to leave. LGBTQ+ individuals raised in religions that reject them would leave. Individuals who pursue advanced education in fields that directly deconstruct religion would leave. People raised in patriarchal religions who adopt more egalitarian views would leave. People who stop believing in religious doctrines would leave. And so on. But that is simply not how people operate. There are LGB individuals who are members of LGB-rejecting religions.[22] There are many highly educated people who are religious,[23] and there are many people who hold progressive views and belong to conservative religions.[24] And, it is worth noting that we aren't trying to argue that people leave religions for rational reasons; we don't really think they do. In a sense, this is us challenging our interviewees who construct rational versions of themselves and the reasons why they left. A closer analysis of their reasons suggests that they are just as much preference-based as the reasons for why people stay.

At some level, it may seem as though we are contradicting ourselves. We are arguing that religious exiting is going to continue in the US—a prediction about societal-level change. But we then turn around and argue that we cannot, with great accuracy, predict which specific individuals are going to leave. This is akin to arguing that we know that tens of thousands of Americans will die in car accidents in a given year based on the number of miles driven and how much time people spend on the road, but we cannot say in advance which Americans are going to die. We know some factors that increase the odds of people dying—how recklessly they drive, the safety features of their car, their age, and whether they engage in riskier driving behaviors. But we cannot perfectly predict who is going to die in car accidents in the US, only that many will. In similar fashion, we can predict that people will continue to leave religion in the US (a macro level claim) but we cannot predict who will leave (a micro level claim) because human behavior at the individual level is just not easy to predict.

Our theoretical argument is based on the assumption that most people are not inherently rational and that they will not always make rational decisions. Certainly, they can rationalize their decision after the fact, but it makes predicting behavior difficult. That assumption holds in the US among Christians and former Christians, but also outside the US and among people in every religion. As a result, we do think our theoretical model is generalizable beyond our primary context. Our point, then, is that our propositions increase the odds of someone leaving, but it is highly unlikely, because of the fact that rationality in humanity is often wanting, that we will ever be able to predict with perfect accuracy who is going to exit religion and who is going to stay.

* * *

This book is the culmination of decades of our research. Our dissertations both focused on people leaving religion and we have continued to publish on that topic—on and off—since we completed our PhDs. During that time, not only have the number of people around the world who have exited religion increased,[25] but so, too, has the research that focuses on religious exiting.[26] The ideas and arguments in this book are not exclusively ours; they build upon the now voluminous research related to religious exiting that has been published in recent decades. We owe a great debt to the many other scholars working in this field and hope that this book will help push research on religious exiting forward.

Our aims with this book were really twofold. First, we wanted to examine in detail why there has been a large increase in people leaving religion and what are both the sociological and psychological forces driving that increase. Second, we wanted to explore the possible consequences for society. We hope we have accomplished these aims.

We also hope that our analyses and interpretations do some justice to the many people who have said "goodbye" to religion.

ACKNOWLEDGMENTS

Like most collaborative projects, this one grew out of our mutual research interests, and from many informal conversations over years. The original idea for this book came from Ryan, who approached Jesse between sessions at the *Society for the Scientific Study of Religion*'s annual conference in 2018. We became convinced it would be worthwhile to explore the synergies we could bring, methodologically and analytically, to a topic we both care about, and that we suspect others care about too. It took some years to move from mere idea to working project, but we eventually made it happen.

Of course, it wasn't really "we" alone that made it happen. The product that is this book extends well beyond the two of us. As such, we'd like to thank the many scholars whose work has informed our own. We have relied on them, and hope we have represented them, fairly and accurately whether we have agreed with them or not. We'd also like to thank the anonymous reviewers of earlier drafts of the book. We benefited greatly from their insights. We are also deeply appreciative of the feedback provided on an early version of chapter 6 at the 2021 Annual Meeting of the Society for the Scientific Study of Religion by Rhys Williams, David Voas, Joel Thiessen, Conrad Hackett, and Phil Zuckerman. And Jennifer Hammer, of NYU Press, for her enthusiasm, high expectations, and critical commentary. She politely helped us realize we were long-winded on our almost-final draft; consequently, we harbor no resentment toward her for having to cut nearly 10,000 words from the manuscript. We are also grateful to James M. Reilly for his careful copyediting.

We thank Debi and Katie, our forbearing spouses, for their generosity in letting us spend large chunks of many weekends on Zoom poring over details of the book.

Finally, we acknowledge and thank the many religious exiters who gave us their time and shared their stories, not always without risk. They have deepened our understanding of this phenomenon, and we wish them the very best.

APPENDIX

Methods

In this methodological appendix, we describe two aspects of our methodology. First, we describe our qualitative sample and the characteristics of our interviewees. Second, we describe in detail why we took the approach we did with our quantitative data to determine who we would consider a religious exiter, and provide more detailed information on how our measure of religious exiting aligns with other ways that we could have selected religious exiters.

QUALITATIVE SAMPLE

We drew upon 120 semi-structured in-depth interviews that took place over a ten-year period between 2008 and 2018. Recruitment for 45 of the interviews began in Colorado through three different secular social groups collectively identified here as the Mountain West Freethinkers. Another 45 interviewees were recruited starting in California and Michigan—the former from an international conference of the Sunday Assembly, an international network of secular congregations that began in the United Kingdom in 2013; and the latter through one of its local chapters. In both settings, recruitment was expanded through a referral system that gained us participants in more than a dozen other states all over the US, including California, Illinois, Maine, Massachusetts, Georgia, Florida, and New York. The remaining 30 interviewees were recruited from a survey posted on Craigslist in 2010 (though interviews continued through 2011). The aim was to find people who reported no religious affiliation but were also not a member of a secular, atheist, humanist, or freethought organization. Using this approach, we were able to recruit 30 individuals who reported no religious affiliation and were also not a member of a secular group. Most of those participants were from Florida, but we also interviewed several individuals from other states who took the initial screening survey, including Louisiana, South Carolina, Virginia, Indiana, Oklahoma, Texas, and Utah. Combined, our sample gave us confidence that we weren't selecting for the exit process by any specific geographic region or any narrow time frame, and that our findings from the interview data reflect the broader process of Americans exiting religion.

As shown in Table A.1, our sample was limited to adults only (18 and up) and the age range of participants was from 18 to 92. By self-identification, 67 were female, 50 were male, 2 were transgender, and 1 was non-binary. From the tables below, readers will see that our sample drew from mostly white (101) and middle-class individuals. However, this leaves 19 non-white (most of whom also identified as middle class) people, including 7 African Americans, 8 Latinx, and 4 of mixed race. As 15.8% of our sample were non-white, and several participants held a minority sexual identity, we took care to highlight the experiences of these participants (especially in chapter 2) to capture both diversity in our sample and diversity in the exiting process. The sample was fairly evenly split regarding marital status. As for education, our sample skewed toward the highly educated, with nearly 40% having obtained a bachelor's degree, and 31% with an advanced degree (most others had at least some college).

All of our formal interviews were in-depth and lasted between 40 minutes and 2.5 hours (averaging just over an hour per interview). About half the interviews were in-person, the other half took place over phone/video conference. Though a structured interview guide was used in every case, we also took an open and conversational approach to the interviews. That is, though we had specific questions to put to every participant, we also allowed them to develop their ideas or individual lines of thinking to capture their unique voice and experience. As alluded in the introductory chapter, our sample included 10 individuals who were not overtly raised within any specific religion (though virtually all participants had at least some casual interaction with religion, such as going to church with a friend or attending a religious funeral service) and did not meet the conditions relative to identity, behavior, and belief that would qualify them as religious at any point in their lives. Why did we include such people in a book about religious exiting? Our original thought was not to; how can one exit something they never really entered? But after we began analysis of the survey data which included

Table A.1. Demographic Characteristics of Interview Participants.

Age Categories	N	Gender	N
18–25	14	Male	50
26–40	44	Female	67
41–55	31	Transgender/Other	3
56 or older	31		
Race/Ethnicity	N	Marital Status	N
Caucasian/White	101	Married	47
Black/African American	7	Single	41
Hispanic	8	Divorced	32
Other	4		
Educational Attainment	N	Raised Religious?	N
Vocational/Technical/Other	3	Yes	110
Some College	31	No	10
Bachelor's Degree	46		
Master's Degree	22		
Doctoral/Professional Degree	14		
Unknown	4		

comparisons across three categorical groups (see Quantitative Analyses on Religious Exiters below), including the "never religious," we realized it would actually give us a reference point in the qualitative data to have a few never religious cases in our sample. We don't rely on these cases to illustrate the exit process; rather, we use quotes from these individuals to supplement points about the never religious and religious exiter categories, and in reference to the different pathways the nonreligious can take (the next section of this appendix describes the surprising similarities between religious exiters and the never religious). The remaining 110 interviewees were clearly religious at one point in their lives, but equally clearly left religion at another. In the end, we determined all 120 interviews would be useful for the analysis, given our definitions and the three groups we compare throughout.

There are a few other data points from the interview sample that bear on the exiting process and are worth considering. For instance, we gave interviewees nearly a dozen identity categories to choose from. Early in the data collection, the original idea was to ask interviewees to choose the term that best describes themselves—that they most identify with. However, several participants stated that a number of the options resonated with them and that they didn't like being restricted to choosing just one. Accordingly, we adjusted the language on this item to allow for participants to choose more than one option (and should they so choose, circle the one they *most* identify with among all those selected). Though it made this particular item a bit messy for analysis purposes, we think it does better reflect the experience of participants. This matters in a book about religious exiting, not because we're so concerned with participants' identities per se, but because changes in self-identification are often important symbolic markers of transition that correspond with the exiting process. Since leaving religion involves abandoning a former religious identity, it, of course, makes sense that many exiters will try on different nonreligious identities as part of this process.

As noted above, we purposefully recruited 30 participants who were not involved with secular groups of any kind in addition to those who, during their interview, noted that they were not affiliated with a secular group. For the others, we asked them about their activism. Though a considerable number of participants for whom we have data thought of themselves as "somewhat" or "absolutely" a secular or atheist activist, this often seemed to be not much more than a proxy for the fact they participated in a secular group of some kind. Many occasionally attended meetings or participated in social gatherings and took this to be a form of outspokenness about their nonreligion, which was construed as a kind of activism. We're not suggesting there weren't true activists in our sample. There were. Some helped organize rallies, gave public talks, set up booths, and engaged in other activities that clearly demonstrate activism. But on balance, the majority of our participants were not what we would consider to be secular activists. Conveniently, our participants were fairly evenly split between the three pathways we described at the beginning of each chapter: the religiously indifferent, religious-secular liminals, and secular activists.

QUANTITATIVE ANALYSES ON RELIGIOUS EXITERS

The aim of this portion of the methodological appendix is to make it clear to readers how we selected those we consider religious exiters in our primary sample, the General Social Survey (GSS). The GSS includes two questions that ask about participants' religious affiliation. One, RELIG, asks about participants' current religious affiliation, "What is your religious preference?" The second, RELIG16, asks about participants' religious affiliation when they were a youth, "In what religion were you raised?" We used these two variables to create the three groups we examine throughout the book. Individuals who were raised with a religious affiliation (i.e., anything other than "none" on RELIG16) but reported no religious affiliation at present were classified as religious exiters. If someone reported no religious affiliation on both variables, they were classified as "never religious." And individuals who reported either a religious affiliation as a youth and a religious affiliation at present or no religious affiliation as a youth but a religious affiliation at present we labeled as stayers or joiners. Throughout this section of the methodological appendix, we use just the 2010 to 2021 waves of the GSS combined (2010, 2012, 2014, 2016, 2018, and 2021) to illustrate why we chose to analyze the data the way we did. Readers can contact us for code that replicates the analyses below with all waves of the GSS (1972–2021).

Table A.2 shows the breakdown of our participants in the GSS from 2010 to 2021. Of note, we originally considered including those who joined religions as a separate category, but they are a relatively small number, just 546 individuals across the 2010 to 2021 waves of the GSS. As a result, we grouped them with those who retained their religious affiliation from their youth.

We recognize that this approach to classifying our participants relies on just a single dimension of religiosity discussed in our introductory chapter—identity or religious affiliation. In what follows, we explore the characteristics of these three groups in greater detail to determine whether our very simple approach to separating out religious exiters

TABLE A.2. Sample Sizes and Percentages for Never Religious, Exiters, and Those Who Stayed or Joined Religions. (Source: GSS 2010–2021)

	N	%
Never Religious	955	6.1
Exiters	2,572	16.5
Stayed or Joined	12,085	77.4

based exclusively on identity is problematic when it comes to the other two dimensions of religiosity: belief and behavior.

In table A.3, we show religious attendance (ATTEND in the GSS), an indicator of behavior, for the three groups. As the table illustrates, for both the never religious (71.4%) and religious exiters (64.9%), the vast majority never attend religious services. The percentage among those who retained a religious affiliation or joined who never attend religious services is just 15.5%. At the other end, there is a small percentage of both the never religious and religious exiters who attend fairly frequently. If we consider frequent attendance more than once a month, 3.8% of the never religious and 5.1% of religious exiters attend more than once a month, compared to 47.7% for those who retained a religious affiliation or joined a religion.

Despite the similarity between the never religious and religious exiters in current attendance, their life experiences have clearly varied. The GSS included in four waves (1991, 1998, 2008, and 2018) a variable asking about religious attendance as a youth (ATTEND12). Given the limited number of times this question was asked, we include those four waves in table A.4 below. Table A.4 shows the frequency of attendance as a youth for our three groups of interest. Religious exiters were not quite as frequent attenders as those who stayed or joined, but they are much closer to those individuals than they are to the never religious in how frequently they attended religious services as a youth. The majority of

TABLE A.3. Religious Service Attendance for Never Religious, Exiters, and Those Who Stayed or Joined. (Source: GSS 2010–2021)

ATTEND	Never Religious (%)	Exiters (%)	Stayed or Joined (%)
Never	71.4	64.9	15.5
Less than once a year	10.8	11.4	7.6
Once a year	9.4	13.3	13.1
Several times a year	2.8	3.6	12.2
Once a month	1.8	1.7	6.9
2–3 times a month	0.8	1.7	9.4
Nearly every week	0.4	0.7	6.6
Every week	1.3	1.8	21.0
More than once a week	1.3	0.9	7.7

the never religious have never attended religious services, but that is not true for religious exiters. Just 12.5% of religious exiters never attended religious services growing up.

We also examined a number of GSS questions that ask about religious belief. Table A.5 breaks down the belief in an afterlife by our three groups of interest. The majority in all three groups report believing in an afterlife, though it is a slight majority for the never religious (55.1%) and exiters (56.6%) compared to those who stayed or joined (86.3%).

Like belief in an afterlife, those who were never religious and exiters are very similar in the percentages who hold particular perspectives toward a god or higher power, as shown in table A.6 below. Around 1 in 5 of the never religious (18.3%) and religious exiters (18.2%) report a confident belief in a monotheistic deity, compared to 66.7% of those who stayed or joined. Atheism and agnosticism are much more common among the never religious and exiters, as is believing in a higher power. Soft agnostic positions (i.e., believing sometimes or believing but doubting) are similar among all three groups.

TABLE A.4. Religious Service Attendance As Youth for Never Religious, Exiters, and Those Who Stayed or Joined. (Source: GSS 1991–2018)

ATTEND12	Never Religious (%)	Exiters (%)	Stayed or Joined (%)
Never	63.8	12.5	4.3
Less than once a year	9.0	4.0	2.0
Once a year	6.9	8.1	4.6
Several times a year	5.9	7.7	7.3
Once a month	2.1	6.1	4.3
2–3 times a month	3.2	8.0	9.1
Nearly every week	3.7	13.1	17.6
Every week	2.7	30.4	38.6
More than once a week	2.7	10.1	12.2

TABLE A.5. Belief in An Afterlife for Never Religious, Exiters, and Those Who Stayed or Joined. (Source: GSS 2010–2021)

POSTLIFE	Never Religious (%)	Exiters (%)	Stayed or Joined (%)
Yes	55.1	56.6	86.3
No	44.9	43.4	13.7

TABLE A.6. Belief in God or Higher Power for Never Religious, Exiters, and Those Who Stayed or Joined. (Source: GSS 2010–2021)

GOD	Never Religious (%)	Exiters (%)	Stayed or Joined (%)
Don't believe	17.7	15.2	1.1
No way to find out	21.7	21.5	2.4
Some higher power	24.3	29.9	7.9
Believe sometimes	4.9	4.4	3.9
Believe but doubts	13.1	10.9	18.0
Know God exists	18.3	18.1	66.7

TABLE A.7. Belief in the Bible for Never Religious, Exiters, and Those Who Stayed or Joined. (Source: GSS 2010–2021)

BIBLE	Never Religious (%)	Exiters (%)	Stayed or Joined (%)
Literal word of God	10.8	8.6	38.3
Inspired word of God	29.6	30.0	48.5
Book of fables	55.3	58.8	12.1
Not part of tradition	4.3	2.6	1.1

Another area where the never religious and religious exiters are quite similar is in their view of the Bible, as shown in table A.7. The majority of both groups consider the Bible a book of fables, though a sizable minority of the never religious (29.6%) and religious exiters (30.0%) consider the Bible the inspired word of god. Close to 10% of each of these groups consider the Bible to be the literal word of god, compared to 38.3% of those who stayed or joined a religion.

Table A.8 examines self-reported spirituality for the never religious, religious exiters, and those who stayed in or joined a religion. There are slight differences between the never religious and religious exiters on the two ends of the continuum. Just 9.2% of the never religious consider themselves very spiritual, while 17.1% of exiters consider themselves very spiritual, compared to 32.1% of those who stayed or joined. A roughly 8% difference between the never religious and religious exiters is also seen on the not spiritual side, with 38.5% of the never religious and 30.2% of exiters reporting they are not spiritual at all, compared to just 5.8% of those who stayed or joined. Table A.8 seems to suggest that those who were raised with religion but left may have retained some elements of spirituality, at least at a slightly higher rate than those who were never religious.

Finally, table A.9 compares the three groups on their self-reported religiosity. The never religious and exiters are quite similar, but there is a gap of about 4% between the two groups in considering themselves not religious, with 74.3% of the never religious and 70.4% of religious exiters reporting they are not religious at all. Just 9.1% of those who stayed religious or joined a religion report that they are not religious.

What does this analysis of our three groups reveal? In many ways, religious exiters look a lot like the never religious, particularly regarding their religious/nonreligious beliefs, like believing in an afterlife, their view of a god, and their view of the Bible. But there are also some small differences. Religious exiters report being more spiritual and slightly more religious, they are more likely to report attending religious services, and they have clearly had different life experiences when it comes to their upbringing in religion. Based on this analysis, we do think it makes sense to analyze the never religious and religious exiters independently of each other.

Additionally, the analysis above does suggest that there is a small percentage of both the never religious and religious exiters, who, while

TABLE A.8. Self-Reported Spirituality for Never Religious, Exiters, and Those Who Stayed or Joined. (Source: GSS 2010–2021)

SPRTPRSN	Never Religious (%)	Exiters (%)	Stayed or Joined (%)
Very Spiritual	9.2	17.1	32.1
Moderately Spiritual	22.4	23.1	40.9
Slightly Spiritual	29.9	29.6	21.2
Not Spiritual	38.5	30.2	5.8

TABLE A.9. Self-Reported Religiosity for Never Religious, Exiters, and Those Who Stayed or Joined. (Source: GSS 2010–2021)

RELPERSN	Never Religious (%)	Exiters (%)	Stayed or Joined (%)
Very Religious	1.6	1.9	20.1
Moderately Religious	7.9	7.0	46.2
Slightly Religious	16.2	20.6	24.6
Not Religious	74.3	70.5	9.1

they report no religious affiliation, exhibit many of the characteristics of religious individuals. We considered whether we should change the classification of those individuals, grouping them with those who stayed religious or joined religions instead. To determine whether that would make sense, we selected just the religious exiters in the GSS and examined to what extent there is overlap on the religious end. For instance, what percentage of religious exiters who report attending religious services regularly (at least once a month) also report that they think the Bible is the literal word of god? If the overlap was substantial, that would suggest that it is the same ~10% of individuals who are highly religious in belief and behavior even though they report not belonging. However, only 23.7% of religious exiters who attend services more than once a month also report being biblical literalists. Similarly, just 11.2% of those who report they are very spiritual also report that they hold a literalistic view of the Bible, while 41.1% consider the Bible inspired and 45.0% consider the Bible a collection of myths. In other words, there is not a clearly distinguishable subset of religious exiters who have all the indicators of being religious in terms of belief and behavior but simply report no religious affiliation. What we find instead are illustrations of human inconsistency: 3.1% of religious exiters who report not believing in a god attend religious services at least once a month, while 50.5% of religious exiters who are confident god exists never attend religious services. Humans are not logically consistent in their beliefs, behaviors, or identities.

If we had found a subset of both religious exiters and the never religious who were consistent in their beliefs and behaviors on the religious end, we would have classified them as religious. Instead, we have chosen to use just our measure of religious change (religious affiliation as a youth and current religious affiliation) to classify our participants. The result is somewhat messy in the sense that religious affiliation does not perfectly predict what individuals believe or how individuals behave. But that messiness is also a reflection of reality. To give a well-known example: Richard Dawkins, the poster child for atheism, has indicated that he enjoys singing Christmas carols[1] and that if he had to choose what record to take with him to a desert island, he'd choose "Mache dich mein Herze rein" from J. S. Bach's *St. Matthew Passion*, a decidedly religious piece of music.[2] As we noted in the previous paragraph, humans are not logically consistent across all life domains and are definitely *in*consistent when it comes to religiosity.

Finally, as advocates of open science, we are providing here the R code used for the quantitative analyses throughout this book: https://osf.io/rq9px/?view_only=b67649b2a812405a9adee1dddf12908b. Should readers find errors or have suggestions, we welcome your feedback.

NOTES

1. INTRODUCTION

1. To be clear, we're not implying that the liminality pathway means people are partly religious and/or partly secular. These participants have left religion. They don't subscribe to religious doctrines, identify with any religion, engage in religious practice, attend religious services in any committed way, or pay religious tithes.
2. Roberts, Keith A., and David Yamane. 2021. *Religion in Sociological Perspective.* 7th edition. Thousand Oaks, CA: Sage Publications.
3. Payne, Seth. 2013. "Ex-Mormon Narratives and Pastoral Apologetics." *Dialogue: A Journal of Mormon Thought* 46, no. 4 (Winter): 85–121.
4. Gervais, Will M., and Ara Norenzayan. 2012. "Analytic Thinking Promotes Religious Disbelief." *Science* 336, no. 6080 (27 April): 493–96. https://doi.org.10.1126/science.1215647.
5. Clark, Mark, and Larry Osborne. 2017. *The Problem of God: Answering a Skeptic's Challenges to Christianity.* Grand Rapids, MI: Zondervan.
6. Bromley, David G., ed. 1998. *The Politics of Religious Apostasy: The Role of Apostates in the Transformation of Religious Movements.* Westport, CT: Praeger Publishers.
7. Zuckerman, Phil. 2011. *Faith No More: Why People Reject Religion.* New York: Oxford University Press.
8. Baggett, Jerome P. 2019. *The Varieties of Nonreligious Experience: Atheism in American Culture.* New York: New York University Press.
9. Baumeister, Roy F. 1982. "A Self-Presentational View of Social Phenomena." *Psychological Bulletin* 91, no. 1 (January): 3–26.
10. Jacoby, Susan. 2005. *Freethinkers: A History of American Secularism.* New York: Holt Paperbacks.
11. Seidel, Andrew L., Susan Jacoby, and Dan Barker. 2019. *The Founding Myth: Why Christian Nationalism Is Un-American.* Illustrated edition. New York: Sterling.
12. Plimpton, Ruth Talbot. 2009. *Mary Dyer: Biography of a Rebel Quaker.* Wellesley, MA: Branden Books; Winship, Michael P. 2002. *Making Heretics: Militant Protestantism and Free Grace in Massachusetts, 1636–1641.* Princeton, NJ: Princeton University Press.
13. Whitehead, Andrew L., and Samuel L. Perry. 2020. *Taking America Back for God: Christian Nationalism in the United States.* New York: Oxford University Press;

Stewart, Katherine. 2020. *The Power Worshippers: Inside the Dangerous Rise of Religious Nationalism*. New York: Bloomsbury Publishing.
14 Jacoby, Susan. 2005. *Freethinkers: A History of American Secularism*. New York: Holt Paperbacks.
15 Brown-Iannuzzi, Jazmin L., Jonathan M. Golding, Will M. Gervais, Kellie R. Lynch, Nesa E. Wasarhaley, and Sierra Bainter. 2019. "Will Jurors Believe Non-believers? Perceptions of Atheist Rape Victims in the Courtroom." *Psychology of Religion and Spirituality* 13, no. 1: 119–126; Gervais, Will M., Dimitris Xygalatas, Ryan T. McKay, Michiel van Elk, Emma E. Buchtel, Mark Aveyard, Sarah R. Schiavone, Ilan Dar-Nimrod, Annika M. Svedholm-Häkkinen, Tapani Riekki, Eva Kundtová Klocová, Jonathan E. Ramsay, and Joseph Bulbulia. 2017. "Global Evidence of Extreme Intuitive Moral Prejudice against Atheists." *Nature Human Behaviour* 1, no. 8 (07 August): 1–6. https://doi.org.10.1038/s41562-017-0151.
16 Finke, Roger, and Rodney Stark. 2005. *The Churching of America, 1776–2005: Winners and Losers in Our Religious Economy*. Revised edition. New Brunswick, NJ: Rutgers University Press; Walker, David. 2019. *Railroading Religion: Mormons, Tourists, and the Corporate Spirit of the West*. Chapel Hill: University of North Carolina Press.
17 Hecht, Jennifer Michael. 2004. *Doubt: A History: The Great Doubters and Their Legacy of Innovation from Socrates and Jesus to Thomas Jefferson and Emily Dickinson*. New York: HarperOne.
18 Jacoby, Susan. 2013. *The Great Agnostic: Robert Ingersoll and American Freethought*. New Haven, CT: Yale University Press.
19 Kruse, Kevin M. 2015. *One Nation Under God: How Corporate America Invented Christian America*. New York: Basic Books.
20 Goldstein, Warren S. 2006. *Marx, Critical Theory, And Religion: A Critique of Rational Choice*. Brill Academic Publishers.
21 Marx, Karl. 2000. *Selected Writings*. 2nd edition. New York: Oxford University Press.
22 Peris, Daniel. 1998. *Storming the Heavens: The Soviet League of the Militant Godless*. Ithaca, NY: Cornell University Press.
23 Kruse, Kevin M. 2015. *One Nation Under God: How Corporate America Invented Christian America*. New York: Basic Books.
24 Rothstein, Richard. 2018. *The Color of Law: A Forgotten History of How Our Government Segregated America*. Reprint edition. New York: Liveright.
25 Weiner, Tim. 2013. *Enemies: A History of the FBI*. 2013 edition. New York: Random House Trade Paperbacks.
26 Jacoby, Susan. 2009. *The Age of American Unreason*. New York: Vintage Books.
27 O'Hair, Madalyn Murray. 1989. *An Atheist Epic: The Complete Unexpurgated Story of How Bible and Prayers Were Removed from the Public Schools of the United States*. Austin, TX: American Atheist Press; O'Hair, Madalyn Murray. 1991. *Why I Am an Atheist; Including, A History of Materialism*. Austin, TX: American Atheist Press.

28 Brown, Callum G. 2012. *Religion and the Demographic Revolution: Women and Secularisation in Canada, Ireland, UK and USA since the 1960s*. Martlesham, UK: The Boydell Press.
29 Eig, Jonathan. 2015. *The Birth of the Pill: How Four Crusaders Reinvented Sex and Launched a Revolution*. New York: W. W. Norton & Company.
30 Stolz, Jörg, Judith Könemann, Mallory Schneuwly Purdie, Thomas Englberger, and Michael Krüggeler. 2016. *(Un)Believing in Modern Society: Religion, Spirituality, and Religious-Secular Competition*. London: Routledge.
31 Rustow, Dankwart A. 1990. "Democracy: A Global Revolution?" *Foreign Affairs* 69, no. 4 (Fall): 75–91. https://doi.org.10.2307/20044497.
32 Hout, Michael, and Claude S. Fischer. 2002. "Why More Americans Have No Religious Preference: Politics and Generations." *American Sociological Review* 67, no. 2 (April): 165–90.
33 Kosmin, Barry A., Ariela Keysar, Ryan T. Cragun, and Juhem Navarro-Rivera. 2009. *American Nones: The Profile of the No Religion Population*. Hartford, CT: Institute for the Study of Secularism in Society and Culture.
34 Thiessen, Joel, and Sarah Wilkins-Laflamme. 2020. *None of the Above: Nonreligious Identity in the US and Canada*. New York: New York University Press.
35 IMDB. *Silicon Valley* "Tech Evangelist"—Episode aired Apr 15, 2018. Accessed December 12, 2023. https://www.imdb.com/title/tt7761624/.
36 Examples of critical documentaries include: *Leah Remini: Scientology and the Aftermath*; the various documentaries about NXIVM, such as *The Vow* and *Seduced*; and the movie *Spotlight*, which focused on sexual abuse in the Catholic Church.
37 Berlinerblau, Jacques. 2013. *How to Be Secular: A Call to Arms for Religious Freedom*. Boston: Mariner Books.
38 Ham, Ken and Bodie Hodge. 2017. "Atheism is Religion." Answers in Genesis, February 20. https://answersingenesis.org/world-religions/atheism/atheism-is-religion/.
39 Maher, Bill. 2012. Real Time with Bill Maher. February 3.
40 Cragun, Ryan T. 2016. "Sociology of Nonreligion and Atheism." In *Handbook of Religion and Society*, edited by David Yamane, 301–20. Cham, Switzerland: Springer.
41 Smith, Jesse M., and Ryan T. Cragun. 2019. "Mapping Religion's Other: A Review of the Study of Nonreligion and Secularity." *Journal for the Scientific Study of Religion* 58, no. 2: 319–35. https://doi.org/10.1111/jssr.12597.
42 In the final chapter, we also revisit the issue of defining religion and problematize it with respect to the implications for future research.
43 Tylor, Edward B. [1873] 1958. *Primitive Culture*, Vol. II. New York: Harper and Row.
44 Kant, Immanuel. [1781] 2004. *Critique of Pure Reason*. New York: Barnes & Noble Publishing.
45 Yinger, J. M. (1970). *The Scientific Study of Religion*. New York: Macmillan.

46 James, William. 2012. *The Varieties of Religious Experience*. Edited by Matthew Bradley. Oxford: Oxford University Press.
47 Durkheim, Emile. 1995. *The Elementary Forms of Religious Life*. New York: Free Press.
48 Geertz, Clifford. 1966. "Religion as a Cultural System." In *Anthropological Approaches to the Study of Religion*, edited by Michael Banton, 1–46. London: Tavistock.
49 To borrow a phrase from scholar and theologian Rudolf Otto. See Otto, Rudolph. 1936. *The Idea of the Holy: An Inquiry into the Non-Rational Factor in the Idea of the Divine and its Relation to the Rational*, trans. John W. Harvey. Oxford: Oxford University Press.
50 This figure is based on a similar one (figure 4.1, p. 98) from: Roberts, Keith A. and David Yamane. 2016. *Religion in Sociological Perspective*. 6th Edition. Thousand Oaks, CA: Sage.
51 Ammerman, Nancy Tatom. 2013. *Sacred Stories, Spiritual Tribes: Finding Religion in Everyday Life*. New York: Oxford University Press; McGuire, Meredith B. 2008. *Lived Religion: Faith and Practice in Everyday Life*. New York: Oxford University Press.
52 Smith, Jesse M. 2017. "Can the Secular Be the Object of Belief and Belonging? The Sunday Assembly." *Qualitative Sociology* 40, no. 1 (March): 83–109. https://doi.org.10.1007/s11133-016-9350-7.
53 We revisit and draw out the implications of functionalist understandings of religion, along with the concept of lived religion, in the conclusion.
54 Lee, Lois. 2015. *Recognizing the Non-Religious: Reimagining the Secular*. New York: Oxford University Press; Quack, Johannes. 2014. "Outline of a Relational Approach to 'Nonreligion.'" *Method & Theory in the Study of Religion* 26, no. 4/5: 439–69. https://doi.org.10.1163/15700682-12341327; Cragun, Ryan T. 2016. "Sociology of Nonreligion and Atheism." In *Handbook of Religion and Society*, edited by David Yamane, 301–20. Switzerland: Springer; Smith, Jesse M., and Ryan T. Cragun. 2019. "Mapping Religion's Other: A Review of the Study of Nonreligion and Secularity." *Journal for the Scientific Study of Religion* 58, no. 2: 319–35. https://doi.org/10.1111/jssr.12597.
55 Lee, Lois. 2015. *Recognizing the Non-Religious: Reimagining the Secular*. New York: Oxford University Press.
56 Tillich, Paul. 1957. *Dynamics of Faith*. New York. HarperOne.
57 Smith, Jesse M., and Ryan T. Cragun. 2021. "Secularity and Nonreligion." In *Secularity and Nonreligion in North America, Bloomsbury Religion in North America*. London: Bloomsbury Academic.
58 Cragun, Ryan T., and Joseph H. Hammer. 2011. "'One Person's Apostate Is Another Person's Convert': Reflections on Pro-Religion Hegemony in the Sociology of Religion." *Humanity & Society* 35, no. 1/2 (February/May): 149–75.
59 For discussion of why we prefer the term "religious exiting" to the term "apostasy," see Cragun, 2016.

60 Of course this doesn't mean it's impossible for religious exiters to once again become religious. So far as we know, none of our participants have "re-entered" religion.
61 Swatos, William H., and Daniel V. A. Olson. 2000. *The Secularization Debate*. Lanham, MD: Rowman & Littlefield Publishers, Inc.; Berg-Sørensen, Anders, ed. 2013. *Contesting Secularism: Comparative Perspectives*. Surrey, England: Ashgate; Dobbelaere, Karel. 2002. *Secularization: An Analysis at Three Levels (Gods, Humans, and Religions)*. New York: Peter Lang Publishing.
62 Berger, Peter L. 2001. "Reflections on the Sociology of Religion Today." *Sociology of Religion* 62, no. 4 (Winter): 443–54; Stark, Rodney. 1999. "Secularization, R.I.P." *Sociology of Religion* 60, no. 3 (Autumn): 249–73.
63 Kasselstrand, Isabella, Phil Zuckerman, and Ryan T. Cragun. 2023. *Beyond Doubt: The Secularization of Society*. New York: New York University Press.
64 Cragun, Ryan T., and Kevin J. McCaffree. 2021. "Nothing Is Not Something: On Replacing Nonreligion with Identities." *Secular Studies* 3, no. 1 (April): 7–26. https://doi.org.10.1163/25892525-bja10017.
65 Cragun, Ryan T., and Joseph H. Hammer. 2011. "'One Person's Apostate Is Another Person's Convert': Reflections on Pro-Religion Hegemony in the Sociology of Religion." *Humanity & Society* 35, no. 1/2 (February/May): 149–75.
66 Keysar, Ariela. 2014. "Shifts Along the American Religious-Secular Spectrum." *Secularism and Nonreligion* 3, no. 1 (March 21): 1–16. http://dx.doi.org/10.5334/snr.am; Cragun, Ryan T., and Kevin J. McCaffree. 2021. "Nothing Is Not Something: On Replacing Nonreligion with Identities." *Secular Studies* 3, no. 1 (April): 7–26. https://doi.org.10.1163/25892525-bja10017.
67 Becker, H. S. 1996. "The Epistemology of Qualitative Research." In *Ethnography and Human Development: Context and Meaning in Social Inquiry*, edited by R. Jessor, A. Colby, and R. A. Shweder, 53–71. Chicago: The University of Chicago Press.
68 A pseudonym for three different secular social and support groups.
69 See the international organization's website: https://www.sundayassembly.org/.
70 Glaser, Barney. [1967] 2017. *The Discovery of Grounded Theory. Strategies for Qualitative Research*. New York: Routledge.
71 Charmaz, Kathy. *Constructing Grounded Theory*. Thousand Oaks, CA: Sage.
72 Brenner, Philip S. 2011. "Identity Importance and the Overreporting of Religious Service Attendance: Multiple Imputation of Religious Attendance Using the American Time Use Study and the General Social Survey." *Journal for the Scientific Study of Religion* 50, no. 1 (March): 103–15.
73 Chaves, Mark. 2011. *American Religion: Contemporary Trends*. Princeton, NJ: Princeton University Press; Voas, David, and Mark Chaves. 2018. "Even Intense Religiosity Is Declining in the United States: Comment." *Sociological Science* 5 (June): 694–710. https://doi.org.10.15195/v5.a29.

74 Putnam, Robert D., and David E. Campbell. 2012. *American Grace: How Religion Divides and Unites Us*. New York: Simon & Schuster; Burge, Ryan P. 2021. *The Nones: Where They Came From, Who They Are, and Where They Are Going*. Minneapolis: Fortress Press.

2. WHO IS LEAVING?

1 Kasselstrand, Isabella. 2015. "Nonbelievers in the Church: A Study of Cultural Religion in Sweden." *Sociology of Religion* 76, no. 3 (Autumn): 275–94. https://doi.org.10.1093/socrel/srv026.
2 Altemeyer, Bob, and Bruce Hunsberger. 1997. *Amazing Conversions: Why Some Turn to Faith & Others Abandon Religion*. Amherst, NY: Prometheus Books; Condran, John G., and Joseph B. Tamney. 1985. "Religious 'Nones': 1957 to 1982." *Sociological Analysis* 46, no. 4 (Winter): 415–23; Feigelman, William, Bernard S. Gorman, and Joseph A. Varacalli. 1992. "Americans Who Give Up Religion." *Sociology and Social Research* 76, no. 3: 138–45; Hadaway, C. Kirk. 1989. "Identifying American Apostates: A Cluster Analysis." *Journal for the Scientific Study of Religion* 28, no. 2 (June): 201–15; Hale, J. Russell. 1977. *Who Are the Unchurched?: An Exploratory Study*. Washington, DC: Glenmary Research Center; Hoge, Dean R. 1981. *Converts, Dropouts, Returnees: A Study of Religious Change Among Catholics*. New York: Pilgrim Press.
3 In many of the figures in this chapter, we aggregate the GSS roughly by decades. We did this because any single wave of the GSS, particularly in the 1970s and 1980s, did not include very many exiters. More recent waves include more. However, natural random variation in any given wave of the GSS can also result in somewhat erratic patterns. Aggregated data by decades provide more reliable, albeit more conservative estimates.
4 Throughout this book, when we refer to "Americans," we mean non-institutionalized adult Americans, since the General Social Survey does not include individuals under 18 nor those who are institutionalized in prisons or hospitals.
5 Atkinson, Michael. 2002. "Fifty Million Viewers Can't Be Wrong: Professional Wrestling, Sports-Entertainment, and Mimesis." *Sociology of Sport Journal* 19, no. 1 (January): 47–66. https://doi.org.10.1123/ssj.19.1.47.
6 Bernstein, Penny, Nicholas Paolone, Justin Higner, Kathleen Gerbasi, Samuel Conway, Adam Privitera, and Laura Scaletta. 2008. "Furries from A to Z (Anthropomorphism to Zoomorphism)." *Society & Animals* 16, no. 3 (January): 197–222. https://doi.org.10.1163/156853008X323376.
7 Strawn, Kelley D. 2019. "What's Behind the 'Nones-Sense'? Change Over Time in Factors Predicting Likelihood of Religious Nonaffiliation in the United States." *Journal for the Scientific Study of Religion* 58, no. 3 (September): 707–24. https://doi.org.10.1111/jssr.12609.
8 Caplovitz, D., and F. Sherrow. 1977. *The Religious Drop-Outs: Apostasy Among College Graduates*. Beverly Hills, CA: Sage.

9 Hadaway, C. Kirk. 1989. "Identifying American Apostates: A Cluster Analysis." *Journal for the Scientific Study of Religion* 28, no. 2 (June): 201–15; Hoge, Dean R. 1981. *Converts, Dropouts, Returnees: A Study of Religious Change Among Catholics*. New York: Pilgrim Press; Roozen, D. A. 1980. "Church Dropouts, Changing Patterns of Disengagement and Re-Entry." *Review of Religious Research* 21: 427–50.
10 Bengtson, Vern L. 2013. *Families and Faith: How Religion Is Passed down across Generations*. New York: Oxford University Press; Bengtson, Vern L., Merril Silverstein, Norella M. Putney, and Susan C. Harris. 2015. "Does Religiousness Increase with Age? Age Changes and Generational Differences Over 35 Years." *Journal for the Scientific Study of Religion* 54, no. 2 (May): 363–79. https://doi.org.10.1111/jssr.12183; Bruce, Steve. 2002. *God Is Dead: Secularization in the West*. London: Blackwell Publishers; Bruce, Steve. 2014. *Scottish Gods: Religion in Modern Scotland*. Edinburgh: Edinburgh University Press.
11 We are aware that the GSS includes a weight variable. We ran these analyses both with and without weights applied and they generally made very little difference, shifting the various population estimates by just small margins. As a result, we opted to show unweighted data, as the relationships are unchanged.
12 Rogers, Everett M. 2006. *Diffusion of Innovations*. 5th Edition. New York: Free Press.
13 Aiello, Thomas. 2005. "Constructing 'Godless Communism': Religion, Politics, and Popular Culture, 1954–1960." *Americana: The Journal of American Popular Culture 1900 to Present* 4, no. 1 (Spring); Hixson, Walter L. 1998. *Parting the Curtain: Propaganda, Culture, and the Cold War, 1945–1961*. New York: St. Martin's Press.
14 O'Hair, Madalyn Murray. 1989. *An Atheist Epic: The Complete Unexpurgated Story of How Bible and Prayers Were Removed from the Public Schools of the United States*. Austin, TX: American Atheist Press.
15 Edgell, Penny, Jacqui Frost, and Evan Stewart. 2017. "From Existential to Social Understandings of Risk: Examining Gender Differences in Nonreligion." *Social Currents* 4, no. 6 (December): 556–74. https://doi.org.10.1177/2329496516686619.
16 Manning, Christel J. 2015. *Losing Our Religion: How Unaffiliated Parents Are Raising Their Children*. New York: New York University Press; Zuckerman, Phil. 2011. *Faith No More: Why People Reject Religion*. New York: Oxford University Press.
17 Bengtson, Vern L., Merril Silverstein, Norella M. Putney, and Susan C. Harris. 2015. "Does Religiousness Increase with Age? Age Changes and Generational Differences Over 35 Years." *Journal for the Scientific Study of Religion* 54, no. 2 (May): 363–79. https://doi.org.10.1111/jssr.12183.
18 Stark, Rodney, and Roger Finke. 2000. *Acts of Faith: Explaining the Human Side of Religion*. Berkeley: University of California Press.
19 Merino, Stephen M. 2011. "Irreligious Socialization? The Adult Religious Preferences of Individuals Raised with No Religion." *Secularism and Nonreligion* 1, no. 0: 1–16.
20 Kasselstrand, Isabella, Phil Zuckerman, and Ryan T. Cragun. 2023. *Beyond Doubt: The Secularization of Society*. New York: New York University Press.

21 Manning, Christel. 2018. "Meaning Making Narratives among Non-Religious Individuals Facing the End of Life." In *New Dimensions in Spirituality, Religion, and Aging*, edited by V. L. Bengtson and M. Silverstein, 59–85. London: Routledge.
22 Zuckerman, Phil. 2020. *Society without God: What the Least Religious Nations Can Tell Us About Contentment*. 2nd edition. New York: New York University Press.
23 Day, Abby. 2022. *Why Baby Boomers Turned from Religion: Shaping Belief and Belonging, 1945–2021*. New York: Oxford University Press.
24 Caplovitz, David, and Fred Sherrow. 1977. *The Religious Drop-Outs: Apostasy Among College Graduates*. Beverly Hills, CA: Sage.
25 Whitmarsh, Tim. 2016. *Battling the Gods: Atheism in the Ancient World*. New York: Vintage.
26 Increasingly, some are working to uproot this assumption. Examples include African American secular activist Sikivu Hutchinson, and the American Humanist Association's recent spotlighting of secular black women and other nonreligious minorities. See: Hutchinson, Sikivu. 2011. *Moral Combat: Black Atheists, Gender Politics, and the Values Wars*. Los Angeles: Infidel Books; Hutchinson, Sikivu. 2013. *Godless Americana: Race and Religious Rebels*. Los Angeles: Infidel Books.
27 Abbott, Dena M., Debra Mollen, Caitlin Mercier, Elyxcus J. Anaya, and Victoria A. Rukus. 2019. "'Isn't Atheism a White Thing?': Centering the Voices of Atheists of Color." *Journal of Counseling Psychology* 67, no. 3: 275–287; Cameron, Christopher. 2019. *Black Freethinkers: A History of African American Secularism*. Evanston, IL: Northwestern University Press; Swann, Daniel. 2021. "Minority Nonreligion in North America." In *Bloomsbury Religion in North America*, edited by Jesse M. Smith and Ryan T. Cragun. London: Bloomsbury Academic.
28 Though see: Cameron, Christopher. 2019. *Black Freethinkers: A History of African American Secularism*. Evanston, IL: Northwestern University Press; Pinn, Anthony B. 2001. *By These Hands: A Documentary History of African American Humanism*. New York: New York University Press; Pinn, Anthony B. 2015. *Humanism: Essays on Race, Religion and Popular Culture*. London: Bloomsbury Academic; Swann, Daniel. 2021. "Minority Nonreligion in North America." In *Bloomsbury Religion in North America*, edited by Jesse M. Smith and Ryan T. Cragun. London: Bloomsbury Academic.
29 Howard, Simon, Kalen C. Kennedy, and Kaylen T. Vine. 2023. "'You don't believe in God? You ain't Black': Identifying as atheist elicits identity denial from Black ingroup members." *Cultural Diversity and Ethnic Minority Psychology* 29, no. 2: 202–7.
30 Edgell, Penny, Jacqui Frost, and Evan Stewart. 2017. "From Existential to Social Understandings of Risk: Examining Gender Differences in Nonreligion." *Social Currents* 4, no. 6 (December): 556–74. https://doi.org.10.1177/2329496516686619.
31 Brown-Iannuzzi, Jazmin L., Jonathan C. Golding, Will M. Gervais, Kellie R. Lynch, Nesa E. Wasarhaley, and Sierra Bainter. 2021. "Will Jurors Believe Nonbelievers? Perceptions of Atheist Rape Victims in the Courtroom." *Psychology of Religion and Spirituality* 13, no. 1: 119–126; Cragun, Ryan T., Barry A. Kosmin, Ariela

Keysar, Joseph H. Hammer, and Michael E. Nielsen. 2012. "On the Receiving End: Discrimination Toward the Non-Religious." *Journal of Contemporary Religion* 27, no. 1: 105–27. https://doi.org.https://doi.org/10.1080/13537903.2012.642741; Gervais, Will M. 2013. "In Godlessness We Distrust: Using Social Psychology to Solve the Puzzle of Anti-Atheist Prejudice." *Social and Personality Psychology Compass* 7, no. 6 (June): 366–77. https://doi.org.10.1111/spc3.12035; Gervais, Will M. 2014. "Everything Is Permitted? People Intuitively Judge Immorality as Representative of Atheists." *PLoS ONE* 9, no. 4 (April 9). https://doi.org.10.1371/journal.pone.0092302; Gervais, Will M., Dimitris Xygalatas, Ryan T. McKay, Michiel van Elk, Emma E. Buchtel, Mark Aveyard, Sarah R. Schiavone, Ilan Dar-Nimrod, Annika M. Svedholm-Häkkinen, Tapani Riekki, Eva Kundtová Klocová, Jonathan E. Ramsay, and Joseph Bulbulia. 2017. "Global Evidence of Extreme Intuitive Moral Prejudice against Atheists." *Nature Human Behaviour* 1, no. 8 (August): 1–6. https://doi.org.10.1038/s41562-017-0151; Hammer, Joseph H., Ryan T. Cragun, Karen Hwang, and Jesse Smith. 2012. "Forms, Frequency, and Correlates of Perceived Anti-Atheist Discrimination." *Secularism and Nonreligion* 1: 43–67. https://doi.org.http://doi.org/10.5334/snr.ad.

32 Abbott, Dena M., and Debra Mollen. 2018. "Atheism as a Concealable Stigmatized Identity: Outness, Anticipated Stigma, and Well-Being." *The Counseling Psychologist* 38: 397–424; Quinn, Diane M., and Stephenie R. Chaudoir. 2009. "Living with a Concealable Stigmatized Identity: The Impact of Anticipated Stigma, Centrality, Salience, and Cultural Stigma on Psychological Distress and Health." *Journal of Personality and Social Psychology* 97, no. 4 (October): 634–51. https://doi.org.10.1037/a0015815; Quinn, Diane M., and Valerie A. Earnshaw. 2011. "Understanding Concealable Stigmatized Identities: The Role of Identity in Psychological, Physical, and Behavioral Outcomes." *Social Issues and Policy Review* 5, no. 1 (December): 160–90. https://doi.org.10.1111/j.1751-2409.2011.01029.x.

33 Hunsberger, Bruce. 2006. *Atheists: A Groundbreaking Study of America's Nonbelievers*. Amherst, NY: Prometheus Books.

34 Quillian, Lincoln, Karen S. Cook, and Douglas S. Massey. 2006. "New Approaches to Understanding Racial Prejudice and Discrimination." *Annual Review of Sociology* 32, no. 1: 299–328.

35 Cameron, Christopher. 2019. *Black Freethinkers: A History of African American Secularism*. Evanston, IL: Northwestern University Press; Swann, Daniel. 2020. *A Qualitative Study of Black Atheists: "Don't Tell Me You're One of Those!"* Lanham, MD: Lexington Books.

36 Discrediting in the Erving Goffman sense, where an identity can put a person at risk of social stigma. See: Goffman, Erving. 1986. *Stigma: Notes on the Management of Spoiled Identity*. New York: Touchstone.

37 The GSS includes a question asking about belief in god (GOD), but it also includes a question asking people how their belief in god has changed over time (GODCHNGE). If one only looks at current belief in god (GOD), just 1.8% of black Americans indicate they are atheists. But the change in belief question

(GODCHNGE) reveals that the percentage is higher; closer to 3.3% of black Americans are atheists. If 3.3% of black Americans are atheists, that's just over 1.5 million black atheists in the US.

38 Swann, Daniel. 2020. *A Qualitative Study of Black Atheists: "Don't Tell Me You're One of Those!"* Lanham, MD: Lexington Books.

39 Collett, Jessica L., and Omar Lizardo. 2009. "A Power-Control Theory of Gender and Religiosity." *Journal for the Scientific Study of Religion* 48, no. 2 (June): 213–31; Hadaway, C. Kirk. 1989. "Identifying American Apostates: A Cluster Analysis." *Journal for the Scientific Study of Religion* 28, no. 2 (June): 201–15; Hadaway, C. Kirk, and Wade Clark Roof. 1988. "Apostasy in American Churches: Evidence from National Survey Data." In *Falling From The Faith: Causes and Consequences of Religious Apostasy*, edited by D. G. Bromley, 29–47. Thousand Oaks, CA: Sage Publications; Hoffmann, John P. 2009. "Gender, Risk, and Religiousness: Can Power Control Provide the Theory?" *Journal for the Scientific Study of Religion* 48, no. 2 (June): 232–40; Lizardo, Omar, and Jessica L. Collett. 2009. "Rescuing the Baby from the Bathwater: Continuing the Conversation on Gender, Risk, and Religiosity." *Journal for the Scientific Study of Religion* 48, no. 2 (June): 256–59.

40 Edgell, Penny, Jacqui Frost, and Evan Stewart. 2017. "From Existential to Social Understandings of Risk: Examining Gender Differences in Nonreligion." *Social Currents* 4, no. 6 (December): 556–74. https://doi.org.10.1177/2329496516686619.

41 Black, Amy, and Stanley Rothman. 1998. "Have You Really Come a Long Way? Women's Access to Power in the United States." *Gender Issues* 16, no. 1/2: 107–34; Bose, Christine E., and Peter H. Rossi. 1983. "Gender and Jobs: Prestige Standings of Occupations as Affected by Gender." *American Sociological Review* 48, no. 3 (June): 316–30; Casper, Lynne M., Sara S. McLanahan, and Irwin Garfinkel. 1994. "The Gender-Poverty Gap: What We Can Learn from Other Countries." *American Sociological Review* 59, no. 4 (August): 594–605; Dobash, R. Emerson, and Russell Dobash. 1979. *Violence Against Wives*. New York: Macmillan; Greenstein, Theodore N. 2000. "Economic Dependence, Gender, and the Division of Labor in the Home: A Replication and Extension." *Journal of Marriage and the Family* 62, no. 2 (May): 322–35; Maume, David J., Jr. 1999. "Glass Ceilings and Glass Escalators: Occupational Segregation and Race and Sex Differences in Managerial Promotions." *Work and Occupations* 26, no. 4 (November): 483–509; Roth, Louise Marie. 2003. "Selling Women Short: A Research Note on Gender Differences in Compensation on Wall Street." *Social Forces* 82, no. 2 (December): 783–802.

42 Miller, Alan S., and Rodney Stark. 2002. "Gender and Religiousness: Can Socialization Explanations Be Saved?" *American Journal of Sociology* 107, no. 6 (May): 1399–1423. https://doi.org.10.1086/342557.

43 Cameron, Christopher. 2019. *Black Freethinkers: A History of African American Secularism*. Evanston, IL: Northwestern University Press; Swann, Daniel. 2020. *A Qualitative Study of Black Atheists: "Don't Tell Me You're One of Those!"* Lanham, MD: Lexington Books.

44 Baker, Joseph O., and Buster G. Smith. 2015. *American Secularism: Cultural Contours of Nonreligious Belief Systems*. New York: New York University Press.
45 Though there is still evidence that a considerable segment of the public considers belief in god a part of being an American: Edgell, Penny, Joseph Gerteis, and Douglas Hartmann. 2006. "Atheists As 'Other': Moral Boundaries and Cultural Membership in American Society." *American Sociological Review* 71: 211–34; Edgell, Penny, Douglas Hartmann, Evan Stewart, and Joseph Gerteis. 2016. "Atheists and Other Cultural Outsiders: Moral Boundaries and the Non-Religious in the United States." *Social Forces* 95, no. 2 (December): 607–38. https://doi.org.10.1093/sf/sow063.
46 Caplovitz, David, and Fred Sherrow. 1977. *The Religious Drop-Outs: Apostasy Among College Graduates*. Beverly Hills, CA: Sage; Hadaway, C. Kirk. 1989. "Identifying American Apostates: A Cluster Analysis." *Journal for the Scientific Study of Religion* 28, no. 2 (June): 201–15; Streib, Heinz, and Constantin Klein. 2013. "Atheists, Agnostics, and Apostates." In *APA Handbook of Psychology, Religion, and Spirituality: Vol. 1. Context, Theory, and Research*, edited by Kenneth I. Pargament, Julie J. Exline, and James W. Jones, 713–28. Washington, DC: American Psychological Association.
47 Analyzing both race and sex in the GSS at different points in time illustrates this point well. Both race (as a dummy-coded variable) and gender (also dummy-coded) were statistically significantly associated with having left religion in the 1980s and in the 2010s. However, neither variable ever accounted for even 1% of the variation observed in who leaves religion. In short, yes, there are minor differences in rejecting religion by race and gender, but those differences are so minor they don't matter much at all and cannot be used to predict who is or is not going to leave religion.
48 Keister, Lisa A. 2008. "Conservative Protestants and Wealth: How Religion Perpetuates Asset Poverty." *American Journal of Sociology* 113, no. 5 (March): 1237–71; Keister, Lisa A., and Darren E. Sherkat, eds. 2014. *Religion and Inequality in America: Research and Theory on Religion's Role in Stratification*. Cambridge, UK: Cambridge University Press; Solt, Frederick, Philip Habel, and J. Tobin Grant. 2011. "Economic Inequality, Relative Power, and Religiosity." *Social Science Quarterly* 92, no. 2 (June). https://doi.org.10.1111/j.1540-6237.2011.00777.x.
49 Roof, Wade Clark, and William McKinney. 1987. *American Mainline Religion: Its Changing Shape and Future*. New Brunswick, NJ: Rutgers University Press.
50 To illustrate this, we regressed religious attendance (from "never" to "more than once a week"), belief in an afterlife (yes or no), and religious affiliation (yes or no) on respondent's income, using GSS data from 1972 to 2021, and looked at the amount of variation in the religious measures that was explained by income. Variation explained—also known as the coefficient of determination—is expressed as R^2 and is measured as a value ranging from 0 to 1, with 0 indicating none of the variation in the dependent variable is explained and 1 indicating that all of the variation in the dependent variable was explained. For attendance, income

explained virtually none of the variation ($R^2 = 0.0002$; or 0.02%). Similarly, for belief in an afterlife, income explained almost no variation ($R^2 = 0.001$; 0.1%). Finally, with religious affiliation, income also explained effectively none of the variation ($R^2 = 0.0003$; 0.03%). What these coefficients mean is that knowing how much money someone makes is not going to tell you anything about their religiosity.

51 Barrett, Justin L. 2012. *Born Believers: The Science of Children's Religious Belief.* New York: Simon and Schuster.

52 Hunsberger, Bruce. 2006. *Atheists: A Groundbreaking Study of America's Nonbelievers.* Amherst, NY: Prometheus Books; Kanazawa, Satoshi. 2010. "Why Liberals and Atheists Are More Intelligent." *Social Psychology Quarterly* 73, no. 1 (June): 33–57. https://doi.org.10.1177/0190272510361602.

53 Braun, Claude M. J. 2012. "Explaining Global Secularity: Existential Security or Education?" *Secularism and Nonreligion* 1 (November 26): 68–93. http://doi.org/10.5334/snr.ae; Sherkat, Darren E. 2011. "Religion and Scientific Literacy in the United States." *Social Science Quarterly* 92, no. 5 (December): 1134–50. https://doi.org.10.1111/j.1540-6237.2011.00811.x.

54 Darnell, Alfred, and Darren E. Sherkat. 1997. "The Impact of Protestant Fundamentalism on Educational Attainment." *American Sociological Review* 62, no. 2 (April): 306–15.

55 Funk, Richard B., and Fern K. Willits. 1987. "College Attendance and Attitude-Change: A Panel Study, 1970–81." *Sociology of Education* 60, no. 4 (October): 224–31; Larson, Edward J., and Larry Witham. 1998. "Leading Scientists Still Reject God." *Nature* 394, no. 6691 (July 23): 313.

56 Johnson, Daniel Carson. 1997. "Formal Education vs. Religious Belief: Soliciting New Evidence with Multinomial Logit Modeling." *Journal for the Scientific Study of Religion* 36 (June): 231–46.

57 Lee, Jenny J. 2002. "Religion and College Attendance: Change among Students." *The Review of Higher Education* 25, no. 4 (Summer): 369–84; Loury, Linda D. 2004. "Does Church Attendance Really Increase Schooling?" *Journal for the Scientific Study of Religion* 43, no. 1 (March): 119–27; Putnam, Robert D., and David E. Campbell. 2012. *American Grace: How Religion Divides and Unites Us.* New York: Simon & Schuster.

58 Putnam, Robert D. 2001. *Bowling Alone: The Collapse and Revival of American Community.* 1st ed. New York: Simon & Schuster.

59 Baker, Joseph O., and Buster G. Smith. 2015. *American Secularism: Cultural Contours of Nonreligious Belief Systems.* New York: New York University Press; Funk, Richard B., and Fern K. Willits. 1987. "College Attendance and Attitude-Change: A Panel Study, 1970–81." *Sociology of Education* 60, no. 4 (October): 224–31.

60 Silk, Mark, and Andrew Walsh. 2008. *One Nation, Divisible: How Regional Religious Differences Shape American Politics.* Lanham, MD: Rowman & Littlefield.

61 Obviously, Native Americans lived in the region before Mormons moved in. We do not mean to imply the region was without people before Mormons moved there.

62 Roof, Wade Clark, and William McKinney. 1987. *American Mainline Religion: Its Changing Shape and Future.* New Brunswick, NJ: Rutgers University Press.
63 Finke, Roger, and Rodney Stark. 2005. *The Churching of America, 1776–2005: Winners and Losers in Our Religious Economy.* Revised edition. New Brunswick, NJ: Rutgers University Press.
64 Wellman, James K., and Katie E. Corcoran. 2013. "Religion and Regional Culture: Embedding Religious Commitment within Place." *Sociology of Religion* 74, no. 4 (Winter): 496–520. https://doi.org.10.1093/socrel/srt046.
65 Table 2.1 is based on GSS data. In order to limit the possibility of identifying specific individuals, the GSS releases the publicly available data set with regional data rather than state-level data. To find which states correspond with which region, please see the GSS Codebook: https://gss.norc.org/documents/codebook/GSS_Codebook_AppendixD.pdf.
66 Silk, Mark, and Andrew Walsh. 2008. *One Nation, Divisible: How Regional Religious Differences Shape American Politics.* Lanham, MD: Rowman & Littlefield.
67 Bramadat, Paul, Patricia O'Connell Killen, and Sarah Wilkins-Laflamme. 2022. *Religion at the Edge: Nature, Spirituality, and Secularity in the Pacific Northwest.* Vancouver: UBC Press; Killen, Patricia O'Connell. 2004. *Religion and Public Life in the Pacific Northwest: The None Zone.* Lanham, MD: AltaMira Press; O'Connell, Nicholas. 2003. *On Sacred Ground: The Spirit of Place in Pacific Northwest Literature.* 1st edition. Seattle: University of Washington Press.
68 Weakliem, David L., and Robert Biggert. 1999. "Region and Political Opinion in the Contemporary United States." *Social Forces* 77, no. 3 (March): 863–86.
69 Sharp, Elaine B., and Mark R. Joslyn. 2008. "Culture, Segregation, and Tolerance in Urban America." *Social Science Quarterly* 89, no. 3 (September): 573–91. https://doi.org.10.1111/j.1540-6237.2008.00549.x.
70 Butler, Sandra S. 2017. "LGBT Aging in the Rural Context." *Annual Review of Gerontology and Geriatrics* 37, no. 1: 127–42. https://doi.org.10.1891/0198-8794.37.127.
71 Weakliem, David L., and Robert Biggert. 1999. "Region and Political Opinion in the Contemporary United States." *Social Forces* 77, no. 3 (March): 863–86.
72 Sharp, Elaine B., and Mark R. Joslyn. 2008. "Culture, Segregation, and Tolerance in Urban America." *Social Science Quarterly* 89, no. 3 (September): 573–91. https://doi.org.10.1111/j.1540-6237.2008.00549.x.
73 Sherkat, Darren E. 2016. "Sexuality and Religious Commitment Revisited: Exploring the Religious Commitments of Sexual Minorities, 1991–2014." *Journal for the Scientific Study of Religion* 55, no. 4 (December): 756–69. https://doi.org.10.1111/jssr.12300; Woodell, Brandi, and Philip Schwadel. 2020. "Changes in Religiosity Among Lesbian, Gay, and Bisexual Emerging Adults." *Journal for the Scientific Study of Religion* 59, no. 2 (June): 379–96. https://doi.org.10.1111/jssr.12653.
74 Sherkat, Darren E. 2019. "Public Opinion and Religion: Gay Rights in the United States." *Oxford Research Encyclopedia of Politics* (March 26). https://doi.org.10.1093/acrefore/9780190228637.013.994.

75 Large, nationally representative surveys have only recently started asking questions that would allow for the identification of transgender individuals. As a result, there is not sufficient data to examine these individuals at this time. For instance, in the 2021 wave of the GSS, there were just 10 individuals who identified as transgender. That was the second year a question about participants' gender identity was included. In the 2018 wave, there were just 2 individuals. We cannot do any meaningful analyses with 12 individuals.

76 Day, Abby. 2022. *Why Baby Boomers Turned from Religion: Shaping Belief and Belonging, 1945–2021*. New York: Oxford University Press.

77 Altemeyer, Bob, and Bruce Hunsberger. 1997. *Amazing Conversions: Why Some Turn to Faith & Others Abandon Religion*. Amherst, NY: Prometheus Books; Thiessen, Joel, and Sarah Wilkins-Laflamme. 2020. *None of the Above: Nonreligious Identity in the US and Canada*. New York: New York University Press.

78 We didn't include sexual orientation/identity in the model because it was not included in earlier decades.

79 Chaves, Mark. 1994. "Secularization as Declining Religious Authority." *Social Forces* 72, no. 3 (March): 749–74.

80 Edgell, Penny, Joseph Gerteis, and Douglas Hartmann. 2006. "Atheists As 'Other': Moral Boundaries and Cultural Membership in American Society." *American Sociological Review* 71, no. 2 (April): 211–34; Edgell, Penny, Douglas Hartmann, Evan Stewart, and Joseph Gerteis. 2016. "Atheists and Other Cultural Outsiders: Moral Boundaries and the Non-Religious in the United States." *Social Forces* 95, no. 2 (December): 607–38. https://doi.org.10.1093/sf/sow063.

3. WHY ARE THEY LEAVING?

1 "Apostasy," is of course a loaded term, one that too often privileges religion. Thus, we don't use it much in this book, preferring instead the more neutral phrase "religious exiting."

2 Zuckerman, Phil. 2012. *Faith No More: Why People Reject Religion*. New York: Oxford University Press.

3 Cragun, Ryan T. 2007. "A Role Conflict Theory of Religious Change: An Explanation and Test." (PhD diss., University of Cincinnati).

4 While this is a problem with the structure of Cragun's dissertation, it's also a problem with ordinary least squares (OLS) regression. In OLS regression, there is a single dependent variable but there can be lots of independent variables. The problem lies in the nature of the relationships that are being modeled. Some factors matter far more for some individuals than for others. OLS regression does not capture such nuance easily.

5 Bromley, David G., ed. 1998. *The Politics of Religious Apostasy: The Role of Apostates in the Transformation of Religious Movements*. Westport, CT: Praeger Publishers; Enstedt, Daniel, Göran Larsson, and Teemu T. Mantsinen, eds. 2019. *Handbook of Leaving Religion*. Leiden: Brill; Ebaugh, Helen Rose Fuchs. 1988. *Becoming an Ex: The Process of Role Exit*. Chicago: University of Chicago Press;

Zuckerman, Phil. 2011. *Faith No More: Why People Reject Religion*. New York: Oxford University Press.

6 A good example is a book by Thiessen, Joel and Sarah Wilkins-Laflamme. 2020. *None of the Above: Nonreligious Identity in the US and Canada*. New York: New York University Press.

7 The Pew Forum on Religion & Public Life. 2009. "Faith in Flux: Changes in Religious Affiliation in the US." Washington, DC: Pew Research Center.

8 Cragun, Ryan T., John Stinespring, and Andrew Tillman. 2019. "Sunday Football or Church? A Case Study in Substitutes and Complements." *Review of Religious Research* 61, no. 2 (June 1): 169–87. https://doi.org/10.1007/s13644-019-00367-0.

9 Cragun, Ryan T., and J. Edward Sumerau. 2015. "The Last Bastion of Sexual and Gender Prejudice? Sexualities, Race, Gender, Religiosity, and Spirituality in the Examination of Prejudice Toward Sexual and Gender Minorities." *Journal of Sex Research* 52, no. 7 (August 12): 821–34. https://doi.org.10.1080/00224499.2014.925534; Darwin, Helana. 2020. "Navigating the Religious Gender Binary." *Sociology of Religion* 81, no. 2 (Summer): 185–205. https://doi.org.10.1093/socrel/srz034; Burke, Kelsy. 2016. *Christians under Covers: Evangelicals and Sexual Pleasure on the Internet*. Reprint edition. Oakland: University of California Press; Thomas, Jeremy N., and Andrew L. Whitehead. 2015. "Evangelical Elites' Anti-Homosexuality Narratives as a Resistance Strategy Against Attribution Effects." *Journal for the Scientific Study of Religion* 54, no. 2 (May): 345–62. https://doi.org.10.1111/jssr.12188.

10 Brown, R. Khari. 2009. "Denominational Differences in Support for Race-Based Policies Among White, Black, Hispanic, and Asian Americans." *Journal for the Scientific Study of Religion* 48, no. 3 (September): 604–15; Emerson, Michael O., and Christian Smith. 2000. *Divided by Faith: Evangelical Religion and the Problem of Race in America*. New York: Oxford University Press; Butler, Anthea D. 2021. *White Evangelical Racism: The Politics of Morality in America*. Chapel Hill: The University of North Carolina Press; Jones, Robert P. 2020. *White Too Long: The Legacy of White Supremacy in American Christianity*. Illustrated edition. New York: Simon & Schuster.

11 Cragun, Ryan T., and Barry A. Kosmin. 2013. "Cheating or Leveling the Playing Field? Rethinking How We Ask Questions About Religion in the United States." *Free Inquiry* 33, no. 4 (June/July), 25–30.

12 We drew upon this book for the list of the 10 largest denominations in the US: Lindner, Eileen W., ed. 2012. *Yearbook of American & Canadian Churches 2012*. Annual edition. Nashville, TN: Abingdon Press.

13 Cragun, Ryan T., and J. Edward Sumerau. 2015. "The Last Bastion of Sexual and Gender Prejudice? Sexualities, Race, Gender, Religiosity, and Spirituality in the Examination of Prejudice Toward Sexual and Gender Minorities." *Journal of Sex Research* 52, no. 7 (August 12): 821–34. https://doi.org.10.1080/00224499.2014.925534; Sumerau, J. Edward, Ryan T. Cragun,

and Lain A. B. Mathers. 2016. "Contemporary Religion and the Cisgendering of Reality." *Social Currents* 3, no. 3 (September): 293–311. https://doi.org.10.1177/2329496515604644.

14 The percentages in this section come from the 2021 wave of the General Social Survey.

15 Avishai, Orit. 2008. "'Doing Religion' In a Secular World: Women in Conservative Religions and the Question of Agency." *Gender & Society* 22, no. 4 (August): 409–33. https://doi.org.10.1177/0891243208321019; Woodhead, Linda. 2012. "Gender Differences in Religious Practice and Significance." *Travail, genre et societes* 27, no. 1: 33–54.

16 Dr. Laura Schlessinger (1947–) is a radio host and author who is known for her conservative views on a number of issues, particularly related to the family.

17 Obviously, this was well before *Roe v. Wade* was overturned in *Dobbs v. Jackson Women's Health Organization* in 2022.

18 Details can be found at their website: https://clergyproject.org/.

19 Waal, Frans de. 2014. *The Bonobo and the Atheist: In Search of Humanism Among the Primates*. New York: W. W. Norton & Company.

20 Chaves, Mark. 1997. *Ordaining Women: Culture and Conflict in Religious Organizations*. Cambridge, MA: Harvard University Press.

21 Avishai, Orit. 2008. "'Doing Religion' In a Secular World: Women in Conservative Religions and the Question of Agency." *Gender & Society* 22, no. 4 (August): 409–33. https://doi.org.10.1177/0891243208321019.

22 Cragun, Ryan T., and Michael Nielsen. 2009. "Fighting Over 'Mormon': Media Coverage of the FLDS and LDS." *Dialogue: A Journal of Mormon Thought* 43, no. 1 (Spring): 65–104.

23 Mauss, Armand L. 1994. *The Angel and the Beehive: The Mormon Struggle With Assimilation*. Chicago: University of Illinois Press.

24 We're not arguing here that secularization is inevitable, only that it *seems* inevitable.

25 Kasselstrand, Isabella, Phil Zuckerman, and Ryan T. Cragun. 2023. *Beyond Doubt: The Secularization of Society*. New York: New York University Press.

26 Fazzino, Lori L., and Ryan T. Cragun. 2017. "'Splitters!': Lessons from Monty Python for Secular Organizations in the US." In *Organized Secularism in the United States: New Directions in Research*, 57–85. Religion and Its Others: Studies in Religion, Nonreligion, and Secularity, edited by Ryan T. Cragun, Christel J. Manning, and Lori L. Fazzino. Berlin: De Gruyter.

27 Addington, Aislinn. 2017. "Building Bridges in the Shadows of Steeples: Atheist Community and Identity Online." In *Organized Secularism in the United States: New Directions in Research*, 135–50. Religion and Its Others: Studies in Religion, Nonreligion, and Secularity, edited by Ryan T. Cragun, Christel J. Manning, and Lori L. Fazzino. Berlin: De Gruyter.

28 Fazzino, Lori L., and Ryan T. Cragun. 2017. "'Splitters!': Lessons from Monty Python for Secular Organizations in the US." In *Organized Secularism in the United*

States: New Directions in Research, 57–85. Religion and Its Others: Studies in Religion, Nonreligion, and Secularity, edited by Ryan T. Cragun, Christel J. Manning, and Lori L. Fazzino. Berlin: De Gruyter; LeDrew, Stephen. 2015. *The Evolution of Atheism: The Politics of a Modern Movement*. New York: Oxford University Press.

29 Hout, Michael, and Claude S. Fischer. 2002. "Why More Americans Have No Religious Preference: Politics and Generations." *American Sociological Review* 67, no. 2 (April): 165–90.

30 Sherkat, Darren E. 2014. *Changing Faith: The Dynamics and Consequences of Americans' Shifting Religious Identities*. New York: New York University Press.

31 Glock, Charles Y. 1965. *Religion and Society in Tension*. Chicago: Rand McNally; Stark, Rodney, and Charles Y. Glock. 1968. *American Piety*. Berkeley: University of California Press.

32 Aarts, Olav, Ariana Need, Manfred Te Grotenhuis, and Nan Dirk De Graaf. 2010. "Does Duration of Deregulated Religious Markets Affect Church Attendance? Evidence from 26 Religious Markets in Europe and North America Between 1981 and 2006." *Journal for the Scientific Study of Religion* 49, no. 4 (December): 657–72; Park, Jerry Z., and Joseph Baker. 2007. "What Would Jesus Buy: American Consumption of Religious and Spiritual Material Goods." *Journal for the Scientific Study of Religion* 46, no. 4 (December): 501–17; Stolz, Jörg. 2010. "A Silent Battle: Theorizing the Effects of Competition Between Churches and Secular Institutions." *Review of Religious Research* 51, no. 3 (March): 253–76.

33 Cragun, Ryan T., John Stinespring, and Andrew Tillman. 2019. "Sunday Football or Church? A Case Study in Substitutes and Complements." *Review of Religious Research* 61, no. 2 (June 1): 169–87. https://doi.org/10.1007/s13644-019-00367-0.

34 Stark, Rodney, and Roger Finke. 2000. *Acts of Faith: Explaining the Human Side of Religion*. Berkeley: University of California Press.

35 Durkheim, Emile. 1997. *The Division of Labor in Society*. New York: The Free Press.

36 Woodhead, Linda. 2012. "Gender Differences in Religious Practice and Significance." *Travail, genre et societes* 27, no. 1: 33–54.

37 Pew Research Center. 2014. *How Americans Feel About Religious Groups: Jews, Catholics & Evangelicals Rated Warmly, Atheists and Muslims More Coldly*. Washington, DC.

38 Pew Research Center's Forum on Religion & Public Life. 2010. *U.S. Religious Knowledge Survey*. Washington, DC: Pew Research Center.

39 Remmel, Atko, and Meelis Friedenthal. 2020. "Atheism and Freethought in Estonian Culture." In *Freethought and Atheism in Central and Eastern Europe: The Development of Secularity and Nonreligion*, edited by Tomáš Bubík, Atko Remmel, and David Václavík, 84–110. Abingdon, UK: Routledge.

40 We thank an anonymous reviewer of this manuscript for suggesting this possibility.

41 Available here: https://www.pewresearch.org/religion/dataset/american-trends-panel-wave-30/.

42 Hout, Michael, and Claude S. Fischer. 2002. "Why More Americans Have No Religious Preference: Politics and Generations." *American Sociological Review* 67, no. 2 (April): 165–90.
43 Egan, Patrick J. 2020. "Identity as Dependent Variable: How Americans Shift Their Identities to Align with Their Politics." *American Journal of Political Science* 64, no. 3 (July): 699–716. https://doi.org.10.1111/ajps.12496; Margolis, Michele F. 2018. "How Politics Affects Religion: Partisanship, Socialization, and Religiosity in America." *Journal of Politics* 80, no. 1 (January): 30–43. https://doi.org.10.1086/694688.
44 Egan, Patrick J. 2020. "Identity as Dependent Variable: How Americans Shift Their Identities to Align with Their Politics." *American Journal of Political Science* 64, no. 3 (July): 699–716. https://doi.org.10.1111/ajps.12496.
45 Frost, Jacqui, Elaine Howard Ecklund, and Christopher P. Scheitle. 2023. "Patterns of Perceived Hostility and Identity Concealment among Self-Identified Atheists." *Social Forces* 101, no. 3 (March): 1580–1605. https://doi.org.10.1093/sf/soab165.
46 Kosmin, Barry and Ariela Keysar. 2006. *Religion in a Free Market*. Ithaca, NY: Paramount Market Publishing.
47 Mauss, Armand. 1969. "Dimensions of Religious Defection." *Review of Religious Research* 10, no. 3 (September): 128–135.
48 Moore, Robert A. 1983. "The Impossible Voyage of Noah's Ark." *Creation/Evolution Journal* 4, no. 1 (Winter): 1–43.
49 Davie, Grace. 2015. *Religion in Britain: A Persistent Paradox*. Second Edition. London: Wiley-Blackwell; Schafer, Markus H. 2018. "Who Talks Religion and What Are the Consequences for Social Ties? Unpacking a Sensitive Discussion Topic in Close Networks." *Sociology of Religion* 79, no. 4 (Winter): 395–424. https://doi.org.10.1093/socrel/srx069.
50 LeDrew, Stephen. 2015. *The Evolution of Atheism: The Politics of a Modern Movement*. New York: Oxford University Press.
51 Bader, Christopher D., F. Carsen Mencken, and Joseph O. Baker. 2017. *Paranormal America: Ghost Encounters, UFO Sightings, Bigfoot Hunts, and Other Curiosities in Religion and Culture*. 2nd edition. New York: New York University Press.
52 Altemeyer, Bob, and Bruce Hunsberger. 1997. *Amazing Conversions: Why Some Turn to Faith & Others Abandon Religion*. Amherst, NY: Prometheus Books.
53 Lauer, Claudia, and Meghan Hoyer. 2016. "Almost 1,700 Priests and Clergy Accused of Sex Abuse Are Unsupervised." *NBC News*, October 4; Saul, Josh. 2020. "Catholic Church Shields $2 Billion in Assets to Limit Abuse Payouts." *Bloomberg.com*, January 8.
54 McManus, Tracey. 2016. "Scientology Policy Enabled Years of Child Sexual Abuse, Lawsuit Says." *Tampa Bay Times*, September 19; Otterman, Sharon, and Ray Rivera. 2012. "Ultra-Orthodox Shun Their Own for Reporting Child Sexual Abuse." *The New York Times*, May 10.
55 Seavey, Gail. 2016. "If Our Secrets Define Us." Presented at the Ministerial Conference of the Unitarian Universalist Church, June 22, Columbus, Ohio.

56 Chaves, Mark, and Diana Garland. 2009. "The Prevalence of Clergy Sexual Advances Toward Adults in Their Congregations." *Journal for the Scientific Study of Religion* 48, no. 4 (December): 817–24. https://doi.org.10.1111/j.1468–5906.2009.01 482.x.
57 See, for example: Moore, Russell. 2021. "Losing Our Religion." Accessed January 22, 2022. https://www.russellmoore.com/2021/04/15/losing-our-religion/; Hansen, Hannah. 2019. "Nine Reasons Why Some People Abandon Christianity (And How to Talk to Them about God)." Accessed January 22, 2022. https://blog.cph.org/read/nine-reasons-why-some-people-abandon-christianity-and-how-to-talk-to-them-about-god; Wirthlin, Joseph B. 1999. "Helping Others in the Lord's Way." Accessed January 22, 2022. https://www.churchofjesuschrist.org/study/ensign/2015/06/helping-others-in-the-lords-way?lang=eng; Davidman, Lynn. 2014. *Becoming Un-Orthodox: Stories of Ex-Hasidic Jews*. Oxford: Oxford University Press.
58 Cragun, Ryan T. 2015. *How to Defeat Religion in 10 Easy Steps: A Toolkit for Secular Activists*. Durham, NC: Pitchstone Publishing.
59 42 is the answer.
60 Beyer, Peter. 2015. "Spirit and Power: The Growth and Global Impact of Pentecostalism." *Sociology of Religion* 76, no. 1 (Spring): 125–26. https://doi.org.10.1093/socrel/srv004.
61 Mencken, H. L. 1982. *A Mencken Chrestomathy: His Own Selection of His Choicest Writing*. Annotated edition. New York: Vintage.
62 Givens, Terryl. 2020. *Mormonism: What Everyone Needs to Know*. New York: Oxford University Press; Hall, John R. 1988. "The Impact of Apostates on the Trajectory of Religious Movements: The Case of Peoples Temple." In *Falling From The Faith: Causes and Consequences of Religious Apostasy*, edited by David G. Bromley, 229–59. Thousand Oaks, CA: Sage Publications; Hall, John R., and Philip Schuyler. 1998. "Apostasy, Apocalypse, and Religious Violence: An Exploratory Comparison of Peoples Temple, the Branch Davidians, and the Solar Temple." In *The Politics of Religious Apostasy: The Role of Apostates in the Transformation of Religious Movements*, edited by David G. Bromley, 141–70. Westport, CT: Praeger Publishers.
63 Schnabel, Landon, and Sean Bock. 2017. "The Persistent and Exceptional Intensity of American Religion: A Response to Recent Research." *Sociological Science* 4 (November): 686–700. https://doi.org.10.15195/v4.a28; Voas, David. 2009. "The Rise and Fall of Fuzzy Fidelity in Europe." *European Sociological Review* 25, no. 2 (April): 155–68. https://doi.org.10.1093/esr/jcn044.
64 Hadaway, C. Kirk. 1989. "Identifying American Apostates: A Cluster Analysis." *Journal for the Scientific Study of Religion* 28, no. 2 (June): 201–15; Speed, David, Caitlin Barry, and Ryan Cragun. 2020. "With a Little Help from My (Canadian) Friends: Health Differences between Minimal and Maximal Religiosity/Spirituality Are Partially Mediated by Social Support." *Social Science & Medicine* 265: 1–9. https://doi.org.10.1016/j.socscimed.2020.113387.

65 Uecker, Jeremy E., Mark D. Regnerus, and Margaret L. Vaaler. 2007. "Losing My Religion: The Social Sources of Religious Decline in Early Adulthood." *Social Forces* 85, no. 4 (June): 1667–92.

66 Griswold, Max G. et al. 2018. "Alcohol Use and Burden for 195 Countries and Territories, 1990–2016: A Systematic Analysis for the Global Burden of Disease Study 2016." *The Lancet* 392, issue 10152 (August 23): 1015–35. https://doi.org.10.1016 /S0140-6736(18)31310-2.

67 Uecker, Jeremy E., Mark D. Regnerus, and Margaret L. Vaaler. 2007. "Losing My Religion: The Social Sources of Religious Decline in Early Adulthood." *Social Forces* 85, no. 4 (June): 1667–92.

68 Gull, Bethany, Jesse Smith, and Ryan Cragun. 2023. "Outcast Women: Gender and Authenticity in Ex-Mormon Women's Disaffiliation Narratives." *Nova Religio* 26, no. 3 (February): 7–29. https://doi.org.10.1525/nr.2023.26.3.7.

69 Dobzhansky, Theodosius. 1973. "Nothing in Biology Makes Sense except in the Light of Evolution." *The American Biology Teacher* 35, no. 3 (March): 125–29. https://doi.org.10.2307/4444260.

70 Baker, Joseph O. 2013. "Acceptance of Evolution and Support for Teaching Creationism in Public Schools: The Conditional Impact of Educational Attainment." *Journal for the Scientific Study of Religion* 52, no. 1 (March): 216–28. https://doi.org .10.1111/jssr.12007; Branch, Glenn, and Eugenie C. Scott. 2008. "The Latest Face of Creationism in the Classroom." *Scientific American*, December. Updated January 1, 2009. https://www.scientificamerican.com/article/the-latest-face-of-creationism/.

71 Baumeister, Roy F., and DiPam M. Tice. 1984. "Role of Self-Presentation and Choice in Cognitive Dissonance under Forced Compliance: Necessary or Sufficient Causes?" *Journal of Personality and Social Psychology* 46, no. 1 (January): 5–13. http://doi.org/10.1037/0022-3514.46.1.5.

72 All credit for this metaphor goes to Rick Phillips, who came up with it. We use it here with his permission.

73 Many living things are able to reproduce without having sex.

74 There were no chariots in the Ancient Americas, as there were no large, domesticated mammals (like horses) to pull them. Horses were brought over by invading Europeans.

75 Do note that we're not arguing here that either of these criticisms would be instrumental in leading these individuals to exit their religions, only that these are not uncommon criticisms of these two religions.

76 Pinn, Anthony B, ed. 2014. *What Is Humanism and Why Does It Matter?* Abingdon, UK: Routledge.

77 Baggett, Jerome P. 2019. *The Varieties of Nonreligious Experience: Atheism in American Culture*. New York: New York University Press; Brooks, E. Marshall. 2018. *Disenchanted Lives: Apostasy and Ex-Mormonism among the Latter-Day Saints*. New Brunswick, NJ: Rutgers University Press; Hunsberger, Bruce. 2006. *Atheists: A Groundbreaking Study of America's Nonbelievers*. Amherst, NY: Prometheus Books.

78 Arli, Denni, Tuyet-Mai Nguyen, and Phong Tuan Nham. 2021. "Are Atheist Consumers Less Ethical? Investigating the Role of Religiosity and Atheism on Consumer Ethics." *Journal of Consumer Marketing* 38, no. 5: 525–39. https://doi.org.10.1108/JCM-04-2020-3755; Galen, Luke W. 2012. "Does Religious Belief Promote Prosociality? A Critical Examination." *Psychological Bulletin* 138, no. 5 (September): 876–906. https://doi.org.10.1037/a0028251; Ståhl, Tomas. 2021. "The Amoral Atheist? A Cross-National Examination of Cultural, Motivational, and Cognitive Antecedents of Disbelief, and Their Implications for Morality." *PLOS ONE* 16, no. 2 (February 24). https://doi.org.10.1371/journal.pone.0246593.

79 Voas, David, and Mark Chaves. 2016. "Is the United States a Counterexample to the Secularization Thesis?" *American Journal of Sociology* 121, no. 5 (March): 1517–56. https://doi.org.10.1086/684202.

80 Do note that we agree with Philip N. Cohen regarding "generations": https://familyinequality.wordpress.com/2021/05/26/open-letter-to-the-pew-research-center-on-generation-labels/. We use the generation labels here only because we wanted to make this as easy to understand as possible, not because we think these labels are meaningful.

81 Close readers will note that we used 3-year moving averages in figure 3.9, which actually hides the fact that Generation Z was already as likely to be nonreligious in the 2018 GSS as were Millennials (34.4% vs 35.2%, respectively) and were more likely to be nonreligious in the 2021 GSS than were Millennials (47.2% vs 40.1%). We used 3-year moving averages because they are less susceptible to a single-year spike and end up showing more substantive trends over time.

82 Some readers may catch the wording here. When we write "religious social scientists" we literally mean that the social scientists are religious, not that they study religion. In the sociology and psychology of religion, being religious (or nonreligious) can make a difference in how scholars think about and frame their subject matter.

83 Smith, Christian, and Amy Adamczyk. 2021. *Handing Down the Faith: How Parents Pass Their Religion on to the Next Generation.* New York: Oxford University Press; Bengtson, Vern L. 2013. *Families and Faith: How Religion Is Passed down across Generations.* New York: Oxford University Press; Smith, Christian, and Melinda Lundquist Denton. 2005. *Soul Searching: The Religious and Spiritual Lives of American Teenagers.* New York: Oxford University Press.

84 Manning, Christel J. 2015. *Losing Our Religion: How Unaffiliated Parents Are Raising Their Children.* New York: New York University Press; Stolz, Jörg, Judith Könemann, Mallory Schneuwly Purdie, Thomas Englberger, and Michael Krüggeler. 2016. *(Un)Believing in Modern Society: Religion, Spirituality, and Religious-Secular Competition.* London: Routledge.

85 Admittedly, our perspective here—that autonomy is a positive value—derives from our worldviews, which lean to the left. Conservative individuals will be less likely to see autonomy in children as a high-ranking value. For more on how conservatives and progressives differ in their values and morality, see: Lakoff,

George. 2016. *Moral Politics: How Liberals and Conservatives Think*. 3rd enlarged ed. Chicago: University of Chicago Press.

86   Edgell, Penny. 2005. *Religion and Family in a Changing Society*. Princeton, NJ: Princeton University Press; Houseknecht, Sharon K., and Jerry G. Pankhurst, eds. 1999. *Family, Religion, and Social Change in Diverse Societies*. New York: Oxford University Press.

87   Denton, Melinda Lundquist, Richard Flory, and Christian Smith. 2020. *Back-Pocket God: Religion and Spirituality in the Lives of Emerging Adults*. New York: Oxford University Press; Smith, Christian, and Amy Adamczyk. 2021. *Handing Down the Faith: How Parents Pass Their Religion on to the Next Generation*. New York: Oxford University Press.

88   Bryant, Seth L., Henri Gooren, Rick Phillips, and David G. Stewart. 2014. "Conversion and Retention in Mormonism." In *The Oxford Handbook of Religious Conversion*, edited by Lewis R. Rambo and Charles E. Farhadian, 756–85. New York: Oxford University Press.

89   Day, Abby. 2022. *Why Baby Boomers Turned from Religion: Shaping Belief and Belonging, 1945–2021*. New York: Oxford University Press.

90   Brown, Callum G. 2012. *Religion and the Demographic Revolution*. Martlesham, UK: Boydell Press.

91   Baker, Joseph O., and Buster G. Smith. 2015. *American Secularism: Cultural Contours of Nonreligious Belief Systems*. New York: New York University Press.

92   Voas, David, and Ingrid Storm. 2021. "National Context, Parental Socialization, and the Varying Relationship Between Religious Belief and Practice." *Journal for the Scientific Study of Religion* 60, no. 1 (March): 189–97. https://doi.org.10.1111/jssr.12691.

93   Smith, Christian, and Amy Adamczyk. 2021. *Handing Down the Faith: How Parents Pass Their Religion on to the Next Generation*. New York: Oxford University Press.

94   Corcoran, Katie E., and James K. Wellman. 2016. "'People Forget He's Human': Charismatic Leadership in Institutionalized Religion." *Sociology of Religion* 77, no. 4 (Winter): 309–33. https://doi.org.10.1093/socrel/srw049; Vermeer, Paul, and Peer Scheepers. 2021. "Church Growth in Times of Secularization: A Case Study of People Joining Evangelical Congregations in the Netherlands." *Review of Religious Research* 63, no. 1: 43–66. https://doi.org.10.1007/s13644-020-00434-x.

95   U.S. Department of Education. 2012. "Parent and Family Involvement in Education, from the National Household Education Surveys Program of 2012." *National Center for Education Statistics*. Retrieved December 12, 2014. https://nces.ed.gov/pubsearch/pubsinfo.asp?pubid=2013028rev.

96   Ganzach, Yoav. "Individual Differences and the Relationship between Education and Religiosity in Longitudinal versus Cross-Sectional Studies." *International Journal of Psychology*. (Online before print). https://doi.org.10.1002/ijop.12828.

97   Bradley, Martha S. 1993. *Kidnapped From That Land: The Government Raids on the Short Creek Polygamists*. Salt Lake City: University of Utah Press; Van

Wagoner, Richard S. 1989. *Mormon Polygamy: A History*. Salt Lake City, UT: Signature Books; Wright, Stuart A., and James T. Richardson, eds. 2011. *Saints Under Siege: The Texas State Raid on the Fundamentalist Latter Day Saints*. New York: New York University Press.
98 Merino, Stephen M. 2011. "Irreligious Socialization? The Adult Religious Preferences of Individuals Raised with No Religion." *Secularism and Nonreligion* 1, no. 0: 1–16.
99 Manning, Christel J. 2015. *Losing Our Religion: How Unaffiliated Parents Are Raising Their Children*. New York: New York University Press.
100 Krause, Neal. 2007. "Evaluating the Stress-Buffering Function of Meaning in Life Among Older People." *Journal of Aging and Health* 19, no. 5 (October): 792–812. https://doi.org.10.1177/0898264307304390; Krause, Neal, and Elena Bastida. 2011. "Church-Based Social Relationships, Belonging, and Health Among Older Mexican Americans." *Journal for the Scientific Study of Religion* 50, no. 2 (June): 397–409.
101 Bengtson, Vern L. 2013. *Families and Faith: How Religion Is Passed down across Generations*. New York: Oxford University Press.
102 Stark, Rodney, and Roger Finke. 2000. *Acts of Faith: Explaining the Human Side of Religion*. Berkeley: University of California Press.

4. WHERE DO THEY GO?

1 Christel Manning. 2015. *Losing Our Religion: How Unaffiliated Parents are Raising Their Children*. New York: New York University Press
2 Klingenberg, Maria and Sofia Sjö. 2019. "Theorizing religious socialization: a critical assessment." *Religion*, 49, no. 2 (April): 163–178.
3 Thiessen, Joel. 2016. "Kids, You Make the Choice: Religious and Secular Socialization among Marginal Affiliates and Nonreligious Individuals." *Secularism and Nonreligion*, 5, no. 1 (April), 6. http://doi.org/10.5334/snr.60
4 Koenig, Harold G., Dana King, & Verna Benner Carson. 2012. *Handbook of Religion and Health*. 2nd edition. Oxford: Oxford University Press.
5 Beider, Nadia. 2023. "Religious residue: The impact of childhood religious socialization on the religiosity of nones in France, Germany, Great Britain, and Sweden." *The British Journal of Sociology* 74, no. 1 (January): 50–69.
6 Smith, Jesse M. 2011. "Becoming an atheist in America: Constructing identity and meaning from the rejection of theism." *Sociology of Religion* 72, no. 2 (Summer): 215–237.
7 Blankholm, Joseph. *The Secular Paradox: On the Religiosity of the Not Religious*. New York. New York University Press.
8 For the most part, we don't correct the claims of our interviewees. However, it is worth noting that Dennis may not have been aware of the religious makeup of the US military. One report from 2010 found that 25.5% of members of the military had no religious affiliation, which was nearly 10% higher than the general public at that time. (Military Leadership Diversity Commission. 2010. *Religious Diversity*

in the U.S. Military. Issue Paper #22: Version 2. Arlington, VA: Military Leadership Diversity Commission.) Dennis was correct in noting that chaplains are disproportionately evangelical Christians, but military personnel are, if anything, less religious than are Americans in general.

9 Scheitle, Christopher P., and Amy Adamczyk. 2010. "High-cost Religion, Religious Switching, and Health." *Journal of Health and Social Behavior*, 51, no. 3 (September), 325–342.
10 Björkmark, Maria, Peter Nynäs, and Camilla Koskinen. 2022. "'Living Between Two Different Worlds': Experiences of Leaving a High-Cost Religious Group." *Journal of Religion and Health* 61 (August 17), 4721–4737.
11 Altemeyer, Bob and Bruce Hunsberger. 1996. *Amazing Conversions: Why Some Turn to Faith & Others Abandon Religion*. New York: Prometheus Books.
12 Klingenberg, Maria and Sofia Sjö. 2019. "Theorizing religious socialization: a critical assessment." *Religion*, 49, no. 2 (April): 163–178.
13 We use the term "cult" here because this is the language of our interviewee. In line with our broader discipline, we would refer to such religions as "new religious movements" or NRMs. See: Olson, Paul J. 2006. "The Public Perception of 'Cults' and 'New Religious Movements.'" *Journal for the Scientific Study of Religion* 45, no. 1 (March): 97–106.
14 This describes the basic pattern found in many studies of people who have left NRMs. See: Bromley, David G., ed. 1988. *Falling From The Faith: Causes and Consequences of Religious Apostasy*. Thousand Oaks, CA: Sage Publications; Bromley, David G., ed. 1998. *The Politics of Religious Apostasy: The Role of Apostates in the Transformation of Religious Movements*. Westport, CT: Praeger Publishers; Lewis, James R., and David G. Bromley. 1987. "The Cult Withdrawal Syndrome: A Case of Misattribution of Cause?" *Journal for the Scientific Study of Religion* 26, no. 4 (December): 508–22.
15 Furseth, Inger, and Pål Repstad. 2006. *An Introduction to the Sociology of Religion: Classical and Contemporary Perspectives*. Aldershot,UK: Ashgate.
16 Thiessen, Joel. 2016. "Kids, You Make the Choice: Religious and Secular Socialization among Marginal Affiliates and Nonreligious Individuals." *Secularism and Nonreligion*, 5, no. 1 (April), 6. http://doi.org/10.5334/snr.60.
17 Though the findings on this question are mixed. Some research shows kids are more likely to follow their mother's lead if the mother is religious and the father is not, while other data suggest it's more about which parent is *more* committed to their (non)religious beliefs. For more on this, see https://www.pewresearch.org/religion/2020/09/10/shared-beliefs-between-parents-and-teens/.
18 Smith, Jesse M. "Becoming an atheist in America: Constructing identity and meaning from the rejection of theism." *Sociology of Religion* 72, no. 2 (Summer): 215–237.
19 Day, Abby. 2022. *Why Baby Boomers Turned from Religion: Shaping Belief and Belonging, 1945–2021*. New York: Oxford University Press.

20 Our definition excludes those who have only made financial contributions to a secular organization. They must have participated in some way beyond writing a check.
21 Blankholm, Joseph. *The Secular Paradox: On the Religiosity of the Not Religious.* New York. New York University Press.
22 Wilkins-Laflamme, Sarah., and Joel Thiessen. 2020. "Religious Socialization and Millennial Involvement in Organized and Digital Nonbelief Activities." *Secularism and Nonreligion* 9(2). http://doi.org/10.5334/snr.126.
23 Cragun, Ryan T., Christel J. Manning, and Lori L. Fazzino, eds. 2017. *Organized Secularism in the United States: New Directions in Research.* Berlin: De Gruyter.
24 Smith, Jesse M. 2017. "Can the Secular be the Object of Belief and Belonging? The Sunday Assembly." *Qualitative Sociology* 40, no. 1 (March): 83–109.
25 Cragun, Ryan T., Christel Manning, and Lori L. Fazzino, eds. 2017. *Organized Secularism in the United States.* Berlin: De Gruyter; Baggett, Jerome P. 2019. *The Varieties of Nonreligious Experience: Atheism in American Culture.* New York: New York University Press.
26 See https://huffman.house.gov/freethought-caucus.
27 Langston, Joseph A., Joseph H. Hammer, Ryan T. Cragun, and Mary Ellen Sikes. 2017. "Inside The Minds and Movement of America's Nonbelievers: Organizational Functions, (Non)Participation, and Attitudes Toward Religion." In *Organized Secularism in the United States: New Directions in Research*, 191–219. Religion and Its Others: Studies in Religion, Nonreligion, and Secularity, edited by Ryan T. Cragun, Christel J. Manning, and Lori L. Fazzino. Berlin: De Gruyter.
28 Durkheim, Emile. 1997. *The Division of Labor in Society.* New York: The Free Press.
29 Cragun, Ryan T., and Kevin J. McCaffree. 2021. "Nothing Is Not Something: On Replacing Nonreligion with Identities." *Secular Studies* 3, no. 1 (April): 7–26. https://doi.org.10.1163/25892525-bja10017.
30 Langston, Joseph A., Joseph H. Hammer, Ryan T. Cragun, and Mary Ellen Sikes. 2017. "Inside The Minds and Movement of America's Nonbelievers: Organizational Functions, (Non)Participation, and Attitudes Toward Religion." In *Organized Secularism in the United States: New Directions in Research*, 191–219. Religion and Its Others: Studies in Religion, Nonreligion, and Secularity, edited by Ryan T. Cragun, Christel J. Manning, and Lori L. Fazzino. Berlin: De Gruyter.
31 Lee, Lois. 2012. "Research Note: Talking about a Revolution: Terminology for the New Field of Non-Religion Studies." *Journal of Contemporary Religion* 27, no. 1 (January): 129–39. https://doi.org.10.1080/13537903.2012.642742.
32 Remmel, Atko, and Meelis Friedenthal. 2020. "Atheism and Freethought in Estonian Culture." In *Freethought and Atheism in Central and Eastern Europe: The Development of Secularity and Nonreligion*, edited by Tomáš Bubík, Atko Remmel, and David Václavík, 84–110. Abingdon, UK: Routledge.

33 Zuckerman, Phil. 2020. *Society without God: What the Least Religious Nations Can Tell Us About Contentment*. 2nd edition. New York: New York University Press.

34 Quack, Johannes, and Cora Schuh, eds. 2017. *Religious Indifference: New Perspectives From Studies on Secularization and Nonreligion*. New York: Springer.

35 A simple calculation can illustrate this. Assuming roughly 30% of American adults have no religious affiliation, that would mean roughly 90 million Americans are not religious. Yet, a generous estimate of the number of Americans involved with organized secular groups in the US would be somewhere between 200,000 and 500,000 based on the reported memberships of the major secular organizations in the US—Freedom From Religion Foundation, American Atheists, American Humanist Association, and Council for Secular Humanism/Center for Inquiry. This suggests that less than 1% of nonreligious Americans are actively involved in organized secularism. For a similar calculation see: Cragun, Ryan T., and Christel Manning. 2017. "Introduction." In *Organized Secularism in the United States: New Directions in Research*, 1–12. Religion and Its Others: Studies in Religion, Nonreligion, and Secularity, edited by Ryan T. Cragun, Christel J. Manning, and Lori L. Fazzino. Berlin: De Gruyter.

36 For discussion of how some young adults are finding meaning in life see: Clydesdale, Tim, and Kathleen Garces-Foley. 2019. *The Twenty-Something Soul: Understanding the Religious and Secular Lives of American Young Adults*. New York: Oxford University Press.

37 Quack, Johannes, and Cora Schuh, eds. 2017. *Religious Indifference: New Perspectives From Studies on Secularization and Nonreligion*. 1st edition. New York: Springer.

38 Wilkins-Laflamme, Sarah. 2022. *Religion, Spirituality and Secularity among Millennials: The Generation Shaping American and Canadian Trends*. Abingdon, UK: Routledge.

39 Indeed, of all our interviews, we don't have evidence of anyone returning to organized religion, though this would of course require long-term tracking and follow-up with every participant, which we haven't done.

40 Do note that the ATUS is only of non-institutionalized American adults. It does not include children or people in prisons or mental institutions.

41 We are aware that a small percentage of individuals—Jews, Muslims, and Seventh-day Adventists, among others—hold religious services on different days of the week. However, collectively, those groups total less than 3% of the US population.

42 As was pointed out by the copyeditor of the book, the ATUS may underestimate the amount of time people spend in religious activities because people can only allot their time to one activity. Thus, if someone prays the Rosary while washing dishes, that will likely get attributed to just washing dishes and not a religious activity.

43 Presser, Stanley, and Linda Stinson. 1998. "Data Collection Mode and Social Desirability Bias in Self-Reported Religious Attendance." *American Sociological Review* 63, no. 1 (February): 137–45.

44 Hadaway, C. Kirk, Penny Long Marler, and Mark Chaves. 1993. "What the Polls Don't Show: A Closer Look at U.S. Church Attendance." *American Sociological Review* 58, no. 6 (December): 741–52; Hadaway, C. Kirk, Penny Long Marler, and Mark Chaves. 1998. "Overreporting Church Attendance in America: Evidence That Demands the Same Verdict." *American Sociological Review* 63, no. 1 (February): 122–30.
45 The ATUS actually does include tobacco and drug use as an option. Those who don't engage in religious activities spend .6 minutes on average consuming tobacco or other drugs while those who do engage in religious activities spend .03 minutes doing this, but the difference was not statistically significant.
46 Pew Research Center. 2014. *How Americans Feel About Religious Groups: Jews, Catholics & Evangelicals Rated Warmly, Atheists and Muslims More Coldly*. Washington, DC; Frost, Jacqui, Christopher P. Scheitle, and Elaine Howard Ecklund. 2023. "Patterns of Perceived Hostility and Identity Concealment among Self-Identified Atheists." *Social Forces* 101, no. 3 (March): 1580–1605. First published February 4, 2022. https://doi.org.10.1093/sf/soab165.
47 Sociologist and politician Daniel Moynihan's phrase to describe society's changing expectations when sufficient numbers of people adopt a behavior.
48 O'Hair, Madalyn Murray. 1989. *An Atheist Epic: The Complete Unexpurgated Story of How Bible and Prayers Were Removed from the Public Schools of the United States*. Austin, TX: American Atheist Press.

5. WHAT HAPPENS TO THEM?

1 Obviously, "spiritual" has some baggage for some religious exiters. Though a few reject the term outright, most were happy to use it if given the chance to explain what they mean by it. We're not imposing it here, nor do we mean any one thing by it. Other terms have been offered to capture the sense of awe, reverence, and wonder about the universe without implication of the supernatural, but for better or worse, "spiritual" seems to be the only one to really stick.
2 Again, we'll note this has to do with the over-representation in our sample of religious exiters who join secular groups. See the appendix for detailed discussion of methods.
3 Taves, Ann, Egil Asprem, and Elliott Ihm. 2018. "Psychology, Meaning Making, and the Study of Worldviews: Beyond Religion and Non-Religion." *Psychology of Religion and Spirituality* 10, no. 3 (August): 207–17. http://doi.org/10.1037/rel0000201.
4 Cragun, Ryan T., Lori Beaman, and Douglas Ezzy. Under Review. "Theorizing Lifestances: Understanding the Substantive Content of Nonreligion." *Sociology of Religion*.
5 Baker, Joseph O., and Buster G. Smith. 2015. *American Secularism: Cultural Contours of Nonreligious Belief Systems*. New York: New York University Press; Thiessen, Joel, and Sarah Wilkins-Laflamme. 2020. *None of the Above: Nonreligious Identity in the US and Canada*. New York: New York University Press; Cragun,

Ryan T., Lori Beaman, and Douglas Ezzy. Under Review. "Theorizing Lifestances: Understanding the Substantive Content of Nonreligion." *Sociology of Religion*.

6 Frost, Jacqui. 2023. "Ritualizing Nonreligion: Cultivating Rational Rituals in Secular Spaces." *Social Forces* 101, no. 4 (April): 2013–2033. Originally published May 15, 2022. https://doi.org.10.1093/sf/soac042.

7 Cragun, Ryan T., Barry A. Kosmin, Ariela Keysar, Joseph H. Hammer, and Michael E. Nielsen. 2012. "On the Receiving End: Discrimination Toward the Non-Religious." *Journal of Contemporary Religion* 27, no. 1 (January): 105–27. https://doi.org/10.1080/13537903.2012.642741; Edgell, Penny, Douglas Hartmann, Evan Stewart, and Joseph Gerteis. 2016. "Atheists and Other Cultural Outsiders: Moral Boundaries and the Non-Religious in the United States." *Social Forces* 95, no. 2 (December): 607–38. https://doi.org.10.1093/sf/sow063; Gervais, Will M. 2014. "Everything Is Permitted? People Intuitively Judge Immorality as Representative of Atheists." *PLoS ONE* 9, no. 4 (April 9). https://doi.org.10.1371/journal.pone.0092302.

8 Hayward, R. David, Neal Krause, Gail Ironson, Peter C. Hill, and Robert Emmons. 2016. "Health and Well-Being Among the Non-Religious: Atheists, Agnostics, and No Preference Compared with Religious Group Members." *Journal of Religion and Health* 55, no. 3 (June): 1024–37. https://doi.org.10.1007/s10943-015-0179-2.

9 See Zuckerman, Phil. 2020. *Society without God: What the Least Religious Nations Can Tell Us About Contentment*. 2nd edition. New York: New York University Press; Zuckerman, Phil. 2009. "Atheism, secularity, and well-being: How the findings of social science counter negative stereotypes and assumptions." *Sociology Compass* 3, no. 6 (June): 949–971.

10 Chapter 6 provides detailed analyses on many of these questions, including differences in meaning between exiters and those who remain religious.

11 Smith, Christian, and Melinda Lundquist Denton. 2005. *Soul Searching: The Religious and Spiritual Lives of American Teenagers*. New York: Oxford University Press.

12 See, for example: https://www.pewresearch.org/religion/2010/02/17/religion-among-the-millennials/.

13 This argument can be found here: https://youthandreligion.nd.edu/related-resources/preliminary-research-findings/sociologists-find-that-religious-teens-are-more-positive-about-life/.

14 By "self" we mean the social self that is constructed through interaction. We're not referring to some intrinsic self that exists apart from interaction. See Stryker, Sheldon, and Richard T. Serpe. 1982. "Commitment, identity salience, and role behavior: Theory and research example." In *Personality, Roles, and Social Behavior*, edited by William Ickes, and Eric S. Knowles, 199–218. New York: Springer-Verlag.

15 Anderson, Benedict. 2016. *Imagined Communities: Reflections on the Origin and Spread of Nationalism*. New York: Verso.

16 A topic that has occupied much of the literature on those who have left religion and are looking for secular "alternatives." See Frost, Jacqui. 2017. "Rejecting Rejection Identities: Negotiating Positive Non-Religiosity at the Sunday Assembly." In *Organized Secularism in the United States: New Directions in Research*, edited by Ryan T. Cragun, Christel Manning, and Lori L. Fazzino, 171–90. Berlin: De Gruyter.

17 See the appendix for a full account of the numbers of respondents identifying with specific terms.

18 Frost, Jacqui. 2017. "Rejecting Rejection Identities: Negotiating Positive Non-Religiosity at the Sunday Assembly." In *Organized Secularism in the United States: New Directions in Research*, edited by Ryan T. Cragun, Christel Manning, and Lori L. Fazzino, 171–90. Berlin: De Gruyter.

19 Goffman, Erving. 1959. *The Presentation of Self in Everyday Life*. New York: Anchor; Goffman, Erving. 1986. *Stigma: Notes on the Management of Spoiled Identity*. New York: Touchstone.

20 Abbott, Dena M., and Debra Mollen. 2018. "Atheism as a Concealable Stigmatized Identity: Outness, Anticipated Stigma, and Well-Being." *The Counseling Psychologist* 46, no. 6 (September): 685–707. https://doi.org.10.1177/0011000018792669; Abbott, Dena M., Debra Mollen, Jessica A. Boyles, and Elyxcus J. Anaya. 2021. "Hidden in Plain Sight: Working Class and Low-Income Atheists." *Journal of Counseling Psychology* 69, no. 1 (July). http://dx.doi.org.esearch.ut.edu/10.1037/cou0000562.

21 Smith, Jesse M., and Caitlin L. Halligan. 2021. "Making Meaning without a Maker: Secular Consciousness through Narrative and Cultural Practice." *Sociology of Religion* 82, no. 1 (Spring): 85–110. https://doi.org.10.1093/socrel/sraa016.

22 Berthomé, François, and Michael Houseman. 2010. "Ritual and Emotions: Moving Relations, Patterned Effusions." *Religion and Society* 1, no. 1 (March): 57–75; Knottnerus, J. David. 2010. "Collective Events, Rituals, and Emotions" In *Advances in Group Processes*. Volume 27. Edited by Kalkhoff, Will, Shane R. Thye, and Edward J. Lawler. Bingley, UK: Emerald Publishing.

23 Much will depend on how inclusive we are with respect to each. If we take rituals to be *any* kind of social activity, symbols to refer to *any* form of representation or communication, or myth to be *any* story one adheres to or finds value in, then to be human is to need the integrating elements of religion. But this is not useful, nor does it jibe with our definition of religion.

24 Hoesly, Dusty. 2015. "'Need a Minister? How About Your Brother?': The Universal Life Church between Religion and Non-Religion." *Secularism and Nonreligion* 4, no. 1 (October 23): 1–13. https://doi.org.10.5334/snr.be.

25 National programs are run by the American Humanist Association and the Center for Inquiry.

26 Formerly known as Campus Crusade for Christ, Cru is an interdenominational Christian parachurch organization represented on many college campuses.

27 Ebaugh, Helen Rose Fuchs. 1988. *Becoming an Ex: The Process of Role Exit*. Chicago: University of Chicago Press; Haire, Fio Selwyn. 2022. "Born again: Narrating the mental health journeys of religious exiters." *Sociology Compass* 16, no. 9 (September).
28 Weinberg, Martin S., Colin J. Williams, and Douglas W. Pryor. 1995. *Dual attraction: Understanding bisexuality*. New York: Oxford University Press.
29 McCauley, Robert N. 2011. *Why Religion Is Natural and Science Is Not*. Illustrated edition. New York: Oxford University Press.
30 One of these exceptions is Colin Campbell's 1971 *Toward a sociology of irreligion*. London: Macmillan. See also: Vernon, Glenn M. 1968. "The Religious 'Nones': A Neglected Category." *Journal for the Scientific Study of Religion* 7, no. 2 (Autumn): 219–29; and Demerath, N. J., III, and Victor Thiessen. 1966. "On Spitting Against the Wind: Organizational Precariousness and American Irreligion." *American Journal of Sociology* 71, no. 6 (May): 674–87.
31 van Mulukom, Valerie, Hugh Turpin, Roosa Haimila, Benjamin Grant Purzycki, Theiss Bendixen, Eva Kundtová Klocová, Dan Řezníček, et al. 2022. "What do nonreligious nonbelievers believe in? Secular worldviews around the world." *Psychology of Religion and Spirituality* (September).
32 Stenmark, Mikael. 2022. "Worldview studies." *Religious Studies* 58, no. 3 (September): 564–582; Taves, Ann. 2020. "From religious studies to worldview studies." Religion 50, no. 1: 137–147.
33 Taves, Ann, Asprem, Egil, & Ihm, Elliott. 2018. "Psychology, meaning making, and the study of worldviews: Beyond religion and non-religion." *Psychology of Religion and Spirituality* 10, no. 3 (August): 207–217.
34 Cottingham, John. 2014. *Philosophy of religion: towards a more humane approach*. Vol. 2. Cambridge, UK: Cambridge University Press.
35 Taves, Ann, Asprem, Egil, & Ihm, Elliott. 2018. "Psychology, meaning making, and the study of worldviews: Beyond religion and non-religion." *Psychology of Religion and Spirituality* 10, no. 3 (August): 207–217..
36 Eidhamar, Levi Geir. 2021. "Dimensions of the relationship between the individual and her unique worldview construction." *Religions* 12, no. 3 (March): 215.
37 See https://americanhumanist.org/what-is-humanism/. Retrieved January 2023.
38 van Mulukom, Valerie, Hugh Turpin, Roosa Haimila, Benjamin Grant Purzycki, Theiss Bendixen, Eva Kundtová Klocová, Dan Řezníček, et al. 2022. "What do nonreligious nonbelievers believe in? Secular worldviews around the world." *Psychology of Religion and Spirituality* (September).
39 For an interesting analysis of the history of the idea of worldview in the social sciences, see Wolters, Albert M. 1989. "On the idea of worldview and its relation to philosophy." In *Stained glass: Worldviews and social science*, edited by Paul A. Marshall, Sander Griffioen, and Richard J. Muow, 14–25. Lanham, MD: University Press of America.

40 Frost, Jacqui. 2019. "Certainty, Uncertainty, or Indifference? Examining Variation in the Identity Narratives of Nonreligious Americans." *American Sociological Review* 84, no. 5 (October): 828–50. https://doi.org.10.1177/0003122419871957.
41 Miller, Joan G. 1997. "Understanding the Role of Worldviews in Morality." *Human Development* 40, no. 6: 350–54. http://www.jstor.org/stable/26767714. See also Habermas, Jürgen. 2012. "'Reasonable' versus 'True,' or the Morality of Worldviews." In *Habermas and Rawls: Disputing the Political*, edited by James Gordon Finlayson and Fabian Freyenhagen, 92–113. New York: Routledge.
42 Ecklund, Elaine Howard, and David R. Johnson. 2021. *Varieties of Atheism in Science*. New York: Oxford University Press.
43 Zuckerman, Phil. 2019. *What It Means to Be Moral: Why Religion Is Not Necessary for Living an Ethical Life*. New York: Catapult.
44 Blankholm, Joseph, Abraham Hawley Suárez, Shakir Stephen, and Ryan T. Cragun. Under review. "Exclusive Empiricism and Mortal Finitude: What 'Atheist' and 'Agnostic' Really Mean." *Sociology of Religion*.
45 Baker, Joseph O. 2015. *American secularism: Cultural contours of nonreligious belief systems*. Vol. 3. New York: New York University Press.
46 Zeller, Benjamin E. 2010. *Prophets and Protons: New Religious Movements and Science in Late Twentieth-Century America*. Vol. 4. New York: New York University Press.
47 Cragun, Ryan T., and David Speed. 2022. "Religiosity and Happiness: Much Ado About Nothing." In *Religious and Secular Perspectives on Happiness and Wellbeing*, edited by S. Sugirtharajah, 167–91. Routledge Studies in Religion. London: Routledge; Smith, Jesse M., and Caitlin L. Halligan. 2021. "Making Meaning without a Maker: Secular Consciousness through Narrative and Cultural Practice." *Sociology of Religion* 82, no. 1 (Spring): 85–110. https://doi.org.10.1093/socrel/sraa016; Edgell, Penny, Mahala Miller, and Jacqui Frost. 2023. "What Makes Life Meaningful? Combinations of Meaningful Commitments Among Nonreligious and Religious Americans." *Sociology of Religion* 84, no. 4 (Winter): 426–46. https://doi.org.10.1093/socrel/srad002.
48 See Cragun, Ryan T., Lori Fazzino, and Christel Manning, eds. 2017. *Organized Secularism in the United States: New Directions in Research*. Berlin: De Gruyter; Zuckerman, Phil, ed. 2009. *Atheism and Secularity*. 2 volumes. Santa Barbara, CA: ABC-CLIO; Zuckerman, Phil, and John R. Shook, eds. 2017. *The Oxford handbook of secularism*. New York: Oxford University Press.
49 Dempsey-Henofer, Helen. 2019. "Death without God: Nonreligious Perspectives on End-of-Life Care." *Diversity and Equality in Health and Care* 16, no. 4.
50 Victor G. Cicirelli. 2011. "Religious and Nonreligious Spirituality in Relation to Death Acceptance or Rejection." *Death Studies* 35, no. 2 (February): 124–46. https://doi.org.10.1080/07481187.2011.535383.
51 Cragun, Ryan T. 2014. *What you don't know about religion (but should)*. Durham, NC: Pitchstone Publishing.

52 Engelke, Matthew. 2015. "Good without God: Happiness and Pleasure among the Humanists." *Journal of Ethnographic Theory* 5, no. 3 (Winter): 69–91.
53 Wilkinson, Peter J., and Peter G. Coleman. 2010. "Strong beliefs and coping in old age: A case-based comparison of atheism and religious faith." *Ageing & Society* 30, no. 2 (February): 337–361.
54 This, and parts of a few other quotes in this book, are also referenced in: Smith, Jesse M., and Caitlin L. Halligan. 2021. "Making Meaning without a Maker: Secular Consciousness through Narrative and Cultural Practice." Sociology of Religion 82, no. 1 (Spring): 85–110. doi: 10.1093/socrel/sraa016.
55 Mayer, Karl Ulrich. 2009. "New Directions in Life Course Research." *Annual Review of Sociology* 35, no. 1: 413–433.
56 Speed, Brandon, Thomas J. Coleman, and Joseph Langston. 2018. "What Do You Mean, 'What Does It All Mean?' Atheism, Nonreligion, and Life Meaning." *Sage Open* 8, no. 1 (January): 1–13; Zuckerman, Phil. 2014. *Living the Secular Life: New Answers to Old Questions*. New York: Penguin Press.
57 Baker, Joseph O., and Buster G. Smith. 2015. *American Secularism: Cultural Contours of Nonreligious Belief Systems*. New York: New York University Press.
58 Ibid.; Uecker, Jeremy E., Mark D. Regnerus, and Margaret L. Vaaler. 2007. "Losing My Religion: The Social Sources of Religious Decline in Early Adulthood." *Social Forces* 85, no. 4 (June): 1667–92.
59 Edgell, Penny, Douglas Hartmann, Evan Stewart, and Joseph Gerteis. 2016. "Atheists and Other Cultural Outsiders: Moral Boundaries and the Non-Religious in the United States." *Social Forces* 95, no. 2 (December): 607–638.
60 Frost, Jacqui, Christopher P. Scheitle, and Elaine Howard Ecklund. 2023. "Patterns of Perceived Hostility and Identity Concealment Among Self-Identified Atheists." *Social Forces* 101, no. 3(March): 1580–1605. First published February 4, 2022.
61 Hammer, Joseph, Ryan T. Cragun, Karen Hwang, and Jesse M. Smith. 2012. "Forms, frequency, and correlates of perceived anti-atheist discrimination." *Secularism and Nonreligion* 1 (December): 43–67.
62 Cragun, Ryan T., Barry Kosmin, Ariela Keysar, Joseph H. Hammer, and Michael Nielsen. 2012. "On the receiving end: Discrimination toward the non-religious in the United States." *Journal of Contemporary Religion*, 27, no. 1 (January), 105–127.
63 Wilcox, W. Bradford, and Nicholas H. Wolfinger. 2008. "Living and Loving 'Decent': Religion and Relationship Quality Among Urban Parents." *Social Science Research* 37, no. 3 (February): 828–843.
64 Nica, Andreea. 2019. "Exiters of religious fundamentalism: Reconstruction of social support and relationships related to well-being." *Mental Health, Religion & Culture* 22, no. 5 (September): 543–556.
65 See: McCaffree, Kevin. 2019. "Atheism, Social Networks and Health: A Review and Theoretical Model." *Secularism and Nonreligion* 8, no. 0 (October): 9. https://doi.org/10.5334/snr.101.

66 Zimmerman, Kevin J., Jesse M. Smith, Kevin Simonson, and W. Benjamin Myers. 2015. "Familial relationship outcomes of coming out as an atheist." *Secularism and Nonreligion*, 4, no. 1 (May).
67 Edgell, Penny, Douglas Hartmann, Evan Stewart, and Joseph Gerteis. 2016. "Atheists and Other Cultural Outsiders: Moral Boundaries and the Non-Religious in the United States." *Social Forces* 95, no. 2 (December): 607–638.
68 Cragun, Ryan T., Kevin McCaffree, Ivan Puga-Gonzalez, Wesley Wildman, and F. LeRon Shults. 2021. "Religious Exiting and Social Networks: Computer Simulations of Religious/Secular Pluralism." *Secularism and Nonreligion* 10, no. 1 (March): 2. https://doi.org/10.5334/snr.129.
69 Lee, Lois. 2015. *Recognizing the Non-Religious: Reimagining the Secular*. New York: Oxford University Press.
70 Mackey, Cameron D., Christopher F. Silver, Kimberly Rios, Colleen M. Cowgill, and Ralph W. Hood, Jr. 2021. "Concealment of nonreligious identity: Exploring social identity threat among atheists and other nonreligious individuals." *Group Processes & Intergroup Relations* 24, no. 5 (August): 860–877.
71 Fang, Ruolian, Blaine Landis, Zhen Zhang, Marc H. Anderson, Jason D. Shaw, and Martin Kilduff. 2015. "Integrating Personality and Social Networks: A Meta-Analysis of Personality, Network Position, and Work Outcomes in Organizations." *Organization Science* 26, no. 4 (July-August): 1243–60. http://www.jstor.org/stable/43661047.
72 Ingersoll-Dayton, Berit, Neal Krause, and David Morgan. 2002. "Religious Trajectories and Transitions Over the Life Course." *The International Journal of Aging and Human Development* 55, no. 1 (July): 51–70; see also Wuthnow, Robert. *After the Baby Boomers: How Twenty- and Thirty-Somethings Are Shaping the Future of American Religion*. Princeton, NJ: Princeton University Press. Accessed March 20, 2023. ProQuest Ebook Central.

6. HOW IS THIS AFFECTING SOCIETY?

1 Hadaway, C. Kirk, Penny Long Marler, and Mark Chaves. 1993. "What the Polls Don't Show: A Closer Look at U.S. Church Attendance." *American Sociological Review* 58, no. 6 (December): 741–52; Hadaway, C. Kirk, Penny Long Marler, and Mark Chaves. 1998. "Overreporting Church Attendance in America: Evidence That Demands the Same Verdict." *American Sociological Review* 63, no. 1 (February): 122–30.
2 Schnabel, Landon, and Sean Bock. 2017. "The Persistent and Exceptional Intensity of American Religion: A Response to Recent Research." *Sociological Science* 4 (November): 686–700. https://doi.org.10.15195/v4.a28; Schnabel, Landon, and Sean Bock. 2018. "The Continuing Persistence of Intense Religion in the United States: Rejoinder." *Sociological Science* 5 (January): 711–21. https://doi.org.10.15195/v5.a30.
3 Voas, David. 2009. "The Rise and Fall of Fuzzy Fidelity in Europe." *European Sociological Review* 25, no. 2 (April): 155–68. https://doi.org.10.1093/esr/jcn044.

4 Voas, David, and Mark Chaves. 2018. "Even Intense Religiosity Is Declining in the United States: Comment." *Sociological Science* 5 (November): 694–710. https://doi.org.10.15195/v5.a29.

5 Burge, Ryan P. 2021. *The Nones: Where They Came From, Who They Are, and Where They Are Going*. Minneapolis: Fortress Press; Putnam, Robert D., and David E. Campbell. 2012. *American Grace: How Religion Divides and Unites Us*. New York: Simon & Schuster.

6 Berlinerblau, Jacques. 2022. *Secularism: The Basics*. New York: Routledge.

7 Pat Robertson. (n.d.). AZQuotes.com. Retrieved December 21, 2023. https://www.azquotes.com/quote/1290949.

8 Green, David. 2012. "Woodstock for Atheists: A Moment for Nonbelievers." National Public Radio Religion Section, March 23. https://www.npr.org/transcripts/149021993.

9 Cragun, Ryan T., Stephanie Yeager, and Desmond Vega. 2012. "Research Report: How Secular Humanists (and Everyone Else) Subsidize Religion in the United States." *Free Inquiry* 32, no. 4 (June/July): 39–46; see also: https://www.irs.gov/charities-non-profits/churches-religious-organizations

10 Chaves, Mark. 2004. *Congregations in America*. First edition. Cambridge, MA: Harvard University Press; Chaves, Mark, and Sharon L. Miller, eds. 1998. *Financing American Religion*. Walnut Creek, CA: AltaMira Press.

11 "Clubs" not in a pejorative sense, but in a straightforward definitional one, as in "a group of persons formally joined together based on some common interest."

12 McBride, Michael. 2007. "Club Mormon: Free-Riders, Monitoring, and Exclusion in the LDS Church." *Rationality and Society* 19, no. 4 (November): 395–424.

13 Partners for Sacred Places. 2016. *The Economic Halo Effect of Historic Sacred Places*. Philadelphia, PA: Partners for Sacred Places.

14 By "secular charities" we mean all charities not based on or affiliated with any religion, not charities with an explicitly nonreligious mission. Doctors without Borders is an example of the former; Humanist Global Charity, of the latter. There is also a third category here: religious charities. These would be organizations that are primarily charities but are affiliated with a religion. In the interest of parsimony, we are not going to address those.

15 Cragun, Ryan T., Alexandra Rodriguez, Jesse Smith, and David Speed. Under Review. "Religiosity is Declining BUT Giving is Increasing: Can the Nonreligious Really Be Less Generous?" *Secularism and Nonreligion*.

16 Partners for Sacred Places. 2016. *The Economic Halo Effect of Historic Sacred Places*. Philadelphia, PA: Partners for Sacred Places.

17 Gervais, Will M., Dimitris Xygalatas, Ryan T. McKay, Michiel van Elk, Emma E. Buchtel, Mark Aveyard, Sarah R. Schiavone, Ilan Dar-Nimrod, Annika M. Svedholm-Häkkinen, Tapani Riekki, Eva Kundtová Klocová, Jonathan E. Ramsay, and Joseph Bulbulia. 2017. "Global Evidence of Extreme Intuitive Moral Prejudice against Atheists." *Nature Human Behaviour* 1, no. 8 (August): 1–6. https://doi.org.10.1038/s41562-017-0151.

18 Edgell, Penny, Douglas Hartmann, Evan Stewart, and Joseph Gerteis. 2016. "Atheists and Other Cultural Outsiders: Moral Boundaries and the Non-Religious in the United States." *Social Forces* 95, no. 2 (December): 607–38. https://doi.org.10.1093/sf/sow063.
19 Sumerau, J. E., Lain A. B. Mathers, and Ryan T. Cragun. 2016. "'Can't Put My Finger on It': A Research Report on the Non-Existence and Meaninglessness of Sin." *The Qualitative Report* 21, no. 6: 1132–44. https://doi.org/10.46743/2160-3715/2016.2385.
20 There is some evidence that nonreligious people have more carefully thought out ethical views that allow for, say, theft when a situation is not just and it would save someone's life (Richards, P. Scott. 1991. "The Relation between Conservative Religious Ideology and Principled Moral Reasoning: A Review." *Review of Religious Research* 32, no. 4 (June): 359–68. https://doi.org.10.2307/3511682.).
21 The data were obtained by Hemant Mehta, an atheist blogger. See here: https://onlysky.media/hemant-mehta/in-2022-atheists-make-up-only-0-09-of-the-federal-prison-population/. The data have also been examined by others, like the FiveThirtyEight website: https://fivethirtyeight.com/features/are-prisoners-less-likely-to-be-atheists/.
22 Mehta, Hemant. February 28, 2022. "In 2021, atheists made up only 0.1% of the federal prison population." OnlySky. Accessed December 20, 2023. https://onlysky.media/hemant-mehta/in-2021-atheists-made-up-only-0-1-of-the-federal-prison-population/.
23 Ream, Geofrey L., and Nicholas R. Forge. 2014. "Homeless Lesbian, Gay, Bisexual, and Transgender (LGBT) Youth in New York City: Insights from the Field." *Child Welfare* 93, no. 2 (January): 7–22.
24 Perry, Samuel L. 2018. "Not Practicing What You Preach: Religion and Incongruence Between Pornography Beliefs and Usage." *The Journal of Sex Research* 55, no. 3: 369–80. https://doi.org.10.1080/00224499.2017.1333569; Perry, Samuel L. 2017. "Pornography Use and Marital Separation: Evidence from Two-Wave Panel Data." *Archives of Sexual Behavior*. https://doi.org.10.1007/s10508-017-1080-8.
25 In our model to estimate these probabilities, we set sex as a constant (male) and race as a constant (white) and used average age, education, and income in order to derive these estimates.
26 Putnam, Robert D. 2001. *Bowling Alone: The Collapse and Revival of American Community*. New York: Simon & Schuster; Sander, Thomas H., and Robert D. Putnam. 2010. "Still Bowling Alone?: The Post-9/11 Split." *Journal of Democracy* 21, no. 1 (January): 9–16. https://doi.org.10.1353/jod.0.0153.
27 This point is made clear in a recent publication: Speed, David, and Penny Edgell. 2023. "Eternally Damned, Yet Socially Conscious? The Volunteerism of Canadian Atheists." *Sociology of Religion* 24, no. 3 (Autumn): 265–91. https://doi.org.10.1093/socrel/srac035.
28 In an ironic violation of the prohibition to do so in Matthew 6:2.
29 For a description, see https://newsroom.churchofjesuschrist.org/article/helping-hands.

30 Abrams, Samuel J. "Perspective: Why even secular people should worry about Gen Z's lack of faith." *Deseret News*, March 4, 2023. Accessed March 8, 2023. https://www.deseret.com/2023/3/4/23617175/gen-z-faith-religious-nones-civic-life-voluntees-charity.

31 Speed, David, and Penny Edgell. 2023. "Eternally Damned, Yet Socially Conscious? The Volunteerism of Canadian Atheists." *Sociology of Religion* 24, no. 3 (Autumn): 265–91. https://doi.org.10.1093/socrel/sraco35.

32 The figures show the predicted probabilities of active involvement in various organizations, holding constant age, sex, income, education, marital status, and number of children. The figures are probabilities, which range from 0 to 1.

33 A description of their activities can be found here: https://www.metromin.org/our-work/food/.

34 See https://feedingtampabay.org/about.

35 If we were, we might note that 98% of Feeding Tampa Bay's revenue goes directly to their programs, with just 2% going to overhead. For Metropolitan Ministries, 89% goes to their programs with 11% going to overhead.

36 Kirk, Dudley. 1996. "Demographic Transition Theory." *Population Studies* 50, no. 3 (November): 361–87; Morgan, S. Philip, Miles G. Taylor, Karen S. Cook, and Douglas S. Massey. 2006. "Low Fertility at the Turn of the Twenty-First Century." *Annual Review of Sociology* 32, no. 1 (August): 375–99.

37 Bartkowski, John P., Aida I. Ramos-Wada, Chris G. Ellison, and Gabriel A. Acevedo. 2012. "Faith, Race-Ethnicity, and Public Policy Preferences: Religious Schemas and Abortion Attitudes Among U.S. Latinos." *Journal for the Scientific Study of Religion* 51, no. 2 (June): 343–58. https://doi.org.10.1111/j.1468–5906.2012.01645.x; Goldscheider, Calvin, and William D. Mosher. 1991. "Patterns of Contraceptive Use in the United States: The Importance of Religious Factors." *Studies in Family Planning* 22, no. 2 (March-April): 102–15.

38 Brecke, Anna. 2018. "Handmaids and Duggars: The Significance of Christian Patriarchy in Pop Culture." *Media Report to Women* 46, no. 3 (Summer):12–18; Hammarberg, Melvyn. 2013. *The Mormon Quest for Glory: The Religious World of the Latter-Day Saints*. New York: Oxford University Press.

39 Morgan, S. Philip, Miles G. Taylor, Karen S. Cook, and Douglas S. Massey. 2006. "Low Fertility at the Turn of the Twenty-First Century." *Annual Review of Sociology* 32, no. 1 (August): 375–99.

40 Shain, Michelle. 2019. "Beyond Belief: How Membership in Congregations Affects the Fertility of U.S. Mormons and Jews." *Review of Religious Research* 61, no. 3 (September): 201–19. https://doi.org.10.1007/s13644-019-00378-x; Weeden, Jason, Robert Kurzban, and Douglas T. Kenrick. 2020. "The Elephant in the Pews: Reproductive Strategy and Religiosity." In *The Oxford Handbook of Evolutionary Psychology and Religion*, edited by James R. Liddle, and Todd K. Shackelford, 182–197. New York: Oxford University Press.

41 Carr, Deborah. 2007. "The Cost of Kids." *Contexts* 6, no. 4 (November): 62. https://doi.org.10.1525/ctx.2007.6.4.62.

42 Pew Research Center. 2015. *The Future of World Religions: Population Growth Projections, 2010–2050.* Washington, DC: Pew Research Center.
43 Ibid.
44 Last, Jonathan V. 2014. *What to Expect When No One's Expecting: America's Coming Demographic Disaster.* New York: Encounter Books.
45 Zeng, Yi, Huashuai Chen, Zhenglian Wang, and Kenneth C. Land. 2015. "Implications of Changes in Households and Living Arrangements for Future Home-Based Care Needs and Costs for Disabled Elders in China." *Journal of Aging and Health* 27, no. 3 (April): 519–50. https://doi.org.10.1177/0898264314552690.
46 Coleman, David, and Robert Rowthorn. 2011. "Who's Afraid of Population Decline? A Critical Examination of Its Consequences." *Population and Development Review* 37(s1):217–48. https://doi.org.10.1111/j.1728-4457.2011.00385.x.
47 Coleman, David, and Robert Rowthorn. 2011. "Who's Afraid of Population Decline? A Critical Examination of Its Consequences." *Population and Development Review* 37, no. 1 (January): 217–48. https://doi.org.10.1111/j.1728-4457.2011.00385.x.
48 Pew Research Center's Forum on Religion & Public Life. 2010. *U.S. Religious Knowledge Survey.* Washington, DC: Pew Research Center.
49 We picked these two examples as nods to people Cragun knows—Carla Sykes, who collects and displays model horses; and Andrew Tillman, who loves his comics!
50 Jödicke, Ansgar, and Andrea Rota. 2014. "Patterns of Religious Education Policy in Switzerland: The Long Arm of Distanced Christians?" *Journal for the Scientific Study of Religion* 53, no. 4 (December): 722–38. https://doi.org.10.1111/jssr.12150.
51 We're not suggesting that educators demand their religious students think about their own religion as fiction; only that, in a public classroom setting, modern religions not be elevated above ancient ones.
52 Krause, Neal. 2007. "Evaluating the Stress-Buffering Function of Meaning in Life Among Older People." *Journal of Aging and Health* 19, no. 5 (November): 792–812. https://doi.org.10.1177/0898264307304390; Li, P. F. Jonah, Y. Joel Wong, and Ruth C. L. Chao. 2019. "Happiness and Meaning in Life: Unique, Differential, and Indirect Associations with Mental Health." *Counseling Psychology Quarterly* 32, nos. 3/4 (April): 396–414. https://doi.org.10.1080/09515070.2019.1604493.
53 Giles, Tyler, Daniel M. Hungerman, and Tamar Oostrom. 2023. "Opiates of the Masses? Deaths of Despair and the Decline of American Religion." *National Bureau of Economic Research Working Paper Series* No. 30840 (January). https://doi.org.10.3386/w30840.
54 Nietzsche seemed to fall into this camp: "If we have our own 'why' of life we shall get along with almost any 'how.'" *Twilight of the Idols.*
55 See, for instance, Peterson, Jordan B. 2018. *12 Rules for Life: An Antidote to Chaos.* Toronto: Random House Canada.
56 https://www.naturalism.org/philosophy/death/death-nothingness-and-subjectivity.

57 Beaman, Lori G. 2017. "Living Well Together in a (Non)Religious Future: Contributions from the Sociology of Religion." *Sociology of Religion* 78, no. 1 (Spring): 9–32. https://doi.org.10.1093/socrel/srw054; Beaman, Lori G. and Lauren Strumos. Forthcoming. "Towards Equality: Including Non-Human Animals in Studies of Lived Religion and Nonreligion." *Social Compass*.

58 Smith, Jesse M., and Caitlin L. Halligan. 2021. "Making Meaning without a Maker: Secular Consciousness through Narrative and Cultural Practice." *Sociology of Religion* 82, no. 1 (Spring): 85–110. https://doi.org.10.1093/socrel/sraa016; Zuckerman, Phil. 2014. *Living the Secular Life: New Answers to Old Questions*. New York: Penguin Press; Zuckerman, Phil. 2020. *Society without God: What the Least Religious Nations Can Tell Us About Contentment*. 2nd edition. New York: New York University Press.

59 Gaffey, Conor. 2015. "Religion Better for Mental Health Than Sport, Study Finds." *Newsweek*, August 5. https://www.newsweek.com/religion-better-mental-health-sport-study-finds-331240; Storrs, Carina. 2016. "Going to Church Could Help You Live Longer, Study Says." *CNN*, May 16. https://www.cnn.com/2016/05/16/health/religion-lifespan-health/index.html.

60 Koenig, Harold G., Michael E. McCullough, and David B. Larson. 2001. *Handbook of Religion and Health*. New York: Oxford University Press; Hayward, R. David, and Neal Krause. 2014. "Religion, Mental Health, and Well-Being: Social Aspects." In *Religion, personality, and social behavior*, edited by Vassilis Saroglou, 255–80. New York: Psychology Press.

61 Collins, Chiquita A., and David R. Williams. 1999. "Segregation and Mortality: The Deadly Effects of Racism." *Sociological Forum* 14, no. 3 (September): 495–523.

62 Jackson, James S., Tony N. Brown, David R. Williams, Myriam Torres, Sherrill L. Sellers, and Kendrick Brown. 1996. "Racism and the Physical and Mental Health Status of African Americans: A Thirteen Year National Panel Study." *Ethnicity and Disease* 6, no. 1 (Winter/Spring): 132–47.

63 Edgell, Penny, Joseph Gerteis, and Douglas Hartmann. 2006. "Atheists As 'Other': Moral Boundaries and Cultural Membership in American Society." *American Sociological Review* 71, no. 2 (April): 211–34; Wallace, Michael, Bradley R. E. Wright, and Allen Hyde. 2014. "Religious Affiliation and Hiring Discrimination in the American South: A Field Experiment." *Social Currents* 1, no. 2 (June): 189–207. https://doi.org.10.1177/2329496514524541.

64 Stavrova, Olga, Detlef Fetchenhauer, and Thomas Schlösser. 2013. "Why Are Religious People Happy? The Effect of the Social Norm of Religiosity across Countries." *Social Science Research* 42, no. 1(January): 90–105. https://doi.org.10.1016/j.ssresearch.2012.07.002.

65 Speed, David, Caitlin Barry, and Ryan Cragun. 2020. "With a Little Help from My (Canadian) Friends: Health Differences between Minimal and Maximal Religiosity/Spirituality Are Partially Mediated by Social Support." *Social Science & Medicine* 265 (November): 1–9. https://doi.org.10.1016/j.socscimed.2020.113387.

66 Griswold, Max G., Nancy Fullman, Caitlin Hawley, et al. 2018. "Alcohol Use and Burden for 195 Countries and Territories, 1990–2016: A Systematic Analysis for the Global Burden of Disease Study 2016." *The Lancet* 392, no. 10152 (September): 1015–35. https://doi.org.10.1016/S0140-6736(18)31310-2; Chang, Cindy M., Catherine G. Corey, Brian L. Rostron, and Benjamin J. Apelberg. 2015. "Systematic Review of Cigar Smoking and All Cause and Smoking Related Mortality." *BMC Public Health* 15, art. no. 390 (April). https://doi.org.10.1186/s12889-015-1617-5; Lee, Peter N., and Barbara A. Forey. 2013. "Indirectly Estimated Absolute Lung Cancer Mortality Rates by Smoking Status and Histological Type Based on a Systematic Review." *BMC Cancer* 13, art. no. 189 (April). https://doi.org.10.1186/1471-2407-13-189.

67 Arli, Denni, Tuyet-Mai Nguyen, and Phong Tuan Nham. 2021. "Are Atheist Consumers Less Ethical? Investigating the Role of Religiosity and Atheism on Consumer Ethics." *Journal of Consumer Marketing* (August—ahead of print). https://doi.org.10.1108/JCM-04-2020-3755.

68 https://human.no/seremonier/konfirmasjon/.

69 Mahabharata 5:1517.

70 La Tzu in *T'ai-Shang Kan-Ying P'ien*.

71 The Bible, New International Version, Matthew 7:12.

72 Guru Granth Sahib, http://www.srigurugranth.org/1299.html.

73 Allport, Gordon W. 1954. *The Nature of Prejudice*. Reading, MA: Addison-Wesley; Laythe, Brian, Deborah Finkel, and Lee A. Kirkpatrick. 2001. "Predicting Prejudice from Religious Fundamentalism and Right-Wing Authoritarianism: A Multiple-Regression Approach." *Journal for the Scientific Study of Religion* 40, no. 1(March): 1-10.

74 Cragun, Ryan T., and J. E. Sumerau. 2017. "No One Expects a Transgender Jew: Religious, Sexual and Gendered Intersections in the Evaluation of Religious and Nonreligious Others." *Secularism and Nonreligion* 6, no. 0 (January): 1–16. https://doi.org.10.5334/snr.82.

75 Preston, Jesse Lee, and Ryan S. Ritter. 2013. "Different Effects of Religion and God on Prosociality With the Ingroup and Outgroup." *Personality and Social Psychology Bulletin* 39, no. 11 (November): 1471–83. https://doi.org.10.1177/0146167213499937; Speed, David, and Melanie Brewster. 2021. "Love Thy Neighbour . . . or Not: Christians, but Not Atheists, Show High In-Group Favoritism." *Secularism and Nonreligion* 10, no. 1 (June): 7. https://doi.org.10.5334/snr.136.

76 Pew Research Center. 2014. *How Americans Feel About Religious Groups: Jews, Catholics & Evangelicals Rated Warmly, Atheists and Muslims More Coldly*. Washington, DC.

77 Note that the statistics in figure 6.10 do not control for demographics.

7. CONCLUSION

1 Strawn, Kelley D. 2019. "What's Behind the 'Nones-Sense'? Change Over Time in Factors Predicting Likelihood of Religious Nonaffiliation in the United States."

    Journal for the Scientific Study of Religion 58, no. 3 (September): 707–24. https://doi.org.10.1111/jssr.12609.
2. Bruce, Steve. 2002. *God Is Dead: Secularization in the West*. London: Blackwell Publishers; Bruce, Steve. 2013. *Secularization: In Defense of an Unfashionable Theory*. Oxford, UK: Oxford University Press.
3. Simon, Stephanie. 2014. "Taxpayers Fund Teaching Creationism." *Politico*. Retrieved January 26, 2023. https://www.politico.com/story/2014/03/education-creationism-104934.
4. Carson v. Makin, 596 U.S. (2022).
5. The situation is of course different when we're talking about individuals who join a religion voluntarily as adults and later exit. This describes very few of our participants.
6. Cragun, Ryan T., Lori Beaman, and Douglas Ezzy. Under Review. "Theorizing Lifestances: Understanding the Substantive Content of Nonreligion." *Sociology of Religion*; Smith, Jesse M. and Ryan T. Cragun. 2019. "Mapping Religion's Other: A Review of the Study of Nonreligion and Secularity." *Journal for the Scientific Study of Religion* 58, no. 2 (June): 319–355.
7. Cragun, Ryan T., Lori Beaman, and Douglas Ezzy. Under Review. "Theorizing Lifestances: Understanding the Substantive Content of Nonreligion." *Sociology of Religion*.
8. Batson, C. Daniel, Patricia Schoenrade, and W. Larry Ventis. 1993. *Religion and the Individual: A Social-Psychological Perspective*. New York: Oxford University Press.
9. Bellah, Robert N., Richard Madsen, William M. Sullivan, Ann Swidler, and Steven M. Tipton. 2007. *Habits of the Heart: Individualism and Commitment in American Life*. 3rd ed. Oakland: University of California Press; Luckmann, Thomas. 2022. *The Invisible Religion: The Problem of Religion in Modern Society*. Abingdon, UK: Routledge.
10. Ammerman, Nancy Tatom. 2021. *Studying Lived Religion*. New York: New York University Press.
11. Salonen, Anna Sofia. 2018. "Living and Dealing with Food in an Affluent Society—A Case for the Study of Lived (Non)Religion." *Religions* 9, no. 10 (October): 306; https://doi.org/10.3390/rel9100306.
12. Salonen, Anna Sofia. 2018. "Living and Dealing with Food in an Affluent Society—A Case for the Study of Lived (Non)Religion." *Religions* 9, no. 10 (October): 306.
13. We don't intend a straw man argument here. We don't think Ammerman or most others working on lived religion would actually embrace the idea that "nothing is not religion." We push the concept to its edge to highlight what we see as a real problem in how some researchers today conceptualize (and privilege) religion and how it's studied.
14. Pew Research Center. 2022. *Modeling the Future of Religion in America*. Washington, DC: Pew Research Center.

15 Berger, Peter L. 1967. *The Social Reality of Religion*. New York: Faber and Faber; Berger, Peter L. 1990. *The Sacred Canopy: Elements of a Sociological Theory of Religion*. New York: Anchor.
16 Guyau, Jean-Marie. 1897. *The Non-Religion of the Future: A Sociological Study*. New York: Henry Holt and Company.
17 For those who care, the model is $Y' = -11.3566 + .005742(YEAR)$. You can insert the year into that model to see what the projected percentage of the population that is nonreligious would be in the future. Do keep in mind that with a linear model, it will eventually cross 100%, which is not what we are actually arguing. We think this approach works up to 2040, but probably not after that. Also, the R^2 for this simple regression was .91, which was rather shocking but also very interesting.
18 Rogers, Everett M. 2006. *Diffusion of Innovations*. 5th edition. New York: Free Press.
19 Kasselstrand, Isabella, Phil Zuckerman, and Ryan T. Cragun. 2023. *Beyond Doubt: The Secularization of Society*. New York: New York University Press.
20 Iannaccone, Laurence, Rodney Stark, and Roger Finke. 1998. "Rationality and the 'Religious Mind.'" *Economic Inquiry* 36, no. 3 (July): 373–89; Iannaccone, Laurence R. 1995. "Voodoo Economics? Reviewing the Rational Choice Approach to Religion." *Journal for the Scientific Study of Religion* 34, no. 1 (March): 76–88.
21 There we go with our pretentious Latin again. *Post hoc ergo propter hoc* means "after this, therefore resulting from it."
22 Bradshaw, William S., Renee V. Galliher, and John Dehlin. 2021. "Differences in Religious Experience between Men and Women in a Sexual Minority Sample of Members of The Church of Jesus Christ of Latter-Day Saints." *Journal of GLBT Family Studies* 17, no. 4 (January): 339–355. https://doi.org/.10.1080/1550428X.2020.1868034; Dehlin, John P., Renee V. Galliher, William S. Bradshaw, and Katherine A. Crowell. 2015. "Navigating Sexual and Religious Identity Conflict: A Mormon Perspective." *Identity* 15, no. 1 (January): 1–22. https://doi.org.10.1080/15283488.2014.989440.
23 Johnson, Daniel Carson. 1997. "Formal Education vs. Religious Belief: Soliciting New Evidence with Multinomial Logit Modeling." *Journal for the Scientific Study of Religion* 36, no. 2 (June): 231–46.
24 Riess, Jana. 2019. *The Next Mormons: How Millennials Are Changing the LDS Church*. New York: Oxford University Press.
25 Kasselstrand, Isabella, Phil Zuckerman, and Ryan T. Cragun. 2023. *Beyond Doubt: The Secularization of Society*. New York: New York University Press.
26 Bullivant, Stephen. 2022. *Nonverts: The Making of Ex-Christian America*. New York: Oxford University Press; Campbell, David E., Geoffrey C. Layman, and John C. Green. 2020. *Secular Surge: A New Fault Line in American Politics*. Cambridge, UK: Cambridge University Press; Cotter, Christopher R. 2020. *The Critical Study of Non-Religion: Discourse, Identification and Locality*. New York: Bloomsbury

Academic; Wilkins-Laflamme, Sarah. 2022. *Religion, Spirituality and Secularity among Millennials: The Generation Shaping American and Canadian Trends*. Abingdon, UK: Routledge.

APPENDIX

1. Dawkins, Richard. 2004. *BBC News*. December 10. http://news.bbc.co.uk/2/hi/uk_news/politics/7136682.stm.
2. Freidman, Jonathan L. 2014. "Thinking on Music." May 22. https://thinkingonmusic.wordpress.com/tag/richard-dawkins/.

INDEX

Page numbers in italics indicate Figures

abortion, 210, 215, *216*, 219; morality and, 66, *66*, 68–*70*, 70, 72–73, 82
abstinence, 114
abuse, 60, 93–94; sexual, 92, 251
activism, secular, 2, 33, 96, 122–23, 137–41, 152, 158, 205, 208, 278
adults, 276
affiliation, religious, 47, 275, 297n50; age and, 38–39, 263; of Americans, 7–10, 253, *261*, 261–64, 312n35; attendance of religious services and, 25; gender and, 44; in GSS, *79*, 279–80, 284; marriage and, 193–95, *194*; political affiliation and, 79–83; prior, 53–55; religiosity and, 9; religious belonging and, 23; self-reported, 9, 58; US military and, 309n8; voluntary, 69. *See also* "nones"
Afghanistan, 229–30
African Americans. *See* Black
afterlife, 85–86, *281*, 281–82, 297n50; Annette on, 184; death and, 12, 89–91, 107–8, 119–20, 237; Luke on, 184–85; Yesina on, 186
age, 53, 227; of interviewees, 27, 33–34, 184, 186, *277*; religious affiliation and, 38–39, 263; of religious exiters, 36–39, *37*, 56, *57*
agnosticism, 7, 108, 212–13, 221, 229, *230*, 281–82; identity and, 129, 133, 162, 170–71
Air Force, US, 167

alienation, 76–77, 83, 183
Altemeyer, Bob, 132
American Atheists, 209
American Humanist Association, 173–74 141, 315n25
American society, 11–13, 26–27, 30, 42, 82, 209, 224, 249. *See also* United States
American Time Use Survey (ATUS), US Census Bureau, 144–46, *147–48*, 148–49, 312nn40–41, 313n45
American Trends Panel Wave 30, Pew, 82
Ammerman, Nancy, 258, 326n13
apologists, religious, 3–4
apostasy, 62, 300n1
ARIS survey, 167
Asian Americans, 32–34
Assemblies of God, 66, *66*, 67n9, 68
Atheism, atheists and, 1, 61, 78, *100*, 281–82, 285; acceptance of, 7–12, *10*, 149; on belief in God, 12, 158, 161–62; Black, 41–43; civic engagement of, 223–26, *225*; communism associated with, 7–10, *10*, 37, 115; defining, 12–13, 17; discrimination against, 37, 41–42; distrust of, 214–15; ethical consumption of, 243; identity, 41, 45, 157–61; on immigrants, 246–47, *247*; media representation of, 11–12; morality of, 214–19, *216*, *217*, *218*; religious knowledge of, 229, *230*; scientific, 181–82; stigma and, 195, 198; under-represented in federal prisons of, 217–18, *218*

ATUS. *See* American Time Use Survey
authenticity, 102–3
authority, *100*, 100–101, 120, 130, 133; religious, 22, 58, 65, 99, 114
autonomy, 51, 98–103, *100*, 252–53, 265; birth control and, 9; for children, 111–12, 116 118, 134–35, 307n85; morality and, 66, *66*

Baby Boomers, 109–10, *110*
Bader, Christopher D., 90
Baguett, Jerome, 181
Baker, Joseph O., 90
baptisms, 32, 158, 183–84 139
Baptists, 32–34, 66, *66*, 67n6, 68, 74, 99, 130, 200–201
BBI. *See* belief, behavior, and identity
Becker, H. S., 26
behavior, 22–25; human, 5, 236, 271; immoral, 102, 214–19, *216*, *217*, *218*; religious, 111, 145, 209, 239–40, 258; self-interested, 243–45; selfless, 243–45, *244*; sinful, 68, 99, 102, 215
belief, behavior, and identity (BBI), 22–25, 48, 59, 137, 155, 238–40
beliefs, 14–15, 23–25; in the Bible, 282, *282*, 284; in hell, 85–86, *87*, 88–89, 98, 108, 127; humanist, 45; nonreligious, 172–73, 176–78; religious, 22, 47, 209, 258; scientific, 178–82, 189; secular, 2, 24, 62, 124, 164; worldview and, 171–93. *See also* God, belief in
belonging, religious, 22–24
Berlinerblau, Jacques, 209
the Bible, 74–76, 85–86, *86*, 103, 107, 130; belief in, 282, *282*, 284
"Bible Belt," 50
biology, 5–6, 104–5, 181
birth control, 9, 98, 227
birth rates, declining, 227
bisexuality, bisexual individuals and, 52–53, 68, 80–81, 83, 219, 269

Black, 44, 130, 238, 276, 294n26; atheists, 41–43; men, 107, 188; Protestants, *230*; religious exiters, 39–45, *40*; women, 33–34, 40–42, 45, 294n26
Blankholm, Joseph, 127, 137
Bob Jones University *versus* the US, 130
Bodzhansky, Theodosius, 104
Book of Mormon, 106
Boy Scouts of America, 211–12
Buddhism, 126, 128, 177, *218*, 268
Bureau of Labor Statistics, US, 144
Bush, George W., 26, 73, 77–78

California, 88, 153, 275
Canada, 10, 209–10, 224
capitalism, 7–8
capital punishment, 75–76
Catholicism, 2, 35, 47, 50, 61, 80, 106, *218*, *230*, 246; on authority, 100–101; Catholic schools, 60, 71, 73, 92; charitable giving and, 213; divorce and, 72; "family values" and, 220; generational changes and, 113–14, 116; on higher education, 48; Hispanic, 153, *230*; marriage and, 194, *194*; of Mexican Americans, 45–46; morality and, 66, *66*, 68; rates of religious exiting and, 53–54; religious exiters and, 101, 133–34, 153–54, 160–61, 185–87, 189, 203; sexual abuse and, 92
causality, 48, 69–71, 102, 193–95
Census Bureau, US, 144, 312nn40–41, 313n45
Center for Inquiry (CFI), 137–38, 315n25
ceremonies, secular, 122, 167–68
CFI. *See* Center for Inquiry
change, religious, 284
chaplains, military, 127–28, 309n8
charities, 211, 214, 223, 225; religious, 226, 320n14; secular, 212–13, 320n14
children/youth, 87, 124, 207, 220, 227–28, 261, 279, 310n17; autonomy of, 111–12, 116, 118, 307n85; faith as, 55, 99, 130–31;

generational changes and, 109–20, *110*; never religious, 38–39; with no religious affiliation, 261–62, 310n17; obedience in, 219; raised religious, 32–35, 53–55, *57, 277,* 280, 282–83, *283*; religion rejected by, 38, 60–61, 219–20; religious socialization of, 125–36; transmission of religion from parents to, 110–13, 116–18, 153–54, 252–53

Chinese Americans, 32–34

Christianity, 2, 61, 219, 248, 259, 267; conservative, 9, 78–83, 230, 269–70; evangelical, 77–79, 81, 83–84, 169–70, 183–84, 197, 201; fundamentalist, 13, 60–62, 77–78, 196, 220–21; God in, 19, 74; on hell, 88–89; liberal, 210; nondenominational, 50, 54, 92; private schools, 74; religious exiting and, 17, 103, 139, 167–68, 170, 176, 192–93, 205, 266

church: attendance, 22, 32, 45, 60–62, 92–93, 125, 128–29; communities, 99, 154, 161, 164, 197; megachurches, 80, 88

church and state, separation of, 21, 30, 140, 251

Church of Christ, 54, 66, *66*, 67n5, 68, 72–73

Church of Jesus Christ of Latter-day Saints (LDS Church), 66, *66*, 68, 117, 224

Cicirelli, Victor G., 182–83

civic engagement, 48, 223–26, *225*

Clark, Thomas, 235

class, social, 46–48, *47*

clergy. *See* leaders, religious

The Clergy Project, 75

clubs, social, 211, 320n11

cognitive: behaviorism, 236; dissonance, 104

cohabitation, 11, 215, 222, *248*

Cold War, 8–10, 37, 110, 115

Coleman, Peter G., 187

college. *See* higher education

commitment: religious, 3, 94, 124–26, 128, 134–35; time, 62, 69, 95–98, 123, 124–25

communism, 7–11, *10,* 37, 58, 65, 115

community, church, 99, 154, 161, 164, 197

Congregationalists, *47,* 54

congregations, religious, 224

congregations, secular, 27, 96, 275

Congressional Freethought Caucus, 141

conscious: awareness, 176; experience, 190, 235

consequentialism, 178–79

conservative religions, 68–69, 71–73; Christianity as a, 9, 78–83, 230, 269–70

conservative religious anti-secular (CRAS) movements, 209

conservative social and political values, 77–84, 169, 265–66, 269–70, 307n85; "family values," 219–23; of Mountain states, 51

Constitution, US, 6–7

consumerism, 225, 242–45, *244*

conversion, religious, 3, 124, 139, 162, 197

CPS. *See* Current Population Survey

Cragun, Ryan T., 300n4, 323n49

CRAS movements. *See* conservative religious anti-secular

creationism, 19, 103, 115, 251

criminal behavior, 216–18, *217*

criticism of religion, 11–12, 58–59, 138, 170

Cru (Christian organization), 169, 315n26

"cults," 182, 310n13

Current Population Survey (CPS), 144

data, 31, 55–56, 82, 167; age related, 36–39, *37*; causality and, 69–71, 194–95; gender related, 43–46, *44*; health related, 240–41; on meaning in life, 232–34, *233, 234*; mixed-effects regression model, 56–58, *57*; morality and, *216*, 216–17, *217*; qualitative, 28–29, 144, 193; quantitative, 28–29, 193–94. *See also specific surveys*

Dawkins, Richard, 42, 284

death, 6, 18–19, 75, 117, 263; afterlife and, 12, 89–91, 107–8, 119–20, 237; capital punishment and, 75–76; funerals, 167–68; meaning of life and, 234–35; mortality and, 39, 119–20, 182–88; murder and, 42, 72, 75, 215; of parents, 119, 184; returning to religion before, 38–39
death penalty, 216
defunct religions, 231
democracy, 140, 173
Democratic Party, 9, 77, 79, 83
demographics: of interviewees, 27, 276–77, 277; nonreligious, 217, 218; religious affiliation and, 261–62; of religious exiters, 29, 34–59, 37, 40, 44, 47, 49, 51, 57, 250
destiny, 19, 174–75
dietary restrictions, 98, 215
disaffiliation, religious, 22, 126, 200, 208. *See also* affiliation, religious
discrimination, 155, 241; against atheists, 37, 41–42; religious, 6, 238–39; against religious exiters, 41–45, 50–51
distrust, 155, 214–15
diversity sampling, 27–28
divine plan, 234, 242
divorce, 72, 96, 128–29, 199, 216, 221–22, 268
Dobbs v. Jackson Women's Health Organization, 302n17
doctrines, religious, 63, 84–91, *85, 86, 87,* 265
drug use, 102, 215 239–40, 247, 248, 313n45
dues, religious, 211–12
Durkheim, Emile, 14–15, 142, 163

"early adopters," 200, 263
Eastern Orthodox religions, 23
Ecklund, Elaine Howard, 179
economics, 7–8, 225; charitable giving and, 212–14; procreation and, 227–28
education, 154, 225, 323n51; boarding school, 104; elementary school, 73, 104; GSS on, 48–49, *49*; higher, 48–49, 72, 95–96, 136, 139–40, 169, 197, 266–68, 315n26; homeschooling as, 116–17, 197, 219; of interviewees, 33–34, 276, *277*; public schools, 251, 268; RE in, 230–31; of religious exiters, 48–49, *49*, 56, *57*, 250; Sunday school, 107, 129, 133–35, 139, 144–45, 184–85, 200. *See also* high school
egalitarian views, 44, 76, 111, 265, 270
empathy, 180–81
employment, 40, 222, 225
end-of-life care, 182–84
Engels, Friedrich, 7–8
environmentalism, 213, 223, 225, 243–45
Episcopalians, 47, 50, 54, 135
Estonia, 23
ethical consumption, 243
ethics, 181, 321n20. *See also* morality
ethnocentrism, 216
Europe, 22, 126, 207, 209–10
European settlers, 6–7, 50
euthanasia, 216
Evangelical religions, 48, 88, 113, 209, 246, 309n8 230; Christianity, 77–79, 81, 83–84, 169–70, 183–84, 197, 201; Lutherans, 66, *66*, 67n7, 68
evolution, 19, 104–5, 107, 181, 251
existential cultures, 18–19
existentialism, 120, 236
exiters, religious ("religious exiting"), 257, 287n1, 291n60, 306n75, 326n5; age of, 36–39, *37*, 56, *57*; on autonomy, 99–100; BBI in, 24; on the Bible, *85*, 85–86; Black, 39–45, *40*; Catholicism and, 101, 133–34, 153–54, 160–61, 185–87, 189, 203; Christianity and, 17, 103, 139, 167–68, 170, 176, 192–93, 205, 266; cliff diving metaphor for, 254–56; on the decline of religiosity, 210; defining, 17, 20, 157; demographics of, 29, 34–59, *37, 40, 44, 47, 49, 51, 57,* 250; discrimination against, 41–45, 50–51;

education of, 48–49, *49*, 56, *57*, 250; "family values" and, 219; functionalist approaches to, 259–60; gender and, 43–46, *44*, 56, *57*, 254; gradual process of, 64–65, 129, 136, 140–41, 185; growth of, 34–35, *35*, 43–44, 51–52; GSS and, 292n3, 297n47; health of, 240–41; homosexual, 53, 131–32, 254, 269–70; identity and, 19–21, 152, 172–73; increase in, 271–72; LGB people as, 52–53; marriage of, 194, *194*; on meaning in life, 231–37, *233*, *234*; motivation for, 30, 61, 64, 139, 197–98; never religious people compared to, 19, 38, 173; pathways to, 2–5, 24–25, 33–34, 152, 205, 208; phenomenon of, 28–29, 84–85, 254; post-religion, 30, 152–76; predictors of, 255–56, 260–64, *261*; prior religious affiliation of, 53–55; push and pull framework for, 30, 64–65, 120–21, 264–66; qualitative sample of, 275–78, *277*; quantitative methodology on, 275, 278–86, *279*, *280*, *281*–*82*, *283*; race of, 39–43, *40*, *47*; regions and, 50–52, *51*, *57*; religiopolitical alignment and, 250–51; religious socialization and, 74, 115, 125–36, 152; on reproduction, 227–28; returning to religion of, 38–39, 118–19, 155–56 171, 312n39; selfless acts by, *244*; self-reported, 43; social class of, 46–48, *47*; social relationships of, 193–206, *194*; spirituality of, 87, 96–97, 143, 282, *283*, 313n1; values of, 69–71, *70*, *71*. *See also* predictors of religious exiting
experts, 98–99
externally-focused civic engagement, 223–26
extramarital sex, 102

faith, 3–4, 91; atheism and, 12–13; as children, 55, 99, 130–31
Faith in Flux survey, Pew, 55, 64, 87, *87*

families, 87, 161, 184–86, 202–6; grandparents in, 113–14; military, 72, 108; multi-faith, 88–89; religious services attended by, 54–55; socialization, 115; trauma and, 131, 196–97; values of, 219–23, *222*. *See also* children/youth; parents
fathers, 54, 60, 93, 153–54, 183–84, 310n17; Glen on, 130, 196–97
Fazzino, Lori L., 182
Feeding Tampa Bay, 226, 322n35
fertility rates, 228
FFRF. *See* Freedom from Religion Foundation
Findhorn Foundation, 132–33
First Amendment, US Constitution, 6–7
Fischer, Claude S., 82
Florida, 131, 226, 275–76
Freedom from Religion Foundation (FFRF), 1, 77, 137
freedom of/from religion, 6–7, 108–9, 268
Freemasonry, 211–12
Free Methodist Church, 199
free will, 181, 236
Frost, Jacqui, 157
functionalism, functionalist definition of religion and, 14–15, 17, 256–60
fundamentalists, religious, 72, 99, 129–30, 209; Christian fundamentalists, 13, 60–62, 77–78, 196, 220–21; Muslim fundamentalists, 77–78, 229–30
funerals, 167–68

gay individuals, 66, 68, *248*; as religious exiters, 53, 131–32, 254, 269–70. *See also* homosexuality
gay rights, lesbian and, 11, 26–27, 71
GDP. *See* gross domestic product
Geertz, Clifford, 15

gender, 66, *66*, 68–71, *71*, 88, 225, 321n25; autonomy and, 9; equality, 68–69, 76–77, 80–81, 115, 219; GSS on, 43–46, *44*, 297n47, 300n75 43–46; of interviewees, 276, *277*; marginalization and, 215; of religious exiters, 43–46, *44*, 56, 57, 254; violence, *217*
gender-fluidity, 88
gender queer people, 198
General Social Survey (GSS), 26, 34–35, *36*, 146, 292n3, 292n4, 293n11, 295n37; age in, 36–39, *37*, 53; on children, 227–28; on divorce, 221–22; on education, 48–49, *49*; gender and, 43–46, *44*; on generational changes, 109–20, *110*; Generation Z in, 207n81; on health, 240–41; on LGB individuals, 52–53; LGB people in, 52–53; on marital happiness, 222–23; on marriage, 194, *194*; on meaning in life, 232–33, *233*; Millennials in, 207n81; on papal infallibility, 101; quantitative analysis in, 278–79; race in, 39–43, *40*; regions in, 50–52, *51*, 299n65; religious affiliation in, 261, *261*; on social class, 46–48, *47*
generations, generational changes and, 120–21, 155–56, 236, 253, 307n80; Catholicism and, 113–14, 116; children and, 109–20, *110*; nonreligious people and, 109–20, *110*; secularization and, 117–18. *See also specific generations*
Generation X, 109–10, *110*
Generation Z, 109–10, *110*, 156, 307n81
Glaser, Barney, 28
God, belief in, 1, 108, 113, 128, 136, 197, 297n45; atheists on, 12, 158, 161–62; Christian, 19, 74; GSS on, 281–82, *281–82*, 295n37; Judeo-Christian, 25, 214–15; meaning in life and, 232–34, *233*
God's Not Dead (movies), 201
Golden Rule, 180–81, 245–48, *247*, *248*
gradual process of religious exit, 64–65, 129, 136, 140–41, 185

grandparents, 113–14
Greatest Generation, 109, *110*
gross domestic product (GDP), 228. 245
Grounded Theory (GT), 28
group membership, 195–96
GSS. *See* General Social Survey
GT. *See* Grounded Theory
Gull, Bethany, 102

Ham, Ken, 12–13, 19
happiness, 190; marital, 222–23; self-reported, 241
Harris, Sam, 43, 77, 178–79
health, 68, 102, 185–86, 237; mental, 111, 170, 231–32, 238–41
hell, belief in, 85–86, *87*, 88–89, 98, 108, 127
Helping Hands program, LDS Church, 224
heterosexuality, 45, 53, 83, 198; "family values" and, 219–20
high-cost religions, 129, 254–55
higher education, 48–49, 72, 95–96, 136, 139–40, 169, 197, 266–68, 315n26
high school, 34, 49, 114, 197, 267; Catholic, 60, 71
Hinduism, Hindus and, *47*, 89, 204, *218*, 245, 267
Hispanic people, 2, 198–99, 276; Catholics, 153, *230*
Holyoake, George, 21
homeschooling, 116–17, 197, 219
homosexuality, 68–71, *70*, 73, 75–76, 131, 216, 219, *248*; fundamentalist Baptists on, 99–100; political affiliation and, 83
House (television show), 11
Hout, Michael, 82
human: behavior, 5, 236, 271; origins, 12, 19, 258
Human-Etisk Forbund (Norwegian Humanist Association), 245

humanism, 23, 47, 107, 153, 158, 171, 173–78, 253; secular, 45, 128, 133, 158, 159, 161–62, 186, 190–91, 197, 199
Hunsberger, Bruce, 132
Hutchinson, Sikivu, 294n26
hypocrisy, religious, 60, 62–63, 91–94, 208, 251

identity, 22–25; agnostic, 129, 133, 162, 170–71; atheist, 41, 45, 157–61; Catholic, 153; community and, 142, 156–71; ethnic, 267; hierarchy of, 156–61; of interviewees, 276–78, *277*; nonreligious, 2, 41, 46, 154, 159–60, 162, 201, 207, 277–78; political, 83; racial, 41, 238; rejection-based, 157; religious, 19–20, 25, 65, 145, 238, 253, 278–80, *279*; religious exiters and, 19–21, 152, 172–73; secular, 13, 21, 140, 167–68, 253; sexual, 276; stigma and, 42–44, 81–82, 295n36; "true," 159; vacuum, 170
immediate gratification, 242
immigration, immigrants and, 64, 94, 190–91, 246–47, *247*, *248*, 250, 266–67
immoral behavior, 102, 214–19, *216*, *217*, *218*
income, 44, 46–48, *47*, *57*, 297n50; charities and, 212; taxes, 214. *See also* class, social
Independents (political), 77, 79
indifference, religious, 2, 19–20, 33, 62, 114, 142, 152, 208, 229, 278. *See also* "never religious" people
indoctrination, religious, 111, 113–14, 129–31, 137–38, 166, 189, 197
inertia, 38, 261–62
infallibility, papal, 100–101
Ingersoll, Robert, 7
ingroup ratings, 246
institutionalized religion (organized religion), 16, 23, 87, 116, 154, 258–59
intelligent design, 251. *See also* creationism

internally-focused civic engagement, 223–26
internet access, 11, 207–8
interviews, interviewees and, 25–26, 28–29, 63, 98, 157–58, 291n68; demographic characteristics of, 27, 276–77, *277*; push factor and, 250; recruitment for, 27, 96, 141, 275–79
introverts, 203
Iran, 78
Islam, Muslims and, 17, 47, 190–91, *218*, 246; Crissy on, 167; fundamentalists, 77–78, 229–30; the Quran and, 106

James, William, 14
Jefferson, Thomas, 7
Jehovah's Witnesses, 47, 47–48, *218*; rates of religious exiting of, 53–54
Jesuit school, 160–61
Jesus Christ, 22, 40, 104–5
joiners, religious, 25, 34–35, *35*, 279, 279–80, *280*, *281–82*; age of, 36–39, *37*; on the Bible, 85; education of, 48–49, *49*; gender of, 43–46, *44*; marriage of, 194, *194*; race of, 39–43, *40*; religious services attended by, 55; social class of, 46–48, *47*. *See also* stayers, religious
Judaism, Jewish people and, 1–2, 17, 35, *47*, 47 246, *218*, 230; conversion to, 124 139, 162; on higher education, 48; marriage and, 194, *194*; rates of religious exiting and, 53–54

Kalamazoo Gospel Ministries, 226
Kant, Immanuel, 14
Kasselstrand, Isabella, 76
knowledge, religious, 32–33, 81, 229–31, 230

labor unions, 224–25, *225*
Langston, Joseph A., 142
Latinx people, 2, 153, 198–99, *230*, 276
Latvia, 113

LDS Church. *See* Church of Jesus Christ of Latter-day Saints
Lee, Lois, 18–19
leisure: marketplace, 252; time, 97, *147–48*, 221–22, *222*
Leon (interviewee), 151–52, 154, 189
Levi-Strauss, Claude, 258
LGB individuals (lesbian, gay, and bisexual), 52–53, 67n3
LGBTQ+ individuals, 11, 51, 66, *66*, 68–69, 253; conservative Christians rejecting, 269–70; "family values" and, 219–21; marginalization of, 215
liberal religions, 80–82, 199–200, 210
Libertarians, 51, 79
lifestances, 153, 172–73. *See also* worldview
liminality, religious-secular, 2, 24, 33, 152, 267n1, 278
linear modeling, 327n17
literalism in religion, 48–49, 85–86, *86*, 251
lived religion, 15–16, 256–60, 326n13
logical consistency, 85, 103–9, 172, 179–80, 265–68
loss, sense of, 156
low-cost religions, 254
Lutherans, 23, 32, *47*, 50, 54, 88–89, 113; Evangelical, 66, *66*, 67n7, 68

Maher, Bill, 13, 19
Manning, Christel, 124
marginalization, 37, 69, 215, 253; discrimination and, 238–39
marijuana, 215
marital status, 276, *277*
marriage, 2, *87*, 223, 227; divorce and, 72, 96, 128–29, 199, *216*, 221–22; gay, 71; heterosexual, 219–20; legalization of same sex, 26–27; religious affiliation and, 193–95, *194*
Marx, Karl, 7–8
masturbation, 215, 219
materialism, *225*, 242–45, *244*

Mauss, Armand, 85
McCaffree, Kevin, 23
McCarthyism, 8
meaning in life, 189–93, 231–37, *233*
megachurches, 80, 88
memberships, religious, 211–12, 224–26
memorial services, secular, 167–68
men, 43–44, *44*, 56; Black, 107, 188; white, 37, 45, 46, 250. *See also* white men
Mencken, F. Carsen, 90
Mencken, H. L., 98
mental health, 111, 170, 231–32, 238–41
Merino, Stephen, 38
Methodists, 50, 54, 74, 77–78, 199
methodology, research, 25–31, 264–72; qualitative, 25–26, 28–29, 275–78, *277*; quantitative, 25–26, 28–29, 275, 278–86, *279*, *280*, *281–82*, *283*
Metropolitan Ministries, 226
Mexican Americans, 45, 153
Michigan, 27, 88, 226, 275
middle school, 74
military, US, 72, 108, 127–28, 309n8
The Military Association of Atheists and Freethinkers, 107
Millennials, 109–10, *110*, 155–56, 307n81
minorities: racial, 42, 46–47, 253; sexual, 52–53
mixed-effects regression model, 56–58, *57*
modernization, 21, 76, 80, 115, 172
modern sensibilities, 76, 112–13, 116–17, 251, 265–67
modern societies, modernity and, 21–22, 64, 80, 97, 265–68
Moorish people, *218*
moral frameworks, 15, 178
morality, 92, 160, 178–81, 214–19, *216*, *217*, *218*; abortion and, 66, *66*, 68–70, 70, 72–73, 82; autonomy and, 66, *66*, 307n85; as a push factors, 28, 66, *66*, 68–77, *70*, *71*; science and, 182
Moral Majority, 69, 72–73

Mormons, 35, *47*, 50, 54, *218*, *230*, 298n61; Book of Mormon, 106; Mauss on, 85
mortality, 39, 119–20, 182–88
mothers, 54, 93–94, 107, 185–86, 310n17
motivation for religious exiters, 30, 61, 64, 139, 197–98
Mountain West Freethinkers, 27, 275
multiculturalism, 51–52
multiple identities, 160–61
multiracial people, 88–89, 204
murder, 42, 72, 75, 215
Muslims. *See* Islam, Muslims and
mutual aid, *225*
myth, 15–17, *16*, 166–67, 230–31

Nation of Islam, *218*
Native Americans, 7, *218*, 298n61
natural disasters, 224
naturalistic worldview, 105, 174–75, 235
Navy, US, 107, 126–28, 159
neighbors, neighborliness and, 245–48, *248*
"never religious" people, 25, 276–77, *277*, 279, 279–84, *281*–*82*; on the afterlife, 90; age of, 36–39, *37*; on the Bible, 85; education of, 48–49, *49*; gender of, 43–46, *44*; health of, 240–41; increase in, 34–35, *35*; marriage of, 194, *194*; on meaning in life, 233, *234*; on procreation, 227–28; race of, 39–43, *40*; religious exiters compared to, 19, 38, 173; religious socialization of, 126–27; selfless acts by, *244*; values of, 69–71, *70*, *71*; wellbeing of, 155
New Atheism, 42
New Deal, US, 7–8
New England, 50–51, *51*, 56, *57*
New Jersey, 72
new religious movements (NRMs), 182, 310n13
New York, 164
Nica, Andreea, 196
Nietzsche, Friedrich, 323n54

nihilism, 233–34, 237, 242
"non-believers," 61, 158
non-denominational Christianity, 50, 54, 92
"nones" (those who claim no religion), 9, 22–23, 25–27, 109, 126, 167, *218*; growth of, 29; marriage of, 194, *194*; religious knowledge of, *230*
nonreligion, nonreligious people and, *100*, *146–47*, 171, 207n81, 252, 257; on autonomy, 102–3; beliefs of, 172–73, 176–78; on birth control, 98; Black, 41; children of, 261–62, 310n17; civic engagement of, 223–26, *225*; consumerism and, *225*, 242–45, *244*; definition of, 18–22; demographics of, 217, *218*; ethics and, 321n20; during European settlement, 7; generational changes and, 109–20, *110*; generational differences, 109–20, *110*; across generations, 109–10, *110*; growth of, 9–12, 82–84, 260–64, *261*; identity and, 2, 41, 46, 154, 159–60, 162, 201, 207, 277–78; on immigrants, 246–47, *247*; linear modeling for, 327n17; lived, 259; minorities, 276–77, *277*, 294n26; morality of, 214–19, *216*, *217*, *219*; organized secularism and, 1, 312n35; political affiliation of, 83; on procreation, 227–28; religious knowledge of, 229; Republicans, 77–79; secular charities and, 212–13; self-identified, 27–28; women as, 44; worldview, 173, 183. *See also* pull factors; push factors
"nonsupernatural sacred," 16
normative values, 153, 178
Northern Europe, 210
Norway, 245
Norwegian Humanist Association (Human-Etisk Forbund), 245
NRMs. *See* new religious movements

Obama, Barack, 26
obedience, 219

organizations, religious, 224–26, 225, 251, 322n32; charity and, 212–14; morality and, 66, *66*, 68. *See also* church
organizations, secular, 27–28, 62, 210, 224–26, *225*, 312n35, 313n2, 322n32; joiners of, 136–44, 149–50, 196; membership of, 77–78; non-joiners of, 136, 141–42, 163
organized religion (institutionalized religion), 16, 23, *87*, 116, 154, 258–59
outgroup ratings, 246
over-representation, 96, 313n2

Pacific states (region), 50, *51*, 56, *57*
Paganism, *218*
Panel Study of Income Dynamics (PSID), University of Michigan, 212–13
parents, parenting and, 11, 114, 120–21, 191–92; Catholic, 60–61; Christian, 19, 219; hypocrisy of religious, 60–62, 93–94; immigrant, 45; Lutheran, 32; mothers as, 54, 93–94, 107, 185–86, 310n17; nonreligious, 38–39; religious, 19, 93–94, 99, 107–8, 111–12, 119, 130–31, 266–68; on religious exiting, 219–20; secular, 19, 75, 117–18, 132, 143; socialization and, 112–13, 116; transmission of religion by, 110–13, 116–18, 153–54, 252–53. *See also* fathers
pathways, religious exit, 2–5, 24–25, 33–34, 152, 205, 208
persecution, religious, 6–8
physical health, 237–41
police brutality, 42
Polish Americans, 154, 186–87
political parties, US, 77, *207*, *225*; religious alignment and, 250–51
politics, political affiliation and, *222*; push factors and, 77–84, *78*
Pope (Catholic), 100–101
population density, 52
pornography, 215, 219
post-religion, religious exiters, 30, 152–76

prayer, 105, 174 197
predictors of religious exiting, 31, 55–58, 195, 200, 255–56, 260–71, *261*; education as a, 49, *57*; income as a, 47–48, *57*; race as a, 40, *40*, 46, *57*
preference, religious, 279
prejudice, 99, 155, 246. *See also* discrimination
pre-marital sex, 4, 11, 72–73, 102, 215, *216*, 227
Presbyterians, 54, 66, *66*, 68
prisoner populations, federal, 217–18, *218*
private schools, religious, 74, 116–17
procreation, reproduction and, 206n73, 227–29
progressive social and political values, 79, 84, 210–11, 265–66; regions and, 50–51
property taxes, 214
prostitution, *216*
Protestantism, 48, 50, 74–75, 194, *194*, *218*, 230; rates of religious exiting in, 53–54
PSID. *See* Panel Study of Income Dynamics
psychological motives for religious exit, 30, 64, 139
psychology, 5–6
public schools, 251, 268
pull factors (toward nonreligion), 94, 172, 250, 252–53, 264–65; autonomy as a, 98–103, *100*; generational changes as, 109–20, *110*; modern worldviews as, 103–9; time as a, 95–97
push and pull framework, 30, 63–65, 118, 120–21, 200, 264–66. *See also* pull; push factors
push factors (out of religion), 65, 95, 250–53, 264–65; hypocrisy as a, 91–94; moral, 28, 66, *66*, 68–77, *70*, *71*; political, *77*, 77–84; religious doctrine as a, 84–91, *85*, *86*, *87*

Quack, Johannes, 18, 142
Quakerism, 90

queer individuals, 68, 198
the Quran, 106

race, ethnicity and, 44–46, 230, 238, 248, 321n25; GSS on, 39–43, 40, 57, 297n47; of interviewees, 276
racism, 40–41
raised with religion, people, 32–35, 53–55, 57, 170, 277, 280, 282–83, 283. See also children/youth
rape, 68
Rastafarians, 218
rational choice framework, 269–71
RE. See Religious Education
Reason Rally (2012), 209–10
Recognizing the Nonreligious (Lee), 18–19
recruitment: interviewee, 27, 96, 141, 275–79; religious, 40–41
Red Scare, 8
rejection-based identities, 157
relationships, social, 30, 151–52, 193–206, 194, 219–23, 222
religion. See specific religions; specific topics
Religion and Health (journal), 237
religiopolitical alignment, 250–51
religiosity, 65, 80 195; BBI and, 22–25, 48, 59, 137, 155, 238–40; decline of, 11–12, 117–18, 209–11, 224, 248; education and, 48–49, 49; gender and, 44; generational, 253; happiness and, 241; level of faith and, 55; race and, 39–44, 40; rational choice framework and, 269–70; religious affiliation and, 9; self reported, 283, 283; of sexual minorities, 52–53; social class and, 46–47
religious: authority, 22, 58, 65, 99, 114; behavior, 111, 145, 209, 239–40, 258; belonging, 22–24; charities, 226, 320n14; commitment, 3, 94, 124–26, 128, 134–35; conversion, 3, 124, 139, 162, 197; disaffiliation, 22, 126, 200, 208; discrimination, 6, 238–39; dues, 211–12;

indifference, 2, 19–20, 33, 62, 114, 142, 152, 208, 229, 278; indoctrination, 111, 113–14, 129–31, 137–38, 166, 189, 197; knowledge, 32–33, 81, 229–31, 230; leaders, 3–5, 91–93, 98; persecution, 6–8; preference, 279; private schools, 117, 251; recruitment, 40–41; retention, 36–39, 37; studies, 23, 256–57; youth groups, 55, 144–45. See also joiners, religious; organizations, religious; services, attendance of religious; skeptics, religious; stayers, religious
Religious Education (RE), 230–31
"religious exiting." See exiters, religious
religious-secular liminality, 2, 24, 33, 152, 267n1, 278
Republican Party, 77, 77–78; religious alignment and, 9, 79–84, 250–51
retention, religious, 36–39, 37
returning to religion, 38–39, 118–19, 155–56, 171, 312n39
Revolutionary War, 6–7
rights: gay, 11, 26–27, 71, 80–81; of women, 73
risk, risk-aversion and, 36–37, 41–43, 45–46
rituals, 16, 17, 19, 122, 165–68, 183
Robertson, Pat, 209–10
Roe v. Wade, 230, 302n17
Romanian-Americans, 135
Roosevelt, Franklin Delano, 7–8
rural environments, 51–52

sacrifices, willingness to make, 244–45
Salonen, Anna Sofia, 260
same sex marriage, 26–27, 66, 66, 68
Santeria, 218
Saudi Arabia, 167
Schlessinger, Laura, 302n16
Schuh, Cora, 142
scientific beliefs, 178–82, 189
scientific-pantheism, 90–91
sectarian religions, 48

secular congregations, 27, 96, 275
secularism, secular people and, 20–22, 153; alternative to religious activities for, 30, 95–98, 122–23, 144–46, *147–48*, 148–50, 312n41, 313n45, 315n16; ceremonies, 122, 167–68; charities, 212–13, 320n14; charities and, 212–13, 320n14; communities, 123–25, 136–38, 144, 163–66, 168–70, 177, 199–200, 210; congregations, 27, 96, 275; memorial services and, 167–68; secular activism, 2, 33, 96, 122–23, 137–41, 152, 158, 205, 208, 278. *See also* organizations, secular
secularity, 12, 20–22, 254–56
secularization, 12, 20, 22, 65, 248, 251, 257, 268; of developed countries, 10; education and, 48; "family values" and, 219; generational change and, 117–18; morality and, 76; religious exiters and, 13; sociology and, 21, 172
secular social groups, 198–99, 275
Secular Student Alliance, 169
self-identification, 9, 27–28, 58, 276, 278
self-image, positive, 4–6
self-interested behavior, 243–45
selfless acts, 243–45, *244*
selfless behavior, 243–45, *244*
separation of church and state, 21, 30, 140, 251
services, attendance of religious, *280*, 280–81, *281*, 283–84, 297n50; alternatives to, 30, 95–98, 122–23, 144–46, *147–48*, 148–50, 312n41, 313n45, 315n16; church, 22, 32, 45, 60–62, 92–93, 125, 128–29; Cold War era, 10; education and, 48; by the extremely devout, 208–9; prior to religious exit, 54–55; religious affiliation and, 25; social class and, 47
Seventh-day Adventists, *47*, 54
sex, *216*, 222–23; casual, *216*, 222–23; extra-marital, 102; pre-marital, 4, 11, 72–73, 102, 215, 227

sexual abuse, 92, 251
sexual orientation, 52–53, 66, *66*, 75–76, 198, 254, 300n78; marginalization and, 215; political orientation and, 83. *See also specific sexual orientations*
shame, 221
Sikhism, 245
Silent Generation, 109, *110*
Silicon Valley (television show), 11
Silverman, David, 209–10
sin, sinful behavior and, 68, 99, 102, 215
skeptics, religious, 40–41, 74, 90, 107, 114–15, 160–61, 165, 237; Megan on, 200–201
Smith, Jesse M., 16
Smith, Joseph, 22
social: class, 46–48, *47*; clubs, 211, 320n11; relationships, 30, 151–52, 193–206, *194*, 219–23, 222
social construction, 156–57, 196, 215, 267; of morality, 218
social forces driving religious exiting, 64, 262–63
"social identity threat," 202
socialism, 8
socialization, 103; family, 115; parental, 112–13, 116; religious, 74, 115, 125–37, 144, 152
social networks, 194–206, 239–40; nonreligious, 265–66
sociology, 5–6, 14, 22–23, 125, 256–60, 269; on nonreligion, 18; secularization and, 21, 172
Southern Baptists, 35, *47*, 54, 66, *66*, 68
Soviet Union, 8–10
spirituality, 105, 165, 202, 243, 259; religious exiters and, 87, 96–97, 143, 282, 283, 313n1
sports, *225*
stayers, religious, 25, *279*, 279–80, *280*, *281*–82; age of, 36–39, *37*; on the Bible, 85; decline of, 34–35, *35*; education of, 48–49, *49*; gender of, 43–46, *44*;

marriage of, 194, *194*; race of, 39–43, *40*; religious services attended by, 55; social class of, 46–48, *47*; values of, 69–71, *70, 71. See also* joiners, religious
stereotypes, 29, 33–34; racist, 40–41
stigmas, social, 50–51, 58, 195, 198; consciousness, 202; identity and, 42–44, 81–82, 295n36
students, 323n50; college, 2 78, 95–96, 169
subjectivity, 235, 266–70
substantive definition of religion, 14–15, 17
suicide, *216*, 219, 221
Sunday Assembly, 27, 124, 137–38, 141, 163–66, 275
Sunday school, 107, 129, 133–35, 139, 144–45, 184–85, 200
supernaturalism, 15–17, 19, 22, 75, 89–90, 151–52, 242–43; American Humanist Association on, 173–74; Buddhism and, 177; Russel on, 169
Supreme Court, US, 130, 230, 251
switching, religious, 3, 20 68–69, 79–81
symbolism, symbols and, 14–15, 17, 166–67

Taliban, 229–30
Taoism, 126, 245
Taves, Ann, 172
taxes, 210–11, 214
technological developments, 11, 36, 64, 207–8, 215
Texas, 92
theology, 87, 98–99
Tillich, Paul, 19
time, 30, 56–57, 122, 144–46, 175; commitments, 62, 69, 95–98, 123, 124–25; leisure, 97, *147–48*, 221–22, *222*; regional differences over, 50–52, *51*
tobacco consumption, 313n45
tolerance, 245–48, *247, 248*
traditional: media, 11–12; views, 265
transcendence, 192–93
transgender people, 2, 68, 276, 300n75
trauma, family, 131, 196–97

tribalism, 149, 248
"true": identity, 159; morality, 180–81
Turkey, 190–91
Tylor, Edward, 14

under-representation, 182, 217–18, *218*
Unitarian church, 119, 129, 185
United Kingdom, 275
United Methodists, *47*, 66, *66*, 68
United States (US), 29, 167, 266–68, 292n4, 297n45; Bureau of Labor Statistics, 144; Census Bureau, 144–46, *147–48*, 148–49, 312nn40–41, 313n45; civic engagement in, 223; Constitution, 6–7; cultural values, 6–11, *10*, 26–27, 110, 115; federal prison, *218*; hierarchy in, 42; military, 72, 108, 127–28, 309n8; Navy, 107, 126–28, 159; political parties, 77, *207*, 225, 250–51; regions, 50–52, *51*, 56; religious affiliations of, 7–10, 253, *261*, 261–64, 312n35; religious landscape, 146, 250, 252, 260–64, *261*; secularization in, 22, 210; Supreme Court, 130, 230, 251
University of Michigan, 212–13
urban environments, 50–52

value misalignment, 69–71, 74, 112
values, 237; autonomy and, 307n85; consumer, 243; cultural, 6–11, *10*, 26–27, 110, 115; family, 219–23, *222*; generational, 236; humanist, 158; of "never religious" people, 69–71, *70, 71*; normative, 153, 178; of religious exiters, 69–71, *70, 71*; secular, 78, 124; social, 68, 80. *See also* conservative social and political values; morality; progressive social and political values
Vietnam War, 9
violence, 93–94, *217*
virgin birth of Jesus, 104–5
voluntary religious affiliation, 69
volunteering, 223–24

Washington, DC, 135
weddings, secular, 167–68
wellbeing, 155, 170, 196
Western Europe, 22, 126, 209–10
What It Means to Be Moral (Zuckerman), 181
white men, 37, 45, 46, 250
white people, 39–43, *40*, *230*, 238, 276
Wiccans, 32, 128
Wilkinson, Peter J., 187
Wittgenstein, Ludwig, 235
women, 43, 225; Black, 33–34, 40–42, 45, 294n26; ordination of, 66, *66*, 68
wonder, sense of, 192–93
World Values Survey, 26, 215–19, *216*, *217*, *218*, 221–23, *222*; on authority, *100*, 100–101; on civic engagement, 224–25; on health, 240–41; on immigrants, 246–47, *247*
worldview, 15–17, *16*, 316n39; belief and, 171–93; humanist, 153, 174–78; modern, 103–9, 172, 174; naturalistic, 105, 174–75, 235; nonreligious, 173, 183; religious, 215; secular, 138, 154, 172–81, 185, 192
World War II, 8

Yinger, Milton, 14
youth. *See* children/youth
youth groups, religious, 55, 144–45

Zeller, Benjamin, 182
Zuckerman, Phil, 62, 181

ABOUT THE AUTHORS

RYAN T. CRAGUN is Professor of Empirical Sociology at The University of Tampa and the author of *Beyond Doubt: The Secularization of Society*.

JESSE M. SMITH is Associate Professor in the Department of Sociology at Western Michigan University and author of *Secularity and Nonreligion in North America*.

www.ingramcontent.com/pod-product-compliance
Lightning Source LLC
Chambersburg PA
CBHW020351080526
44584CB00014B/979